Interfaith Treasures Uncovered - 1

Hindu Nationalism and the Indian Church

Towards an Ecclesiology in Conversation with Martin Luther

R. Sahayadhas

Christian World Imprints™

Edition: 2016

Christian World Imprints(TM)
Christian Publishing & Books from India
H-12 Bali Nagar, **New Delhi-110015**
info@christianworldimprints.com
www.ChristianWorldImprints.com
Phone: +91 11 25465925

ISBN-13: 978-93-5148-184-3 ISBN-10: 93-5148-184-0

Cataloging in Publication Data--DK
Courtesy: D.K. Agencies (P) Ltd. <docinfo@dkagencies.com>

Sahayadhas, R., 1958-
Hindu nationalism and the Indian church : towards an ecclesiology in conversation with Martin Luther / R. Sahayadhas.
p. cm. -- (Interfaith treasures uncovered ; 1)
Revision of the author's thesis (D.Th.--Senate of Serampore College, 2009) under the title: Towards an ecclesiology in the contemporary Indian context of Hindu nationalism in critical interaction with Martin Luther's ecclesiology.
Includes bibliographical references (p.) and indexes.
ISBN 9789351481843
ISBN 9351481840

1. India--Church history. 2. Christianity--India. 3. Nationalism--Religious aspects--Hinduism. 4. Luther, Martin, 1483-1546. I. Title. II. Title: Towards an ecclesiology in the contemporary Indian context of Hindu nationalism in critical interaction with Martin Luther's ecclesiology. III. Series: Interfaith treasures uncovered ; 1.

DDC 262 23

Printed in India.

Dedicated to:

J. Usha, *my wife, and* ***Benil Sahayadhas,***
my son, who stood with me with unflinching support throughout the completion of this project.

THE BOOK

In this book, the author attempts to re-construe an Indian ecclesiology *vis-à-vis* the narrowly defined ideals of Hindu nationalism in contemporary India by analyzing and investigating the ecclesiological thoughts of Martin Luther, the 16th century Protestant Reformer. The book brilliantly places the teachings of the Reformer within 'the social and historical travails of that time and brings them to bear on the ongoing constructive task of living into a relevant and appropriate Indian ecclesiology (and thereby, Indian Christian theology) today'. In this process, it is being maintained that the Indian Church must transform itself into a "*Perichoretic Communion*", in which the diverse Christian ethnic groups and the plurality of cultures of India must interpenetrate in order to form one unit, while keeping their respective ethnic, linguistic and cultural identities intact. The author draws his insights from Luther's fundamental theological/ ecclesiological principle: ***unity of the opposites*** or ***distinction and integration***, and passionately proposes that it must be the principle of the Indian Church today.

This theological writing presents an important and pioneering opus. It clearly focuses on contemporary contextual issues, concerns and challenges, and offers insights of general validity, not only for the Indian world but also from a global perspective. It is a timely volume and is well advised for the worldwide Church and the public at large.

THE AUTHOR

Rev. Dr. R. Sahayadhas is an ordained minister of the India Evangelical Lutheran Church (IELC). Currently he is Professor, teaching ***systematic theology***, and the Dean, Division of Graduate Studies at the United Theological College, Bangalore. Prof. Sahayadhas affirms himself as an ecclesial person with a deep-rooted passion and commitment for the mission/ministry of the Church, especially in India. He has come to academia after having a long stint of pastoral experience to his credit. What is the relationship between ecclesia and academia? With the emergence of Enlightenment rationalism, there was an attempt to thrust religion within the limits of reason and a good number of theologians developed a kind of scepticism with regard to the ability of ecclesia to stand rational scrutiny. But Prof. Sahayadhas iterates not only the indispensable inter-connection but also their inter-dependence. This volume represents his passion to be a genuine bridge-builder or interlocutor between ecclesia and academia. He can best be caricatured as a 'Middle-Path' theologian. He is the recipient of Dr. Frank Collision Award (2012) for the best published article by an Indian theologian entitled: "Religion-State Relationship: Significance of a Middle-Path in Contemporary India". Prof. Sahayadhas is married to ***J. Usha***, a High School Teacher, teaching Tamil language, and they are blessed with a son, ***Benil Sahayadhas***, who is studying in college now.

LIST OF ABBREVIATIONS

AIADMK	All India Anna Dravida Munnetra Kazhagom
ATC	Asia Trading Corporation
ATESEA	Association of Theological Education in South East Asia
BC	*Book of Concord*
BJP	Bharatya Janata Party
BTE-SSC	Board of Theological Education-Senate of Serampore College
CAB	Catholic Association of Bombay
CCA	Christian Conference of Asia
CMS	Church Missionary Society
CPH	Concordia Publishing House
CSS	Christava Sahitya Samiti
CTCR	Commission on Theology and Church Relations
CUP	Cambridge University Press
DMK	Dravida Munnetra Kazhagom
EPW	*Economic and Political Weekly*
INC (I)	Indian National Congress (Indira)
INC	Indian National Congress
ISPCK	Indian Society for Promoting Christian Knowledge
JDDJ	Joint Declaration on the Doctrine of Justification
LCMS	Lutheran Church Missouri Synod

LW	*Luther's Works* - American Edition
LWF	Lutheran World Federation
NDA	National Democratic Alliance
NT	New Testament
OBC	Other Backward Classes
OT	Old Testament
OUP	Oxford University Press
PCPCU	Pontifical Council for Promoting Christian Unity
RSS	Rashtrya Swayamsevak Sangh
SATHRI	South Asia Theological Research Institute
SCM	Student Christian Movement
TPI	Theological Publications of India
UBS	Union Biblical Seminary
UK	United Kingdom
UPA	United Progressive Alliance
US/USA	United States of America
UTC	United Theological College
VHP	Vishwa Hindu Parishad
WA	*D. Martin Luthers Werke.* Kritische Gesammtausgabe, Weimer, 1883ff.
WARC	World Alliance of the Reformed Churches

ACKNOWLEDGEMENTS

It is quite obvious that a volume of this nature cannot emerge without the support, encouragement and strength from various people. Here, I would like to place on record my sincere thanks and appreciation to all those who played a role, direct or indirect, in my theological journey thus far. With a grateful heart and a profound sense of respect, I thank Prof. O. V. Jathanna, whom I always regard as one of the finest Indian Christian theological minds, for his guidance in the process of the making of this volume. His meticulous and untiring reading of the script and his candid, stimulating, sharp and challenging comments on the entire work are unparalleled. In my interaction with him in the course of this work, I have experienced his deep sense of commitment and depth of knowledge in matters academic; it has been an inspiring and enriching learning experience indeed. I am also privileged that he has written the "FOREWORD" for this volume. However, if there is any discrepancy in this volume, I am fully responsible for the same.

I also acknowledge the valuable contributions of Prof. Sathianathan Clarke, a well-known contemporary theologian, who mentored me as a student of theology at the United Theological College, Bangalore. Prof. Jayakiran Sebastian is another prominent theologian, a friend and philosopher, who had shared his theological knowledge and resources with me in my academic journey. He continues to support and encourage me in my theological journey and I place on record my sincere appreciation and thanks to him. I am glad that a brief blurb of Dr. Kiran Sebastian appears on the back cover of this volume. A special word of thanks is due to the Prof. Christopher Duraisingh who had offered his valuable suggestions and shared a great deal of resource materials in the process of this research.

I also take this opportunity to place on record my indebtedness to him as he was inspirational in creating a special interest in me towards Christian Theology in my academic pursuit. Dr. S. Muthuraj and Prof. Sham P. Thomas are the two people with whom I had extensive dialogue on various issues and they enabled me to clarify many of those issues and I thank them for their valuable contributions.

I also express my sincere thanks and appreciation to all my faculty colleagues and the Library staff at the United Theological College, Bangalore, for their support and strength in the course of my research. My thanks are also due to Mrs. Delphin George who read through the Manuscript and offered valuable suggestions on English Language.

This book in its original form was my doctoral dissertation submitted to the Senate of Serampore College towards the D. Th. (Doctoral of Theology) degree and is published with written permission. I am grateful to the Senate of Serampore College for extending permission to publish it. It comes in this form after thorough revision and the author is responsible for the changed title, contents and the opinions expressed in it.

I thank the Rev. J. Isaac Moon, President Emeritus, India Evangelical Lutheran Church (IELC), who encouraged me to pursue my higher theological education and also arranged partial financial support from the Lutheran World Federation for my research. I also take this opportunity to thank Christ Lutheran Church at Vellore and all the members of this congregation, with whom I served as a pastor for over fifteen years, for their unflinching love and support in my spiritual and academic journey. I have to mention here that it is my long stint of pastoral experience that has provided me with a great deal of insights to be a bridge builder between the academia and ecclesia, which will be conspicuous, at least sporadically, in this volume. Last, but not the least, my profound sense of gratitude goes to my wife, J. Usha, and my son, Benil Sahayadhas, who stood with me with their unfailing love and support, especially during the times of frustration in the course of my research. Finally, I submit this volume with a profound sense of humility before and gratefulness to God whose ever-abiding grace has been the sustaining force throughout my journey in this research.

R. Sahayadhas
September 2016

PREFACE

Has the Church become obsolescent in the context of the Hindu nationalist politics in modern India? Has religion come to be blunted and relegated to human private realms with the onset of modernisation and secularisation? How can the Church respond to modernity's attempt to reshape the world within the limits of technical/technological reason alone? What is the relationship between religion and the 'secular' state? What is our response to Hindutva's aggressive posture to hijack India's pluralistic texture in order to re-construe the nation through the instrumentation of the dominant religion? This volume revolves around such vital questions that have serious consequences to the life and mission of the Church (and thereby the life of the Indian Christians) in contemporary India. It is the outcome of my intense research and passionate theological reflections towards understanding the nature of the Church, its life and mission/ministry in the contemporary Indian context of Hindu nationalism. To be sure, ecclesia has never been a perfect institution since its inception in world history. In its worldwide journey, the Church has, time and again, been tormented by various heresies (controversial teachings), schisms, internal conflicts, and self-contradictions. It could never exhibit an ideal image as the body of Christ for the world. Hence, for the critics and detractors, ecclesia cannot evoke in them any sense of special interest as a theme of theological ratiocination.

Nevertheless, the Church can never be dispensed with from the world because it is a vital force in history that has influenced and shaped (and continues to do so) numerous structures, systems, cultures, worldviews and lifestyles across the globe. My own commitment to ecclesia and ecclesiological reflections stems from my firm conviction that despite all its self-contradictions, ecclesia still stands as a definite and indispensable referral point for Christian self-identity, especially in contexts like India; and it is a veritable instrument of God on earth to proclaim the new quality of life – the life of the perichoretic warmth and plenitude of the Trinity – God has made available in Jesus Christ for the entire world amidst all that attempts to fragment the world of humans. Of course, a critical question is: how is this message going to get translated in the Indian public domain, which, even though is characterized by incredible pluralism at all level of its existence, yet is saturated with the Hindutva ideology with its aggressive anti-other stance?

In India, secularism plays an important role in holding the diverse people groups together with their variegated faith persuasions, cultural and linguistic affiliations and ethnicities within the principle and framework of 'unity in diversity'. But the emergence of the Hindu nationalism in Indian politics as a veritable force, scaffolded by Hindutva ideology, has become a serious concern for the minority communities, especially Christians and Muslims, as they are benchmarked as the definite others or outsiders or even enemies of the (Hindu) nation. In this process, the ominous signs are that Hindutva is going to unleash an all out attack on the secular fabric of the nation, and thereby on the minority communities, under the cover of 'development'. The invocation of the 'uniform civil code' in the recent debates within Hindutva politics even at the slightest possibility of its resurgence as a decisive force, for instance, can be seen as an important indicator in this direction. The ominous signs are that Hindutva would strategically marginalize the more moderate and liberal forces who would lend their voice for an all-inclusive politics even within its own fold for the sake of a more aggressive and exclusive politics. It has serious ramifications for the life of the Church and the minority communities in the days ahead.

It then prompts us to ask certain disturbing questions and concerns about the meaning of ecclesia and its ongoing mission/ministry in this part of the world. Hence, my reflections on the Indian Church begin from the Hindu nationalist situation of the Indian politics, which is in no way sympathetic towards the minority communities

– Christians and Muslims to be precise – because of their unrelenting endeavours to resist Hindutva's attempt to re-construe India as a Hindu Rāshtrā, the land or nation of the Hindus. In this context, a proper self-understanding of ecclesia is a pressing need because it alone can provide a strong theological/spiritual foundation for the self-understanding and empowerment of the Indian Christians to live in this land of theirs as Christians and engage in the Church's mission for the wider world.

Ecclesia has various designations: it has come to be described as an institution, a communion, a sacrament, a herald, a servant and a community of disciples (of Jesus). There are other designations as well. Notable among them are: 'the Church in the round', which is a feminist vision of an inclusive ecclesiology that would foster equality of gender relations within its boundaries; 'Church as a people's movement' with a special focus on the base communities; and also the notion of 'Churchless Christianity'. Church is recognized as a universal entity with particular expressions. These designations raise a fundamental question pertaining to the relationship between ecclesia and the kingdom of God. While critics find the Church as a detour of what Jesus had intended, others, while acknowledging the fundamental difference between the Kingdom of God and the Church, do lend credence to the Church as an important entity that bears traits of the kingdom of God and continues to represent it on earth albeit its historical incongruencies.

All the above designations, representations and definitions are valid expressions of the Church indeed and, to the most part, they are very meaningful to the context in which they emerged. Nonetheless, if we ask the question whether such designations are meaningful expressions of the Church in the Hindu nationalist context, the answer might not be in the affirmative. Quite obviously the Church needs to take on a new form in this context and this volume is a modest attempt to recapture the image of the Church, using the 16th century German Reformer's thoughts on the Church. It is an attempt to enter into critical conversation with Luther's thoughts on the Church, which, I believe, have the potential spiritual/theological resources to navigate our own contemporary imaginations of the Church. Having said that I rush to add that, in this ecclesiological exercise, my endeavour is neither to privilege the Reformer nor to uncritically validate his theological thoughts. Rather, I intend to glean certain helpful insights, which emanated from his fundamental theological principle as he intervened in the Church and society as a Reformer.

Martin Luther's central theological principle can rightly be sketched as unity of the opposites, which is posited on the central theological axiom: God's acceptance of the unacceptable. It is a principle that critiques and undercuts many of our assumptions in contemporary societies, more specifically the one Hindutva attempts to create in India. Can Hindu nationalist discourse and politics conceive of a unity of the opposites? I think the central ideology that navigates Hindu nationalist politics in India is 'unity though uniformity', for Hindutva regards diversity as a serious impediment to progress. The progressive idiom Hindutva promotes is not premised on social justice and, hence, it cannot be inclusive. It will look for an-other India, a homogenous India, that would embrace only those who can catch up with the kind of progress Hindutva envisages, eyeing on a homogenous nation at the expense of diversity, plurality and multiplicity.

In the face of these developments, the Indian Church cannot be complacent. It has to be proactive rather than reactive. It has to proclaim its central message of embrace – a message that springs from God's acceptance of the unacceptable in Christ – in a world that is characterized by exclusion, especially of the differently others. It is an important ecclesiological task that the Church becomes a 'sign-post' that points to the possibility of a harmonious human communion in the midst of all that attempts to fragment and lock up human existence within rigid boundaries. This volume, therefore, attempts to understand those components of ecclesiology with the specific purpose of moving towards an appropriate vision of ecclesia in the contemporary Indian context. In the process, it also seeks to address several key issues and concerns that are crucial and critically important for the secular fabric of the nation and also for the life and mission of the Indian Church in the 21st century. Prominent among them are: Church's response to (a) organized violence, especially when the Church is subjected to brutal violence; (b) gender inequality within the Church and society; (c) caste discrimination within and without the Church; (d) religion-state interface; (e) diversity of cultures, linguistic affiliations, ethnicities and faith persuasions and their co-existence; (f) the issue of dealing with the differently 'others' in contemporary societies and so on. Herewith, I seek to place these concerns of local, national, and global significance in the public domain with an earnest hope that they would generate informed and healthy discussions for the transformation of the world into a harmonious aboard of the entire creation of God. It heralds that what ultimately concerns us is 'life in all its fullness' that is premised on the truth and plenitude of the Divine Trinity.

September 2016

R. Sahayadhas
Professor of Systematic Theology &
Dean, Division of Graduate Studies
United Theological College
Bengaluru, India

FOREWORD

R. Sahayadhas' *Hindu Nationalism and the Indian Church: Towards an Ecclesiology in Conversation with Martin Luther* is an important and timely study. In this volume, the author attempts to critically engage himself, both analytically and creatively, with the 16th century reformer Martin Luther's ecclesiological thought, with a view to gain helpful insights for the task of constructing a meaningful ecclesiology in the present-day Indian context, especially in view of the challenges posed by the Hindu nationalistic ideology known as Hindutva.

This attempt in itself is significant particularly for two reasons:

(1) In the recent times, there is a tendency to overlook the rich Christian theological heritage—both historical and contemporary ecumenical—under the misconceived premise that a contextual theology has to take primarily or even predominantly the contextual dimension of the situatedness of theological thinking, often understood in terms of context-related experience of the people in a given situation to the detriment of other dimensions of Christian theology. Thus, the helpful recognition as well as the right emphasis that Christian Theology worth the name at any time and in any place has to be contextual, i.e., context-related, has, in the recent past, tended to increasingly narrow down the scope of theological thinking, especially in the Protestant theological scenario in the Indian context. This renders theology poorer and leads to a particular kind of stagnation in theological thought.

(2) Even in the contextual dimension of theology certain aspects become dominant and others become neglected. This in itself has to be seen partly as a corrective to the lack of emphasis on these particular issues in the theological thinking of our theological forebears, recent as well as distant, which are now seen to be both

important and urgent for various reasons. Seen from this perspective, the above-mentioned phenomenon has to be recognized as having certain legitimacy because of its corrective value. At the same time, the problem with this tendency is that only a couple of contextual aspects get recurrent highlighting and others tend to be overshadowed or even ignored outright so much that, over a period of time, theology faces the danger of not addressing persons in the totality of their being. The point here is not that every theologian has to take all contextual aspects equally meticulously and seriously, which is not feasible. On the other hand, theology in a given period of time has to pay sufficient attention in its totality to the various contextual aspects and not just to a select and preferred few aspects. The phenomenon of religio-socio-political challenges posed by the Hindutva ideology, by and large, belongs to the category of such neglected ones, when it comes to systematic-constructive theology.

With regard to both aspects, Sahayadhas' present volume is to be seen as an earnest effort to remedy this deficit to an appreciable extent, within the scope of the present volume. It is to be hoped that this work will encourage others to take the various other aspects that are more or less consigned to oblivion, but nevertheless are important in the life-situation of the church and the society in a given context, and, therefore, need to be taken into account in theological research and reflection.

Sahayadhas sees Martin Luther as the originating voice of the Protestant Ecclesiology and argues that there are certain similarities between Luther's context and the present-day Indian context, characterized by Hindutva, especially as regards the relationship between religion and state, particularly with regard to usurping and wielding political power for self-preservation and vested interests, which proved to be disastrous to the medieval church and society-at-large. It is commendable that, in the present volume, Luther's ecclesiological thought is not studied or presented in isolation, but is seen in its integral relation to Luther's overall theological framework as well as his key theological concerns.

What the author is particularly interested in Luther's ecclesiological thought are the insights that would be of help, when, through critical and creative interaction, are taken further in relation to the present-day Indian context. As a result of such an interaction with Luther's ecclesiological thinking, Sahayadhas highlights the following as helpful insights gleaned from Luther's theological thought:

- Luther's principle of "distinction and integration" in guiding the religion-state relationship;
- the critical perspective provided by the "Theology of the Cross" in shaping theological thought and expression;
- the hermeneutical key found in the doctrine of justification by grace through faith, over against emphasizing work-righteousness that paved the way to corrupt practices in the structures and functioning of the ecclesial institutions that vitiated the ecclesial and the societal life and thought;
- the emphasis on the equality of all believers that found expression in the "Priesthood of all Believers;"
- and the understanding of the church as *Communio Sanctorum*, which, in the final analysis, is derived from the perichoretic or co-inherent communion of the Trinity.

With this, the author constructively seeks to present his proposal for a "communion ecclesiology," understanding the church "as the *perichoretic* communion of the people of God that promotes relationship, reconciliation, and healing in an overwhelmingly fragmented, hurt and hurting world". This is proposed vis-à-vis the *Hindutva*'s repudiation of 'unity in diversity,' and its single-minded promotion of 'unity in uniformity' or homogeneity, and its aggressive project of either "assimilating" or "annihilating" those who do not submit themselves to its view and way of being what it considers as the only manner to be authentically Indian, which by definition and design is intended to exclude especially Muslims and Christians, marking them as the "other," i.e., as outsiders. The author takes care to point out that this communion is not confined to the Christian community, but is open to all who, in the Spirit of Jesus Christ, are ready to embrace the "other," and strive towards communion, healing and fullness of life for all. For, what we see in Jesus Christ—his life and teachings, death and resurrection—is God's will to accept what is considered to be unacceptable, by extending the loving concern across all human-made divisions and boundaries, so that there will be a new quality of life and relationship. The present work is, thus, also an invitation to those who are influenced by Hindutva ideology to reflect afresh in the light of a communion ecclesiology. This being the inaugural volume of the author, later he will have to expound further on how the sociological and the anthropological dimensions of "communion" will be integrated into the communion ecclesiology, as theology has to take into account the ecclesial and societal dimensions of life in a concrete life-situation.

To the credit of the author, it should be said that the work seeks to steer clear of hagiographical tendencies, uncritically extolling the Reformer's thought in every respect. Aspects of Luther's thought or action which the author thinks are not helpful or negative, especially in view of developing a communion ecclesiology, are pointed out candidly: for example, Luther's *ad hoc* response to the Peasants' Revolt, and his act of putting the administration of the church in the hands of the political rulers of the land. At the same time, in a number of cases the popular misperceptions and misrepresentations of Luther have been corrected with helpful interpretations and appropriate documentation.

Through the publication of this volume, which will be both rewarding and challenging to read, Sahayadhas has given a clear and a hopeful sign that one can expect from him further profound theological writings in the future, as he is willing to learn from the theological treasures of the past, as well as from the contemporary ecumenical world, and, at the same time, he is concerned with thinking theologically through contemporary contextual issues, concerns, and challenges, especially the ones, which though important, tend to be overlooked and by-passed. I wish him well in his present and future theological endeavours.

O.V. Jathanna
Professor of Systematic Theology and Principal (Retired)
United Theological College, Bengaluru

CONTENTS

Chapter Five

Chapter Six

Chapter One

INTRODUCTION

Indian Church in Crisis Phase

The Indian Church currently undergoes a crisis situation, perpetrated by the right wing Hindu extremism, which came to make its veritable manifestation in terms of Hindu nationalism effectively scaffolded by the formidable Hindutva ideology. The Christian presence in India is as old as the religion itself if we lend credence to the theory of Apostle Thomas' visit to India. The St. Thomas Christians of Kerala emerged as an indigenous Christian community and co-existed with other communities for several centuries. However, this ambience gradually changed with the western missionary enterprises in India, which coincided (and to some extend collaborated) with colonialism, leading many Hindus to develop a strong suspicion about the very intention of the Church and culminating into a sort of a strong anti-Christian syndrome in the minds of the Hindu right. Consequently, the Church came to be viewed with great prejudice as having only one purpose of conversion – a view that completely overlooks the enormous contribution the Church had made in the life of the nation. One of the serious invectives leveled against Christians is that their loyalty to the nation is split, which emanates from the mischievous insinuation that their *God-man is not the son of the soil but of an alien soil.* Some of the serious fallouts of this emergent trend are that (a) the very identity and purpose of the Christians are called into question;

(b) they are regarded to be second class citizens in their own country by the Hindu right; and (c) the Christian community is subjected to hatred, hostility and brutal violence by Hindu extremists. Truly, it is a transition of Hinduism from its mostly tolerant mould to a totally alien posture of intolerance, aggression and ostracism.

The crisis has worsened with the attacks on Christians, Churches and Christian institutions in various parts of the country including the brutal violence against Christians in Kandhamal in Orissa, and Karnataka in 2008. These attacks on the Church are not "sporadic outbursts due to provocations" as has often been described by some of the state authorities. Rather, they are the visible manifestations of certain deep-rooted anti-Christian sentiments that had been hatched over a period of time; and these sentiments are further intensified by continuous hate-campaigns. Undeniably, the seeds of hatred that had been sown by the likes of V. D. Savarkar have come to their bitter fruition in our time. Consumed by hate, Hindutva makes use of certain central features of the Church, such as its Christo-centric theology and missions and conversion – *forceful conversion*, according to Hindutva – as pretexts to intimidate the Church.

Hindu Nationalism

Hindu nationalism is an interventionist discourse, emanating mostly from the modern English educated Hindu elites who are relentless in their attempt to catapult themselves to the ruling bloc of Indian politics through the instrumentation of Hindu religion. In other words, Hindu nationalism took shape not as a struggle for social justice, but as a veritable political feature in order to safeguard the interests of the Hindu elites. A deeper analysis of the current situation points to the fact that Hindutva and Hindu nationalism are the political underpinnings of certain emergent phenomena within Hinduism – a sense of victimhood,[1] a sense of loss of Hinduism's erstwhile authority over the civil society, and an attempt to re-inscribe Hindu culture as the essential and overarching way of life that alone would make India a strong Hindu nation. For a long time, Brahminic Hinduism held its supremacy over the masses through its dubiously canonized caste system in the name of upholding social dharma that had locked people within the hierarchically ascribed communities.[2] This was a cleverly devised long-term strategy of the Hindu lawmakers of antiquity in order to ensure that no one would dare to challenge this divisive system because of its overt religious sanction.

But this draconian system of discrimination came to be challenged with the emergence of modernization, secularization and the new awareness among the marginalized and subjugated communities. Undeniably, Christianity did play a vital role towards this new consciousness, and this emergent subversive voice of protest and resistance poses a real challenge to the Hindu hegemony.[3] Arguably, then, Hindutva's warpath against the minority Christians is fuelled not by conversions but by the Church's engagement with the marginalized that had enabled them to raise their voice against oppression and claim their fundamental rights. Hindu nationalism, undergirded by the aggressive Hindutva ideology, thus, is a carefully worked out project towards the cultural homogenization of the pluralistic texture of India through political impositions for the re-inscription of the Brahminic hegemony, and it has been successful to a large extent, at least in states where the saffron brigades are in power. It has established itself as a veritable political force, having its ideological roots deeply entrenched in Brahminic Hinduism. The great pace with which Hindutva ideology could disseminate among the Indian public, in fact, falsifies the 'melting pot' theory that has predicted the dissolution of religion from the public sphere with the onset of modernization and secularization.[4]

Hindutva's Diatribe against the Church

Hindutva identifies and benchmarks those who resist its sinister designs as the 'others' or 'enemies' and works relentlessly to demonize, exorcise or even annihilate them. Clearly, Muslims and Christians are the two communities who stand firm in their resistance to Hindutva's homogenization drive and they are the targets of Hindutva's anger. Faced with such resistance, Hindutva intensifies its discourse on reality in oppositional categories – something similar to Huntington's clash of civilizations – creating a kind of an *insider-outsider* syndrome among the Hindus. In this kind of hate-filled discourse, the Church becomes a definite 'other' and an *outsider*. In relation to the Church the most appalling attitudes of Hindutva are manifold: (a) the way it calls into question the very meaning and purpose of the life and missions of the Church, (b) its deliberate intentions to create a crisis of identity and meaning among the Christians, and (c) its hate-filled ideology that spews venomous hostility towards the Church.

The resurgence of Hindutva (as an ideology) and Hindu nationalism[5] (as its political manifestation) has, thus, assumed dangerous proportions in our time. Its hate-filled ideological campaigns, acute hostility towards the 'other', and intolerance of differences clearly point to a kind of fascist-elitist political programme couched in religion. In the event of Hindutva's encounter with the Church and the brutalities that have been perpetrated against Christians, the stereotypical response from the Hindutva ideologues is that they are due to 'provocation', which implies conversion. But then, there is a strange but conspicuous paradox with regard to Hindutva's activism in the event of conversions, i.e., the self-styled Hindutva warriors become furious and run into mad rampage mostly when people from the marginalised communities decide to convert. It indicates that Hindutva demands people, especially those who have been assigned a lower status by Brahminic Hinduism, not to overstep their ascribed boundaries. In other words, Hindutva is totally intolerant when people prefer to be different, and the attacks on the Church and Christians must be seen in the light of the above developments.[6]

The alarming hatred, hostility and crude violence against the Indian Church become cause for great concern and the trauma becomes even worse when we realize that, on many occasions, the state authority, which is supposed to protect and uphold the secular fabric of the nation, throws its weight behind the Hindu extremists against Christians. These are serious conditions created by Hindutva proponents, which would even deny Christians their rightful place in this land. Golwalkar, for instance, reiterated:

> The foreign races [Muslims and Christians] in Hindustan must either adopt the Hindu culture and language, must learn to respect and hold in reverence Hindu religion, must entertain no ideas but those of glorification of the Hindu race and culture...or may

> stay in the country, wholly subordinated to the Hindu nation, claiming nothing, deserving no privileges, far less any preferential treatment; not even citizen's rights..."[7]

This view has not undergone any serious transformation over the years; rather it has got further intensified as evidenced, for instance, by the Janatha Party chief Subramanian Swamy's reiteration in one of his media articles that those who refuse to subject themselves to the Hindu identity must forfeit even voting rights.[8] Further, it has been alleged that the *singular* objective of all church people in India is conversion or "harvesting of souls for Jesus" and everything they do "is and should be an instrument for attaining this singular objective".[9] Christians are identified as enemies of India,[10] having no loyalty to their 'fatherland'.[11] Central to all these negativised campaigns against the Christians is an apprehension that the 'Hindus will become minority in their own country and their culture will get erased from their own land'.[12] This is a tenuous but mischievous propaganda for the simple fact that despite its presence in this land for about two millennia and its active missions for well over five centuries, the Christians are still a small minority, accounting to about 2.5% of the population. The negative propaganda of the Hindutva forces infuses a sense of zeal among the right wing Hindus to protect their religion and culture from erosion by adopting a warpath. [13] Therefore, whenever there are violent outrages against the Church in India, the Hindutva forces are quick enough to justify those incidents as the reaction of the Hindus due to provocation, which is mostly identified as "forcible conversion". Thus the growth of the Church will be viewed as formidable to the peaceful coexistence of the nation based on the simple arithmetic: "a convert from Hinduism is not only one Hindu less, but an *enemy* more"[14]

Nationalism Couched in Religion

Hindu nationalism in India represents a deliberate use of the dominant religion laced with an extremist mode of discourse in order to impose a corporatist religious/cultural identity on all those who inhabit this land, which dumps pluralism as an impediment to the realization of a strong and unified nation. Hindu nationalism can, thus, be identified as a defining category of contemporary India for specific reasons.

(i) It has enunciated itself as a prominent feature of modern Indian politics, which has transformed the political ambience with the activities of the *sangh parivar* that dangerously polarize communities.

(ii) It attempts to homogenize particular identities into a broad based Hindu national identity based on a 'sacred geography'.[15]

(iii) It demands that every 'patriotic' Indian must learn to put the 'nation before the self',[16] which is a strategic move to downplay the more contradictory aspects of Hindu religion: untouchability, caste discriminations, subordination of women, and so on.[17]

(iv) Hindu nationalism is relentless in its attempt to de-secularise the Indian polity and re-sacralise the nation state by essentialising certain religious tenets, and denouncing the state secularism for its attempt to treat all faiths alike.[18]

(v) Hindu nationalism is founded on the explicit and insistent exclusion of those defined as 'others', particularly targeting the minorities – the Muslims and Christians.[19]

(vi) Sociologists generally acknowledge that Hindutva is the resurgence and revitalization of the Brahminic hegemony to re-establish itself from the heavy loss it has experienced of its strongholds by way of re-construing and reconstructing the nation.[20]

(vii) Hindu nationalism is intolerant towards multiplicity and differences. That is why Hindutva forces selectively use religious symbols, undercutting the religious and spiritual core of Hinduism, and forge out of it a "hate-filled ideology of nationalism".[21]

Hindu nationalist situation exhibits a kind of discomfiture over plurality and a deep-rooted suspicion about the minorities. As far as the hardcore Hindutva proponents are concerned, plurality/difference is something that stands as an obstruction to (Hindu) national unity and this discomfiture leads to suspect the minorities as divisive. A crucial factor that constitutes the general Hindu consciousness is the partition of Pakistan from India on religious lines on the eve of independence, and the agony and trauma of partition are still part of the Indian consciousness.[22] Therefore, the Hindu mind is suspicious of the minorities, and the Christian presence (and mission) in India is viewed as standing in the way of Hindutva's ultimate goal of creating a homogenous Hindu nation, either by assimilating the religious and ethno-cultural minorities into its Brahminic construction of an Indian nation or by excluding/annihilating those identified as the 'others'.[23] It is, thus, an urgent task for the Indian Church to understand itself, especially its nature and function in this hostile situation, empower the Christians to affirm their identity as Christians and engage in the mission of the Church, and make an appropriate response to the suspicious Hindu minds in and through its theology and praxis.

Significance of the Church in India

As viewed by O. V. Jathanna, the Church is one of the most important and indispensable components of Christianity and Christian faith. It is the referral point and a definite constituent of the identity of the Christians in India.[24] In its origin, the Church typified a new reality that emerged from the death and resurrection of Jesus Christ and continuously nourished by the Holy Spirit. It was characterized by its bearing witness to Christ through the believers' service to one another, sometimes even at the risk of their life. It was a new communion, which was Christ-centered, Spirit-guided and neighbour-oriented with a new life-style of love, self-sacrifice and humble service in imitation of Christ.[25] In this sense, then, the Church (not as an institution[26] but in the sense of the communion of believers) is an instrument of God to fulfill God's eternal will for the entire world, especially in the midst of brokenness and suffering.[27] There can be no doubt that the Indian Church has made substantial contributions to the life of the nation and its people in several areas, especially in their brokenness and suffering. But Hindutva calls into question the very integrity and purpose of the Church, and the identity of the Indian Christians. It is against this background that the present study is undertaken with the fundamental question: in such a context, how should the Church understand itself, especially its structure, style of living, and mission?

History tells that Christianity took shape from the crucibles of the rejection and martyrdom of its central faith figure, Jesus Christ. The early followers of Jesus also were rejected by their own community and subsequently subjected to brutal violence by the Jewish religious authority and the Roman colonial state. This hostile environment forced them to disperse to different parts of the world, of course, with their unflinching zeal to proclaim the good news of the risen Christ. The enthusiasm and zeal of these itinerant missionaries further increased as the message of the risen Christ found greater receptivity among the new audience, referred to as Gentiles. What attracted the new audience towards the Gospel and to make a decision for Christ was the central Christian message of *God's acceptance of the unacceptable*, i.e., 'in Christ God has made available a new quality of life – a new quality of relationship – to the entire humanity'. It was truly appealing to the hearers who lived in a context of brokenness, misery and incertitude. This reception of the message of Jesus Christ across boundaries made Christianity to quickly transcend its Jewish enclaves and transform itself into a universal faith. It suggests that the missionary character is something that can never be dispensed with from Christianity, for it is a character that was deeply entrenched in it from its very birth as a religion on the move.

Nonetheless, the missionary nature of the Church is not without its own difficulties, especially when it encounters the revival and revitalization of other religious persuasions. Thus, while acknowledging the missionary character as something that is constitutively inherent and, hence, cannot be dispensed with from the Church, we also need to bear in mind that the Church of Christ must be sensitive to the fact that (a) ours is an age that witnesses the dissemination of secularist and liberal democratic ideals (guided by technical reason) as the most appropriate way of life in the public domain; (b) it is, at the same time, an age that experiences the revival, resurgence and, at times, the dangerous manifestations of the world religions that have become capable of pitching peoples, communities and cultures against each other; and (c) it is an age that announces the demise of all meta-stories and hegemonies. The

Church of Christ must be conscious of these new developments and re-construe and reconstruct its theology in order to make sense to the immediate context of its expression. This task requires adequate theological resources and the present study has identified Martin Luther's thoughts on ecclesia as a viable resource for our ecclesiological imaginations in the contemporary Hindu Nationalist situation in India.

Martin Luther – Our Conversation Partner

The present study is done in *critical* conversation with Martin Luther's thoughts on the Church and my preference has certain specific reasons.

i. Luther's ecclesiology is an originating voice of a Protestant ecclesiology, which emerged as a voice of 'protest' against the distorted life of the medieval Church. In many respects, his ecclesiology became foundational to a substantial section of the Indian Church, shaping its life and mission.[28] Implicitly, then, his ecclesiological constructions need to be critically studied and appropriated in the present context even if we differ from his thoughts.

ii. Luther brought the universal significance of the Gospel of God's unconditional, suffering and redeeming acceptance of the unacceptable to the forefront. If we take this Gospel seriously, then, it becomes inevitable to understand the Church as fundamentally different from other social groups, which normally draw sharp lines of separation between 'we' and 'they', based on certain rules, rituals, traditions, and patterns of behaviour, promoting clear distinction between those *inside* and *outside*. In this schema, those defined as 'outsiders' may be considered as strangers and enemies and not as part of the group. Hindutva does exactly the same; it identifies the Church as a definite 'other' and, hence, liable to be ostracized, excluded or assimilated. In this context, Luther's understanding of *communio* undercuts this hegemonic trait of Hindutva. In his understanding, the communion of the faithful is open by definition, always willing to expose itself to the risk of being interfaced with people who are not only different, but also unacceptable (Gal 3:26-28). In this model of ecclesia, those whom God has accepted into the communion will be in relationship with those whom God has also invited, whether one finds them acceptable or not. Further, in this model, when God invites those who respond to God's Word into the communion, the differences do not melt away; rather, while differences prevailing, the believers are held together in a bond of unity in faith and in the Word of God.[29] Here, the fundamental theological principle is *unity of the opposites* or *distinction and integration* because God has dismantled the wall of separation (Eph 2:14f). This is one of the most significant contributions of the Reformer, which is seldom realized in our theological/ecclesiological reflections.

iii. Luther's understanding of the ministry with special reference to the 'priesthood of all believers' is an important resource for us to understand the Church's vocation (mission/ ministry) and also the vocation of the Christian person within and outside the boundaries of the Church, especially in the context of the marginalized communities who are kept outside the boundaries of the Hindu sacred scriptures, not to mention the priestly functions, by the Hindu priestly class.

iv. Luther's ecclesiology emerged in a context in which the state was dominated by religion (Church) and he was attempting to disconnect the Church from its political-economic powers and abuses and to renew the Church for the service of the Gospel. His theology of Church-State relationship is predicated on two sets of principles: whereas the normative principles of the Church are faith and love, the normative principles that govern the civil order are reason and justice.[30] Hence, his interpretation of the Church-State relationship needs to be critically evaluated, especially in the context of Hindutva's attempt to dominate the nation state based on Vedic Hinduism.

v. In Luther's perception, the Church is called to participate in God's creative authority, redemptive concern and comprehensive vision for a fuller human existence. Luther believed that within God's communion, there is no hierarchical distinction in terms of human dignity as everyone is equal before God. Further, in his view, authority is meant to serve and empower and not to oppress and exploit. We need to rediscover this effect of the Gospel in the context of Hindu nationalism.

vi. An important feature of Luther's theology is the freedom of the religious person, an aspect that finds its clearest expression in his tract, "The Babylonian Captivity of the Church". This freedom was an important tool for him to critique the Roman hegemony, which held people captive under the sea of Rome, both religiously and politically. Contemporary Hindu nationalism exhibits a similar trait, which attempts to keep the variegated peoples and cultures under the sway of Brahminic Hinduism, disallowing even the freedom that has been engendered in the constitution. Here, the idea of freedom is a credible tool to critique Hindutva's hegemony over the different religious persuasions of the people of this country. As Otto Hermann Pesch aptly puts it, "Luther needs only to eliminate some of the medieval presuppositions which he takes for granted and his God question becomes ours."[31] Hence, it is no exaggeration to say that his ecclesiology is more capable of witnessing to the biblical message in today's context than many of its classical counterparts.

vii. Luther's theology of the Church, which was carefully constructed around the idea of *communio sanctorum*, is a vitally important resource for us to navigate our own ecclesiological discourse in the context of Hindu Nationalism's anti-other discourse in contemporary India.

Having said the above, we do acknowledge that Luther's ecclesiology must be studied critically in order to avoid falling into theologically questionable and historically obsolete patterns of thought or authority. A critically important point in reading Luther's ecclesiology in the present context is that we must be able to distinguish between his *theological reasons* and *final judgments*. While we do not concur with his final judgments, it is necessary to understand his theological reasons and the principles on which he constructed his theology. His engagement with the peasants' agitation, for instance, is a typical case in this regard. Critics expressed their total disagreement with Luther's position with regard to the Peasant war in Germany. They are of the opinion that he unambiguously stood with the princes against the peasants, which, however, is found not to be the entire truth. In Gerhad O. Forde's view,

> As a medieval man he [Luther] was completely caught up in a mythology of status quo. He was afraid of change and revolution and had no faith in popular movements. This he did not see. If he had been more aware of his own blind spots perhaps his decision [concerning peasants' agitation] might have been different. At least, even though we come to understand his theological reasons, we need not concur with his final decision – especially not in the cruel and intemperate manner in which it was expressed.[32]

It suggests that Luther himself was not a perfect man and his theology cannot be taken as an already finished product. But, then, these cannot be the reasons to reject his theology as a whole, because such a rejection would amount to losing sight of the many and varied insights of his theology of the Church.

Intended Readers and Structure of the Study

As I commenced this study, I had three sets of audience in mind. *First*, the (beleaguered) Indian Christians, drawn from different ethno-cultural and linguistic traditions and social strata from across the nation, who constitute about 2.5 % of the total Indian population of over 1.2 billion people. I would like to commend this study to provide a viable and meaningful spiritual/theological basis for them *to affirm their Christian identity and live as Christians* in this hostile environment created by Hindutva. *Second*, it is intended to be a resource for the people of different faith persuasions (with special focus on the 'majority' Hindus) in India for their engagement in the pluralistic Indian public space in a spirit of mutual conversation. *Third*, it is also envisaged to be a critical theological/spiritual resource to the members of the worldwide Christian communion, especially those who are involved in active mission, to redefine and reconstruct their mission in the changed climate in the 21st century.

The study is structured into seven chapters. The first chapter is *Introduction*, which sets forth the theme of the study. Chapter two is "*Hindu Nationalism in Contemporary India*", which analyzes the contemporary Hindu nationalist situation – its historical roots, its encounter with Indian nationalism, various trajectories, the modes of consolidation of its political base, its contemporary manifestations and its impact on the life and mission of the Church. Chapter three is *Emergent Image of Ecclesia*, which makes an analytical survey of the Biblical, historical and theological roots of the Church, and various theological developments that occurred in its journey up to the Protestant Reformation in the 16th century. The fourth chapter is an analytical study of *Ecclesia in Martin Luther's Thoughts*, which examines the important themes that the Reformer dealt with in his thoughts on the Church and the fundamental theological principle with which he engaged in his ecclesiological reflections. Chapter five is *Luther's Thoughts on Ecclesia – A Contextual Critique*, which offers a contextual critique of Luther's ecclesiology, taking cognizance of the context of the Reformer, the contemporary Hindu nationalist situation and the situation of the Indian Church. The sixth chapter is *Church – The Perichoretic Communion of the People of God*, which proposes *perichoretic communion* as a relevant mode of discourse on the Church in the given context. Chapter seven is Conclusion, which recaptures the study and opens up new vistas of ecclesiological reflections closely attuned to the contemporary situation. I earnestly hope that this study is a potential resource for the renewal of the Church, both Indian and worldwide, to be a living force that engenders new hope and direction to the fragmented, hurt and hurting world in order to build mutually enriching and loving relationships between human beings and human communities across boundaries, hoping and working together for the fullness of life for all, including God's wider creation.

Notes

1 See Vinayak Damodhar Savarkar, *Six Glorious Epochs of Indian History* (Bombay: Bal Savarkar Publishers, 1971). The fundamental premises of this volume are: India's glorious past under the 'Hindu' rulers that had stretched from Afghanistan to Sri Lanka; the alien invasions from the Greeks, the Moguls and the British; and the ways in which the valorous Hindu kings defeated the invaders and established their supremacy. The most insidious part of this whole exercise is the clever way in which Savarkar was able to interpret those invasions in terms of 'clash of civilizations' in which, the Hindu civilization was the victim of alien aggressions. But the Hindus were able to resist the aggressors with valour and might. Undoubtedly, this is a strategically devised treatment of history. Savarkar is furious about the whole idea of Hindu tolerance and invites Hindu's to dispel their tolerance and 'pay back' the aggressive forces in the most fitting manner. Incidentally, the idea of the 'clash of civilizations' forms the central theme of Samuel P. Huntington's recent influential work, *The Clash of Civilizations and the Remaking of the World Order* (New York: Simon & Schuster, 1996). Huntington's central thesis in this volume is that if there is a third clash on the global level, it will be the clash of civilizations. Opinions are divided. September 11, for instance, has been viewed as a vindication of Huntington's thesis by a section of the intellectuals, which was also repudiated by others. (CNN-IBN debate on Huntington's thesis, involving eminent sociologists and columnists like Christophe Jeffrelot, M. J. Akbar, Ashish Nandy and Tarun, 30 January 2009).

2 T. K. Oommen, "Religious Nationalism and Democratic Polity in India: Impossibility of Reconciliation" in Mark T. B. Laing, ed., *Nationalism and Hindutva: A Christian Response* (Delhi: ISPCK, 2005), pp. 37ff.

3 See Pralay Kanungo, "Hindutva's Fury against Christians in Orissa" in *Economic and Political Weekly* (September 13, 2008), pp. 16-19.

4 One of the perceptions of the sociologists a generation ago was that the effect of modernization and secularization would eliminate the prominence of religious and cultural identifications. See Harvey Cox, *The Secular City* (London: SCM Press, 1965). Cox's theory has been challenged by Michael Novak in his volume *The Rise of the Untenable Ethnics* (New York: Macmillan, 1972). However, Cox himself had to revise his theory in his volume *Religion in the Secular City* (New York: Simon & Schuster, 1984).

5 Deshpande posits the historical roots of Hindu nationalism in two crucial locations: (i) the emergence of Hindutva, pioneered by Savarkar (1923), which has become the ideological basis for contemporary Hindu nationalism; and (ii) the elite middle class of the postcolonial India, and according to Deshpande, it is this elite middle class that produces and transmits legitimizing ideologies and the masses (mainly the lower middle class) play the role as the sincere consumers of these dominant ideologies. Satish Deshpande *Contemporary India: A Sociological View* (Delhi: Viking, 2003), pp. 74-97 & 125-150.

6 The anti-Christian campaigners are particularly agitated against the works of the Church among the Dalits, Tribals and other marginalized communities. These activities of the Church are interpreted as divisive and anti-national. See Arun Shourie, *Missionaries in India: Continuities, Changes, Dilemmas* (Delhi: ASA Publications, 1994), pp. 234ff. For a detailed case study on communal riots, specifically targeted against the minorities, see Pradeep Manadev, *Communalism in India: A Paradigm Shift to Indian Politics* (Delhi: Authors Press), pp. 191-277.

7 M. S. Golwalkar, *We, or Our Nationhood Defined* (Nagpur: Bharat Prakashan, 1939), p. 62.

8 *The New Indian Express* (28.12.08), p. 6.

9 Arun Shourie, *Harvesting Our Souls: Missionaries, Their Design, Their Claims* (Delhi: ASA, 2001), p. 49. See Ch. 5: "The Singular Objective *vs.* the law of the land", pp. 42-53.

10 *Religious Conversions: Frequently Asked Questions* (Mumbai: Hindu Vivek Kendra, 1999), p. 11.

11 V. D. Savarkar, *Hindutva*, p. 113.

12 *The New Indian Express* (Bangalore: 28 Sept. 2008), p. 10.

13 Two instances can be cited as examples here. *First,* commenting on the 24.01.2009 outrage against women in Mangalore, the Sri Ram Sene chief Promod Mutalik and its functionaries heaped praises on the attackers as doing a wonderful job of "protecting India's culture". The Sene warriors openly declared that they would do it again. *Second,* the same Mutalik commended those involved in the Malagaon blast case as having done a holy job and hinted that the Malagoan blast was an example of what they are capable of. (Source: CNN-IBN News Reports and Analyses since 24 January 2009). For more details on this issue, see *Religious Conversions,* p. 24; Ashok V. Chowgule, *Christianity in India: The Hindutva Perspective* (Mumbai: Hindu Vivek Kendra, 1999); Arun Shourie, *Harvesting Our Souls,* pp.7-68.

14 *Religious Conversions,* p. 11.

15 For a discussion on the origin and development of the ideology of 'sacred geography', see Satish Deshpande, *Contemporary India*, pp. 74-97.

16 Madhu Kishwar, *Religion at the Service of Nationalism and Other Essays* (Delhi: OUP, 1998), p. 251.

17 Satish Deshpande, *Contemporary India*, p. 78.

18 Ibid., p. 83. Hindutva's specific mode of attack on secularism is to describe it as 'pseudo-secularism' and accuse it of 'pampering the minorities' and 'denying Hindus the dominant status they ought to have in India', based on the claim of Hindu majority. But it has been challenged as being inconsistent with the heterogeneity of the socio-religious practices of those who constitute the majority. See K. N. Panikkar, *Before the Night Falls: Forebodings of Fascism in India* (Bangalore: Books for Change, 2003), pp. 35ff.

19 S. Deshpande *Contemporary India*, p. 83.

20 Rajni Kothari, *Communalism in Indian Politics* (Ahmedabad: Rainbow Publishers, 1998), p. 126.

21 Madhu Kishwar, *Religion at the Service of Nationalism*, p. 252.

22 Gerald James Larson, *India's Agony over Religion* (Delhi: Oxford University Press, 1997), pp. 32f.

23 Sathianathan Clarke, "Hindutva, Religious and Ethnocultural Minorities, and Indian-Christian Theology" *Harvard Theological Review* 95:2 (April 2002), p. 200. According to Hansen, "The Hindu nationalists desire to transform Indian public culture into a sovereign, disciplined national culture rooted in what is claimed to be a superior ancient Hindu past, and to impose a corporatist and disciplined social and political organization upon society". Thomas Blom Hansen, *The Saffron Wave* (Delhi: Oxford University Press, 2004), p. 4. According to Hindu nationalists, "India was always and will remain fundamentally Hindu in a civilized sense, just as (it implies) Muslims and other non-Hindus always were alien to India and will remain so for ever." Ibid., p. 11. See also Vinayak Damodhar Savarkar, *Hindutva: Who Is a Hindu?* (Bombay: Veer Savarkar Prakasan, 6th ed. 1989), p. 25.

24 O. V. Jathanna, "Ecclesiology in Context: Reflections from an Indian Perspective in the Light of Current Ecumenical Deliberations" *Bangalore Theological Forum* Vol. 28, Nos. 3-4 (Sep-Dec 1996), pp. 3-11.

25 Lucius Nereparampil, "The Church in the Johannine Literature" *Indian Journal of Theology* Vol. 28, Nos. 3 & 4 (July-Dec, 1979), p. 177.

26 One of the major criticisms against the Church is that it has become too institutionalized. But it has to be acknowledged that the Church, in order to exist in this world as an embodied entity, needs certain

structures. The last period (roughly 100-140 CE) of NT history is characterized by certain new demands and difficulties that were developing within the newly emergent Church, which prompted the Church towards institutionalization. For more details see Norman Perrin, *The New Testament: An Introduction* (New York: Harcourt Brace, 1974), pp. 253-254 & John Macquarrie, *Principles of Christian Theology* (London: SCM Press, 1986), pp. 373-378 & 401-416.

27 M. J. Joseph, "The Church in Paul" *Indian Journal of Theology* Vol. 28, 3-4 (July-Dec, 1979), p. 157.

28 For an informative reading on the impact of Reformation theology on a number of theological/ ecclesiological traditions, see John Dillenberger and Claude Welch, *Protestant Christianity* (New York: Charles Scribner's Sons, 1954), pp. 311ff.

29 Klaus Nürnberger, *Martin Luther's Message for Us Today: A Perspective from the South* (Pieter-Martizburg: Cluster Publications, 2005), pp. 143-144.

30 Robert Kolb, "Christian Civic Responsibility in an Age of Judgment", *Concordia Journal* Vol. 19, No. 1 (Jan 1993), p. 20.

31 Otto Hermann Pesch, *The God Question in Thomas Aquinas and Martin Luther* (Philadelphia: Fortress Press, 1972), p. 27.

32 Gerhard O. Forde, *Where God Meets Man: Luther's Down-to-Earth Approach to the Gospel* (Minneapolis: Augsburg Publishing House, 1972), pp. 109-110.

Chapter Two

HINDU NATIONALISM IN CONTEMPORARY INDIA

The Point of View

In a great variety of ways the Indian sub-continent has become a boiling pot of widely divergent mindsets, cultures, communities, and linguistic and religious traditions[1]. A critically important aspect of contemporary India is the impact of colonialism, imperialism and modern capitalist liberalism, which had led to a tacit interplay between various forms of traditionalism and that of modernity. India is a multifaceted reality, characterized by incredible pluralism and contrasting (and often conflicting) diversity at all levels of its existence. India stands as a unified entity on the principle of *unity in diversity* and not on *uniformity* or *homogeneity*. It is known as the largest democracy of the world with a population of over 1.2 billion people from at least six different racial types with some amount of predominance of the Aryan race in the Indo-Gangetic plain in the North and the Dravidian race in the South. Almost 35% of the total population is illiterate and an equal segment lives in abject poverty.[2] It has 18 official languages (including English) and 1652 dialects. Indian society is stratified into 4635 castes and 641 tribal communities and a number of them were marginalized and confined within their hereditary occupations, legitimized by Vedic Religion as *vranashrama dharma* (the basis on which caste system is constructed). India is the cradle of many religions and the minority religious communities

(Muslim, Christian, Sikh, Buddhist, Jain, Jewish, Parsee and Animist communities, who constitute almost 40% of the population) coexist with the dominant Hindu community till this day.[3] This coexistence has, however, been threatened by the resurgent Hinduism in the form of Hindu nationalism, which, in fact, has caused great alarm among those traditions that are identified as 'others', especially the religious minorities. As P. B. Mehta maintains, "The threat posed to minorities lies not only in singular conceptions of nationalism, but in the very quest for benchmarking identities, in search for something that makes us one thing rather than another". [4]

When we analyze the Indian reality, both its historic past[5] and the present, it is possible to discern the constellation of a number of discourses emanating from the distinct particularities that intersect in the social domain with each one having its own claims and counter-claims, making deeper influences and impacts in the nation's life. Even though the different particularities attempt to coexist, yet, often times, they were at loggerhead with each other, causing inexplicable trauma that have become typical of this ancient sub-continent. Among the various elements that are characteristic of India, of late religion (which Whitehead regarded as something to do with an individual's own "solitariness"[6]), with its emotive and cultural affiliations, has, somehow, come to play a key role in the Indian polity, making deeper inroads into all spheres of its life. It has given rise to the issue of religion-state relationship that has become an important subject of political and academic debate in the recent times. Critics opine that the issue is crucial not simply because of the fact that there is a convergence of a number of distinct and living religious traditions within the texture of Indian consciousness, but because religion has become the root cause of several of its current problems.

Any enquiry into the Indian reality must take into account the dense texture of India's cultural heritage(s) as it will put the present crises of India in a very different light. In this regard, Gerald James Larson identifies certain crucial factors that influence the contemporary Indian context such as: (a) the ancient layers of India's religious life are alive and active in contemporary India; (b) even the discourse on 'secular state' is a hybrid one and it is nothing but a religious discourse in modern India, given the fact that the so-called post-independent 'secular state' is projected, in many respects, a forward caste Neo-Hindu state. In other words, the 'secular state' is loaded with a number of religious components; and (c) India's current difficulty over religion is instructive for rethinking some of our most general notions of religion and secularization.[7] To understand the contemporary Indian situation further, we need to take a look at some of the theoretical tools employed by analysts that would facilitate our task of analyzing the Hindu nationalist situation of India by developing/deploying our own tools.

Theoretical Devices

Theorists of South Asian studies employed a number of viewpoints[8] and also developed certain theoretical devices that best suited their purpose. Larson lists out four prominent theoretical devices: modernization-secularization theory, orientalist theory, world-systems theory and subaltern theory.[9]

Modernization-Secularization Theory

The new awakening and the quest for enquiry that emerged with Enlightenment modernity resulted in the breakdown of many of the old institutionalized ideas and customs.[10] This was followed by a new revolution in natural science that became a great challenge to religion, for until then religion was in control of human affairs: both spiritual and mundane. But in the changed milieu, religion found itself being pushed to the private realm of the individuals (a sacred-secular divide). This can be seen as the beginning of the process of *modernization* and *secularization*.

There are certain basic assumptions behind this form of theorizing. (a) The process of modernization and secularization begins from an emerging dissatisfaction over the traditional ways of human social life, mostly dictated by religion. In the new climate, religion accounts for a completely negative caricature, i.e., religion and religious ideas are viewed as impediments to reform and development. (b) Progress is contingent solely on industrialization and economic growth, which are possible only by new forms of rationalization, i.e., the free play of ideas in the intellectual centers or academies, free flow of commodities in the market, and a thoroughly this-worldly humanistic orientation. (c) What the modern world requires is a steady upward mobility from *less advanced* traditional societies to *more advanced* modern societies. Humanity has come to maturity to plan and bring to perfection the transition from the former to the latter. (d) The paradigm for modernization and secularization is provided mainly by the industrial countries of the west. (e) The backwardness of the traditional societies become explicit when evaluated in comparison with the modern western societies and their development from the 16th century onward.[11] The philosophical/epistemological roots of this mode of theorizing go back to the Neo-Kantian and Neo-Hegelian schools and its economic roots can be located in capitalism or democratic socialism. Modern India is shaped by the ideas derived from these western intellectual traditions by Nehru and other secularists.[12]

Orientalist Theory

What Enlightenment modernity did was, above all, to establish a kind of Euro-centrism that has become hazardous to the non-western world in many ways, and it has prompted critics from the southern hemisphere to develop their own rationality that could unsettle the Euro-centric bias and make the suppressed and obscured voices from the margins heard in the mainstream. Orientalism is such a pioneering theoretical work that emerged within this climate of western dominance of the rest. In his volume entitled *Orientalism*, Edward Said discusses extensively about the intricacies and polarities of this Orient-Occident dynamism. Orientalist theorizing, according to him, "is a style of thought based upon an ontological and epistemological distinction made between 'the Orient' and 'the Occident'".[13] It is a "way of coming to terms with the Orient that is based on the Oriental's special place in European Western experience...The Orient, as far as the European was concerned, was almost an European invention and had been since antiquity a place of romance, exotic beings, haunting memories, landscapes and remarkable experiences". The Orient is not only adjacent to Europe, but it is also the place of Europe's greatest, richest and oldest colonies and 'one of its deepest and most recurring images of the 'other''. In fact, the Orient enabled Europe 'to define itself as contrasting image, idea, personality and experience' (of superiority). Thus, Orientalism is a way of thought based on an ontological and epistemological differentiation created between the "Orient" and the "Occident". From a historic and material point of view, Orientalism was a western academic project for administering, restructuring and subjugating the Orient. Orient, as far as the Occident is concerned, is not just out there; but it is a human creation and, as such, it has a history, ideology, imagery, vocabulary, and a tradition of thought that have given it a reality and presence in and for the west.[14]

The Orientalist theory derives its epistemology from the intellectual traditions that include anthropology, sociology, philology, history, archeology, art history, ancient history, language, poetry, novels, philosophy, political science, history of religions and so forth.[15] The fundamental difference between the modernization-secularization theory and orientalist theory is that, while the former is concerned with its trajectory of future-oriented development, the latter focuses on the 'classical' and essentialist formulations that have come from the world's great non-western civilizations and religions as they are set forth primarily in textual, art-historical and archeological sources. Many Indian scholars showed greater inclination and fascination over this kind of theorizing but the interest is rapidly diminishing in the recent times.

World-Systems Theory

The salience of this theory is its *modes of production-consumption* discourse. There are certain fundamental features that distinguish this way of theorizing from that of the modernization-secularization approach. (a) It stresses the importance of a holistic systemic approach when we analyze the context of a nation. In this approach, for instance, one cannot speak about a particular country or state in isolation from the rest of the world for the simple fact that nations form parts of the whole. India as a nation, according to this theory, clearly remains in the semi-periphery as a potential mediating power between the core and the periphery in terms of the core world of economy. (b) In contrast to the modernization-secularization theory (which relies mostly on Max Weber's "elective affinity" model of interfacing ideas and political movements with economic institutions or 'modes of production') world systems theory stresses the underlying significance of the material or economic growth.[16] As such, in this mode of reasoning, the emergence of active religious groups, their ideas and intellectual content are more or less reduced as 'anti-systemic movements' within the larger exploitative "world system", which typifies a naïvely reductive analysis of religion in line with the conventional Marxian analysis. The important content, rather, is a veiled symptom of changing modes of material production-and-consumption within a national economy and the world system as a whole. Interestingly, the world-systems theorizing and its Marxian orientations could not make much headway in the European and American academia except forming only a tiny part of the intellectual traditions, which emerged in the wake of the end of the cold war and the collapse of Soviet system. But such leftist theorizing is quite rampant in the Indian intellectual circles despite the fact that neither the Indian society is structured on class lines nor is its economy structured on a socialist pattern[17] – an irony indeed.

Subaltern Theory

In a provocative essay entitled "Can the Subaltern Speak?" G. C. Spivak has to come to a rather reluctant but challenging conclusion that in the given situation of the elite dominance, the subaltern can hardly speak.[18] Nevertheless, "Subaltern Studies" continues its relentless toils to retrieve the voices from the margin and to reinscribe them in the mainstream. Subaltern theory is one of the most stimulating theoretical devices that emerged from 'Subaltern Studies' and it is typically Indian, developed by a collective of young scholars and intellectuals, which has given the name '*Subaltern Studies Collective*' for its well-developed theoretical response to the onslaught of elite historiography.

The primary purpose of the scholars involved in this collective is to undertake research in an attempt to unsettle what they term the 'elite historiography' of India both by the western and native historians. Quite amazingly, in their theorizing, they have picked up oft-obscured issues, events and themes from specifically local contexts from rural India or from the underside of history, which were otherwise unheard of or regarded to be insignificant.[19] They represent the struggles and voices of the subalterns, systematically subdued by the elitist historiography. The subaltern scholars have called into question the predominant assumptions and presuppositions of the earlier three ways of theorizing because, in their view, they do not represent the Indian reality in its entirety. Spivak, for instance, recaptures the basic intent of this collective in the very title of her review essay: "Subaltern Studies: Deconstructing Historiography".[20] Commenting on the task and purpose of this group, she affirms that this collective moves beyond the broad mainstream and biased overview of the 'official' or 'elitist' history of India in order to trace the concrete and particular historical struggles of the subaltern masses.

This sort of theorizing looks for "an-other" India, which is not yet a "nation" or, as Dipesh Chakrabarty described, "Subaltern Studies begins by questioning the category of the nation and poses the failure of the 'nation' to come to its own as a fundamental problem of modern Indian history."[21] To put it more clearly, the primary purpose of the Subaltern Studies Project is "to understand the consciousness that informed and still informs political actions taken by the Subaltern classes on their own, independently of any elite narratives".[22] It unearths an important factor, i.e., the 'religious consciousness' of the subalterns, which remains as an important subject of study.[23] There are two major criticisms directed against the Subaltern theory: (a) even though this way of theorizing has the credit of recognizing the significance of religious consciousness in the life of the Subalterns, it has not made much headway in its treatment of this consciousness towards a systematic conceptualization; and (b) epistemologically and intellectually, it is a derivative of the postmodernist and poststructuralist western critical theories and thereby runs the risk of being little more than a kind of Neo-Orientalist theorizing.[24]

Towards a Multi-Civilizational Approach

The various modes of theorizing that we have seen above are developed by the analysts of South Asian studies from specific viewpoints that helped them understand the Indian context for their own specific objectives. As is evident from our analysis, the above theories fall short of our requirement, especially our task of analyzing the contemporary Indian context of Hindu nationalism. The modernization-secularization theory anticipates the dissipation of religious perspectives with the dissemination of modern-secular worldviews. In independent India, Nehru, for instance, posited his 'economistic and deterministic approach' on the dissolution of the hold of religion over the lives of the people with economic affluence, the spread of education, and science and technology.[25] But time and again we are reminded that it is not so facile to dispense with religion from human consciousness and its expression in the public domain, for religion is capable of making a comeback with a vengeful mood as in the case of religious fundamentalism[26] and fanaticism.[27] Orientalist theory does talk about the great pre-modern world religions, especially describing these classical traditions as the belief systems of the great textual traditions. But seldom have these approaches taken us beyond the essentialist formulations.[28] World-Systems theory recognizes the importance of religious perspective as a crucial component in many "anti-systemic movements", but treats religious perspectives in a reductive manner. Finally, Subaltern theory, though acknowledges the religious consciousness of the Subalterns, frankly admits that it has not made substantial progress in treating it. These setbacks in the various traditions of theorizing, then, prompt us to go beyond them, especially in our attempt to look at certain historically and existentially important issues that have ramifications for all walks Indian of life. Therefore, in this study, I propose to explore the contemporary Indian context from a *multi-civilizational* point of view towards proper approximation, conceptualization and articulation.

This study identifies Hindu nationalism as a challenging issue that has consequences for the life of all segments of the people of India, and more specifically, to the minority communities like the Christians. Hence, Hindu nationalism's claims of 'Hindu majority', 'dominant status' in India and its attempt to exclude those who do not conform to or fall within the parameters of its claims become the fundamental points of departure in the present analysis of the Indian context. This, I believe, is particularly useful as we attempt to locate ecclesia within the wider Indian context. The multi-civilizational approach serves as a tool to look at and bring to light the various attempts of Hindu nationalists to obscure, down play, and even deny several other vital issues, namely, caste discriminations, gender inequality, poverty, pluralism, and cultural diversity by projecting the Hindu culture as the homogenous entity to build a strong nation.

The root of multi-civilizationalism goes back to anti-colonial movements in India. One of the colonial projects was to 'civilize' the natives with modern western ways of life – western knowledge systems, educational methods, life-styles and religion – with the presupposition that the non-west was completely caught up in darkness and the colonizers' task was to dispel this darkness with the light from the West. In this context, another form of civilizational idiom was made prominent by the native upper caste intellectuals, aiming at retrieving and re-establishing the pristine form of native culture that was seen as the most essential component of anti-colonial movements, a process that can aptly be called 're-civilizationalism'.[29] It was a mode of discourse that emerged from within the colonized sites as a counter to the civilizational idiom of the colonizers.

In India, nationalism and re-civilizationalism operate from two different premises: while nationalism operates from the vantage point of the nation-state, re-civilizationalism functions from the wider context of Hindu civilization. It works relentlessly to reinscribe the traditional Hindu culture as an overarching entity by erasing the different traditions and distinct particularities of religious and ethno-cultural minorities. There are two crucial ways in which the dominant attempt to bring the country under the sway of the ascriptive ideology of the old order: *structural unification* and *cultural uniformization*. The re-civilizational idiom maintains that the reinvention of the subdued and obscured Hindu traditions would be an authentic means to combat the onslaught of western colonialism, because the west has now permeated every walk of life – both structures and minds.[30] In this project, the colonial public space (which provided the upper caste elites with ample opportunities such as: English education, their occupations in the key decision-making and value enforcing positions, and their self-assumed role as the liaison between the colonial masters and the masses) was effectively used by the upper caste elites in order to disseminate their legitimizing ideologies and also to maintain control over the masses.[31] The new re-civilizational idiom within the nation-state certainly creates some kind of suspicion among those who adhere to particular cultural practices, namely, the minorities and the marginalized, who view it as an attempt to dominate their ways of life by the dominant communities. This has driven the local civilizations to be locked in a conflict of establishing their pre-eminence over the others, which in turn has created a kind of an identity politics among the different communities.

Multi-civilizationalism is a critical category – a strategic theoretical device – developed specifically for the present study. It stands as a resistance or a challenge to the Hindutva forces, who, in the name of re-civilizing the natives are engaged in forcefully erasing the different identities in order to impose a singular dominant identity on them. A typical example of this insidious project is Hindutva's efforts to 'reconvert' those who had converted to other religions, especially to Christianity, often with brutal force. *India Today* reports[32] that the Hindu revivalists are on a big conversion spree among the Christian Tribals in Madhya Pradesh. While the Hindus choose to describe their reconversion spree as "homecoming", the Christians view that the Hindu revivalists have a free hand because they enjoy the tacit support of the (then) BJP government of the state. In this backdrop of the alarmingly ascriptive re-civilizational discourse of Hindutva, a multi-civilizational approach serves, among others, two important objectives: (a) as a strategic theoretical device to resist the menacing onslaught of Hindutva ideology that threatens to erase the pluralistic texture of India in order to re-construe and reconstruct it into a mono-cultural entity; and (b) as a way of reaffirming plurality, multiplicity and differences of religious, cultural and ethnic affiliations of the people, which is the essential characteristic of India. Further, when Hindutva's re-civilizationalism attempts to exclude 'others' as "unfits" and establish one dominant religion as the *only* legitimate way of life; when it operates from the vantage point of Brahminic-Hindu hegemony; and when it turns out to be impervious and insidious to other ways of life that are integral to this sub-continent, multi-civilizationalism is a counter-consciousness that reaffirms heterogeneity, which is the salience, beauty and richness of this sub-continent. From a Christian point of view, multi-civilizationalism is a critical category that could locate ecclesia within the larger context of the diverse Indian reality.

Reality of India

In a way, India can be viewed simply as one among a number of other modern nation-states, as it is possible to treat India in the same general manner that one would treat other nation-states. Thus, there is a possibility to set forth the social and cultural realities of contemporary India, the history of India, and the philosophic and religious traditions of India in a direct, conventional manner.[33] Nevertheless, in some other ways, India is remarkably different and distinct from other nations, not simply because of its sheer antiquity and continuity of its civilization, but because of the complex density and texture of traditions that exist side by side in the sub-continent, ranging from archaic traditions to the most sophisticated developments in the 21st century high-tech culture.[34]

Construing the Nation Religiously

Amidst the co-existence of these variegated traditions, the challenge of Hindu nationalism is so acute that their co-existence is put to severe test. In the given situation, one wonders whether the co-existence will have a smooth sail in the long run at all, because the turn of events in the socio-political arena of the country has taken new trajectories to infuse a specific way of imagining the nation, i.e., from a dominant (or majoritarian) Hindu religious perspective, which has claimed to be an all-embracing way of life for *all* those who inhabit this part of the world that is called 'India'. In such a milieu, it is pointed out that an *ascriptively-particularized* way of viewing the nation by denying its wide variety of ways of life will be hazardous to those who do not subscribe to that particular way of life. As Hindu nationalism has the potential to stake its claims in all facets of Indian life, it would be apt here first to deal with its 'secular' counterpart, Indian nationalism and the discourses connected with it and, then, to take a look at how Hindu nationalism attempts to tame the minorities, especially the Christians in India.

Rise of Nationalism

Nationalism is a typically European product, which emerged within the context of the fragmentation of the western societies and people's languishing under feudalism. At the outset it aided people to shift their focus from the local to the wider nation state. In this sense, it appears that it had provided certain degree of respite to the people who were gasping under the yoke of feudalism. Nationalism, however, had the notorious distinction of abetting catastrophic effects on the lives of people across the globe wherever it has been invoked, for nationalism often works through people's emotive affiliations towards the nation, which is promoted as patriotism. Often the proponents of nationalism invoke patriotism for their selfish ends. Thus, it could be argued that nationalism encapsulates discursive meanings and traits that make it a difficult task to define it in simple terms.

Nationalism – Definition

Defining nationalism, Ernest Gellner says:

> Nationalism is primarily a political principle, which holds that the political and the national unit should be congruent. Nationalism as a sentiment, or as a movement, can best be defined in terms of this principle. Nationalist *sentiment* is the feeling of anger aroused by the violation of the principle, or the feeling of satisfaction aroused by its fulfillment. A nationalist *movement* is one actuated by a sentiment of this kind.[35]

In this definition, nationalism encapsulates at least two aspects, namely, a sentiment and a movement, and yet it is defined mostly in political terms in the contemporary times, albeit the difficulties involved in defining contemporary nationalism in such terms. Benedict Anderson is right when he asserts, "Nation, nationality, nationalism – all have proved notoriously difficult to define, let alone to analyse."[36] The complexity that is involved in defining nationalism has, in fact, driven many historians and theorists to conclude that devising a single definition of nation/nationalism is impossible. Yet the phenomenon has existed and still exists. Anderson, however, provides a stunning definition: "it [nation] is an imagined political community – and imagined as both inherently limited and sovereign".[37] In this sense, nationalism is a discourse on an imagined space called 'nation' that demands absolute loyalty of the citizens towards this imagined space, even to the extent of placing the self only next to the nation. As a matter of fact, Hindu nationalism expends much of its energy to popularize this ideology.

Contemporary critics are not at ease with the conventional definitions of nation because of the tendency among theorists to lump all the ethnic movements together and categorize them as 'ethno-nationalist',[38] based on the assumption that 'nation' and 'ethnos' imply a group of people who adhere to the belief that they are genealogically related. For these theorists, the nation-state is essentially a post-medieval, post-industrial product, i.e., a product of modernity. Most of the modern critics are influenced by the idea that nationalist movements are the result of the breaking up of the hold of traditional culture and religion over public life, and, in that process, this space has been usurped by modernity (science, technology and industrialization), making religion and religious questions virtually obsolescent for modern humanity.[39]

Eric Lott views this as a naïve perception of religion. According to him, the hold of religion is still alive and active on people's consciousness across the globe and as such it is not so facile to discard religion from the public domain, a fact that is clearly demonstrated, for example, by the contemporary Indian nationalism that "is very close to religion in its form and scope".[40] Eric Lott, here, places Adrian Hastings' arguments on the role of religion in shaping a nation's identity as quite apposite: (i) Religion provides the formative shape and a sacral sense to the origins of particular ethnic groups and defines their identity in opposition to the other groups they confront or come into contact with. (ii) This kind of identity formation, then, leads them to mythologize any threat to their identity and creates a kind of a deep sense of differentiation between 'us' and 'them'. (iii) In this kind of identity formation, the 'faith-figures' act as a community's representatives, interpret the community's special faith-identity and take a leading role in the affirmation of what a 'nation' means. (iv) Religious faith has prompted the generation of vernacular literature, which firmly establishes the consciousness of a national identity. This is in sharp contrast to Benedict Anderson's thesis that only in the decline of the influence of religion and the sacred language that nationalism emerges. (v) In the Case of the Jewish nation, for instance, the Hebrew Scripture provided a clear image of what a theocratic nation would look like and it inspired the belief in God's preferential liking for a particular people. (vi) The development of national/state Churches led by religious leaders who were separate from the state is the final development that reflects the relationship between rulers and faith-leaders. These arguments make a strong case for the powerful role of biblical faith in developing national identities in subsequent centuries leading up to modern Europe.[41]

The relationship between ethnicity and nationalism is another important point. For the postmodernists, ethnicity is a welcome sign but nationalism is not. There is also the strivings for internationalism or trans-nationalism, perhaps the highest possible form of the state, for which the international socialists, certain religious communities like (certain sects of) Muslims, Christians and the globalizing capitalists will aim at. In Deshpande's view, for the influential elite fraction of the middle class "the nation is no longer the canvas for their dreams and aspirations. This is due to the decline of old ideologies as much as the rise of new ones – the emergence of sub-national loyalties as well as the lure of transnational identities".[42] There is a strong criticism that nationalism went out of control to the extent that even its proponents could not tame it.[43] Nationalism, then, is such a complex phenomenon, created by several factors, configured in different ways and used and abused by groups and (vested) interests.

Nationalism – Its Historic Roots

Nationalism, it is said, is a peculiarly modern phenomenon, originating from the assumption that nations are the primary focus of political allegiance (of course, a view not so widely accepted). From the available evidence, it is possible to locate the origin of the concept of nationalism in the 18th century, in which the primary focus of nationalism was on the loyalty of the citizens towards smaller and homogenous political units such as the fiefdom, religious groups, city or immediate locality.[44] This focus of loyalty gradually shifted from the immediate local to the wider Sovereign State for a number of reasons: the demise of feudal structures, the rise of large, centralized states, the tyranny of the feudal lords, and so forth. In the changed climate, the ruler was no longer identified with the state, which was in sharp contrast to the feudal structures in which the local rulers were identified with the fiefdom. But now in the context of the wider nations, the rulers were seen as only the *temporary heads* of states, which gave the citizens some kind of respite from the tyrannies of their cruel over lords. According to Gellner, nationalism emerged from the crucibles of the transition of the agrarian society to the industrial society. The crucial question was whether the agrarian way of life was sufficient to sustain anything like the present and the anticipated number of inhabitants of the planet earth, and the kind of standard of living which humans now aspire to achieve. This tendency has driven humanity to commit to industrial society, marginalizing the agrarian societies and without even responding to many of the problems created by that shift (as peasants were driven off the land to feed the ever-hungry industry). The Industrial society certainly demanded some kind of cultural homogeneity, which was typical of European nationalism.[45]

Another form of nationalism is cultural nationalism,[46] which does not nurse any political objectives (at least in principle), but is interested in certain national cultural expression through activities such as art, literature, music dance and so on. This sort of 'cultural nationalism' must not, however, be confused with the 'cultural nationalism' preached in India by the Hindutva ideologues. For, in this type of *cultural nationalism*, the predominant tendency is to promote (Brahminic) Hindu culture as the only culture that must be embraced by all those who inhabit or intend to inhabit this land because it is this culture that determines the way of life of the Indians. For the Hindu elites of the 19th century, the concept of national identity was indistinguishable from Hindu identity. This is what is dealt with in this study as *Hindu (cultural) nationalism*. It is indicative of the fact that the current Indian public space is occupied by two key conflicting discourses: Indian nationalism and Hindu nationalism.[47] The proponents of Indian nationalism were mostly the western educated liberal elites who sought to distance themselves from the cultural heritage of Hindus for all practical purposes; and Hindu nationalism emerged as a reaction to Indian nationalism and it is deeply rooted in the Hindu cultural revival and social reform movements of the 19th century.

Two early nationalist thinkers were Jean Jacques Rousseau and Johan Gottfried Herder. Inspired by the examples of the Greek city-states, Rousseau attempted to envision how modern political communities could once again become the nodal points of human public activities in their various manifestations – a transition from annual public festivals to a civil religion – in order to heal the split between the spiritual and the temporal. Hence, his specific interest was to highlight the contributions of all citizens towards a common goal, in which the political constitutions would reflect the peculiarities of each community for which it is held together. Herder's contribution, on the contrary, was to stress the need for the cultural unity of a community, in which the prominent discourse was on the role played by folklore and popular traditions.[48] By the end of the 19th century, European nationalist movements became more conservative and even reactionary. There is consensus among critics that the progressive intensification and parochialism of these nationalist movements culminated into world war. In Partha Chatterjee's assessment:

> Nothing, it would seem, was left in the legacy of nationalism to make people in the Western world feel good about it. This recent assessment of the idea explains why nationalism is now viewed as a dark, elemental, unpredictable force of primordial nature, threatening the orderly calm civilized life...In light of current discussions on the subject in the media, it is surprising to recall that not many years ago nationalism was generally considered one of Europe's magnificent gifts to the rest of the world. It is also not often remembered today that the two greatest wars of the twentieth century, engulfing as they did virtually every part of the globe, were brought about by Europe's failure to manage its own ethnic nationalisms.[49]

After World War II, the nationalist fervor began to dissipate in many European nations. But in Asia and Africa, nationalism resurged mainly as anti-colonial movements.

Nationalist Discourse in India

There are certain elemental factors that contributed to the emergence of nationalism especially within the colonized sites. In these sites, nationalism was developed primarily from within the doctrines of freedom/independence, sovereignty of the nation-state and patriotism. When colonialism was in force, nationalistic/patriotic sentiments were used extensively in anti-colonial movements in the third world countries.[50] Within the colonized cites, thus, nationalism was invoked to keep abreast the patriotic sense of the masses towards the nation that favours political freedom from alien domination. This, however, does not imply that nationalism has only these limited traits and objectives. Rather it encompasses a whole lot of other issues in our context. According to Y. K. Malik and V. B. Singh, there are two versions of nationalism in India: Indian nationalism and Hindu nationalism with several overlapping as well as distinctive traits in their ideological and functional modes.[51] Incidentally, these intense discourses on Indian and Hindu nationalism cannot ignore the existence of Islamic and Subaltern nationalisms as well. In all these discourses, the proponents were predominantly the educated (most of them Western educated) middle-class Indian elites. As far as Indian nationalism is concerned, the early proponents were mainly secular and utilitarian in their approach, having an anti-traditional, liberal democratic, secular and politically oriented concept of the nation with an ideology that could encompass, within its parameters, all cultures and religions that are practiced within this sub-continent.[52] For all practical purposes, the early nationalists sought to distance themselves to a great extent from the cultural legacy of Hindu religion. The origin of Hindu nationalism, conversely, is rooted in the Hindu religious and cultural revival and reform movements that emerged in the 19th century.[53]

There is a general view among the historians and theorists that the beginning of Indian nationalism proper can be located in 1885, the year of the founding of the Indian National Congress,[54] which was a constellation of a number of strands of mindset, interest and discourse. This rather limited political initiative was replete with a sort of a representative idiom. It has generally been accepted that one of the pioneering figures, who was instrumental in the founding of the INC movement was Allan Octavian Hume.[55] To begin with, it was an organization of eminent lawyers, teachers, journalists and other professionals, who assumed to represent the social and political interests and aspirations of the Indian people as a whole. The symbolic invocation of representation was persistently expressed as central to the self-image of the organization in order to give it meaning and purpose within the public sphere in which it operated.[56] In its early phases, nationalists who subscribed to the ideals of the INC chose to promote 'secular democracy' as the most appropriate way of nationalism.

Nationalism and Secularism – Contemporary Dilemma

Within the nationalist discourse, India is defined as a 'secular' democratic country – by the people, for the people and of the people. Even though it seems to be outwardly so, the (often compelling) inner dynamics are different. The State power, for instance, affirms these rhetorics, but even the most 'vociferous guardians' of secular democracy succumb to the pressure from the other quarter (religion) when it comes to gaining or retaining power. It clearly points to the hidden potencies of religion in influencing the nation. That is the reason why many theorists like to address the discourse on secularism in India as "hybrid" discourse.[57]

The 1950 version of the preamble of the Indian Constitution affirmed independent India as a "Sovereign Democratic Republic", and later it came to be modified in the 42nd amendment in 1976 as a "Sovereign Socialist Secular Democratic Republic". India has never been a monolithic state in terms of its cultural, linguistic or ethnic identities. Independent India was conceived in a *secular* manner and it lived as a *secular* state. What is typical of India is its diversity, which is the watershed of its life. However, there is an ongoing debate between those who argue for maintaining its identity as a secular state without compromising its *secular* credentials by succumbing to the pressures from various religious communities to have special privileges and those who argue that the modern nation-state of India must give greater prominence to its specifically "Hindu" heritage. This line of argument claims that since the *majority* of the Indian population consists of *Hindus*, naturally they deserve the dominant status in the affairs of the nation. But there is strong resistance to such majoritarian discourse.

Benedict Anderson is right as he ascribes greater importance to the newly emergent institutions in the creation of nationalism, which he called "print capitalism".[58] During the colonial rule, the print media played a vital role in creating an 'imagined community', especially through news items related to marriages, shipping trade, and Church services. These news items not only kept people informed about the day-to-day events, but also established an unseen communion among them and, it was only a matter of time that political elements would enter in. It became true of colonial India where the activities associated with the public space became an effective agent for the spread of the nationalist discourse deeply entrenched in religion.[59] This discourse, in the first phase, was closely connected with the process of linguistic/vernacular modernization. Rejuvenation of vernacular and the philological study of Sanskrit were all within the project of British orientalism, in which intellectuals (including missionaries) took keen interest in the study of Indian languages primarily for the purpose of the spread of Christianity. The start of the printing press in Serampore by the Baptist missionaries (1801) was intrinsically related to this larger orientalist project.[60]

The Orientalist project played its own role in polarizing various communities in colonial India in which the most striking way of understanding Indian life was to identify it with Hinduism, especially of its negative aspects. This conflation of the negative aspects of Hinduism with India was strongly contested and it motivated the Hindu society to organize itself into various *Sabhas* and associations that had enormous impact on Indian nationalist discourse.[61] Further, 19th Century was characterized by a number of reform movements within Hinduism. The prominent ones were: the *Brahmo Samaj* of Rammohun Roy, the *Arya Samaj* founded by Swami Dayanand and later made into an organization by Lala Lajpat Rai, and the Ramakrishna Mission (started by his disciple Vivekananda). Most often, the reformers were identified as modernizers, attempting to inculcate a more 'humane' or ethical religiosity with a more rational approach to religious truths and a rejection of the contradictions of Hinduism, such as, caste discriminations, *Sati*, and idol worship. There are commentators who identify these reform movements as a kind of an Indian version of Protestant Reformation in Europe.[62] But I think the Indian reformers were greatly influenced by liberal Protestantism that emerged after Enlightenment modernity. Orientalist scholars define such reform movements in terms of the proximity of the reformers to European conceptions of modern society that provided greater scope for social reforms like eradication of caste discriminations, emancipation of women, condemnation of idolatry, and encouraging individual communion with God.[63] Of course, contemporary scholars do not fully subscribe to such perceptions.[64] A notable point here is an emergent discursive trend in which terms such as *Hindu* and *Indian* came to be collated as having some form of metonymical relationship with one another. Thus, it can be stated that the emergence of nationalist discourse coincided with the intense religious discourse as well, and it continues to cast its unmistakable shadows on the nation's life.

Yet another key contestant that came to intersect in the colonial public space with a strong and lasting impact on the formation of the Indian (Hindu) consciousness and socio-political texture was Islamic (nationalist) discourse. At the outset, we need to bear in mind that Islamic Scripture, theology, symbols, rituals and traditions engendered a kind of a worldview and value system that had shaped the Islamic community (*umma*) with certain personal and social gestalt of cultural exclusion and intolerance towards other religious/ cultural persuasions, generating a great deal of mutual rivalry and hatred between Muslims and Hindus.[65] Islam emerged from the Semitic religious traditions, and more specifically within the context of Judaism and Christianity. Prophet Mohammad unequivocally claimed that the revelation he had received was the fulfillment of Jewish and Christian religious traditions.[66] An important concept embedded in Islam is 'jihad' (holy war),[67] which allows killing in a *holy war* for the sake of Islamic theocracy – a religious state with Allah as the only ruler. The Arabic term *Islam* means submission or surrender, not only voluntary but also forceful.[68] Islam, thus, purposes to conquer the world for Allah, using violent force if required ('jihad of the sword'). The rapid expansion of Islam was mind-boggling that within a century of its emergence it was able to spread to Spain, France, Egypt, Syria, Iraq, Iran, India, Africa, China, Java and Philippines,[69]and the spirit of jihad manifested itself wherever Islam came to encounter other faiths.[70]

Islam arrived in India through invaders and conquerors. Islamic rulers like Muhammad Ghazni, Qutub-ud-din, and Aurangzeb followed the principle of jihad, destroyed Hindu temples and converted many to Islam. This policy of Islamisation gave birth to two communities with exclusive cultures – Hindus and Muslims – with too little scope for mutual love. During the British rule, the chasm between these two communities further widened and the mutual hatred continued even after partition.[71] The hostility between these two communities had cast its definite shadow on the prolonged discussion on the kind of nation that had to emerge in the wake of the departure of the colonial rulers. We will have more discussion on these factors in the later part of this chapter and at the moment suffice it to say that the social and political texture of India has been so characterized by these factors that they formed part of the identity politics, on the one hand, and the 'secular' character of the nationalist discourse, on the other.

It is in this context that we discuss the issue of secularism in India. It certainly raises some important questions. What are the predominant modes of discourse that characterize secularism in India? Does secularism mean a total absence of religions? Can we perceive of a discourse with the binary divisions of secular/sacred or material/ spiritual, especially in the Indian context? Is secularism synonymous with materialism and is it an opposite of communalism? Secularism is a nebulous terminology, especially when it is applied in the Indian context, which prompted most commentators to term it as a 'hybrid' discourse.[72] This fluidity calls for an explanation of the term 'secular/ secularism' and the way it operates in contemporary India.

Secularism has come to mean different things to different people at different times. Its wide usage had never rendered any univocal meaning. In his attempt to decipher an Indian meaning to the term,

S. Radhakrishnan maintained: "Secularism here [in India] does not mean irreligion or atheism, or even stress on material comforts. It proclaims that it lays stress on the universality of spiritual values which may be attained by a variety of ways".[73] M. R. Masani equated secularism with atheism and asserted that only communist countries can be truly called secular.[74] According to Donald Eugene Smith, India is a secular state precisely because of the fact that it is enshrined in the constitution and practiced by a strong parliamentary system despite the fact that there are a few anomalies, which, in his view, may be dispelled over time.[75] Smith seems to be working with a set of principles, which, in his view, would safeguard secularism if those principles could be applied in a proper perspective. His theoretical principles have three distinct but interrelated sets of relationships between the *state*, *religion* and the *citizen*. *First*, the secular state guarantees individual and corporate freedom of religion when it pertains to the citizen's relationship to religion. *Second*, when it comes to the relationship between the state and the citizen, the secular state deals with the individual as a citizen irrespective of his/her religion. *Third*, with regard to the relationship between the state and religion, the secular state is not *constitutionally* connected to any particular religion, nor does it seek to promote or interfere with religion.[76]

Secularism in India exhibits discursive meanings than it does in many of the western nations. Even though these nations have an official religion (Christianity), they are more secular (if secularism means irreligious) than India in their temper and working. For the fundamental criterion for secularism is not whether they have an official religion, but whether religion in any way influences or impinges upon the public policies and the relationship between individuals, groups and the state. In India, however, the application of secularism exhibits certain discursive traits. The Indian constitution, offers no privileged treatment to any religion; rather the state will treat all religions equally. This, however, does not mean that the state will desist from extending financial assistance to the educational institutions run by religious bodies. The state also reserves the right to interfere in the religious practices of various communities for the peaceful co-existence and cultural development of these communities. Further, the constitution contains a special clause enunciating the banning of cow-slaughter as a desirable policy to be adopted and implemented by the constituent states of the Indian Union.

Now, in relation to religion and religious sentiments, the Indian Union seems to be lukewarm in its approach. Even in the matter of cow-slaughter, it tries to pass the buck to the constituent states to make necessary provisions for implementation. The reasons are numerous. While the Indian state professes to be secular, the Indian society is mostly religious in its essential nature. Almost all communities invoke certain myths and practices enshrined in their religions in all walks of their life[77] and it has been further perpetuated by electoral politics because no politician in India will dare to do anything that would harm the religious sentiments of the people as it will have serious repercussions in their electoral fortunes. The state heads and politicians will participate in various religious ceremonies (in their official capacities) that would enhance their chances of winning people's support. Thus, in A. B. Shah's view, the state, instead of providing leadership in promoting secularism in India, in fact, plays a half-hearted role that reflects the prejudices and often vested interests of various communal groups.[78]

Another trajectory of secularism in India is the use of the term *secularism* synonymously with the term nationalism. Interestingly, these terms are understood to be the opposites of the term 'communal'. It is in this sense the term 'communal' has a profoundly different connotation than its original meaning in the west. Politically speaking, within contemporary India, there is a general tendency to categorize the Congress (I), its allies and the left parties as *secular* parties and the BJP and its allies as *communal* parties because of their professed religious disconnection and connection respectively. In most instances in the electoral politics, political polarization takes place along these lines. As an illustration, the attitude of the Christians in Tamilnadu towards politics, especially electoral politics, can be cited. Most of the Christian Churches in Tamilnadu are sympathizers of the DMK because it has all along been supporting the minorities. But during the 2001 Assembly elections, the DMK was in alliance with the BJP and the Churches switched their support over to the AIADMK because, in their estimation, the DMK then was in alliance with the 'communal' party. The 2006 Assembly elections in Tamilnadu took yet another turn in which the Christian support swung back to the DMK because it broke away from the BJP and forged an alliance with the Congress, the 'secular' party.[79] A closer reading of the context, thus, exhibits an entirely different picture of secularism in India, which involves a dense religious texture that calls into serious question our usual penchant to identify 'secular' and 'communal' on the basis of what we see on the surface. Because, deep down, at every political move, there is a tint of communal element (in the pejorative sense), as all political parties play communal cards in their political games, often pitching people from different background against each other for their electoral gains.[80]

As regard to the contemporary dilemma over secularism that hovers over the Indian polity and public life, one need only to look at the way Gandhi construed the nation, which constitutes a typical example of the hybrid discourse on secularism. He promoted a thoroughly Neo-Hindu reformist and nationalist vision,[81] mostly influenced by neo-Hindu traditions from Rammohun Roy and the Brahmo Samaj in the 19th century through Keshub Chandra Sen, Dayananda Sarasvati and the Arya Samaj, Ramakrishna, Vivekananda and Aurobindo in the 20th century. Further, his western English education, the liberal democratic ideas he gained from his education, Enlightenment rationalism, liberal humanism, socialist ideology, the practice of the parliamentary democracy, the Christian missionary activities and the Hindu-Muslim tensions had all come to play in his notion of secularism. Describing the salience of Gandhi in Indian politics, Nehru states:

> Gandhi was essentially a man of religion, a Hindu to the innermost depths of his being, and yet his conception of religion has nothing to do with any custom or dogma or ritual. It is basically concerned with his firm belief in moral law, which he calls the law of truth or love. Truth and non-violence appear to him to be the same thing, or different aspects of one and the same thing, and he uses these words almost interchangeably. Claiming to understand the spirit of Hinduism, he rejects every text or practice which does not fit in with his idealist interpretation of what it should be.[82]

Pertaining to Gandhi's vision of India, Nehru quotes him again:

> I shall work for an India in which the poorest shall feel that it is their country, in whose making they have an effective voice, an India in which there shall be no high class and low class of people, an India in which all communities of people shall live in perfect harmony...There can be no room in such an India for the curse of untouchability or the curse of intoxicating drinks and drugs... Women will enjoy the same right as men...this is the India of my dream.[83]

Gandhi's attempt was to provide a kind of a universal attire to Hinduism by way of a synthesis of various religious traditions within the framework of truth as he interpreted.

> Indian culture, he wrote, is neither Hindu, Islamic, nor any other, wholly. It is a fusion of all...I want the culture of all lands to be blown about my house as freely as possible. But I refuse to be blown off my feet by any. I refuse to live in other people's house as an interloper, a beggar, or a slave.[84]

But today we encounter the discursive and aggressive mode of Hindu nationalist discourse, which even attempts to identify Hindutva with secularism. This aggressive posture has motivated critics to draw some parallels between European fascism (1920s) and that of the Hindu right in India in the recent times. They have brought to light some of the bewildering similarities between fascism in Italy and Nazism in Germany and the right wing Hinduism in India that are truly alarming.[85] The most recent one is Justice Markandey Katju's appeal to the nation not to commit the mistake of Nazi Germany (1933) in his reaction against the attempts within a section of the BJP to project Narendra Modi as the next prime ministerial candidate.[86] It, then, leads us to ask a somewhat disturbing question: is secularism a viable, or even adequate, alternative to meet the challenges of Hindu nationalism?

Partha Chatterjee has problematised the very notion of secularism in India. He maintains that the current thinking of the Hindu nationalists has emerged as a re-examination of the very foundations of liberal democratic India and its relation to the history and theory of modern state in Europe and Americas. It has to be noted that none of the leadership of the Hindu nationalist movement utters anything serious that contains an advocacy of theocratic institutions. It would be quite unlikely that a conception of a *Hindu Rāshtrā* with a serious demand for framing the laws of the state in conformity with the general spirit of any *dharmasashtra* would explicitly be put forward. Rather, the campaign of the Hindu right seeks to mobilize the will of an 'interventionist modernizing state' in order to obliterate the presence of the religious or ethno-cultural particularities from the public sphere. Thus, there is a very real possibility of the Hindu right locating itself very firmly in the political domains and using all of the material and ideological resources of the state to deal with those who do not conform to its version of the 'national culture' according to its own standards, including intolerance and violence. Further, the current campaign of the Hindu right is directed not against the principle of the secular state but towards mobilizing the legal powers of the state in order to systematically terrorize religious minorities. In this context, the question of the adequacy of 'secularism' to deal with the claims of Hindu right becomes vitally important.[87]

Here, Chatterjee raises a startling question: is the defense of secularism an adequate and appropriate ground for meeting the challenge of the Hindu right, or should it be fought at the root of the attack, i.e., should the response be the duty of the democratic state to ensure policies of religious toleration? Of course, Chatterjee's concerns, questions and arguments are well taken, especially his very attempt to bring out the nuances of secularism. Nevertheless, I differ from his views, especially his argument that rather than relying on secularism (because of its inability to address the challenges of the Hindu right), the state has to ensure policies of religious toleration. It sounds to be an idealistic expectation. Given the fact that when the state apparatus itself has been used to intimidate the minorities, in what way can we expect the state to ensure religious tolerance? Hence, till a viable alternative is evolved, 'secularism' must be preserved as a counter to the claims of Hindutva; and in the present circumstances such an alternative is not apparent.

The above comments on secularism in India invite us to answer a pertinent question as to whether India a truly secular state. In response to this question, D. E. Smith offers not a straight but qualified answer as he remarks: "Is India a secular state? My answer is a qualified "Yes". It is meaningful to speak of India as a secular state, despite the existence of the problems...India is secular in the sense in which one can say that India is a democracy. Despite various undemocratic features of Indian politics and government, parliamentary democracy *is* functioning, and with considerable vigour. Similarly, the secular state; the ideal is clearly embodied in the constitution, and is being implemented in substantial measure. The question must be answered in terms of a dynamic state which has inherited some difficult problems and is struggling hard to overcome them along generally sound lines".[88]

Let me conclude our discussion on 'secularism' in contemporary India with one final point. What emerges from the above discussion on secularism in India is a hybrid discourse that attempts to hold together tradition and modernity, which has a broad-based neo-Hindu (an inclusive Hindu) vision of a civilization-state. Among others, it has an extraordinary vision of Gandhi, a liberal philosophical touch of Nehru and the terrible impact of partition. Whether this is a modified version of a "civil religion" as defined by Robert Bellah[89] is a question for further debate. But suffice it to say that in the course of the last few decades Gandhian vision dissipated and Nehruvian adventures to lead the nation to modernity by breaking with the past withered away; but the memories – the bitter memories – of partition are still alive (or deliberately kept alive). Possibly then, the bitter memories of partition have become a strong point for the Hindu extremists to make a shift in the discourse on nationalism – from *Indian* nationalism to *Hindu* nationalism – in its vigorous and violent manifestations.

Partition and Its Impacts on Contemporary India

Any debate on nationalism in postcolonial India must take into account the most important defining moment of its history, the partition of Pakistan from India. When the British left this subcontinent, they left not one but two independent, sovereign nation states – India and Pakistan. India became a 'Sovereign Democratic Republic' on 26 January 1950, following the adoption of the draft constitution in its constituent assembly on 26 November 1949; and Pakistan became the 'Islamic Republic of Pakistan' on 23 March 1950, when its first constitution came into effect followed by its adoption in its constituent assembly on 29 February 1950. The bitterness of the events that followed partition has gone so deep into the consciousness of both these nations that all attempts to find a lasting solution remain a mirage. The crucial point to note in this strained relationship between the two neighboring countries is that the issue has been emotionally interiorized with religious sentiments and political overtones.[90] It is this aspect of 'religious-sentiment', which has become an important issue that continues to haunt the nation, casting its shade on everything that has a public connotation.

Partition was effectuated on *religious* grounds and the bitterness, suspicion, anger and hatred generated by it continue to occupy the centre of a series of crisis situations that India confronts today. At this point, it would be worth noting certain events and movements that preceded partition, which generated conflicting ideas and attitudes between the two partners. The idea of partition had its base on the (rather inchoate) formation of two opposing groups – the Neo-Hindu and Neo-Muslim – that emerged in the later part of the 19th century. On the Neo-Hindu side, there were both 'Hindu reformist' and 'Indian nationalist' movements, which included such figures and organizations as Rammohun Roy, the Brahmo Samaj, the Arya Samaj, Ramakrishna-Vivekananda movement, Aurobindo Ghose, V. D. Savarkar, M. K. Gandhi and others. This side was also represented by 'Neo-Hindu revisionist and internationalist movements', which included such figures and movements as Paramahamsa Yogananda, Mehr Baba, Satya Sai Baba, Swami Narayana movement and others. Similarly, on the Neo-Muslim side, there were 'Neo-Muslim reformist and accomodationist movements', which included such movements and figures as the Deoband School of 'ulama', the Jami'at al-'ulama'-i Hind, Hasan Ahmed Madani, and Abul Kalam Azad. There was also on this side the 'Neo-Muslim modernist and separatist movements', which included such movements and figures as Anglo-Oriental College at Aligarh, Sayyid Ahmad Khan, Muhammad Iqbal, the Muslim League, and Muhammad Ali Jinnah.[91]

It was the Aligarh tradition (Neo-Muslim modernist and Separatist) that had sown the seeds of separation,[92] which, of course, emerged in many respects as a direct response to the 'Neo-Hindu reformist and nationalist' traditions, which were gradually moving towards consolidation throughout the 19th century and eventually, reached a landmark with the founding of the INC in 1885.[93] During this time, the clearest spokesperson on the Muslim side was Sayyid Ahmad Khan. He was quite suspicious about the very intentions of the INC that was staking its claims to represent and speak for India as a whole. In his view, it was an attempt to establish Hindu hegemony over the (Muslim) minorities. Expressing his apprehensions, Khan said:

> Friends, in India there live two prominent nations which are distinguished by the names of Hindus and Mussalmans. Just as a man has some principal organs, similarly these two nations are the principal limbs of India.[94]

In 1888, he commented as follows about the INC, which is not without its own shift:

> The aims and objects of Indian National Congress are based upon an ignorance of history and present day realities; they do not take into consideration that India is inhabited by different nationalities; they presuppose that Muslims, the Marathas, the Brahmins, the Kshatryas, the Banias, the Sudras, the Sikhs, the Bengalis, the Madrasis, and the Peshawaris can all be treated alike and all of them belong to the same nation. The Congress thinks that they profess the same religion, that they speak the same language, that their way of life and customs are the same...I consider the experiment which the Indian National Congress wants to make [is] fraught with dangers and suffering for all the nationalities of India, especially for the Muslims. [95]

Sayyid Ahmad Khan's views were not so widespread at this stage, as other Muslim movements were sympathetic towards the INC, which was broadly inclusive of a great variety of peoples, groups and ideas. Its meeting in 1887, for instance, was attended by Hindus (965), Muslims (221) and others (62 including European Christians,

Indian Christians, Jains, Jews, Parsis and Sikhs).[96] It largely accepted the liberal-democratic principles of Britain's parliamentary democracy and viewed the British rule basically as benevolent to India. The approach of the Muslims towards the INC at this stage was generally sympathetic, which was to change later and to give way to a more reactionary mode, especially by the dawn of the 20th century, when in 1905, the British viceroy, Lord Curzon, separated Bengal by creating a largely Muslim East Bengal and Assam and a largely Hindu West Bengal, Bihar and Orissa. This was claimed as done purely on administrative grounds, which was finally rescinded in 1911-12 when the administrative capital was shifted from Calcutta to Delhi.[97] But we cannot forget the 'divide-and-rule' tactics of the British, given the fact that even this administrative division had to put two rather recalcitrant communities on either side of the fence.

This partition coincided with the emergence of a more radical and extremist nationalist movement with people who were deeply resentful about the partition and also extremely angry with several other issues such as the issues emerging from the Northwest region of Punjab and in the Western region of Maharashtra. Aurobindo Ghosh (1872 – 1950) and Bankim Chandra Chatterjee (1838 – 1894) from Bengal, Bal Gangadhar Tilak (1856 – 1920) from Maharashtra, and Lala Lajpat Rai (1865 – 1928) were some of the prominent representatives of the extremist wing in the Congress. They were more inclined to use Hindu religious imageries in their fiery rhetorics that had in a way distanced the Muslim supporters who were somewhat skeptical about the Hindu dominance in the Indian nationalist movement. It has to be noted that it was around this time, i.e., in 1906, a group of Neo-Muslims from Aligarh and Dacca made an appeal to the viceroy to create separate electorate for Muslims in India, and it was in the same year the All-India Muslim League was founded in Dacca. But eventually, the extremists in the INC had lost their influence and the congress leadership fell into the hands of more moderate and liberal leaders, which paved the way for Gandhi to assume the leadership of the nationalist movement in 1920, following the demise of B. G. Tilak. Along with this transition of leadership, there was also a shift of perception about the British rule in which the important attitude was to seek political freedom rather than accepting the British rule as a beneficial one. Recalling Gandhi's principle, Nehru states:

> The call of action was two-fold. There was, of course, the action involved in challenging and resisting foreign rule; there was also action which led us to fight our own social evils. Apart from the fundamental objective of the Congress (the freedom of India) and the method of peaceful action, the planks of the Congress were national unity, which involved the solution of the minority problems, and the raising of the depressed classes and the ending of the curse of untouchability.[98]

These developments also were marked by the increasing alienation of the Muslims from within the Congress, which coincided with the increasing radicalism of the older Arya Samaj and the emergence of the more conservative Hindu Mahasabha (Great Assembly of Hindus), which was politically active after 1923, led by the conservative Neo-Hindu reformer, Pandit Madan Mohan Malavya, partly in response to the founding of the Muslim League and partly as a pressure group to keep the Hindu interest abreast within the nationalist movement and to check unnecessary concessions to the Muslim groups and their demands. This was exacerbated with the electoral reforms brought out by the colonial rulers, including the Morley-Minto Reforms of 1909, the Montague-Chelmsford Reforms of 1919, and the Government of India Act of 1935. These steps, even though regarded by some as important for the eventual self-governance of India, nevertheless, became tools for the provision of separate electorate, at first only for the Muslims, and then extended to the Sikhs, Anglo-Indians, Indian Christians, and the Depressed Classes by 1935. This division by creed, especially in electoral politics, was viewed with great regrets, as for instance, the Montague-Chelmsford report observed: "Division by creeds and classes means the creation of political camps organized against each other, and teaches men to think as partisans and not as citizens".[99]

An important issue that merits our attention here is that the roots of communalism in contemporary India can be traced to two important camps, namely, the emergence of radical Islamic movements and the extremist Hindu reform movements. Mention has to be made here about an important change that Gandhi brought about in the 1935 system of separate electorates. Bhim Rao Ambedkar (1891 – 1956) was aiming at attaining separate electorate for the depressed classes but Gandhi vehemently opposed this move, viewing it as a serious threat to the integrity of the Hindu community and he began a 'fast-unto-death'; and eventually Ambedkar had to arrive at a compromise for some 'generous' reserved seats for the depressed classes. It seemed acceptable to the British Government and when Independent India's Constitution came into effect in 1950, the separate electorate was abolished and in its place 'reserved seats' were allowed – Scheduled Castes 15% and Scheduled Tribes 7%. This has generated at least two opposing viewpoints: those who appreciated the Gandhian cause viewed it as his vision for the emancipation of the depressed classes; and those who were critical about the Gandhian cause, like Ambedkar and others, viewed it as an example of his incorrigible caste-ism.[100]

By the end of 1930s, when Gandhian consolidation of the nationalist movement was almost establishing a strong base, some Muslim leaders, especially from the extremist camp, began contemplating a definite independent status for the Muslim community, more specifically in the Muslim populated regions. In the annual meeting of the Muslim League in 1930, Muhammad Iqbal observed:

> We are seventy million and far more homogenous than any other people in India. Indeed the Muslims of India are the only Indian people who can fitly be described as a nation in the modern sense of the word.[101]

Muhammad Ali Jinnah, in his speech at the annual meeting of the Muslim League in 1940 made a clarion call:

> If the British government are really earnest and sincere to secure peace and happiness of the people of the subcontinent, the only course open to us all is to allow the *major nations* separate homelands by dividing India into *autonomous national states*... It is extremely difficult to appreciate why our Hindu friends fail to understand the real nature of Islam and Hinduism. They are

> [not] religions in the strict sense of the word, but are, in fact, different and distinct social orders, and it is a dream that the Hindus and Muslims can ever evolve a common nationality, and this misconception of one Indian nation has gone far beyond the limits and is the cause of most of your troubles and will lead India to destruction if we fail to revise our notions in time. The Hindus and Muslims belong to two different religious philosophies, social customs, and literatures. They neither intermarry nor interdine together and, indeed, they belong to two different civilizations which are based mainly on conflicting ideas and conceptions.[102]

Reacting sharply to Jinnah's call, Gandhi maintained:

> My whole soul rebels against the idea that Hinduism and Islam represent two antagonistic cultures and doctrines. To assent such a doctrine is for me denial of God. For I believe with my whole soul that the God of Koran is also the God of Gita, and that we are all, no matter what name we designated, children of the same God.[103]

Despite all these and other vigorous debates, claims and counter-claims, the inevitable had happened. Exhausted by the Second World War, Britain decided to leave India when the Labor government of Clement Richard Atlee came to power, defeating Winston Churchill's Tory Government. Atlee appointed Lord Louis Mountbatten as the new viceroy to transfer the governance to the indigenous leadership. Finally, by the order of the House of Commons in London, two independent nations were created with the allocation of 82.5% of the territory and resources to India and 17.5% to Pakistan. It was a time of sheer uncertainty, confusion and holocaust, which forced millions of people to change their land of occupation along religious lines. It is reported that in the process of the transition from one territory to the other, about a million people perished in the hands of the bloodthirsty warriors of the Gods. Religious loyalties couched in emotions led extremists to engage in butchery, loot, arson and rape. As described by Wolpert:

> The terror, the anguish of millions of Hindus, Muslims, and Sikhs who feared that they would awaken next morning to find

> themselves trapped in a nation fundamentally hostile to their faith and were thus driven to take what pitiful possessions they could carry and abandon their fields and homes, can barely be imagined. An estimated ten million people changed lands that summer of 1947, and approximately one million of them never reached their promised nation alive. A totally inadequate boundary force of fifty thousand troops, most of them infected with communal fever, had been assembled in the Punjab to help make the transition a peaceful one. For the most part they stayed in their barracks, cleaning their weapons and boots, while trainloads of Sikh refugees moving east were slaughtered by Muslims in Pakistan and Muslims headed west were butchered by Sikhs and Hindus in India. The stream became a flood, the flood of a holocaust of pain, looting, rape and murder.[104]

Without doubt then, partition, a creation of acute nationalist impulse and intense religiosity, became a definite marker of contemporary Hindu nationalism, not simply because it has created two opposing nations, but because of the kind of feelings it has created among the Hindu elites. Is it not a sheer trouble with religion, which the nation has to endure for generations to come? Even after six decades since independence, the scar that has been left behind by partition still creates painful moments, often acute, in the life of the nation. For the right wing Hindus, it has provided a powerful ammunition to hit at the minorities by accusing them of being unpatriotic and divisive – a lasting suspicion about the minorities as if they are a permanent threat to the interests of the 'majority' Hindus. It has been taken as enough proof of the anti-national activities of the minorities and sufficient justification to tame them in Hindutva's own terms.

Partition is at the heart not only of the conflict in the bordering states (of Punjab and Jammu and Kashmir), but also of a whole series of religious-cum-political conflicts reaching down to the present time. These crises include: (a) the founding of the People's Republic of Bangladesh in 1971 by the separation of Pakistan's Eastern Province; (b) the social unrest generated by the resentment of 'backward classes' following the Mandal Commission Report of 1980 calling for 49.5% of compensatory discrimination for the OBCs; (c) the deep rooted suspicion about the Muslims in India as a pampered and, at the same time, alien community, typified by the furor among the Muslims over the Shah Bano case[105] and even greater furor among certain Hindu groups over the passage of the Muslim Women (Protection on Divorce) Bill of 1986; and (d) the Babri Masjid-Ramjanmabhoomi controversy in Ayodhya that culminated in the demolition of the Mosque in 1992. In addition, India at the moment encounters a strained relationship with Pakistan, its neighboring state. All these issues are in some way related to religion and it is in this context that we are dealing with Hindu nationalism in India.

Hindu Nationalism

Hindu nationalism, a prominent feature in Indian politics in recent times, is a reactionary and often violent mode of discourse against certain developments in the social, religious and political domains in the Indian sub-continent. In the past couple of decades, the Hindu nationalist movement, pioneered by the militant organization, the RSS, with its branches and subsidiaries has sunk its firm roots in many domains of Indian life.[106] It is generally viewed that Hindu nationalism emerged out of a sense of 'victimhood' of the Hindus that has driven the Hindu think-tank to redefine and reassert the Hindu identity[107] and recapture the lost status of the Hindu dominance due to certain developments in the socio-political milieu, namely, alien invasions, modernization, secularization, and the new awakening among the marginalized communities.[108] Pratap Bhanu Mehta, for instance, argues that Hindu nationalism is an attempt to make the Hindus self-conscious of their own history and create a common identity, to mobilize this identity to protect and glorify the claims of Hindus, and, most importantly, to assert the cultural primacy of Hindus in the territorial entity called India and define India primarily as a land belonging to the Hindus.[109] Hindu nationalism has thus become a veritable and permanent force in Indian politics. Its phenomenal development, then, prompts us to ask as to where, when and how Hindu nationalism has taken shape and permeated into the mainstream of Indian public life.

Colonial Public Space and Hindu Nationalist Discourse

Public space is a potential site that provides ample room for the coming together, coalescence and configuration of peoples, temperaments, ideas and attitudes. It is a space that becomes a potential breeding ground of various legitimizing ideologies as well. This is particularly true of Hindu nationalism, for it was the colonial public space that had provided ample opportunities for the educated middle-class Hindu elites to come together and produce the formative ideology that undergirds and perpetuates Hindu nationalist discourse in India today. To put it succinctly, Hindu nationalist ideologies emerged as middle-class ideologies coterminously with the nationalist discourse.

Class as a concept is not a favorable theoretical category in contemporary intellectual discourses mainly because it defines society mainly on economic terms. Even Marx could conceive of only two classes – the bourgeois and the proletariat – and the intermediary classes were not a favored grouping because they stand as impediments to the growth process. In our context, we need to go beyond Marx's anti-capitalist and pro-labor class critiques because of the important role the middle class plays in the social and political realms. According to Deshpande, the importance of the middle-class lies in its location – the middle axis of the society. It is an increasingly differentiated class that specializes in the production and dissemination of ideologies: its elite segment specializes in the production of ideologies and its mass segment engages in the exemplary consumption of these ideologies, thus, investing them with social legitimacy.[110]

As identified by Mishra, Indian middle-class is not a class that emerged out of technological or industrial revolution, as, for instance, in the case of Britain or the other European countries. Rather, it is predominantly a professional class – a class of people emerging from the educational, judicial and administrative developments under colonial rule, occupying important positions as lawyers, public servants, teachers, scholars, writers, and members of other recognized occupations.[111] What provided them greater impetus in evolving their ideologies was the proximity they had to the structures of colonial rule, which was critically important in the process of the consolidation of their ideas and ideologies. How they gained access to the structures of colonial rule is an important point to note. One of the key elements that drew many of the middle-class elites together was their engagement with the cultural hegemony of the colonial state. This was a potential and key site, which can be termed as the civic or public space of the colonial politics. This has close resemblance to what Jürgen Habermas construed as public space in the context of the Bourgeois Europe.[112] Habermas' public represented the people who played a kind of an intermediary role independent of state authority. This public emerged as a central feature of a functioning democracy – "the public organized as a discursive and decision making public". But then, there is a basic difference between Habermas' public sphere and the public sphere of colonial India. Whereas Habermas' public sphere enjoyed autonomy and exerted considerable influence in decision making, the colonial public sphere was limited and it had to function within the limits of the surveillance of the colonial masters. Even though, many of the public spheres: the judiciary, press and other institutions had several semblances of Habermas' public space, the ability of these institutions to express themselves freely was severely curtailed. It was a space over which the colonial state attempted to wield self-conscious authority – "widening or narrowing the space, changing its shape in various areas as it saw it fit, and according to what it perceived as the susceptibility of those who used it".[113]

These limitations notwithstanding, the colonial public space was incredibly broad in another sense, i.e., even though it was a space with curtailed freedom of expression, it was a cross-regional space in which ideologies could emerge and make their own impact across colonial India. Events or movements in one part of India had their direct consequences in other parts of the country. It is in this context of the dynamics of the public sphere that our attention is drawn, for instance, to Nagpur, the administrative centre of the Central Provinces from 1861, as the city of one of the pioneering Hindu organizations (RSS) was founded in the year 1925. It was a city that had a concentration of strong, predominantly high-caste, middle-class people and a good number of them occupied key positions in the educational, judicial and administrative institutions in that region.

These elites can be aptly termed as the 'prime movers' of legitimizing ideologies precisely because of their coveted positions in the public sphere. This privileged position provided them with enough impetus to involve actively in the events and issues in British India and beyond through petitions to the administration, discussions in recognized organizations, literary comments and through the print media.

The cross-regional potential of the public sphere was also a significant area for the development of indigenous critiques of colonial dispensation. Members of the middle-class made potential use of their positions in the public sphere to translate, transform, and even subvert the mechanics of colonial discourse. An example of the elite intervention in the colonial discourse is proffered by the state's attempt to codify religion and caste through census. The administrative positions of the elite became a major factor in deciding who belongs to which group, for in this sort of decision-making the census enumerators had the propensity to make their own judgments on such issues.[114] The census enumerators, mostly school teachers and other local professionals, thus, were able to use their own mental frameworks and integrate them into colonial discourse. This clearly illustrates that the colonial public space was a critical area of ideological struggle where the colonial discourse was subjected to the scrutiny and interpretation of the middle-class mental frameworks. This elite intervention in the colonial discourse has far reaching consequences and the legacy of which we experience even today.

Another important point that emerges from this analysis of the colonial public space is the *representative* role the middle-class assumed for the 'benefit' and 'on behalf' of the other segments (the non-elites) of the society. According to Haynes, the non-elites had to depend heavily on the 'symbolic specialists' as mediators between them and the civic domain as they had no proximity to the public space.[115] This inaccessibility of the public sphere to the non-elites prompted the middle-class elites to take on representative roles that became effective tools to promote certain ideologies in the name of 'public interest', which turned out to be a way of legitimizing the claims of certain organizations as a means to provide meaning to the public space. As an illustration, we can look at the way *The Nagpur*

Gaurakshini Sabha took it on itself to petition the Government of India on the issue of cow protection in 1894, which was claimed as done 'on behalf of' the inhabitants of Nagpur and the adjoining districts. The notable point in this representative mode of discourse is the kind of people who were involved in the *Sabha* and who claimed representative roles – lawyers, bankers and landowners and so on. Thus the colonial public space turned out to be a virtual breeding ground of Hindu nationalist discourse. Hindu nationalist discourse from this point onwards must be analyzed from two broad but interrelated levels – (i) its ideological constructs, and (ii) its political agenda – from a historical as well as multi-civilizational perspective. At both levels, the Hindu nationalists were confronted with the fundamental question: What is Hinduism? In all probability, it is at this level emerged the ideological basis of Hindu nationalism – Hindutva.

Hindutva – The Backbone of Hindu Nationalism

Hindu nationalism, in a sense, is an attempt to take advantage of a somewhat inchoate but very widespread sentiment of the Hindus, a process that has been on the move since a long time. Many people who identified themselves as Hindus experienced an extraordinary sense of a lack of identity. It was further intensified by a sense of injury of being the victims of history and at the receiving end. According to this view, India is a land of conquests and the invaders conspired to ensure that the Hindus could not claim cultural hegemony over a sacred territory they regard as their own.[116] One can, then, argue that this sense of 'victimhood' forms the basis of Hindu nationalism and consequently it involves a kind of an aggressive, reactionary, and violent mode of discourse that is intended to salvage the wounded consciousness of the Hindus and organize them into a community that can do justice to them as Hindus. Quite logically, then, these burdens exercise their strong influence on the newfound notion of a Hindu nation. That is why contemporary Hindu revivalists define Hinduism with a sense of superiority – as the highest achievement of spirituality – and do everything possible to enlist this superior spirituality into the cause of nationalism.[117] This phenomenon, then, involves, at the outset, a concerted effort to redefine *Hinduism* and the *Hindus*, and that is exactly what Vinayak Damodar Savarkar did in his most provocative work, *Hindutva, Who is a Hindu?*

The term *Hindutva*, as coined by Savarkar,[118] encapsulates within itself a whole range of meanings, motives and programs, ranging from its religious connotation of Hinduness up to its national outlook of defining 'Hindu people' as a homogenous *Hindu-Rāshtra*.[119] Basically, Hindutva attempted to provide, "a broad basic foundation or bedrock on which a consolidated mighty Hindu Nation could take a secure stand".[120] This comprehensive project involves motivating and facilitating the configuration of religion, culture, society, and politics.[121] Formulated with a high sense of 'victimhood' and charged with emotional appeals, Hindutva forms not only the ideological[122] basis for Hindu nationalism, but also provides a neat mapping of a Hindu nation and the preconditions for those who intend or claim to be Indians. Savarkar formulated it from his colonial prison cell and it contains strong reactions against the alien rule and the psychological and socio-political ordeals it has caused on the nation as a whole.

The colonial power in India did two things that became conducive to the Hindu nationalists: (i) it construed India as a "unitary and homogenous entity held together by its essential religiosity, which can be captured under the label Hinduism",[123] making it an effective means to administer this vast subcontinent; and (ii) quite paradoxically, it encouraged the identification of the people into numerous communities distinguishing them according to their religious and cultural cleavages, which was effectively carried out through the census projects.[124] In this 'divide-and-rule' tactic, the colonizers almost succeeded in making the natives clearly understand themselves as a loosely held collective of human tribes within the territorial entity called 'India'. Of course, ever since the Vedic times, the indigenous communities had been divided into numerous caste groups. But then, what the colonial census projects did was to clearly demarcate various communities, which provided greater possibilities to identify particular communities, especially at the times of conflicts, and intimidate the vulnerable. It enmeshed the indigenous communities into a kind of an identity crisis, as they were broken up, fragmented and confined within the enclaves of their particular cultures, religions and regions. Contrary to the colonial divisive politics, Hindutva sought to *consolidate* the fragmented indigenous communities into one homogenous, unitary and uniform Hindu nation. In this project, the colonizers' attempt to imagine the nation with specific geographical territories was tactfully transformed and incorporated into the Hindutva ideology in order to project India as a composite and unified Hindu nation. This homogenizing drive of Hindutva involves several key components[125] and we will unravel some of them here.

Instrumentation of Religion

Religion became an effective agent of consolidation and homogenization drives of the Hindu nationalists. In Madhu Kishwar's opinion, "The Sangh leadership is selectively using gods from the Hindu pantheon while destroying or undercutting the religious and spiritual core of Hindu dharma and forging out of it a hate-filled ideology of [Hindu] nationalism".[126] One of the ways in which Hindu nationalists perpetuate their ideology is to interpret Hinduism as a *Sanatana Dharma* that transcends time and space and to demand that those who engage in the study of this religion would do well first to dispel their western notions of 'time' and 'history'.[127] Further, in order to advance and disseminate the Hindutva ideology, the predominant tendency is to glorify the 'superior' Indian spirituality in contrast to the western materialism,[128] coupled with a fervent appeal to the Hindu sentiment of victimhood, which becomes an effective means to mobilize the masses to rise above their differences and stand for the cause of Hindu religion. In this schema, Hindutva does two things: *first*, it effectively promotes the idea that Hindus must stand united to fight against the onslaught of the invaders, modernity's secularizing drive and the onslaught of alien religions (Islam and Christianity); and *second*, it interfaces religion with politics with the fundamental claim that India is the 'fatherland' and holy land of the Hindus as enshrined in the Vedas, and it is precisely at this point that Savarkar extends the clarion call: 'back to the Vedas', to the national revivalists.[129] This, then, compels Savarkar to redefine the terms *Hindu* and *Hinduism*, specifically from a Hindutva perspective.

Re-construal of Hindu/Hinduism

Hindutva, according to Savarkar, is different from Hinduism as he asserts:

> Hindutva is not a word but a history. Not only the spiritual or religious history of our people as at times it is mistaken to be by being confounded with the other cognate term Hinduism, but a history in full. Hinduism is only a derivative, a fraction, a part of Hindutva.[130]

Savarkar seems to be extremely discontent with the popular use of the term Hindu/ Hinduism, for, in his opinion, it essentially carries with it a sectarian connotation since it is couched in certain dogmatic and creedal constructions, and it is a definite hindrance to the task of claiming India as specifically belonging to the Hindus. It, therefore, necessitates a re-construal of the term Hindu in unambiguous terms, which will logically lead to the re-construal of the nation in consonance with Hindutva ideology.

According to the publishers of the *Hindutva, Who is Hindu?*, the emergence of this tract coincided with a passionate longing among the cross section of the Indian society – from eminent scholars to the poorest of the poor – to understand the term Hindu[131] and Hindutva sought to provide a comprehensive interpretation of the term Hindu in response to this longing. The demand for a redefinition of the term Hindu/Hinduism was felt due to the fact that the previous attempts did not yield the desired outcome and it was almost given up as indefinable.[132] Further, even when defined, it was understood within the strict dogmatic forms, which could provide no unity or uniformity. *Unity* of Hinduism and *uniformity* of Hindus were seen as the most essential aspects that could encompass the beliefs, dogmas and symbols 'owned by the millions of people who constituted the Hindu community'. Thus there emerged a strong sense that the absence of the *dogmatic unity* of Hinduism and the *cultural uniformity* of the Hindus made them unable to "grasp the full import of the national aspects implied in the word 'Hindu'". Realization of this fact drove Savarkar to approach the term Hindu from a historical perspective in order to "trace the development of the Hindu race, religion and polity ever since the Vedic period".[133]

G. M. Joshi, in his "Introduction" to the 6th edition of the *Hindutva*, makes the political motives of Savarkar clear as he states:

> Savarkar knew that, though there were differences among the sects of Hindus, yet there was a golden thread that kept them united... The Hindus are tied together by bonds of a common fatherland, ties of blood, a common culture and civilization, common history, and above all, the will to remain united as a nation...India is the fatherland and holy land of Hindus. *Loyalty* and devotion to India would unite Hindus to achieve freedom and to defend it against foreign aggression.[134]

It would be helpful to understand the way Savarkar unfolds the depth of the term Hindutva. As he expounds, Hindutva is not identical to any religious dogma or creed. Rather it is a broader and wider concept that encapsulates "all the departments of thought and activity of the whole Being of our Hindu race" and Hinduism, as such, is a sectarian term.[135] Here, in order to provide a wider base for Hinduism, Savarkar locates the term *Hindu* in the prehistoric period of antiquity, which is "so remoter than the first that even mythology fails to penetrate". He argues that *Hindu* must have been the name by which this land and the people that inhabited it were known, considering the fact that "Indus was known as Hindu to the original inhabitants" and due to the vocal changes of words it must have become 'Sindhu' in the Sanskritised form because 'S' seems to be the equivalent of 'H' in Sanskrit. Thus, as Savarkar argues, even before the Aryans came and settled in this land, the term *Hindu* was in vogue to indicate India and the Indians[136] – a deliberate twist of history indeed. According to Nehru, the term Hindu originated in a much later period, i.e., 8th century BCE, and it appeared first in a *Tantric* literature. The term Hindu, according to him, never occurred at all in any of the ancient literature and even when it first appeared in the *Tantric* literature, it originally meant a people and not the followers of a particular religion.[137]

Spatial Strategy

Savarkar, further, moves away from treating Hinduism as a religion and in that he is the most innovative interpreter and promoter of a

Hinduism that is entirely different from its traditional mode and meaning. He redefines Hinduism in more comprehensive terms – as a religion that encompasses not simply the spiritual but, most importantly, the material, i.e., geography, society, politics and culture. Space (geographical area) becomes a key site of struggle and, as is well known, humans are willing to pay any price to safeguard or grab a piece of land as their own possession precisely because it is in possessing a piece of land lies their identity and address. Savarkar is no different when he attempts to unfold the boundaries that mark the land of the Hindus – their address and the primary component of their identity. In demarcating the boundaries of the land of Hindus, Savarkar first identifies present day Afghanistan (far beyond the Indus) up to the sea in the southern-most tip as parts of the Indian state. He affirms:

> Right from these Indian states [from Afghanistan], all along the banks of the Indus, straight up to the place where it leaps into the sea, was a *long and unbroken chain* of Indian states which followed strictly the Vedic religion.[138]

When was this great nation born? Savarkar answers:

> At last the great mission which the Sindhus had undertaken of founding a nation and country found and reached its geographical limit when the valorous Prince of Ayodhya [Ram] made a triumphant entry in Ceylon and actually brought the whole land from the Himalayas to the Seas under one sovereign sway. The day when the Horse of Victory returned to Ayodhya unchallenged and unchallengeable...that day was the real birth-day of our Hindu people. It was truly our national day: for Aryans and Anaryans knitting themselves into a people were born as a nation.[139]

These emotionally charged rhetorics take us further to Hindutva's spatial strategy in contemporary times.

While expounding the ways in which Hindutva attempts to construct the nation predominantly by translating certain purported scriptural injunctions into concrete historical realities, we are once again reminded not only of Benedict Anderson's thesis that nations are collectively imagined or constructed but also led to arrive at the conclusion that even such a physical entity as 'space' is not natural but socially constructed.[140] Edward Said would argue that long before this subcontinent assumed the form of a modern nation, 'India' appeared on the Western imagination as a land of imperial desires, as manifested by the economic expeditions of Christopher Columbus and Vasco da Gama. Imperialism is nothing but an ideology of space *par excellence*, which can effectively fuse abstract (ideas of) space and concrete places within the mental frameworks of politics. It is a desire to maintain control over an actual place.[141] Hindutva's contemporary path leads to a cultural hegemony over an imaginatively and socially constructed space called 'India' by completely obliterating the traces of all 'others' as a land belonging predominantly to the Aryan descendants.

Savarkar takes great pains to stress the geographical boundaries of Sindhustan, especially the versatility of the sanctified term *Sindhu*. These boundaries that mark the land of the Aryans range from "Sindhu to Sindhu, from the Indus to the Seas".[142] Again Savarkar makes scrupulous attempts to club the land within this territory with three crucial prerequisites or conditions that would determine who a Hindu is, namely, *pitrabhoo, jati,* and *sanskriti*. The first condition, *pitrabhoo*, insists that a 'Hindu' must be born within Hindustan and thus have a legitimate claim to this nation-space as the fatherland.[143] The second condition invokes the trope of blood and makes it obligatory for a Hindu to inherit Hindu blood through natural parents, because Hindus "are not only a Nation but also a race – jati".[144] The third is the most crucial strategic and interpretive move, which insists that "[w]e [Hindus] are one because we are a nation, a race and own a common Sanskriti (civilization)".[145] Savarkar here gives a new meaning to culture, namely, allegiance or loyalty to a particular geography. Thus, the all-important criterion to be included in the shared Hindu culture is that one's *punyabhoo* (holy land) must unmistakably correspond to the *pitrabhoo*, so carefully outlined earlier.

It is at this pivotal point comes Savarkar's clever and tricky interpretation of *Hindu* and *Hindutva*. According to him, even though those who adhere to other faiths (Christians and Muslims to be precise) fulfill the first two conditions, they certainly fail in the third, because according to this criterion their *punyabhoo* is an alien land and their heroes are not the sons of this soil. In this regard, Savarkar is unambiguous and unequivocal in his assertion:

> "...in the case of some of our Mohammedan and Christian countrymen who had originally been forcibly converted to a non-Hindu religion and who consequently have inherited, along with Hindus, a common Fatherland and a greater part of the wealth of a common culture...are not and cannot be recognized as Hindus. For though Hindusthan to them is Fatherland as to any other Hindu yet it is not to them a Holyland too. Their holyland is far of in Arabia or Palestine. Their mythology and Godmen, ideas and heroes are not the children of this soil. Consequently, their names and their outlook smack of a foreign origin. Their love is divided".[146]

It is important to note that, among the three criteria, as outlined by Savarkar, the third one, i.e. the *punyabhoo*, clearly takes precedence over the others. One can, thus, conclude that the first two are neither necessary nor sufficient, but the criterion of *punyabhoo* is both necessary and sufficient. This is clearly illustrated by the exceptions that Savarkar considers: the Buddhists, the Sikhs, the Sindhis and the Indians in diaspora. These groups are regarded to be Hindus no matter what they believe and where they live because their *punyabhoo* is still Hindustan.[147]

It would be helpful in this context to understand the two kinds of spatial strategy that have been operant in independent India, namely, Nehruvian *economic geography* and Hindutva's *sacred geography*. While Nehru dreamt of an economic nation-space, which claimed that dams and steel plants were the temples of modern India, Hindutva insists that temples are to contemporary India what steel plants and dams to Nehruvian India.[148] Nehru believed that a legal guarantee of equality to all citizens irrespective of their communal affiliations would root out communalism from modern India.[149] The developmental idiom was popularized precisely with this perception. But all the idealism that surrounded this economistic deterministic perception remained only a dream and once this perception failed to yield its desired results, people were once again locked into their vicious circle, giving way for communal forces to stake their claims. Contemporary communal conflicts in India, which are closely associated with their spatial strategies, must be understood from this backdrop.

The spatial strategy that has been vigorously promoted by Hindutva in the recent times certainly involves a 'de-secularization and re-sacralization' process of the Indian nation state and polity. It is a kind of *re-civilizationalism* – a process through which Vedic Hinduism has been brought back through political impositions, essentializing its inherent tenets to the nation building. Deshpande argues in a similar line while he affirms that the process of "de-secularization is directly dependent upon the strategic deployment of essentialism".[150] It is in the name of religious essences – uncontestable and self-evident truths – that the state secularism is denounced as "pseudo-secularism". Hindutva's diatribes against the secular state are to accuse the state of 'pampering' the minorities and 'denying' the Hindus the dominant status they deserve in India. Unlike the Nehruvian era, when the exclusionary efforts of the dominant were unseen, contemporary Hindu communalism is founded on the explicit exclusion of those defined as 'others'. Viewing from this vantage point, one can understand the intensity of the utterances of certain Hindu nationalist leaders. Golwalkar (2nd chief of the RSS), for instance, iterated:

> The *foreign races* [Muslims and Christians] in Hindustan must either adopt the Hindu culture and language, must learn to respect and hold in reverence Hindu religion, must entertain no ideas but those of glorification of the Hindu race and culture...or may stay in the country, wholly subordinated to the Hindu nation, claiming nothing, deserving no privileges, far less any preferential treatment; not even citizen's rights...[151] [emphasis added]

Obviously, then, Hindutva's intention is to re-construe the nation through religious essentialism, in which the 'geographical space' becomes a crucial component. It is a site of intense struggle, a struggle to gain supremacy over certain chosen space or spaces, and the predominant criterion in the selection of a particular space is that it must in some way implicate the 'other' so that it can become a battle ground where Hindu 'pride' or 'self-respect' can be firmly established by inflicting an insult of some kind on the 'other'.[152] This is certainly designed on an inexorable 'victor-vanquished' dynamism (*my* victory lies in *other's* defeat) in order to postulate Hindus in the victor's position vis-à-vis the 'others' (Muslims and Christians), who are considered as enemies or aggressors or, at least, the infiltrators. Now, it is not so difficult to find the definite link between the ideological gamut of Hindutva and the *sporadic* incidents of violence and intimidations unleashed on the minorities in India.

Hindutva's spatial strategy is one of its most successful modes of operation in the recent times as, for instance, in the cases of (a) the struggle for the 'liberation' of Ayodhya (the purported birth place of Ram); (b) the unprecedented increase of pilgrimages and religious processions in various parts of India over the past decade or so; and (c) the brutal violence let loose on the Christians and their Churches, institutions, houses, properties and business establishments in Kandhamal, Orissa, and the series of vandalism unleashed on Churches in many parts of Karnataka. It would be helpful, I believe, to probe a little further into the above incidents.

The Ayodhya Issue: It is one of the most successful stories of the Hindu nationalist strategy to invoke a site-based politics by fanning communal frenzy. It is a story of the demolition of *Babri Masjid* (the Mosque built by Babar purportedly demolishing an existent temple in Ayodhya, which is considered to be the birth place of lord Ram) on 06 December 1992. Here it is pertinent to note that the mosque was demolished in defiance of the court verdicts, which is indicative of the ulterior motive of the Hindu nationalists to whip up communal clashes as occasions to deal adequately with the "aggressors". The sudden constellation of interest around Ayodhya raises certain startling questions. Do the belligerent soldiers of Hindutva politics allow any space for thoughtful discussions on the authenticity of the birthplace of Ram, an icon from prehistoric antiquity? What veritable proof is available to ascertain that the (demolished) mosque stood exactly at the spot of an earlier temple? Even if these theories are taken for granted, how can such theories authorize vandalism that had rendered the nation into communal clashes? The answer is simple: it is to construct a space of confrontation where the all-embracing native Hindu faith collides with an alien faith and the enemy is thoroughly defeated and inflicted with insults – a principle derived from none other than Savarkar's legacy indeed.

For Tagore, the story of Rama is a 'marvelous parable of reconciliation', and not to be taken as a matter of historical facts, i.e., in the realm of ideas.[153] But such argumentative standpoints would be fiercely contested by the intolerant Hindutva proponents. In this precarious situation, we need to ask yet another crucial practical question: Will the Hindutva forces allow any lasting solution to the Ayodhya issue? The current mood of the Hindu nationalists obviously suggests that there is no room for any optimism in this regard. The Hindutva warriors intent to keep this issue alive and active for generations to come, which is made clear by the assertion of L.K. Advani in his recently published self-vindicative and much publicized autobiography.[154] Recalling the demolition of the Mosque, Advani attempts to convince his readers that he was against the destruction of the mosque! However, one can identify certain amount of covering up in what Advani has to say, for he has conveniently forgotten to tell us that (a) the Ayodhya incident was but the culmination of his *rath yathra*, a march towards Ayodhya, which he began from Kanyakumari in order to reclaim this site for constructing a magnificent Ram Temple as a national symbol of unification; (b) it was he who campaigned and mobilized the *kar sevaks* (physical labourers) from all corners of the country to move towards Ayodhya and it is these *kar sevaks* who indulged in vandalism. It is quite surprising to hear from him that leaders like Uma Bharti, Ashok Singhal and he himself attempted to dissuade the *kar sevaks* from vandalism – quite unbelievable indeed. His tactic of obscurantism is made clear in his interview to *India Today* following the publication of his autobiography. Here is a brief text of his interview:

> "*Q.* Most of the issues you touch in the book still remain unresolved, like cultural nationalism. *A.* I was hopeful that the Ayodhya issue would be resolved. We were confident that we would come back to power. On the basis of our talks, I thought they would agree... after all, everyone realizes that Ayodhya cannot be built again. *Q.*

> Everybody realizes Ayodhya cannot be built again. *A.* No. *I said the Masjid cannot be built again.* Not that Ayodhya will not be built again. Of that I have no doubt. *The Masjid cannot be built again*". [Emphases added][155]

The irresistible question at this point is: if he was not in favor of the demolition of the mosque, why is he not in favor of its reconstruction?

The increasing number of Hindu pilgrimages and religious processions: For a casual observer, the increasing number of pilgrimages and processions may seem to be the result of the revolution in modern communication network that includes the transportation facilities. But deep down, there are concerted efforts to organize and popularize these phenomena, which serve well to further Hindutva's site based politics in which, on the one hand, the Hindu supremacy is firmly established and, on the other hand, the benchmarked 'other' is either made to suffer or made to experience some sort of humiliation. To cite just one instance, in the year 2006, the Dangs in Gujarat witnessed a sudden creation of a pilgrim centre that generated great panic among the Christian community there. The VHP created a new *Shabari Kumbh Mela* in the Dangs District of Gujarat in a remote village called Jasrol. The site that had been made prominent is a small pond called Pampa Sarovar where pilgrims take their holy dip. Reporting on the event, the *Frontline* says: "The Shabari Kumbh Mela was not just an innocuous religious festival. It was organized to create a religious tourism site to intimidate Christians." Here, again, the identified site is associated with a myth that it was at this spot that Saint Shabari fed Ram with berries while he was on the way to Lanka to liberate Sita. Hindutva could make an easy appeal among the Tribal community in this sort of spatial strategy, because St. Shabari was an *Adivasi*, which the VHP hopes, would lead to the re-conversion of the Christian *Adivasis*.[156] These are clear signs of the drifting away of tolerance that was characteristic of Hinduism.

Violence against Christians in Kandhamal, Orissa: This began hitting headlines since Christmas 2007 when there were attacks on them during their Christmas celebrations. The climax of such pre-meditated brutality was let loose on them, their Churches and institutions in Kandhamal on 24 August 2008 following the funeral procession of Swami Lakshmanananda, a VHP leader, who was actively involved in the mission of *reconverting* or *re-civilising* the Christians. As Anto Akkara recaptures:

> The sum total of the death and devastation in Kandhamal speaks for itself: more than 75 Christians killed over weeks of continued violence, over 5,000 Christian houses looted and destroyed along with 250 Christian Churches and Christian institutions desecrated, looted and reduced to ashes. To cap it all, nearly half of the 117,000 Christians in jungle district have been rendered refugees with the Supreme Court itself reminding the Orissa government on January 5, 2009 that "It is the duty of the state government to protect the minority community. You (State) have done that only after 50,000 people of the minority fled to the jungles."[157]

In fact, the Maoists claimed responsibility for the killing of the swami, but the Hindutva brigades found it an apt pretext to carry out their pre-planned assault on Christians. It was nothing short of the Roman persecution of the early Christians. It made the Indian Prime Minister to admit openly that it was a "national shame".[158]

It has been reported that the funeral procession of the slain Swami covered a mammoth distance of more than two-hundred kilometers inciting violent riots, killing of innocent people and burning Churches and Christian institutions.[159] According to the Hindu extremists, the slain swami was not involved in *re-conversion*, but *de-conversion*, i.e., he was involved in bringing those who had been converted to Christianity back to their original religion. But the activities of the Ashram established by Lakshmanananda in Kandhamal clearly tell us that it was re-conversion because the regular activities in the Ashram involve, among other things, a meticulous attempt to teach Vedic Hinduism to the inmates, a phenomenon, which we have identified as re-civilizationalism earlier.

The violence in Kandhamal was nothing but the bitter fruition of the prolonged hate-campaign carried out against Christians by the Hindutva forces. Probing further, it becomes explicit that what angers Hindutva most is, among others, the Church's engagement with the poorest of the poor, the Dalit and Tribal communities, who had been driven to the peripheries by none other than Vedic Hinduism. In fact, Hindutva cannot tolerate the empowerment of the voiceless. Here is an excerpt from a media article:

> Kandhamal is poor, very very poor. The poverty stares at you from every nook and corner: no electricity, no drinking water, no roads, tiny huts, minimal live stock, no crops, just miles and miles of forest land. The villagers...while had heard of violence against Christians in other parts of the state never thought it would happen to them. They were taken by surprise, as village after village was attacked by rampaging mobs...belonging to the Viswa Hindu Parishad and Bajrang Dal, on August 23-24 (2008)... The people have been mobilized on lies and falsehoods spread by a well-oiled VHP/RSS machinery. The mobs taking revenge for the Swami's murder did not stop even when the Maoists came out with official statement claiming responsibility for the deed. ***No one also stopped to ask why the poorest of the poor were being made to pay the price for a death in which they played no part***...But what is worse,... they [Christians] are not being allowed to return to the villages... 'They tell us, first you become Hindus; then only you can come back,' has become a chorus in Kandhamal...The Christians have become a target of the RSS/VHP/Bajrang Dal that is seeking to consolidate its position, and is using the poison of communalism to mobilize the dalits and the tribals. The worst kind of political machination is being used to make the poor fight for the poor. The recent violence, contrary to some reports, is not casteist in nature. It is religious cleansing with all Christians, their houses, and their places of worship becoming the focus of generated mob violence...They were crying for help all this while from Orissa, but none [in the administration] was willing to listen. The cry did not become a shout as the victims in Kandhamal are too helpless, too weak and too traumatized. It has just become an echo in the remote jungles of Kandhamal where the huts are still burning and the Christians are being driven out.[160] [Emphasis added]

As for as the reasons behind this and several other attacks on Christians in India, the common theory floated is '*forcible conversion* aided by *foreign funds*'. The Hindutva brigades conveniently use this theory as a pretext to brutalize innocent Christians with impunity because the state machinery throws its weight behind them.[161] Ironically, "the Orissa Freedom of Religion Act" has been in force for the past forty years and the state officials could not give any evidence of even one single case of 'forcible conversion' being registered under this act over the last ten years.[162] These are clear signs that Hinduism is gradually drifting away from one of its most fundamental characteristics, i.e., tolerance, in order to assume an alien posture of aggression.

From Tolerance to Aggression

Tolerance has a lot to do with acceptance – acceptance of difference, of opposing viewpoints – that nourishes from diverse traditions, which helps self and collective growth. Hinduism, in the view of many scholars and critics, has an amazing feature of acceptance and it allows a rich variety of 'well developed but diverse religious arguments'. This approach of Hinduism promoted a kind of a value system that laid greater stress on human *dharma* (roughly translated as the personal basis of behavior) and not necessarily their religion.[163] That magnanimity and pride in liberality and tolerance are vitiated by the belligerently sectarian interpretation of Hinduism that is now being popularized by Hindutva. Eric Lott's comments on the leadership of the Sangh Parivar provide us with some important insights. Most of the Sangh leaders have not been primarily products of authentic Hindu tradition (e.g., K. B. Hedgewar, M. S. Golwalkar), however successfully they use symbolisms from Hindu tradition. They are rather modern individuals endowed with western education. Even the most influential RSS leader, V. D. Savarkar, was a 'cultural' Hindu, having least personal commitment to Hindu practice and faith. His was essentially the nationalist stance of a politically minded modernist.[164] Similarly, drawing sources from the Vedas, Amartya Sen argues that there has been a long tradition of accepting skepticism, diversity and disagreement in Hinduism. But the unfortunate developments in recent Hinduism, especially through its political aspirants, have ushered in a tendency to erase or dispense with or sacrifice this age-old tradition of Hinduism on the altar of homogeneity.[165]

Take, for instance, the case put forward in favour of Ram, the epic hero of *Ramayan*. First, the extremist Hindu activists refuse to see the multiple versions of this epic that are in vogue in various regions, not only in India, but also in other parts of Southeast Asia. Second, even if we accept the centrality of Ram in Hinduism (which is not the case at all because many of the Hindu schools of thought do not even mention Ram) as a divine manifestation who was born almost nine hundred thousand years ago and existed at the identified spot, it is not clear as to Who or What provides the authority to the extremists to indulge in religious vandalism or sectarian destruction? What motivates them to favour the narrow interpretations of Hinduism? Without doubt, the Hindutva forces have identified Ayodhya as a potential site that could create confrontation between different faiths. This then leads us to the contemporary interpretation of Hinduism that promotes a different path, i.e., aggression.

If tolerance is acceptance, then, aggression is intolerance *par excellence*. Aggression upholds the deployment of force/power, either persuasive or coercive and it can be defined in terms of a number of pejorative 'isms' – exclusivism, fundamentalism, communalism, fanaticism and fascism. Aggression looks upon the 'other' as its 'object' to be conquered or assimilated or excluded or destroyed and the predominant mode of its function is either violation or violence. In fact, all these and other similar traits are fully embodied in Hindutva as propounded by Savarkar and perpetuated by his Hindu nationalist cohorts. Savarkar laments for the 'unfortunate' tradition of Hinduism that propagates tolerance as its essential virtue and proposes the opposite, i.e., aggression, as the most essential need of Hinduism today (especially on the face of the onslaught of the aggression of other religions and modernity's drive of secularization). To use a popular idiom, "pay it in the same coin as it is paid to you." It is in this context that Savarkar, in extreme anger, curses traditional Hinduism for its principle of tolerance.[166] Hinduism, without doubt, is an ancient religion. But Hindutva is a recent political phenomenon. The dominance of the extremists would eclipse or marginalize, if not totally obliterate, traditional Hinduism of its legacy of diversity.[167]

Considering the belligerent views advanced by the likes of Savarkar, Hedgewar and Golwalkar, it is pertinent to note that there is enough justification in identifying Hindutva and Hindu nationalism with fascism in Italy and Nazism in Germany. Certainly there are varying degrees of agreement and disagreement concerning the identification of the Sangh Parivar with Fascism or Nazism. Nevertheless, a strong case that has been made out to trace the close interconnections between the Parivar and Fascism/Nazism, whereby some critics have attempted to brand the Parivar as 'communal outfits'.[168]

With regard to the connection between the Parivar and Fascism/Nazism, one line of argument points to the direct contacts that had existed between Hindu nationalists and Mussolini and Hitler. Pointing to the direct contact between Mussolini and B. S. Moonje (the mentor of Hedgewar), Casolari argues:

> No doubt, beginning with the early 1920s, and up to the Second World War, Hindu nationalists looked at the political reality of fascist Italy, and subsequently of Nazi Germany, as a source of inspiration...Such influence is still alive in today's militant Hinduism.[169]

Another line of argument points to the coincidence of the time of the origin of Hindu nationalism in India and fascism/Nazism in Europe in the 20th century. Is it a mere coincidence or a strategic attempt to navigate the entire climate of the rising nationalism to usher in a totalitarian, fascist, authoritarian polity? Here, it suffices to point to the coincidence of the emergence of Hindu communalism and the authoritarian regimes of Mussolini and Hitler because it was around this time that Savarkar made two clarion calls to the Hindus: 'back to the Vedas'[170], and 'be aggressive and vengeful', discarding the usual penchant for tolerance, which according to him, is a "perverted virtue" to be done away with.[171] It is important to note that during the colonial period, anti-colonial movement was the predominant agenda of nationalism. But it is an irony that in the context of construing a Hindu Rashtra, the RSS, one of the most prominent entities within the sangh parivar, identified the Muslims, rather than the British, as the prime enemy. Hindutva's construction of the Hindu identity, thus, is dependent on the identification of enemies and threats: as for as this study is concerned, Christians are identified as enemies and threats.[172]

Hindu Nationalism – Its Organization and Consolidation

The early 20th century was a period of intense ideological struggles in Indian politics. Within the colonial public space, a variety of ideologies, which emerged in the course of previous centuries, came together, engaged with one another and attempted to establish their preeminence over others, especially with the aim of gaining a dominant position in national politics. Perhaps, two of these discourses are notable: the Nationalist discourse and the Hindu nationalist discourse. In the course of the freedom struggle the Nationalist discourse took precedence over the Hindu nationalist discourse, and the latter had to wait for its chances to assert itself as a veritable political entity until 1998 when the BJP, the political manifestation of Hindu nationalism, took precedence over the Congress,[173] which was in the fore front of freedom struggle (of course, to identify the present day Congress with the Congress of the freedom movement will cause some uneasiness among critics). Atal Behari Vajpayee became the first BJP prime minister of a fragile coalition government constituted by twelve minor regional parties in March 1998. Within months, (May 11 and 13) the BJP government tested five nuclear bombs in Pokhran, making clear the intentions of Hindu nationalists, i.e., to enlist India among the strong nations of the world. The exuberance, exhilaration and euphoria over the newfound national pride seemed to resonate with Hindutva's imaginations of a strong nation and India's place as a super power on the global map.

There are certain perceptional differences with regard to Hindu nationalism and its recent success. One view understands its success more in cultural and historical terms and argues that it was successful because its leaders were able to draw on 'religious nationalism', which was quite rampant in all the nationalist discourses.[174] Another argument suggests that the current position of the Hindu nationalists became a reality through at least a century of systematic, painstaking organizational and consolidation work that made it possible for them to enunciate themselves as the successful contenders to decide the destiny of the nation.[175] A third argument suggests that Hindu nationalism emerged and consolidated itself neither through the political system nor through religious discourses, but in the broader realm of what we can call 'public culture' – the public space in which individuals and communities 'imagine, represent and recognize themselves through political/commercial expressions and representations of the state and civic organizations'.[176] These are valid arguments indeed about the consolidation of Hindu nationalist forces. However, they miss out an important point, i.e., the coincidence of the disintegration of the secular nationalist discourse that gave rise to a kind of a weariness and discomfiture of the public over the failure of the rulers to fulfill their aspirations and the consolidation of Hindu nationalist forces. Hence, it can be argued that it is the disintegration of the Congress and the secular forces and their utter failure to meet the needs of the masses that have become an easy entry point of the already existent Hindu nationalism within the main stream of Indian politics.

To push our argument further, let me highlight three important stages of this development in which the beginning point was Gandhi's entry into the nationalist movement itself. First, as Nehru describes, the entry of Gandhi marked a definite turning point in national politics, because it was he who transformed the INC, which was otherwise an elite-led organization into a mass-based organization.[177] As Nehru states:

> Gandhi for the first time entered the Congress organization and immediately brought about a complete change in its constitution... Now the peasants rolled and, in its new garb, it began to assume the look of a vast agrarian organization with a strong sprinkling of the middle class.[178]

It offered high promises to resist colonialism, to fight social evils, to solve minority problems, to uplift the depressed classes, to end the curse of untouchability and so forth. Nevertheless, within a short span of time after independence, the INC was reduced to INC (I) and those who were dissatisfied with this trajectory formed separate regional parties. With this transition, its focus also changed and it failed to fulfill its promises of development. To a large extent, it turned out to be a party of sycophants who, in fact, reaped the fruits of Nehruvian modernization and industrialization, leaving the masses in a state of despair.

Second, the disgruntled masses, the strong support base of the Congress, had also to shift their faith to others and they made a few experiments. (a) The Indian electorate defeated Indira Gandhi and brought the Janata Party (a short-lived amalgam of several *like-minded* parties) to power in 1977 subsequent to her declaration of a state of internal emergency in 1975, following the Allahabad High Court's verdict against her election from Rae Bareilly in 1971 (the emergency was clamped on 25 June 1975 and it extended up to 21 March 1977).[179] (b) The people also tried the Vishwanath Pratap Singh experiment in 1989 defeating Rajiv Gandhi on the ground of graft charges. But it could not last long because of his implementation of the Mandal Commission recommendation of 27% affirmative reservation for the OBCs. (c) It was followed by the Narasimharao coalition experiment. These experiments also failed to meet the aspirations of the masses and it is in this context emerged the BJP as the single largest party (though not with absolute majority).

In the third phase, the people did not allow the BJP to continue its hold on politics because they came to realize that the BJP's agenda was not the welfare of the common people or social justice, but something different, as typified by the nuclear testing down to the saffronizing mission until the end of its office in 2003. Even in the 2009 elections, the BJP's manifesto projected the building of Ram Mandir in Ayodhya as the central agenda of governance (and the *temple plank* resurfaces as BJP's central election agenda as the 2014 general elections fast approach). These developments clearly illustrate that the masses are neither enthused nor mesmerized by the rhetorics of either secular nationalists or Hindu nationalists. They are looking for "an-other" India, to borrow the term from subaltern scholarship, in which their voices shall be heard in the mainstream. It can be affirmed that the Indian masses will not invest their faith consistently on any organization or political party until and unless their aspirations are taken into account as the main agenda of governance.

At this crucial juncture, the most important question before us is: what would be the future of Hindu nationalist discourse? In this regard, J. Kruvachira argues:

> ...judging from the aggressive, fundamentalist and militant nature of the ideology its [Hindu nationalism's] survival in the future is seriously in doubt, for it does not possess in itself any enduring values that can take the ideology forward into a distant future. History reminds us that in spite of the might and muscle of Adolf Hitler, the Nazi dictatorship lasted only for [a] little over a decade – 1933-1945![180]

This, however, does not trivialize the inherent potencies of the *Sangh Parivar* to make a comeback, which is demonstrated by the *Parivar's* latest attempts to create 'vote banks' in all the assembly and parliamentary constituencies in order to balance the 'minority vote banks', which are often identified as swing votes with the inherent potencies to decide the political fortunes of major political parties. Among these vote banks, the Muslim and Christian votes are crucial in electoral politics. This, according to the *Sangh Parivar*, is due to the "demographic shift caused in India by the machinations and growth of (minority) Muslim and Christian population". Hence, the right wing Hindu think-tank also plans to create their own vote banks in order to pressurize political parties to protect and advance the interests of the Hindus across caste boundaries. According to Pravin Togadia, the *Parivar* envisages enlisting three thousand Hindus in every assembly constituency and fifteen thousand Hindus in every parliamentary constituency, who would pledge to support only candidates who give an unambiguous public assurance to protect and promote Hindu interests.[181] Thus, even though the BJP is out of power now, the *Parivar* is very much alive and active, renewing its energy and making all out efforts to capture power[182] either by winning or by pressurizing the ruling organization in order to promote its agenda. Further, Hindutva is subtle and it can woo and wound; it can unite and divide to the extent of permeating to the ends of this land with its ideology vitiating the diversity of this nation. It is this aspect of Hindu nationalism that becomes cause for great concern to the minorities, especially the Christians in India.

Hindu Nationalism – Its Challenges to the Church in India

Among the contemporary Hindu extremists who perpetuate an aggressive form of Hindu revivalism, Arun Shourie is an intelligent and prolific writer and is noted for his 'anti-other' attitude, which is demonstrated in almost all of his writings. His diatribes against Christian community in India are acute. Two major planks on which Shourie attacks the Christians are the mission (conversion) of the Church and the Christo-centrism of the Church's theology, a view that is shared by many others also among the Hindu extremists in order to attack and intimidate the Church in India.

The debate over conversion has a long history but no solution to this issue is apparent until now. Here, it is important to bear in mind that, unlike Hinduism, the missionary character is something that is inherent in Christianity, which cannot be dispensed with (a point, which will be discussed in more detail in the ensuing chapter). Those who are involved in missionary activities both past and present, point to the fact that conversions take place mostly among the marginalized communities because of their plight in their home, i.e., their traditional religious practices, which are oppressive. But the opponents accuse missionaries for their 'fraudulent' means to convert the socially and economically marginalized section of the people.[183] According to this view, whatever the Church does, it does with one and the only purpose, i.e., conversion. This is a real challenge to the Church's mission in the contemporary world, and it necessitates the Church to rethink its mission/ministry in the changing contexts.

Another point on which the Church is challenged is its affirmation of the centrality and uniqueness of Christ. In Hindu Vivek Kendra's perception:

> Christianity believes that Jesus Christ is the ONLY son of god. He is supposed to have been sent to earth to wash away the sins of the people, and so redeem them. Of course, this happens only to those who accept him as the ONLY son of god. All the others do not get the benefit, and so will be consigned to that place where one is eternally barbecued.
>
> Christianity says that it has a unique path to salvation, and all other paths are false. While there is supposed to be some

> modification in these views, the acceptance that all other paths may at most be second best. Therefore, it is better if people accept Christianity and not take a chance.
>
> Christians believe that they have been commanded by Christ to go and convert people of this world. This is also supposed to give them special merit when it comes to the day of final judgment.
>
> Christianity is a hierarchical religion, and the commands of the clergy are supposed to be final. It is also this clergy that is supposed to be a link between man and god through Jesus Christ. So, if a person has sinned, and wants god to forgive him/her, he/she has to go to a priest, to ask him to [sic] god on his/her behalf.
>
> While there are many Christians who do not believe in this exclusivity, the statements of the clergy leave no doubt that the clergy believes in exclusivity, and the concept of saving souls.[184]

Thus, it has to be kept in mind that the Church or the Christians in India can hardly hope for any goodwill from the Hindu nationalists, which is made clear from the fact that they are not ready to take the recent paradigm changes in Christian theology and more specifically in Christological constructions seriously because, in their view, the official theology of the Church remains essentially unchanged.

The third point that calls for our attention is Hindu nationalism's attempt to create a corporate identity either by assimilating or excluding the minorities in order to form a monolithic, homogenous Hindu culture. As recognized by many scholars, one of the greatest challenges to the Christians in India is "benchmarking" their identity – an identity that would mark them out as permanent 'others' and potential enemies either to be driven out or annihilated. P. B. Mehta, for instance argues succinctly:

> Hindu nationalism is not so much about defending a way of life, as it is about creating litmus tests of true allegiance. These litmus tests are designed in such a way that it is almost over determined that minorities, especially Christians and Muslims will fail. They remain the permanent 'other' of Hindu identity that either need to be encompassed by bringing them under the sign of a common ethnicity, or else they remain, on this view, a permanent threat to Hindu identity and claims".[185]

Going by the thesis of Savarkar, one can only get the feeling that those identified and certified as Hindus by Hindutva alone have the moral-political right to constitute the nation. The basic strategy behind Savarkar's notion of Hindutva is the redefinition of the nation as the sacred space – a *punyabhoo*. This serves well to describe the Indian nation with a religious essence or value that is beyond all scientific analyses or critical questions. It certainly creates an 'insider-outsider' dichotomy in which the outsider is entitled to exist in this land only at the will of the insider.

This sort of identity formation is a clear indication of a re-civilizationism that attempts to invest all its efforts to construct the nation through the Vedic religious tenets, regarded to be the "eternal law" – a kind of phylogeny wherein all sorts and conditions of people are encompassed in a holistic, hierarchically ranked system of patterned and ritualized exchange of Hindu nationalist discourse. Partha Chtterjee's critique is apt here:

> [I]n its most sophisticated forms, the campaign of the Hindu right often seeks to mobilize on its behalf the will of an interventionist modernizing state, in order to erase the presence of religious or ethnic particularisms from the domains of law or public life, and to supply, in the name of 'national culture', a homogenized content to the notion of citizenship. In this role, the Hindu right in fact seeks to project itself as a principled modernist critic of Islamic or Sikh fundamentalism, and to accuse the 'pseudo-secularists' of preaching tolerance for religious obscurantism and bigotry.[186]

In Rajni Kothari's assessment, the recent interpretation of Hinduism as a majority religion is a gross distortion and a complete misrepresentation of both the social and spiritual realities of India, and more specifically of Hindu religious tradition itself. In his view, the majoritarian syndrome is the Neo-Hindu tendency to *semitize* Hinduism, modeling it along the line of Islam, Christianity or Judaism with one common doctrine, one book, a common clergy, common Church, or Masjid or Temple.[187] Thus, it can be further argued that the modern Indian notion of religion has gone through a transition in which it has derived many of its conceptual categories from a synthesis of Christian (mainly Protestant) models, Orientalist and largely western reconstructions of India's religious past, and the 19th century indigenous reform movements, most of which were defensive reactions against the onslaught of Westernization and Christian Missionising. Therefore, the Church cannot be complacent if it intends to make sense, both to the believers and the wider world, in this precarious situation.

Summary

Hindutva is trying to project itself to be changing towards inclusivity. If this change is for better or for worse, time alone will testify. A current development (early 2012) within the BJP is its search for a suitable person to be projected as the prime ministerial candidate in the general elections 2014. One prominent personality is Narendra Modi, the Gujrat chief minister. Nonetheless, he has been haunted by the Godhra riots 2002 and with the Godhra ghost around his neck, Modi or the BJP can hardly think of his successful entry into the national politics. There are meticulous attempts to make over the image of Modi to be a charismatic leader. His *Sadbhāvanā* is an example of this image building mission. Meanwhile, the Special Investigation Team (SIT), appointed by the apex court of India, to investigate the 2002 riots in Gujrat headed by Raghavan submitted its reports with the conclusion that there is no prosecutable evidence against Modi in the 2002 riots in Gujrat as against the report of the *amicus Curiae* Ramachandran, who found Modi culpable.[188] While the BJP is quick to claim the SIT report as a vindication of Modi, it is contested by citizens' groups and NGOs, including a retired judge of the Bombay High Court. According to *TIME* magazine's internet opinion poll (of course the BJP contests the negative votes against him as rigged) Modi is seen as the most polarizing person in Indian politics. In this milieu, while the victims of 2002 riots demand justice, the BJP has come out with a proposal of '*forgetting the past and moving beyond 2002*' towards progress.[189] However, there is a lot of irony and cynicism about BJP's intentions because its politics revolves around the bitter memories of the partition of India in 1947. Is it not an irony that the BJP, while keeping the memories of bygone past alive, expects the victims of the riots to forget the (recent) past?[190]

Hindu nationalist situation represents a clearly defined political agenda couched in Brahminic Hinduism, which is posited on defining reality in oppositional terms (e.g. *insider* and *outsider*) in order to re-construe India as a monolithic Hindu nation following the dominant religious tenets by excluding or assimilating the 'other', circumventing or down-playing the pluralistic or multi-civilizational texture of India. This is untenable and tenuous for the simple fact that the Indian reality is marked by diversity in all facets of its existence. Hindutva, however, is engaged in a discourse that first identifies the 'other', demonizes the 'other' and then it assimilates the 'other' wherever possible (e.g. Buddhism) and ostracizes the 'other' wherever it finds that the 'other' resolutely remains different (e.g. Christians and Muslims). This is a project that can be termed as a kind of systemic integration through assimilation or ostracism. In this process, Hindutva does not embrace differences as something to be celebrated; rather differences are viewed as something to be erased in order to create an ambience of uniformity or homogeneity. Over against Hindutva's reactionary, extremist, assimilatory/exclusionary mode of discourse, we would like to employ *unity of the opposites* as a veritable and relevant theological principle in our reflections on ecclesia. It provides ample scope to move away from exclusion to embrace of differences in a spirit of *perichoretic* relationship, which is the basis of our ecclesiological reflections in the Hindu nationalist situation.

It has been noted that nothing is more dangerous than the spread of Hindutva, which is a specific mode of religiously-charged political discourse on the nation. Therefore, it indulges in erasing differences through either assimilation or exclusion and annihilation. Hindu nationalism's particular mode of discourse to assimilate or ostracize the 'others' must be resisted. First, the very attempt to claim that the Hindus are the majority in India is a strategic way of befogging truth. How can the Dalits be included within the fold of Vedic Hinduism, when they are virtually excluded from the sacred scriptures?[191] Second, the Tribal communities can in no way be considered to be Hindus, because their worldview and religion are different from that of Hinduism. Third, Savarkar's invocation of the trope of blood is a clever ploy to woo various communities because the Aryans and

Dravidians (leave alone the other races) are ethnically, culturally and racially different. In their trenchant advocacy for a Hindu nation, cotemporary right wing Hindus are predominantly concerned about a nationalism that would be beneficial to the elite middle class, a class that would not tolerate anything that would impinge upon its comforts. Quite conspicuously, the discourse on Hindu nationalism is not constructed around social justice, especially the vices like caste and gender discriminations.[192] It is an open challenge to Christian theology as we engage in reflections on the Church's life and mission in this subcontinent called 'India'.

In the present milieu, we need to constantly remind ourselves that what we encounter now is *not* another religion, but a veritable, influential and religiously loaded political ideology with an avowed agenda to erase the different identities and replace them with a corporatist Hindu identity to make India a strong monolithic Hindu nation. Its operational agenda is consolidation of different and distinct particularities, which, in Francesco Alberoni's terms, might be understood as "unanimity through symbolic integration".[193] One needs to be cautious in understanding 'integration' as a conceptual category, since the term *integration* has a different connotation of bringing together different categories on a common platform for the common good. The best Indian example in this regard is the principle of "unity in diversity" on which hinges national integration. But Hindutva does not believe in this type of integration, but in consolidation of the different communities in order to serve the interest of a particular segment at the expense of others. In the 2009 general elections the BJP has experienced one of its worst defeats in the past two decades. An important observation that the media has made with regard to the poll verdicts is notable here. It has been observed that the UPA's victory (with Congress as the main alliance partner) came against two ideologically well-defined fronts: the NDA (with BJP as the main partner), and the third front (with the Left Parties as the major partners). The notable point is that the people of India had rejected the ideological rigorisms and rigidities of the BJP and the Left as untenable and gave their verdict in favor of a centrist coalition with flexibility. In other words, the people of India reposed their faith in a political configuration that provides space for differences, pluralities, multiplicities or the co-existence of different civilizations, and not on those who believed in homogeneity and bigotry.[194] Do not the election results indicate a passionate cry of the people for a truly human communion amidst all that attempts to divide humans in oppositional terms? Is it not true that the people of India look for a viable alternative that would embrace differences and work for the welfare of all who are part of this great nation? It is from this background we move on to understand the origin, life, theology and mission of the Church up to the time of the protestant Reformation in the ensuing chapter.

Notes

1 Gerald James Larson, *India's Agony Over Religion* (op. cit.), p. 158 (also see pp. 44-141).

2 It is estimated that about 421 million of our fellow Indians live in deplorable conditions. See Rajiv Chandrasekhar, "National Priority Issues and You" in *The New Indian Express* (Tuesday, November 09, 2010, Bangalore), p. 2. For further discussions, see Ashish Nandy, *Bonfire of Creeds* (Delhi: Oxford University Press, 2004); R. W. Stern, *Changing India* (Cambridge, UK: Cambridge University Press, 2nd edition, 2003); Romila Thapar, ed., *India: Another Millennium?* (Delhi: Penguin Books, 2001); and V. S. Upadhyay and V. P. Sharma, *Contemporary Indian Society* (Delhi: Amol Publications, 1995).

3 Augustine Kanjamala, "Seven Images of the Church in India", in Thomas D'Sa, ed., *The Church in India in the Emerging Third Millennium* (Bangalore: NBCLC, 2005), p. 27.

4 Pratap Bhanu Mehta, "Introduction to the Omnibus", in *Hindu Nationalism and Indian Politics* (Delhi: Oxford University Press, A 'three books in one volume' edition, 2004), p. xiv.

5 Some people view the history of India in terms of its glorious past: See V. D. Savarkar, *Six Glorious Epochs of Indian History*; A. L. Basham, *The Wonder that was India* (Fontana: Collins, 1975); and Praphullachandra Basu, *Indo-Aryan Polity during the Period of the Rig Veda* (Allahabad: The Pioneer Press, 1919). This tendency is either a naïve perception of India or it may be a willful attempt to romanticize the historic past of India with a hidden and/or ulterior motive.

6 A. N. Whitehead, *Religion in the Making* (Cambridge: Cambridge University Press, 1927), p. 6.

7 See Gerald James Larson, *India's Agony Over Religion*, p. x.

8 See, for instance, Amartya Sen, "On Interpreting India's Past" in Sugata Bose and Ayesha Jalal, eds., *Nationalism, Democracy & Development* (Delhi: OUP, 1998), pp.10-35. For a "fragmentary" viewpoint against the "subject-centered" universal reasoning, see Partha Chatterjee, *The Nation and Its Fragments: Colonial and Postcolonial Histories* (Delhi: OUP, 1995), p. xi.

9 See Gerald James Larson, *India's Agony Over Religion*, pp. 37-43.

10 Enlightenment geared all its resources towards a higher and enlightened order of society with three fundamental principles, namely, (a) a strong confidence in the powers of human reason and an inclination to natural enquiry to uncover the core truth in every field; (b) a preparedness to open the vistas of religious discussions transcending the rigid enclaves of Christianity and Paganism to include the possibility of a religion 'natural' to the entire humanity; and (c) well defined educational and social goals and objectives to aid the development process towards an enlightened order of society. See Immanuel Kant, "*Was ist Aufklärung?*" (What is Enlightenment?) in Peter Gay, ed., *The Enlightenment: A Comprehensive Anthology* (New York: Simon and Schuster, 1973), p. 384.

11 G. J. Larson, *India's Agony Over Religion,* p. 38. Here, Larson identifies the following schools responsible for the new metamorphoses: Modern Liberal Social Scientific School represented by Emile Durkheim and Max Weber; the sociological and social-anthropological schools represented by the works of people like Peter Berger, Milton Singer, Louis Dumont, McKim Marriot, M. N. Srinivas, and Andre Beteille; and the 'critical theory' tradition of Jürgen Habermas and the Frankfurt School.

12 Jawaharlal Nehru, *The Discovery of India* (Delhi: Penguin Books, 2004, first in 1946), pp. 16ff & 573ff.

13 Edward Said, *Orientalism* (New York: Vintage Books, 1979), p. 2.

14 Ibid., pp. 1-5.

15 Ibid., p. 2. See also G. J. Larson, *India's Agony over Religion*, p. 39.

16 For a fair discussion on this mode of Max Weber's theorization, see Reinhard Bendix, *Max Weber: An Intellectual Portrait* (Berkeley, California: University of California Press, 1977), especially chapters II & III, pp. 13-79; & Sung Ho Kim, *Max Weber's Politics of Civil Society* (Cambridge, UK: Cambridge University Press, 2004), especially pp. 1-56, 133-172. See also Max Weber, *The Protestant Ethic and the Spirit of Capitalism*, Tr. by Talcott Parsons (London York: Routledge, 1992), especially chapter 5 "Asceticism and the Spirit of Capitalism"

pp. 101-125; Max Weber, *The Sociology of Religion*, Tr. by Ephraim Fischof with an Introduction by Talcott Parsons (London: Methuen & Co., 1963), Especially Chapter XV "Judaism, Christianity, and the Socio-Economic Order", pp. 246-261.

17 For an informative reading on this sort of theorizing in India, see Sugata Bose, ed., *South Asia and World Capitalism* (Delhi: Oxford University Press, 1990).

18 G. C. Spivak, "Can the Subaltern Speak?" in Carey Nelson and Larry Grossberg, eds., *Marxism and the Interpretation of Culture* (Uraba: University of Illinois Press, 1988), pp. 271-313.

19 A cursory glance at some of the themes they have dealt with will illustrate this point: "The Bhils and Shahukars of Eastern Gujarat" (*SS V*, 1-54), "Chandra's Death" (*SS V*, 135-165), "Approver's Testimony, Judicial Discourse: The Case of Chauri Chaura" (*SS V*, 166-202), "The Slave of MS. H.6" (*SS VII*, 159-220), "Power, Religion and Community: The Matobo Case". (*SS VII*, 221-246).

20 Gayatri Chakravarty Spivak, "Subaltern Studies: Deconstructing Historiography" in Ranajit Guha, ed., *Subaltern Studies IV* (Delhi: Oxford University Press, 1985), pp. 330-363.

21 *SS IV*, p. 373.

22 Ibid., p. 374.

23 Ibid., p. 375.

24 G. J. Larson, *India's Agony Over Religion*, p. 42.

25 See Jawaharlal Nehru, *Discovery of India*, pp. 567-583. Also see George Mathew, "Fundamentalism in India: A Sociological Perspective" in John S. Augustine, ed., *Religious Fundamentalism: An Asian Perspective* (Bangalore: SATHRI/CCA/ WARC, 1993), p. 21.

26 The tern 'fundamentalism' is used here in its pejorative sense, which is defined somewhat simplistically by Palkivala as "the triumph of letter over spirit", which reminds us of the lesson taught two thousand years ago that "the letter killeth but the spirit giveth life" N. A. Palkivala, *We, the People* (Bombay: Strand Book Stall, 4th print, 1984), p. xiv.

27 See Prabhakar Bhattacharyya, *Fanaticism* (Kolkata: Samik Prakashan, 2004). In this booklet, the author defines fanaticism as a "mental tendency to indulge in wild and extravagant notions, in religious, social and political matters which result in unreasonable enthusiasm among people", p. 1.

28 For an excellent analysis of such essentialist outlook, see Ronald Inden, *Imagining India* (Oxford: Basil Blackwell, 1990.) See also one of his

interesting articles "Orientalist Constructions of India" *Modern Asian Studies* Vol. 20, No. 3, (1986), pp. 401-446.

29 Kuan-Hsing Chen, "The Decolonization Question" in Kuan-Hsing Chen, ed., *Trajectories: Inter-Asia Cultural Studies* (London and New York: Routledge, 1998), pp. 1-47.

30 Ashis Nandy, *The Intimate Enemy: Loss and Recovery of Self under Colonialism* (Delhi: Oxford University Press, 1983), p. xi.

31 G. Aloysius, *Nationalism without a Nation in India* (Delhi: Oxford University Press, 1997), pp. 44-46. For an analysis of the way in which the British contributed to the renewal of Brahminism, see Swami Dharma Theertha, *The Menace of Hindu Imperialism* (Lahore: Happy Home Publications, 1946).

32 See *India Today* (15 May 1992), pp. 11 & 96-97. This has been openly acknowledged by Hindutva ideologues through their publications and public assertions. See *Religious Conversions*, Answer to Question No. 34, p. 32.

33 For a fair understanding of the general manner of treating India as a nation-state, see Donald Eugene Smith, *India as a Secular State* (Princeton: Princeton University Press, 1963).

34 For a brief discussion, see Leroy S. Rouner, *To be at Home: Christianity, Civil Religion, and World Community* (Boston: Beacon Press, 1991), Ch. 6: "Christianity and the New India", pp. 77-95.

35 Ernest Gellner, *Nations and Nationalism* (Oxford, UK, Cambridge, USA: Blackwell, 1996), p. 1.

36 Benedict Anderson, *Imagined Communities* (New York: Verso, 1996, 7th Impression), p. 3.

37 Ibid., p. 6.

38 Walter Connor, *Ethnonationalism: The Quest for Understanding* (Princeton: Princeton University Press, 1994), p. xi.

39 Some of the influential works in this sort of theorizing are: Benedict Anderson, *Imagined Communities;* Eric Hobsbawm, *Nations and Nationalism Since 1780* (Cambridge: Cambridge University Press, 1990).

40 Eric Lott, *Religious Faith, Human Identity: Dangerous Dynamics in Global &Indian life* (Bangalore: ATC/UTC, 2005), p. 235; Also see the entire chapter: "Imagining the Nation Religiously", pp. 220-236.

41 Adapted from Eric Lott, *Religious Faith, Human Identity*, pp. 223f. Also see Adrian Hastings, *The Construction of Nationhood: Ethnicity, Religion & Nationalism* (Cambridge: CUP, 1997), pp. 188-197.

42 Satish Deshpande, *Contemporary India*, p. 148.

43 Nehru, for instance, affirms: "[N]ationalism was and is inevitable in the India of my day; it is a natural and healthy growth." See *The Discovery of India*, p. 44. But in Kishwar's opinion, nationalism has caused more bloodshed and the bloodiest of wars of all time. See *Religion at the Service of Nationalism*, p. 252.

44 See "Nationalism" in Robert McHenry, Gen. ed., *The New Encyclopedia Britannica* (Chicago: University of Chicago, 15th Edition. 1992), p. 552.

45 Ernest Gellner, *Nations and Nationalism*, pp. 39-52.

46 See Yogendra K. Malik and V. B. Singh, *Hindu Nationalists in India: The Rise of Bharatiya Janata Party* (Delhi: Vistaar Publications, 1994), p. 3.

47 For a glimpse of the intersecting discourses in the Indian public domain, especially around nationalism, see R. Sahayadhas, "Religion-State Relationship: Significance of a Middle-Path in Contemporary India", *Bangalore Theological Forum*, Vol. XLIII, No. 1 (June 2011), pp. 55-82 – esp. 57-61.

48 *The New Encyclopedia Britannica,* p. 552.

49 Partha Chatterjee, *The Nation and Its Fragments: Colonial and Postcolonial Histories* (Delhi: Oxford University Press, 1995), pp. 3-4.

50 See Jim Masselos, *Nationalism on Indian Subcontinent: An Introductory History* (Melbourne, Australia: Thomas Nelson, 1972), Chapters 4 & 5, pp. 43-73.

51 Yogendra K. Malik &V. B. Singh, *Hindu Nationalists in India,* p. 3.

52 Charles H. Heimsath, *Indian Nationalism and Hindu Social Reforms* (Princeton: Princeton University Press, 1964), p. 139. To provide a brief definition of secularism: "Secularism often denotes a way of life and conduct guided by materialistic considerations devoid of religion." M. C. Setalvad, *Secularism*, Patel Memorial Lecture (Delhi: Ministry of Information and Broadcasting, Govt. of India, 1965), p. 3.

53 Y. K. Malik & V. B. Singh, *Hindu Nationalists in India,* pp. 3ff.

54 Some critics argue that anti-colonial nationalism evolved its own domain of sovereignty well ahead of its political battle against the colonizers, i.e., well before the founding of the INC. See Partha Chatterjee, *The Nation and its Fragments*, pp. 3-13.

55 Jim Masselos, *Nationalism on the Indian Subcontinent: An Introductory History*, p.62. The origin of INC is a contested point. For an opposing view point, see John Zavos, *The Emergence of Hindu nationalism in India* (Delhi: Oxford University Press, 2004), Ch. 3, pp. 68-98.

56 For a detailed discussion on this representative base of the Congress and its democratic proceedings, see Jim Masselos, *Nationalism on the Indian Subcontinent*, pp. 62-73.

57 See G. J. Larson, *India's Agony over Religion*, pp. 178-277.

58 Benedict Anderson, *Imagined Communities*, p. 62.

59 Shamita Basu, *Religious Revivalism as Nationalist Discourse: Swami Vivekananda and New Hinduism in Nineteenth-Century Bengal* (Delhi: Oxford University Press, 2002), p. 17.

60 It also involved, within its scope, a critique of Indian society and its ways of life. For a typical example of this kind of orientalist project, see David Kopf, *British Orientalism and the Bengal Renaissance: The Dynamics of Indian Modernization 1793-1835* (Berkeley: University of California Press, 1969). See also R. S. Sugirtharajah, *Asian Biblical Hermeneutics and Postcolonialism* (Sheffield, UK: Sheffield Academic Press, 1999), pp. i-ix & 1-52; and R. S. Sugirtharajah, *Postcolonial Criticism and Biblical Interpretation* (Oxford, UK: Oxford University Press, 2002), pp. 200-207.

61 Nehru was wary about this way of perceiving India. According to him 'Hindu' means a people and not the followers of a religion and in no sense can India be identified with Hinduism. *The Discovery of India* (op. cit.), pp. 69-72. See also Shamita Basu, *Religious Revivalism as Nationalist Discourse* (op. cit.,), p. 18.

62 Susan Bayly, for instance, makes such a comparison in one of her essays "Hindu Modernizers and the Public Arena: Indigenous Critiques of Caste in colonial India" in W. Radice, ed., *Swami Vivekananda and the Modernization of Hinduism* (Delhi: Oxford University Press, 1998), pp. 93-137, especially pp. 135ff.

63 A typical example of this line of thinking is J. N. Farquhar, *Modern Religious Movements in India* (Delhi: Munshram Manoharlal, 1967, First published in 1915).

64 For a critique of this view see, John Zavos, *The Emergence of Hindu Nationalism in India*, pp. 34-50.

65 P. L. John Panicker, *Gandhi on Pluralism and Communalism* (Delhi: ISPCK, 2006), pp. 117ff.

66 According to Zakir Naik, the *Koran* is the "final revelation of God". Source: Lectures, Speeches and Disputations of Dr. Zakir Naik in Q TV.

67 There are four kinds of *jihad*, namely, jihad of the heart (spiritual warfare), jihad of the hand (physical labor), jihad of the tongue (warfare of preaching and disputation), and jihad of the sword (holy war).

See Harold Coward, *Pluralism: Challenges to World Religions* (Delhi: Satguru Publications, 1996), pp. 45-47.

68 P. L. John Panicker, *Gandhi on Pluralism and Communalism*, p. 122.

69 Ibid., p. 124.

70 As critics point out: “Islamic law recognizes no other nation than its own since the aim of Islam was the subordination of the whole world to one system of law and religion to be enforced by the supreme authority of the Caliph”. Majid Khadduri and H. J. Liebesny, eds., *Law in the Middle East*, Vol. I (Washington: Richmond William Byrd Press, 1955), p. 359.

71 P. L. John Panicker, *Gandhi on Pluralism and Communalism*, p. 125ff.

72 For an informative reading on how various elements come into play within the ‘secular’ practices of India, see Thomas Blom Hansen, *The Saffron Wave: Democracy and Hindu Nationalism in Modern India* (Delhi: Oxford University Press, 2004), pp. 52-57.

73 Sarvapalli Radhakrishnan, “Foreword” in Abid Hussain, *The National Culture of India* (Bombay: Asia Publishing House, 2nd edition, 1961), p. vii.

74 V. K. Sinha, “Introduction” in V. K. Sinha, ed., *Secularism in India* (Bombay: Lalvani Publishing House, 1968), p. vii.

75 D. E. Smith, *India as a Secular State*, pp. 149 & 499-500.

76 D. E. Smith, *India as a Secular State*, p. 4. For a critique of Smith’s assumptions on secularism in India, see, Marc Galanter, “Secularism East and West” in V. K. Sinha, ed. *Secularism in India*, pp. 159-191. An assessment of the application of secular principles in governance reveals that often state governments offer their tacit support to religious fanatics. The *Frontline* (March 10, 2006), for instance, reports that in the Dangs in Gujarath, the VHP is organizing a Kumbh Mela in a remote Tribal village called Jarsol, aiming at converting the Adivasi Christians to Hinduism by force. The state administration fully backs and even aids the designs of the VHP (see pp. 39-41).

77 Describing the Asian reality, Aloysius Pieris states that the Asian reality is characterized by acute poverty and intense religiosity. India being part of Asia certainly shares this trait. See Aloysius Pieris, “A Theology of Liberation in Asian Churches?” in S. Arokiasamy & and G. Gispert-Sauch, eds., *Liberation in Asia: Theological Perspectives* (Delhi: Vidhyajyoti Faculty of Theology, 1987), pp. 17-38 & 36.

78 V. K. Sinha, ed., *Secularism in India*, p. 3.

79 In the 2009 general elections, there has been a serious debate about secular-communal divide. While Prime Minister Manmohan Singh

iterated that the secular-communal divide is a serious issue in this election, Advani countered it by saying that the real issue is not secular-communal divide, but between *true and pseudo secularism* (Source: CNN-IBN, 21.04.2009).

80 For an excellent analysis of this kind of political gymnastics in India, See W. H. Morris-Jones, *The Government and Politics of India* (Bombay: B.I. Publications, 1964).

81 Various neo-Hindu reformist and nationalist traditions came to be united on certain common interests: (i) developing a self-confident national identity, (ii) redefining out-dated, parochial, and superstitious Hindu practices, (iii) reforming, re-interpreting or rejecting caste system, (iv) improving the condition of women, (v) encouraging the economic development of all sections of the people, and (vi) utilizing the techniques of modern communication network, especially derived from the Protestant missionary models to accelerate the speedy development of the nation. G. J. Larson, *India's Agony Over Religion*, p. 193.

82 Jawaharlal Nehru, *The Discovery of India*, pp. 397-398. In a footnote to this text Nehru quotes Gandhi's affirmation: "Gandhi told the Federation of International Fellowships in 1928, that 'after long study and experience I have come to these conclusions that (1) all religions are true, (2) all religions have some error in them, (3) all religions are almost as dear to me as my own Hinduism. My veneration for other faiths is the same as for my own faith. Consequently, the thought of conversion is impossible...Our prayer for others ought never to be: 'God give them the light thou has given to me!' But: 'Give them all the light and truth they need for their highest development.' " (Ibid.)

83 Ibid., p. 398.

84 Ibid., p. 398.

85 See Sumit Sarkar, "The Fascism of the Sangh Parivar" *Economic and Political Weekly* (30 Jan. 1993), pp. 163-167; Casolari, Marzia. "Hindutva's Foreign Tie-up in the 1930s: Archival Evidence" *Economic and Political Weekly* (22 Jan 2000), pp. 218-228; Jan Breman, "The Hindu Right: Comparisons with Nazi Germany" *Times of India* (15 March 1993).

86 Markandey Katju, "All the Perfumes of Arabia" *The Hindu* (February 18, 2013).

87 Partha Chatterjee, *A Possible India: Essays in Political Criticism* (Delhi: OUP, 1998), pp. 228-231.

88 Donald Eugene Smith, *India as a Secular state*, pp. 499-500.

89 For a discussion, see Robert N. Bellah, et al., *Habits of the Heart: Individualism and Commitment in American life* (New York: Harper and Row, 1986).

90 *Frontline*, (March 10, 2006), p. 44.

91 These are but a few names and movements that were active in the events that led to the partition. A full treatment of all the names and movements is not possible in this study. Readers may find detailed treatment of them in various works produced in the historic study of India. Owing to the scope and limitation of this study, suffice it to mention such selective names and movements here. See also G. J. Larson, *India's Agony Over Religion*, pp. 178-191.

92 Some theorists opine that the seeds of separation were sown by V. D. Savarkar long before Jinnah could invoke the idea. See Amartya Sen, *The Argumentative Indian: Writings on Indian Culture, History and Identity* (London: Penguin Books, 2005), p. 51. The following are the actual words of Savarkar: "India cannot be assumed today to be a unitarian and homogenous nation, but on the contrary there are two nations in the main; the Hindus and the Muslims...There are two antagonistic nations living side by side in India." Savarkar's Presidential address to the Hindu Mahasabha in 1937, cited by D. E. Smith, *India as a Secular State*, p. 459.

93 G. J. Larson, *India's Agony*, p. 196.

94 As cited in Stephen Hay, ed., *Sources of Indian Tradition* Vol. II (New York: Columbia University Press, 1988), p. 192.

95 As cited in Stephen Hay, ed., *Sources of Indian Tradition* Vol. II, p. 195.

96 Donald Eugene Smith, *India as a Secular State*, pp. 88-89.

97 G. J. Larson, *India's Agony Over Religion*, p. 185. Also see John R. McLane, "The Decision to Partition Bengal in 1905" *Indian Economic and Social History Review*, Vol. 2, No. 3 (July 1965), pp. 221- 237; and Gordon Johnson, "Partition, Agitation and Congress: Bengal 1904 To 1908", *Modern Asian Studies*, Vol. 7, No. 3 (May 1973), pp. 533-588.

98 Jawaharlal Nehru, *The Discovery of India*, p. 395.

99 Cited from D. E. Smith, *India as a Secular State*, p. 86.

100 See Stanley Wolpert, *A New History of India* (Delhi: Oxford University Press, 1993), pp. 301ff.

101 As cited in Stanley Wolpert, *A New History of India*, p. 317.

102 Cited in Stephen Hay, *Sources of Indian Tradition*, Vol. 2, pp.229-230.

103 As quoted in D. E. Smith, *India as a Secular State*, pp. 148-149 from M. K. Gandhi, *To the Hindus and Muslims*, ed. by Anand T. Hingorani (Allahabad: Law Journal Press, 1942).

104 Stanley Wolpert, *A History of India*, p. 348.

105 In order to have a fair grasp of the intricacy of this particular case, we need to go through the rulings of the Supreme Court in two other similar cases: (i) the case of Bai Tahira *VS* Ali Hussain Fissali, 1979 (judgment by the bench comprised of Krishna Iyer, Tulzapulkar and R. S. Pathak), and (ii) the case of Fuzlunbi *VS* K. Khader Vali, 1980 (judgment by Krishna Iyer, Chinnappa Reddy and A. P. Sen). In both the cases, the right of the divorced woman to maintenance was upheld and that had never created any uproar. Conversely, in the Shah Bano case (judgment by the bench comprised of Chandrachud, Desai, Venkatramaiah, Chinnappareddy, and R. Misra), even though the same right was upheld, it created such an uproar. The reason, according to some analysts, was that in the previous cases the judges dwelt mostly upon the issue of *social injustice* meted out to women, and they hardly mentioned the word 'Muslim' in their judgments. But in the Shah Bano case, invariably every paragraph of the judgment dwells almost obsessively upon 'Muslim' and 'Muslims'. To quote one statement from the judgment as an illustration: "Undoubtedly, the Muslim husband enjoys the privilege of being able to discard his wife whenever he chooses to do so, for reasons, good, bad or indifferent. Indeed, for no reason at all." If the word 'Muslim' were deleted from this statement, would it not hold well? To be sure, it was to send wrong signals among the Muslim community as if it was an attempt to single out Muslim men and Islam in general. And it came to be interpreted that it indirectly vindicated the Hindu men and Hindu community. The immediate question that arises is: do not most husbands in Indian society enjoy this privilege, irrespective of religion or no religion? By one stroke, justice Chandrachud and his companions converted what was essentially a women's rights issue into a communal issue. The entire tone of the judgment gave a wrong impression that other communities in India have a perfectly secular egalitarian law. For a detailed discussion on this case and its aftermath, see "Pro-Women or Anti-Muslim? The Shah Bano Controversy" in Madhu Kishwar, *Religion at the Service of Nationalism and Other Essays*, pp. 206-232.

106 To understand the kind of political clout the RSS has over the BJP, one needs only to look at the quick reaction of the RSS to the 2009 election debacle of the saffron party by assigning a three men commission to

enquire into the factors that had led the party's defeat on the very day of the election results, i.e. on 16 May 2009 itself. (Source: Election Bulletins of *Headlines Today* & *Times Now*, 16 May 2009). Even in the event of the vey recent corruption charges against the current BJP president, Nitin Gadkari, It is said that the RSS is shielding him for its own political reasons (Source: Media Debates on the issue October-November 2012).

107 Commenting on the intellectual constructions of Hindutva, Ashis Nandy observes: "The writings (of the likes of Savarkar) tell one much about their feelings of inferiority *vis-à-vis* Christianity and Islam, their confusion of self-definition in the wake of British colonization of India, and their sexual anxieties and deep masculinity strivings. But they tell you next to nothing about where they – as representatives of the semi-westernized, decultured, upper-caste, urban, tertiary sector in India – stand in terms of the contents of Hinduism. Their knowledge of Hinduism is third-rate, permeated by 19th century colonial scholarship, that too usually acquired second-hand, and their theology is invariably bogus. Like their presentday followers, they can outshoot everybody, out-think none." Ashish Nandy, "Fundamentalism" in John S. Augustine, ed., *Religious Fundamentalism,* p. 5.

108 This sense of victimhood has been subtly and cleverly twisted to show the indomitable courage of Hindus and the crushing defeat inflicted on the Muslim and Christian invaders by the valorous Hindu heroes as exemplified by Savarkar's *Six Glorious Epochs of Indian History*, in which Savarkar aims at achieving two things at one stroke: (i) to refute the charge that the history of Hindus is one of perpetual defeats at the hands of non-Hindus; and (ii) to show that the Hindu history is one of glorious victories against the alien aggressors. See Ibid., pp. 1-5 & 124-126.

109 Pratap Bhanu Mehta, "Introduction to the Omnibus", p. vii.

110 For a detailed discussion on these aspects, see Satish Deshpande, *Contemporary India*, pp. 125-150.

111 B. B. Mishra, *The Indian Middle Classes: Their Growth in Modern Times* (London: Oxford University Press, 1961), pp. 106, 307.

112 C. Calhoun, *Critical Social Theory: Culture, History and the Challenges of Difference* (Oxford: Blackwell, 1995), p. 241. See also Jürgen Habermas, *Structural Transformation of the Public Sphere: An Inquiry into a Category of Bourgeois Society* (Cambridge, Massachusetts: MIT, 1989), pp. 27-30.

113 John Zavos, *The Emergence of Hindu Nationalism in India*, p. 12.

114 John Zavos, *The Emergence of Hindu Nationalism in India*, p. 14.

115 D. Haynes, *Rhetoric and Ritual in Colonial India: The Shaping of a Public Culture in Surat City, 1852-1928* (Berkeley, CA: University of California Press, 1991), p. 15.

116 P. B. Mehta, "Introduction to the Omnibus", p. viii.

117 Take, for instance, the works of Vivekananda. In his fiery rhetorics, he attempted to heap diatribes against the west and to glorify Indian cultural and religious traditions as the highest and pristine form of life. See Swami Vivekananda, *The East and the West* (Calcutta: Advaita Ashrama, 1963).

118 V. D. Savarkar, *Hindutva,* p. iv.

119 Savarkar, *Hindutva,* p. v.

120 See "Preface by the Publisher of Second Edition" in Savarkar, *Hindutva,* p. vii.

121 S. Clarke, "Hindutva, Religious and Ethnocultural Minorities and Indian-Christian Theology", p. 200.

122 Marx's insight on ideology popularized the notion that ideology is culturally and/or socially conditioned and as a consequence, at the beginning of the 20th century the *sociology of knowledge* postulated ideology as a necessary condition of all rational thinking. See Karl Marx, "Preface to a Contribution to the Critique of Political Economy" in *Karl Marx and Frederick Engels: Selected Works* (New York: International Publishers, 1969) p. 182. In the context of the dominant power, ideology forms the very foundation of normativity that has been used like a whip against the vulnerable by the powerful for centuries, despite the fact that a particular ideology is given birth by specific historical and cultural context. The general opinion about *ideology* is that it is built around a "lie" which is projected and promoted to serve the *purpose(s)* of a particular people group. See David J. Krieger, *The New Universalism: Foundation for a Global Theology* (Maryknoll, New York: Orbis Books, 1991), p. 82.

123 S. Clarke, "Hindutva, Religious and Ethnocultural Minorities and Indian-Christian Theology", p. 200.

124 John Zavos, *The Emergence of Hindu Nationalism in India*, pp. 14ff.

125 Savarkar meticulously uses his wit to construe the geographical boundaries of India with the claim that these boundaries were drawn by the ancient seers and not by the British. Nevertheless, the boundaries he alludes to closely correspond with the boundaries drawn by the British. See Savarkar, *Hindutva*, pp. 27-34.

126 Madhu Kishwar, *Religion at the Service of Nationalism and Other* Essays, p. 252.
127 Peter Van der Veer, *Gods on Earth: Religious Experience and Identity in Ayodhya* (Delhi: Oxford University Press, 1997), p. 268.
128 For this kind of treatment of Hinduism, See *The Complete Works of swami Vivekananda* (Calcutta: Advaita Ashrama, 10th Edition, 1963); Sarvapalli Radhakrishnan, *The Heart of Hindusthan* (Madras: G. A. Natesan & Co., 2nd Edition, 1932) & *Our Heritage* (Delhi: Hind Pocket Books, 1973).
129 See V. D. Savarkar, *Hindutva*, p. 29.
130 Ibid., p. 3.
131 Ibid., p. i.
132 Ibid., p. ii.
133 Ibid., pp. ii -iii.
134 Ibid., pp. xi-xii.
135 Ibid., p. 4.
136 Ibid., p. 10.
137 Jawaharlal Nehru, *The Discovery of India*, pp. 69-72.
138 V. D. Savarkar, *Six Glorious Epochs of Indian History*, p. 6. [Emphasis added]
139 V. D. Savarkar, *Hindutva*, pp. 11-12.
140 Satish Deshpande, *Contemporary India*, p. 74.
141 Edward Said, *Culture and Imperialism* (New York: Alfred Knopf, 1993), p. 78.
142 V. D. Savarkar, *Hindutva*, p. 82.
143 Ibid., p. 82.
144 Ibid., p. 84.
145 Ibid., p. 92.
146 Ibid., p. 113.
147 Peter van der Veer, R*eligious Nationalisms: Hindus and Muslims in India* (Delhi: Oxford university Press, 1996), p. 126.
148 This is demonstrated by the statements of the BJP leaders that if the BJP comes to power with absolute majority, it would build the *Ram Mandir* in Ayodhya by appropriate constitutional amendments. See the News item "BJP vows to build temple", *The New Indian Express* (08 February 2009), p. 1 & the editorial, "It's the temple plank, again", *The New Indian Express* (09 February 2009), p. 10.
149 Jawaharlal Nehru, *The Discovery of India*, pp. 387ff.
150 Satish Deshpande, *Contemporary India*, p. 83.
151 M. S. Golwalker, *We, or Our Nationhood Defined*, p. 62.

152 See the pages of Savarkar's *Six Glorious Epochs of Indian History*, which is nothing but a narrative of the victorious battles the Hindu Kings of India fought against the alien invaders. In this volume, Savarkar repeatedly laments and regrets that the Hindu kings failed to inflict the same kind of insult on the Muslim population, especially women, after their victories as the Muslims kings had done to the Hindu women when they invaded Hindu kingdoms. (See especially pp. 255-258 & 444-448)
153 Rabindranath Tagore, *A Vision for India's History* (Calcutta: Vishvabharathi, 1951).
154 L. K. Advani, *My Country, My Life* (Delhi: Rupa & Co., 2008).
155 *India Today* (March 24, 2008), pp. 32-33.
156 *Frontline* (March 10, 2006), pp. 39-41.
157 Anto Akkara, *Kandhamal: A Blot on Indian Secularism* (Delhi: Media House, 2009), p. 15.
158 Anto Akkara, *Kandhamal: A Blot on Indian Secularism*, p. 25.
159 CNN-IBN News Analysis, 31 August 2008.
160 Seema Mustafa, "Partners in Criminality" *The New Indian Express* (Tuesday, Sept 23, 2008), p. 10.
161 For a brief discussion, see Pralay Kanungo, "Hindutva's Fury against Christians in Orissa" *EPW* (September13, 2008), pp. 16-19.
162 Anto Akkara, *Kandhamal: A Blot on Indian Secularism*, p. 115.
163 Amartya Sen, *The argumentative Indian*, p. 46.
164 Eric Lott, *Religious Faith, Human Identity*, p. 302. See also Sudhir Kakar, *The Colours of Violence* (Delhi: Penguin Books, 1995.)
165 Amartya Sen, *The Argumentative Indian*, p. 48.
166 V. D. Savarkar, *Six Glorious Epochs*, p. 245 & 444. To understand his extreme impulse for aggression, read the anecdote he uses in pp. 125-126.
167 Amartya Sen, *The Argumentative Indian*, pp. 3-33.
168 To understand the specific trajectory of the meaning of the term 'communalism' when it is used in the Indian context, see Gyanendra Pandey, *The Construction of Communalism in Colonial North India* (Delhi: Oxford University Press, 1992), p. 6.
169 Marzia Casolari, "Hindutva's Foreign Tie-up in the 1930s: Archival Evidence" E*conomic and Political Weekly* (22 January 2000), p. 227.
170 V. D. Savarkar, *Hindutva*, p. 29.
171 V. D. Savarkar, *Six Glorious Epochs*, p. 444.
172 Brutalization and social ostracism are not uncommon to Christians, especially in areas where they are very few in number. Christians are

more vulnerable if they happen to be from the subaltern communities. See the news report: "Dalit Christians living in fear after attack" *The Hindu*, City edition, Bangalore (Sunday, January 29, 2012), p. 1.

173 As Anita Saluja reports, "The Ram Mandir agitation in 1989 made the then BJP president L. K. Advani a hero. He succeeded in turning around the fortunes of the party. The BJP which had just two Lok Sabha MPs in 1984 increased its tally to 86 in the 1989 elections and to 119 in 1991and was the single-largest party in 1996, 1998 and 1999. In fact the BJP owes its ascendance to the Hindutva agenda, with Advani taking the lead in fanning communal emotions. *The New Indian Express* (24 Nov. 2008), p. 11.

174 See Peter van der Veer, *Religious Nationalism*: *Hindus and Muslims in India*.

175 For a fair understanding of this view, see Christophe Jaffrelot, ed., *The Sangh Parivar: A Reader* (Delhi: Oxford University Press, 2005); Jaffrelot, "The Sangh Parivar Between Sanskritization and Social Engineering" in Thomas Blom Hansen and Christphe Jaffrelot, ed., *The BJP and the Compulsions of Politics in India* (Delhi: Oxford University Press, 2004), pp. 22-71. Take, for instance, the growth of the RSS. It has been a well-established fact that the RSS grew to its present stature through its concerted efforts in organizing the Hindu society at various levels. The base units, branches and subsidiaries of the RSS is generally known as its network that includes the *shakhas* (branches), the *pracharaks* (propagators), the *Rashtra Sevika Samiti* (women's propaganda wing), the *Akil Bharatiya Pratinidhi Sabha* (all India Representative Forum), the *Akil Bharatiya Vidhyarti Parishad* (the students' wing of the RSS) and so on and so forth. For an informative reading on the phenomenal growth of the RSS since 1925 till the recent times, see "Introduction" in Christophe Jaffrelot, ed., *The Sangh Parivar: A Reader*. The RSS, in a sense, is carrying out the will of its founder, Keshav Baliram Hedgewar, in all sincerity and with devotion. In his last speech in 1940, he charged the RSS cadres with the following words: "Remember, we have to organize the entire Hindu society from Kanyakumary to Himalayas." See B. V. Deshpande and S. R. Ramaswamy, *Dr. Hedgewar, the Epoch Maker* (Bangalore: Sahitya Sindhu, 1981), p. 188.

176 See Thomas Blom Hansen, *The Saffron Wave: Democracy and Hindu Nationalism in Modern India*.

177 Jawaharlal Nehru, *The Discovery of India*, p. 395.

178 Ibid., p. 395.

179 For a detailed analysis see Pratap Bhanu Mehta, "The Rise of Judicial Sovereignty", *Journal of* Democracy, Vol. 18, No.2 (2007), pp. 70-83; and Katherine Frank, *Indira: The Life of Indira Nehru Gandhi* (Houghton: Mifflin Company, 2002).

180 J. Kuruvachira, *Roots of Hindutva: A Critical Study of Hindu Fundamentalism and Nationalism* (Delhi: Media House, 2005), p. 64.

181 For the detailed report, see *Frontline* (10 March 2006), pp. 37-38.

182 L. K. Advani, for instance, was quite confident that the BJP would return to power after 2009 general elections. See *India Today* (March 24, 2008), pp. 32f. But the Indian electorate proved him wrong.

183 Arun Shourie, *Harvesting Our Souls*, p. 49. See also the entire Ch. 5: "The Singular Objective *vs.* the law of the land", pp. 42-53; and another volume of Shourie, *Missionaries in India: Continuities, Changes, Dilemmas*, especially Ch. 12: "But Have We No Right?" pp. 231-242.

184 *Religious Conversions*, Answer to Question No. 2, p. 7.

185 Pratap Bhanu Mehta, "Introduction to the Omnibus", p. xiii.

186 Partha Chatterjee, *A Possible India*, p. 230.

187 Rajni Kothari, *Communalism in Indian Politics* (Delhi: Rainbow Publishers, 1998), p. 9.

188 The 2002 Gujrat riot victims did not get justice even after ten years. There are reports in the media that the Chief Minister of the state asked the police force to allow Hindus to vent their anger. See the statement of the then Deputy Commissioner Sanjiv Bhatt (now under suspension): Manas Dasgupta, "Your closure report a bid to shield Modi, Bhatt tells Raghavan" in *The Hindu* (Thursday May 17, 2012), p. 16. With regard Modi's *sadhbhāvanā* mission (24 February 2012) around the 10th anniversary of the 2002 Gujarath communal riots, we need to ask: did Modi's *sadhbhāvanā* smack of a human touch? For a brief analysis see Rajdeep Sardesai, "Modi's 'Sadhbhavana and the horror of 2002" Rajdeep Sardesai's Blog (Friday, February 24, 2012 at 00:31)

189 Sources: Media Debates on the issue on NDTV & Times Now 10-11, April 2012

190 In this regard, the Hindutva brigades adopt a double standard. Four months after the series of attacks on the Churches in the BJP ruled Karnataka, the then Chief Minister (B. S. Yeddyurappa) asked the Christians to "forget the past incidents and move on", for according to him, "such incidents were the work of a few fringe elements". *The New Indian Express* (Monday, Feb.2, 2009), p. 3.

191 For a fair discussion on this issue see Sathianathan Clarke, "Viewing the Bible through the Eyes and Ears of Subalterns in India" *Biblical Interpretation* Vol. 10, No.3 (2002), pp. 245-266.

192 Ram Punyani, *Fascism of Sangh Parivar* (Delhi: Media House, 2000), Ch. 5, pp. 81-107.

193 Francesco Alberoni, *Movement and Institution* (New York: Columbia University Press, 1984), pp. 152ff.

194 Source: *Times Now* (TV), 16 May 2006.

Chapter Three

EMERGENT IMAGE OF THE CHURCH

Perspective

> Only the ignorant can claim that all religions are the same. On the contrary, it is extremely important for members of every religion and especially every prophetic religion, whether Christianity, Judaism or Islam, to ask, 'What is the difference between my religion and other religions? What is the special, the typical, the essential character, indeed the "essence" of this or that religion?' I now want to raise this question for Christianity...in an ecumenical spirit, without polemic against other religions.[1]

Hindu nationalism, as we have seen, is built on the untenable but insidious assumption that religious/cultural homogeneity constitutes the nation and what is even more untenable is Hindutva's claim that India is the land of Hindus.[2] Hence, the realization of the multi-civilizational composition of India, its pluralistic texture, its diverse religious, cultural and ethnic identities and its secular fabric angers Hindutva because these elemental factors truly hamper its endeavours to ascribe a corporatist (Hindu) identity to all Indians. This anger turns into hatred, hostility, enmity, and violence against those particularities that resist Hindutva's objective of construing the nation religiously. Undeniably, the Church is one of those vital particularities that is consistent and defiant in resisting Hindutva's objectives of erasing differences in order to reconstruct India as a monolithic Hindu nation. Moreover, the Church is resolute in its commitment to embrace various communities and, more importantly, to be in solidarity with the communities excluded from the Vedic religion and kept under dehumanized conditions for ages by the caste hierarchy. Hindutva's identification of the Church as the definite 'other' and/or 'enemy' to be ostracized, and its malicious insinuation that the Church cannot find a rightful place in India must be understood in this wider context.

This trend raises a pertinent issue concerning the contemporary human experience of negotiating multiple worlds, worldviews and boundaries, and what it means for the Church in India today. Given the kind of Hindu nationalist engagement with the pluralistic texture of Indian reality, it is pretty clear that Hindu nationalism, scaffolded by Hindutva ideology, is a clearly worked out programme of lumping people belonging to different backgrounds into one corporatist, homogenized, ascribed mould. The question of negotiating difference is not so facile and it would be pretentious if we try to solve this issue with our usual categories such as brother/sisterhood, love, compassion, and so forth, because the way contemporary Hindu nationalism negotiates difference is characterized by certain pernicious modes of discourse that makes the current social terrain of India a highly complicated one. It is a mode of discourse that regards difference as something to be erased and the differently 'other' as someone to be ostracized or annihilated.[3]

In his analysis of contemporary human experiences of negotiating differences, Christopher Duraisingh identifies four important ways in which 'otherness' is dealt with. *First,* there is a pervasive tendency towards *centering* and *essentializing* one's own construal of one's self, nation, values, and norms in a way that they are mystified as universal and true. *Second,* there is a strong inclination to the *bifurcation of reality* in oppositional terms that provides the necessary impetus to marginalize the 'other'. *Third,* there is a strong tendency to construct *rigid boundaries or borders* in order to protect the 'self' from the enemies. *Fourth,* the dominant normally *silences* and even *eliminates* the voice of the 'other'.[4] Hindutva's construal of India unmistakably represents these traits. The most menacing aspect of Hindutva ideology is its construction of the 'other' that fosters an insider-outsider syndrome. When Hindutva realizes that the 'other' does not conform to its construal of the nation after Vedic religion, it demonizes the 'other' and works relentlessly to exorcize or annihilate the 'other'. With its religiously charged political discourse, it also erects borders, both geographical and ideological, in order to project India as a unified, monolithic and homogenized entity, belonging only to the Hindus. In this process, it claims that the 'other' cannot aspire to have a rightful place in this country, not even citizenry right – a dangerously poisonous stance indeed.[5]

Incidentally, this trend coincides with the emergent global phenomenon of alarming disintegration of human relationships. The predominant trend is to pitch humans and human communities against each other, which creates an ambience of endemic hatred, hostility, enmity and fragmentation in the human social domain. It is an atmosphere conducive enough for the vested interests to hatch enmity and unleash gruesome violence against fellow humans.[6] In this milieu, the Church has to demonstrate that its life is founded on a new quality of relationship, which begins with the biblical teaching that we are united in Christ and therefore in fellowship with each other. It is a communion that proclaims that our differences of sex, race, culture, nation, ethnicity, and social positions are transcended by our unity in Christ. Therefore, the old lines of conflict are becoming redundant and a new quality of *mutually indwelling* relationship is made possible by God in Jesus Christ by *accepting the unacceptable*. The Church of Christ exists to mediate this relationship in the midst of the disintegration of human relationships. The relationship that we talk about is posited on the fertile theological principle of *unity of the opposites* or *distinction and integration*, which operates from the vantage point of making clear distinctions, i.e., fully recognizing the genuine differences that are characteristic of variegated people groups and communities, and embracing them to be in communion with all the differences. Without doubt, this proffers a new consciousness in the context of Hindutva's project of integration through symbolic assimilation, for the Church of Christ represents this mode of existence that always embraces the 'other' with all that differentiates him/her.

Anyone acquainted with the research on 'Church history' would quickly recognize the metamorphoses that occurred in the field of Church history *vis-à-vis* 'history of Christianity' and 'history of world Christian movement'.[7] For a theologian, the issue is far more complex than what meets the eye due to the fragmented expression of the Church in numerous forms and yet claiming to have faith in the same Lord. A few examples of the various approaches to ecclesiology employed by theologians would help us to understand the situation better. Hans Küng has a threefold approach to ecclesa: (i) the ideal picture, (ii) the hostile picture, and (iii) the real picture.[8] For Alister McGrath, Christianity has three core components: a set of beliefs, a set of values, and a way of life.[9] Avery Dulles identifies six prominent models of the Church: as an institution, communion, sacrament, herald, servant, and community of disciples.[10] For an ecumenical theologian, the visible unity of the Church is a matter of urgent concern, especially in multi-faith contexts.[11] The Church is also understood as 'people's movement'.[12]

While recognizing the legitimacy and credibility of all these approaches to ecclesiology, we also need to acknowledge the limitations of these approaches because, even though they are helpful to understand the nature and function of ecclesia, it cannot be imprisoned within any one of these approaches. Rather, we need to approach ecclesia from different perspectives and, for the purpose of the present study, I would like to understand the origin, life, mission and theology of the Church from a *relational* perspective, i.e., Church as a paradigm of a new *perichoretic* relationship, which is realized in and through the communion of the people of God, held together by the principle of the *unity of the opposites* or *distinction and integration*. To accomplish such a task, we would investigate the emergence of the Church in this chapter, identifying (a) the historical-theological foundations of the Church, (b) the central theological suppositions that hold ecclesia together as a universal entity with particular expressions, (c) the trajectories that occurred in its life and mission with its expansion up to the Protestant Reformation.

Historical-Theological Foundations of the Church

In its journey over the past two millennia, Christianity has crossed boundaries of culture, language and identity, affecting, and being affected by these factors. As some historians opine, "The Christian movement is one that has continuously diversified itself through its expansions, all the while claiming to remain the same".[13] It implies that ecclesiology represents certain conscious variations in accordance with the historical forms the Church had taken, which prompts us to track the historical/ theological roots of the Church.

Origin of the Church

Did the idea of the Church originate from Jesus? This question is crucial for the self-understanding of the Church today. Until 1960s, many scholars worked with the simple proposition that either Jesus had founded the Church or he had intended a Church be established after his resurrection.[14] But this view came to be challenged in the subsequent times.[15] In order to establish the authenticity of the Church, it is customary to invoke Matthew 16:18: "And I tell you, you are Peter, and on this rock I will build my church, and the gates of Hades will not prevail against it." However, there is hardly any evidence in the New Testament to demonstrate what Jesus really meant or intended by this declaration. There is also considerable skepticism among scholars as to whether this is an authentic saying of Jesus. Alfred Loisy argues:

> If Christ had Himself drawn up a statement of His doctrine, and summary of His prophecy, a detailed treatise on His work, His Mission, His hopes, the historian would submit it to a most attentive examination, and would determine the essence of the gospel, according to irrefutable testimony. But no such treatise has ever existed, and nothing can take its place. In the Gospels there remains but an echo, necessarily weakened and a little confused, of the words of Jesus, the general impression He produced upon hearers well disposed towards Him, with some of the more striking of His sentences, as they were understood and interpreted; and finally there remains the movement which He initiated.[16]

Admittedly, it is difficult to deal with this central issue without some amount of prejudice with regard to the nature of the Church order and organization, not to privilege the present structure and style of function of the Church, but to provide an adequate theological basis for the identity of the Christian community and also to aid ecclesia in its life and mission in India. For, it is impossible to demonstrate satisfactorily the validity of the Church if it did not originate from Jesus himself because it would raise serious objections against the credibility of the Church. Hence, it would be fair to maintain that, even though the direct evidences to the ecclesia sayings from the mouth of Jesus are sparse, it does not totally negate the authenticity of ecclesia, because from the available evidences, it is possible to locate the origin of the Church in the life and teachings of Jesus himself.[17]

Keeping such uncertainties and skepticisms aside, we approach the life of the Church from a relational perspective, i.e., the Church as a paradigm of a new quality of relationship. It is no exaggeration to say that more than ever before, the world is passionately crying for an authentic model of relationship that can hold humans together. Therefore, as a starting point, we like to begin this inquiry with the proposition that the Church originated with the life and ministry of Jesus who, according to the New Testament tradition, is the Christ, the Son of the living God (Mt 1:16, 16:16; John 11:27, 20:31), sent into the world by God in order to redeem the fallen humanity from sin and restore them to fullness of life (Gal 4:4-5) – a life in *intimate(perichoretic) communion* with God and fellow humans. Our contention (and conviction) is that this relationship, with its variants, must assume top priority in our ecclesiological reflections, more specifically in the Hindu nationalist context.

In the eyes of the skeptics and critics, the visible manifestations of the Church might appear to be a set of distortions,[18] and, hence, cannot claim any credibility. But the Church is an important force that had made enormous contributions for the shaping of the world history.[19] Undeniably, Christianity is a vital agent that continues to play a major role in shaping the lives, hopes and aspirations of a major segment of human populace the world over. Within the Indian context, for instance, the Church continues to make its vital contributions in a number of areas in the public domain, which include: (a) stimulating awareness among the most neglected classes of the Indian society of their essential humanhood; (b) bearing the torch of education to the remotest parts of India, enabling a significant number of subalterns to obtain high social positions through education; (c) taking health care to the most neglected sections of our society (which was otherwise out of their reach) through numerous medical missions;[20] (d) stimulating religious and social reforms in the Hindu society; (e) giving female education and thereby acting as a stimulus to the new awakening among women; and (f) opening of community centers and industrial schools that had enabled people from marginalized communities to find employment. These are the veritable contributions of the Church towards nation building.[21]

When Jesus began his ministry, his first task was to announce the inauguration of God's rule (Mark 1:15); and when he called a small band of disciples, he sent them out to proclaim the dawn of the new age or the rule of God (Mt. 10:7) to all nations (Mt 28:19-20). Moving on to the *Book of Acts*, we come across the early communion of the disciples engaging itself in acts of worship, proclaiming the Gospel of the risen Jesus and acts of charity (Acts 2:42-47; 6:1-6). These early believers were Jews who were worshippers in the synagogues and individual homes. The point of departure at this stage was their proclamation of the risen Jesus as the Christ over against the continued expectation of the Jews for the promised Messiah.[22] It clearly represents a break with the Jewish religion because of the new focus on the life and ministry of Jesus. The idea of ecclesia was not a theme for intense theological/spiritual reflection among the early believers up to this point.

A more detailed exposition of the theme 'ecclesia' emerged from the apostle Paul, whose primary concern was to take the Gospel of Jesus Christ beyond the strictly Jewish enclaves to the wider world. As a consequence, people of other faith persuasions, popularly known as the 'Gentiles', became believers. Perhaps, this is the point of the emergence of the body metaphor as a brilliant expression of ecclesia – a metaphor that explains the reality of the Church as the true communion of believers intimately held together in Christ as different organs to an organism in order to demonstrate the unity of the believers and for the proclamation of the Gospel of God's saving act in Christ (Rom. 12:4; 1 Cor. 6:15; 12:12, 27; Eph. 1:23; 5:30). Historically, Paul's Gentile mission and the hostile political situation in the Roman Empire (which resulted in the persecution of Christians and their eventual dispersion) saw the expansion of Christianity far and wide. The driving force behind the spread of the Gospel of Jesus Christ was the fundamental self-understanding of the early believers that God has decisively acted in Jesus Christ for the *salvation* of the world. A brief note on the idea of salvation is in place here, as it would through more light on the emergence of the missionary nature of the Church.

The idea of salvation is central to all theistic religions. Even though it means different things to different religions, the issue of ethics in the economy of human salvation is a common problem in all religions. As Christianity came to interact with various cultures and religious traditions, the issue of ethics came to the fore with greater emphasis on human moral/ethical accomplishments in the economy of salvation,[23] which has strong Stoican overtones. According to Stoicism, there exists a fundamental harmony among all things – a supreme law that governs everything. In this schema, the goal of human existence is to reach the point of conformity to this truth. Now to achieve this, a human person is bestowed with reason or will at his/her disposal. By using this faculty a human person must protect him/herself, so that he/she might not drift away from the universal law that governs the whole.[24] Incidentally, this school of thought came to meet head on with Christianity in the early 5th century in the form of Pelagius, a British monk and a contemporary of Augustine.[25] In summary, Pelagius' thought does not identify nature with good, but it does so with freedom – a freedom that stands in between two precise and complete human possibilities: *good* and *evil* and humans are capable of both. If human beings do good or evil, they do it voluntarily. They are always free to choose one of the two alternatives, which is entirely within their limit or power. Augustine in the 5th century and Luther in the 16th century wrestled with this issue and propounded *healing grace* and *justifying grace* respectively in their understanding of the economy of salvation.

Soteriological motif has been deeply entrenched in the theology of the Church and, more than anything else, it is this motif that has become the central thrust of the Church's mission ever since its inception in world history. The Christian conception of salvation embodies a curious synthesis of two apparently antagonistic categories: God and the world (of humans and nature). Thus, the historical and theological roots of the Church can be traced back to God's decisive relationship with humanity that has found its expression first in the Hebrew Scriptures and then in the Christ event as testified by the New Testament.

Biblical Images of the Church[26]

Understanding ecclesia from a relational perspective requires: (a) a deeper understanding of the embodiment of this relationship in two phases, namely, the life of the Jewish people and the life of the Christians as represented in the Old and New Testaments; (b) a critical look at the way this relationship came to be represented by the Church in its more '*successful*' and institutionalized existence; and (c) the reconstruction of the Church's representation of this relationship in a way that would enable the Church to make sense in the contemporary context in which it makes its particular expression. In this chapter we would undertake the first two tasks and reserve the third one to be done towards the end of this study.

Divine-Human Relationship in the Old Testament

The social fabric of the Jewish people was built on a set of relationships whose concrete expression is found in the covenant relationship between God and the Israelites and the relationship that bonded them together as a people of God as illustrated by the Decalogue, which was given as a mark of the covenant between God and the Jewish people. It is this relationship that runs right across the Bible like an unbroken chain, connecting both the Testaments. Jesus reiterated this relationship through his summation of the Decalogue in terms of 'love for God' and 'love for the neighbors' (Mt. 22:37-40). Christianity had promptly appropriated this relationship, which is demonstrated by at least two aspects of its visible expression: (a) the relationship that existed among the early Christians, which was not simply about sharing of ideas or feelings but real sharing of life through specific practices as expressed in and through the *koinonia*; and (b) it was an intimacy that involved tangible material expressions of relationship, in that they had volunteered to share their material possessions according to the needs of the members of the communion. As L. T. Johnson observes, the early Christians formed among themselves a network of associations involving shared beliefs, commitments and practices that were critical for their survival as a communion of the faithful in a hostile environment and for the proclamation of the new life, which God had inaugurated in Jesus Christ. Such networks also enabled them to be recognized as *a people* endowed with the ideal of a communion of persons that had the inner spirit of relationship.[27]

The Israelites constantly recalled, cherished and treasured this intimacy, especially in their self-understanding as "the people of God" (Jer. 31:1, 31-34).[28] A brief note on the term 'Judaism' is in place here. In fact, Judaism is not a prominent name for the religion of the Jewish people. Scholars show considerable reluctance to use 'Judaism' to refer to the Jewish religion. Instead, they prefer to use the expression 'the faith of Israel'.[29] Judaism as a proper name for the religion of the Israelites emerged within the two centuries prior to the arrival of Christianity. It was a time of intense inculturation between Greek civilization and the ancient oriental cultures of Asia Minor, Syria, and Egypt. This is known as the process of Hellenization. Part of the Hellenization project was to establish cities modeled in Greek patterns by transforming the existing cities and introducing new patterns of education in conformity with the Greek spirit.[30] This elicited mixed reactions: while the urban elites espoused this change, the pious groups strongly resisted it, as is evident from the books of Maccabees. Two crucial factors might have led the pious groups to resist the Hellenisation process: (i) the new trend had posed a serious threat to their monotheistic belief system, which is foundational to Judaism; and (ii) it attempted to rock the basic social unit of the Jewish people, i.e., their family patterns.[31]

For the Israelites, the Exodus event represented the concrete expression of the divine initiative to restore the relationship between God and humanity. It was an event in which God chose a people from the underside of history – a bunch of slaves – to be the subjects of God's redemptive purpose and these gullible Hebrew slaves were chosen not simply to accord them political freedom; rather to take them further to the eschatological future when the whole world would taste the reign of God. It has provided a new consciousness and a new paradigm for the rest of the history of Israel and beyond. This new consciousness of God's preferential option for the victimized has been carried through with careful precision in the Biblical accounts of the life of Israel and it has been extended to the New Testament. For instance, when Jesus announced that 'the Son of Man came to seek out and save the lost' (Luke 19:10), it signified God's universal salvific will with a special focus on the 'lost'. This special privilege within the realm of God's relationship provided sufficient theological substance to the Church to come to a specific self-understanding of itself as an inclusive communion in Christ Jesus – an intimate communion that embraces even the differently 'others'.

From Exclusion to Embrace

When the Church came into being, it represented the embodiment of the divine relationship that had found its expression in the intimacy that existed in the early communion of believers, an intimacy that could take them beyond their self-interests in order to be a sharing, caring and serving communion (Acts 2). Two clear marks of the nascent Church were: the proclamation of the message of God's salvific acts in Jesus, and building up of their own communion because the early believers understood themselves as a *chosen people of God* for a specific vocation (1 Peter 2:9-10). Without doubt, this self-understanding had emanated from their Jewish roots,[32] even though the specific term 'Church' (*ekklesia*) had its origin elsewhere. The term *ekklesia* originated in classical Greek literature, where it had the secular meaning of the 'assembly of citizens' of a Greek city-state for administrative and judicial purposes.[33] In the Hebrew Bible, this sort of the 'gathering of people' had assumed certain sacred or theological meaning as demonstrated by terms such as *edhah* and *qahal*, especially when they are combined with phrases like "of Israel" and "of Yahweh", which indicate that this sort of 'congregating' was the religious/cultic assembly of Israel. The root meaning of *edhah* is 'to appoint' and that of *qahal* is 'to call'. They suggest that Israel is a people appointed or called by God for a specific purpose. Thus, it can be affirmed that ecclesia[34] in Christian history has drawn a considerable portion of its theological substance from these sources. The theological significance of these terms is that they represent Israel as a chosen people, brought into being and set apart by divine initiative to participate in the plan of salvation.[35]

The distinctive faith identity of Israel originated from God's covenant with the patriarch, Abraham. According to the Old Testament, Abraham trusted God and God promised to make him a great nation whose descendents would be as multitude as the stars of the sky (Gen 12:1-2, 15:5) – a covenant that would embrace a multitude of nations.[36] It is important to note that Abraham was a key figure in three living religious traditions: Judaism, Christianity, and Islam. He was called "the ancestor (or father) of a multitude of nations" (Gen 17:5) and a "friend of God" (2 Chr. 20:7). Some of the cultic/cultural practices that emerged with him had lasting influence in many Semitic religious traditions. Certain important aspects of the story of Abraham are: it originated in Ur followed by his sojourn to the land of Canaan on divine instructions (Gen 12:1-8); Abraham's instruction to Sarah not to reveal her identity as his wife and to pretend to be his sister on the face of the impending threat to his life (Gen 12: 10ff); the ethnological story of Lot that demonstrates the character and origin of the Moabites and the Edomites (Gen 13:2-18); the birth of his son Ishmael through Sarah's maid servant Hagar (Gen 16); the emergence of the practice of circumcision (Gen 17:27); and the birth of Isaac (Gen 21) followed closely by offering a ram as a substitution for the sacrifice of Isaac (Gen 22).

Now, there are scholars who subscribe to the view that Abraham was a historical figure; and there are others who argue that he was an eponymous figure – a name taken to identify a people. Early Christian writings, however, present Abraham as the Patriarch who is the pioneer of their faith in God (Acts 7:2-50; Rom 4:1-25; Gal 3:1-29; Heb 7:1-10). As the story further unfolds, his descendents were eventually made into forced slavery in Egypt, and it is their deliverance from Egypt under the leadership of Moses that has become the foundation and the defining event of Israel's salvation history. It has further been remembered as a proto-type of the Christian salvation story by the followers of Jesus.

This is what constitutes the continuity and discontinuity between the Old Testament 'People of God' and the New Testament 'Church'. Here, the continuity stems from the fundamental Christian consciousness of being the descendents of Abraham and the discontinuity is brought about by the Christian belief of Jesus as the expected Messiah. This consciousness enabled the Christians to coin new terms to describe the Church, involving Christ and his centrality in the life of the new communion. It has to be borne in mind that the earliest interpreter of Jesus was Paul and his was a selective interest. For in his interpretation of Jesus, he paid only petite attention to Jesus' teachings and deeds on earth and focused mainly on the risen Christ and his ascension into heaven, which confirmed Jesus' divine status and proved that he was part of God's plan of salvation for the entire world. Thus, according to Paul, the purpose of the creation of the first Adam has found its fulfillment in the second Adam, Jesus Christ (1 Cor. 15:22, 45-47). Obviously, Paul had drawn his theological materials greatly from the Jewish tradition and interpreted the resurrection as God's intervention in history to bring everything to a glorious consummation.

The Church, in its earliest form, had entertained an exclusivist mode of faith identity, i.e., it originated with a band of Jewish disciples of Jesus and there had been strong inclinations to preserve its exclusive Jewish identity (Acts 10). At this stage, Church was an exclusively Jewish *community* of believers, bearing witness to the resurrected Christ as the Messiah.[37] The term '*Messiah*' indicates a person anointed and sent by God for a specific task, which has both political and religious connotations. Politically, it refers to the kings who would continue the Davidic dynasty (Ps 18:50, 89:20) and religiously, 'anointed one' refers to an Aaronic priest (cf. Lev 4:3-5). Since there was a strong belief among the Israelites that the Davidic king was the chosen ruler (2 Sam 7:8-16), 'Messiah' is often associated with the prophetic expectation that God would raise an ideal king to occupy the throne of Israel in the line of David. The irony is that, in time, David's weakness was forgotten and his greatness was extolled, just as tradition has idealized such figures of Indian history as Gandhi, Nehru, and Ambedkar.

David was considered to be the ideal combination of power and goodness and remembered as "Yahweh's servant", the God-fearing king who "executed justice and righteousness unto all his people" (II Sam 8:15) and his dynasty would be established forever. The bitter political experiences of Israel after the death of David gave rise to the hope that a messiah would come from David's lineage, reunite the tribes of Israel, and restore Jerusalem to a position of prestige among the nations (Is 9 &11). Scholars show great reluctance to accept the idea that these messianic ideas point to an eschatological king. Isaiah's reference to the 'anointed' (45:1), for instance, refers to Cyrus as God's agent. The Dead Sea Scrolls also contain texts referring to the coming of two figures – a priestly 'anointed' of Aaron and a kingly 'anointed' of Israel.[38]

The early believers were deeply inclined to hold on to the view that Jesus was the expected messiah,[39] closely following the Jewish belief (Acts 1: 6), which might have firmly constructed an exclusive Jewish identity to the Church and locked it within the confines of a closed *community*. But the Church showed remarkable ability to transcend this exclusively particularized understanding in order to assume a more inclusive vision, i.e., a shift from an attitude of *exclusion* to *embrace*. It was a trajectory that demonstrated Church's incredible ability to embrace differences within a relatively short span of time. In all probability, this might have been the point of the emergence of *communion* as an important mode of ecclesiological discourse, because previously the Church had remained as a closed *community* of the Jewish believers who were keen to preserve their Jewish identity intact. But now the closed community of believers could transcend this particularized identity to become a truly open *communion*, embracing a variety of identities and transform itself into a truly universal phenomenon. Paul was the key player of this mode of discourse, for, in his view, the life of a Christian is contingent on the renunciation of the ways of the world to be embraced into the body of Christ. It suggests a 'new life' lived for God in Christ and for one another in love (Rom 12:1-2; 2 Cor. 5:17; Eph. 4: 17-32; 5:1).

With this message, Paul advocated a new form of religion, bringing Jewish and Hellenistic sources together, a religion that transcended the existing forms of local cults and placed its emphasis on the universal salvific will of God in Christ[40] that could embrace all people, both Jews and Gentiles, into its territory. It was a universal vision in which humanity as a whole would exist in harmony as children of the one God. An important posture of ecclesia in this vision is its ability to transcend the differences that are normally regarded to be divisive: "There is no longer Jew or Greek, there is no longer slave or free, there is no longer male and female" (Gal. 3:28). In this mode of ecclesiological discourse, even though the faith of the followers of Jesus underwent a definite change, they were never forced to abandon their cultural roots and accept another culture. The fiercely contested issue of circumcision is a clear case for our consideration here. When there was an insistence on circumcision, i.e., accepting the Jewish culture as a definite marker to be accepted within the Christian household, the Church clearly negated it by saying, "Circumcision is nothing, and uncircumcision is nothing; but obeying the commandment of God is everything" (1 Cor. 7:19); "For in Christ Jesus neither circumcision or uncircumcision counts for anything; the only thing that counts is faith working through love" (Gal 5: 6; 6:15). Therefore, in its earliest expression, the Church was not insisting on lumping people of different cultures into one uniform mould; rather it embraced differences without discriminating the believers on the basis of their cultural practices. This disproves the criticism that conversion to Christianity involved *cultural alienation*.[41] Nonetheless, there was a definite call for the Christians to be different as the mark of being transformed by their faith in Christ (Rom. 12:2) – a transition from the old to a new life. Perhaps this might have been a strong factor that motivated people cutting across cultures to embrace Christian faith, making it a universal phenomenon.

Universality of the Church is one of the four marks of the Church (unity, purity, catholicity and apostolicity) as enunciated in the Nicene Creed. It, however, does not make the Church a monolithic and homogenous superstructure. Nor does it make the Church a grand canopy that incorporates and assimilates the multiple expressions of peoples' faith in Christ across borders and frontiers into a single institution. Rather, the universalism of the Church is contingent on its inter-connectedness across cultures in its faith in the one Lord that enables it to be at the service of those in need, both from within and without. The earliest expression of this 'service-based' inter-connection of the Church is found in the book of Acts (11:27-30) – the communion of the *Gentile* believers in Antioch taking the initiative to send relief to the communion of *Jewish* believers in Judea. Further, when the issue of circumcision threatened to rock the Church, the Church could quickly get together, debate the matter at length and sort out the issue with a simple, but noteworthy formula: "For it has seemed good to the Holy Spirit and to us to impose on you no further burden" (Acts 15:28). It has further been reported that the early believers derived great joy in embracing the gentiles into their communion (Acts 15:3). Clearly, it was a definite mark of the Church's nature of embracing differences, multiplicities, and pluralities – a feature that had provided space for the 'other' to remain in his/her own cultural practices even though he/she had been embraced into the body of Christ. Within this body differences and pluralities are not assimilated or erased but embraced and celebrated as a reflection of the divine reality, making the Church a unique institution in human history. Thus, the Church could persist as a strong and effective focus of a variety of people's faith across the globe.[42] The transcendence of the Church from exclusion to embrace also marks another important nature of the Church, i.e., its missionary character.

Missionary Nature of Ecclesia

Christianity emerged in a religiously plural situation and it had to negotiate a largely hostile world. To begin with, Christians were not accepted as equal citizens in the society. Rather, they were viewed with prejudice, hatred, hostility, (Acts 17:5-9, 1Thess 2:14-16, 1Pet 1:6; Heb 10:32-34, Rev 2:10) and eventually subjected to organized violence. They became targets of persecution for two reasons: *first*, their faith affirmation and proclamation of Jesus as the promised messiah earned them the wrath of the Jewish religious authorities; and *second*, their withdrawal from a number of day-to-day practices connected with the worship of other deities and, more particularly, the emperor worship because of their new faith in Christ elicited the anger of the state. Quite remarkably, this hostile situation, instead of disintegrating the believers, in fact, enabled them to become a closely-knit group with a difference. Hostility of the fellow Israelites and the persecution (sponsored by the Roman colonial state and the Jewish religious authority) never deterred them from preaching Jesus as the Christ, and drawing others into their fellowship.

The early Christians, thus, exhibited great defiance and determination to preach Jesus as the Christ in the midst of acute hostility. It illustrates the fact that the missionary nature is something that cannot be divorced from the life of the Church wherever it is placed, for it is a nature that the Church had inherited from the time of its inception in the world history. It began with Jesus when he first converted Simon, Andrew, James, and John who followed him, responding to his call. The Christians' missionary zeal got further intensified with the rejection and eventual martyrdom of Jesus and the hostility and persecution that forced them to disperse to different parts of the world. These early believers, who experienced the bitterness of rejection, alienation, and brutal violence unleashed on them by their own fellow-Jews in collaboration with the Roman colonial rulers, moved out of their own land proclaiming the new quality of life God had engendered to humanity in Jesus Christ and the process continues until the present day. The early itinerant missionaries, mostly fugitives who fled their hometowns for fear of life, thus, played a major role in the expansion of Christianity. The Church represents a worldwide phenomenon today precisely because of the fruit of the conversions that have been carried out throughout its history. Thus, Christianity has been a missionary religion (Acts 1:8, 2:41) and conversion has been an essential part of its mission. Having said that we need to realize that it is a real challenge for the Church today, as it has to engage in its mission in India in the midst of Hindutva's acute hostility.

It is unfortunate that the critics of the Church (even from within) easily buy the idea of 'forcible conversion', little realizing that 'forcible conversion' is a bogey used by Hindutva forces to intimidate Christians and polarize communities for political gains – a fact that has been attested by the tacit support rendered by the state law enforcing machinery to the perpetrators of violence in a number of incidents. It has almost become a regular feature to demand a national debate on 'forcible conversion' following every attack on Christians. There are certain crucial issues involved here: *First*, little attention is paid when people change political loyalties mostly lured and/or coerced by political parties. But there is too much noise and furore over people changing their religion. It strikes at the very root of fundamental human rights. *Second*, Hindutva forces are angered only when the subalterns change their religion and they interpret such episodes as 'forcible conversion', i.e., as passive acts and not the outcome of the people's conscious choice. But conversions are people's clear choice to be different, which represent the political will of the people and it is this determination to be different that angers Hindutva because such choices of the people have the serious implication of their daring to overstep the boundary ascribed to them by Vedic Hinduism.[43]

The issue of 'forcible conversion' has been in the air for quite some time now. Certain self-criticizing Christians also join Hindutva's *forced-conversion* bogey and justify these attacks.[44] But the anti-conversionists completely downplay some of the facts. *First*, anti-conversion laws are in force in those states where the attacks took place and one wonders how many cases were registered against forced conversions. Critics opine that the alleged 'forced conversions' is a pretext for the militant Hindus to take law into their hands to show their strength. Prof. G. M. Krishnan, Political Science Dept of Bangalore University, thinks that "Hindu fundamentalists hate Christian missionaries more, as they do much better work in education and health and are better organized". With regard to the recent attacks on the Churches in Karnataka, political analyst Sandeep Shastri opines that "The Government (in Karnataka) is led by fellow ideologues, so the Bajrang Dal and other related outfits feel they can do anything and get away with it".[45] Shastri further opines that there is reason to suspect the ruling BJP's tacit support for the attacks on the Church in Karnataka because the attacks coincided with the three-day national executive committee meeting of the BJP in Bangalore and its top leaders were in the city on the day before the attacks. A clear indication is that Hindutva is trying to employ the method of saffronizing the state "by engineering attacks on the minorities and profiting from the polarization".

The issue of conversion is a sensitive one and it has to be approached sensibly. If someone claims that ('forceful') conversion is enough justification for the *sangh parivar* to kill innocent Christians, it raises a very pertinent question: What course of action befits against the dominant Hindus who have been forcefully keeping the 'untouchables' in wretched and dehumanized condition for centuries in the name of caste system? According to Gothandarama, the president of the *Ambedkar Yuva Sena* (Ambedkar Youth Army), conversion is a fundamental right and it would continue as long as the *varṇā* system of Vedic Hinduism prevails.[46] Therefore, there is reason to believe that it is not conversion but the new awakening among the 'untouchables' that enrages the Hindu right because the Church has all along been expressing its solidarity with the Subalterns in India.

In the midst of severe persecutions, the early Christians did not indulge in violent retaliation. Rather, they got themselves together wherever possible and served those in need, following their master's command to shun violence and do good to even those who persecuted them (Mt. 5:38-44). As Harnack understands:

> Patience, meekness, readiness for service, renunciation of one's own right – these are the virtues which ought to distinguish the Christian; even self defense was not recognized...Peace is proclaimed to all people, and the Gospel itself is called the 'Gospel of peace'. The disciples of Jesus are not to behave the way the mighty and powerful do; their attitude was supposed to be opposite to the attitude of the ones who rule.[47]

Of course, it is a debatable point in the contemporary situation as to what course of action – patient endurance or violent reaction – befits the Church when cold blooded violence is unleashed on the innocent Christians by the dominant religious fanatics.[48] But non-violence is the fundamental Christian principle and if there are voices that express the need for a kind of 'Christian militia' out of frustration over the unjustifiable violence against the vulnerable Christian minority in India, those voices do not represent the essential spirit of Christianity.

The persecutions, instead of disheartening, in fact, strengthened the early Christians to endure suffering and engage in mission – proclaiming the Gospel and serving the needy. This is a crucial point that must arouse our interest as Christians encounter similar situations in India. It raises a pertinent question as to the kind of attitude Christians must demonstrate when the Church is subjected to unjustifiable violence. An appropriate Christian response to the above issue of unjustifiable violence must take into account at least two crucial factors: (a) contrary to the situation of the early Church, the Christians in India have constitutional protection within the limits of the secular democracy; and (b) despite the constitutional protection, the Church has to encounter the hatred and hostility generated by Hindutva through its intense hate campaign against the minorities.

The above comments on the Church in the context of Hindutva might appear to be a flirtation with a thorough going historical relativism of the Church. Any such reductionism would potentially minimize ecclesia into a mere sociological entity. The Church, however, is not a mere social entity because it encapsulates certain vital components that make it both a historical and a trans-historical reality. In the ensuing sections we would enumerate two of those elemental and inter-connected factors, namely, the idea of transcendence and Christian understanding of suffering, in order to carry our discourse on the Church further.

Idea of Transcendence

The idea of transcendence iterates that there is something that surpasses empirical verification. As a matter of fact, it was the ancient philosophic schools that had prepared the ground for a Christian understanding of transcendence. Plato and Aristotle were the key influences. Plato, for instance, spoke of "ideas" (*ousia*) as the true essence of things. According to Platonic and later Neo-Platonic traditions, the material world has no ultimate value in comparison with the essential world. The ultimate aim of human existence is to discard its bondage to the world and become like God, who is the spiritual domain; and the inner *telos* of human existence is to participate in the spiritual realm. This component occupied an important place in the theology of the Capadocian Fathers, especially in their attempt to understand the ultimate aim of human existence. The idea of human soul as having fallen from its essence, i.e., from the essential or spiritual world into the world of existence was another element from the Platonic tradition that was prominently used by those early theologians. According to Platonism, from this condition of being on the earth in a body, the human soul tries to dispel its bondage to the body and finally reaches an elevation from the material world. The idea of providence that was in the Platonic tradition was also used extensively in early Christian thought as an attempt to overcome anxiety (Rom 8). Another element that was incorporated into Christian theology was Aristotle's understanding of the divine as a *form* without a substance. This highest form moves the world, not from outside, but by moving everything finite towards this form, which is called "God", the highest form or 'pure actuality' (*actus purus*) by means of love.[49] In fact, all the visible expressions of the Church were to point to its central purpose, namely, to "put on Christ" (Rom 13:14) in order "not to be conformed to the world, but be transformed by the renewing of...minds" for discerning "the will of God" (Rom 12:2) to be in communion with God.

Admittedly, a number of spiritual/theological attitudes that have been in vogue in the Church are the outcome of these influences. As early as in the mid first century itself, Paul, in his first letter to the Corinthians challenged the followers of Christ not to be content exclusively with the concerns of this age as he warned them: "If for this life only we have hoped in Christ, we are of all people most to be pitied" (15:19). This futuristic hope, especially the hope for a life of eternal peace and joy devoid of all turbulences of the present age, is an endemic theme in the theology of the Church. Paul repeats this theme in Romans as he passionately affirms: "I consider that the sufferings of this present time are not worth comparing with the glory about to be revealed to us" (8:18). It is possible that these attitudes might have provided substance to certain new modes of discourse on suffering (martyrdom to be more precise) as the early believers in Christ had been subjected to organized violence.

For a contemporary mind, the idea of transcendence and the attitudes attached to it might sound untenable and obstructing the human struggle for liberation from historical bondages as these attitudes legitimize the suffering of the victims and hasten to maintain status quo. But we need to bear in mind that the idea of transcendence and the consequent spiritual/theological attitudes did not emerge from the sophisticated ivory towers of the emperors and rulers, but from the margins, i.e., from the site of trampled humanity. They were not intended to make the broken humanity to remain in perpetual struggle; rather they were aimed at providing them hope in the midst of their struggle through which they anticipated a transformation of their present lives.[50] As Sebastian Kappen understands, as human beings, we encounter the Holy under two conditions: in our *nakedness* and in our *glory*. He further argues that in the midst of pain, brokenness and anxiety, humans experience a genuine God-human encounter; and in the innermost experience of beauty, love and human togetherness, we experience God in glory.[51]

Of course, the idea of transcendence has come to be interpreted as a kind of utopianism with a strong dose of individualism in the more sophisticated theology that emerged in due course. Nonetheless, in its original form, setting and substance, the idea of transcendence was a mode of discourse that proffered the necessary force and power to the victims to hold on to their struggle that would enable them to overcome their suffering. It was not an individual exercise, but a collective struggle to realize the fullness of life that God has prepared in Christ; and once again we are drawn to the relational aspect of the life and theology of the Church, which we need to re-discover in our collective struggle to respond to the hostile situation in which the Indian Church has been thrust into by the Hindutva forces in the contemporary time.

Church's Attitude towards Suffering

The hostile situation the Church had to negotiate was an important factor that contributed greatly to the understanding of suffering. A predominant view of suffering was 'self-mortification'. Christianity had inherited its monotheistic belief system from Judaism, which, however, was not compatible with the traditional religions or with the 'divine honors' bestowed upon the emperors.[52] This led them to be at risk for about three centuries, for they were liable to be executed often with dreadful cruelty but fully within the statutory provisions for their refusal to worship the Roman gods and emperors. In most cases of torture, the Christians endured suffering and even death as dying for Christ. Tertullian captures the Christians' zeal for martyrdom as he writes:

> Your cruelties, each more refined than the last, achieve nothing. They attract others to our school. Each time you mow us down, you increase our number: the blood of Christians is seed. Many of you preach endurance of pain and death: Cicero in the *Tusculans*, Seneca in *Chances*...but their words do not find as many followers as the Christians do in teaching by action.[53]

From a Roman point of view, the Christians' refusal to offer worships to their local deities amounted to jeopardizing the welfare of the State, and from a Christian point of view, it was a particular form of martyrdom, i.e., dying for one's belief, which became part of Christian self-understanding and was commemorated and venerated as the Church's history of championing the cause of the Gospel. The same tendency continues to exist even today in the Church. Christian response to the brutal killing of the Australian missionary, Graham Steins, and his two minor sons by the Hindu extremists in Orissa, for instance, reflects this tendency. It re-echoes the exhortation found in Matthew 10:28: "And do not fear those who kill the body but cannot kill the soul; rather fear him who can destroy both soul and body in hell".

Martyrdom was so important for Christian self-understanding, both before and after persecutions, as Christianity originated from the martyrdom of its saviour figure, Jesus.[54] The term *martyr* is a derivative from Greek *martures*, meaning "witness", and hence, a martyr is the one who bears witness to his/her principles (faith for Christians) by choosing to die rather than to renounce them.[55] Traditional accounts of martyrdom can be described as hagiography (writings about saints). Such accounts, in fact, enabled successive generations of people to withstand torture for the cause of faith. In such instances, the victims confidently defied the torturers even to their amazement. In its Christian connotation, 'martyr' has a distinctive meaning because Christians died out of the sheer confidence of the reward that they believed to be waiting for them in the future (Rom 8:18). In the events of martyrdom, Christians were subjected to torture and death mostly as public spectacles in Roman amphitheatres, which was a form of sentence that declared them outcasts from the Roman society.

What is the theological significance of the accounts of the pain inflicted on Christians? From a Roman point of view, it was extremely degrading to die as a sentenced criminal. The community (spectators) that eagerly watched the death of the convicted expressed its utter scornfulness and rejection of the condemned. The victims in the arena, thrown before the gladiators or wild beasts were regarded to be social outcasts. Conversely, the Christian accounts of these incidents claimed that the crowds who watched them were awe-inspired by the amazing courage of the martyrs and many of them turned to Christianity. Here comes the significance of Tertullian's famous statement: "The blood of the Christians is seed." It implies that those Christians were not done away with; rather they beget new life and generate renewed vigor and zeal for Christ.[56]

For the contemporary readers, especially with critical minds, the martyr stories might appear to be a commercial technique in order to promote the new faith with greater appeal. They would express shock and contempt to the textual display of the tortured or mutilated bodies and the stylization of torture. It might appear to them as something similar to producing, marketing, and watching video nasties or, even worse, snuff movies in which people actually die. On the contrary, a positive reading of such narratives would argue that the purpose of such textual display of torture is to show the triumph of the victims over the worst that the torturers could inflict on them. In this perception, the viewers identify themselves with the victims and not with the torturers.[57] The martyr's pain is neither forgotten nor degraded but admired, commemorated, and even venerated with a new interpretation that the final outcome of martyrdom is just the opposite to the intended degradation by the perpetrators.

Historically, Christians were targeted mostly during natural calamities. Since such calamities had no rational explanations, Christians would be scapegoated with the charge that the gods were infuriated due to their refusal to offer sacrifices and placate their anger. Consequently, any punishment inflicted on Christians would normally diffuse public uproar against the State's apathies. During the mid third century (249CE), Emperor Decius decreed all Roman citizens to offer sacrifices to the Roman gods and obtain official certificates as proof of compliance to the decree by the citizens. This had enormous effect on the Church, especially in the later periods of Christian history. In the African province of Carthage, for instance, there were mixed responses to the emperor's edict. Some Christians obtained token certificates; some others presented themselves at the sacrificial ceremony; and yet others obtained certificates without actually taking part in such ceremonies. But those who openly repudiated were either imprisoned or executed. This resulted in schisms within the Church between the 'lapsed' and the 'rigorists'.[58]

The physical suffering of the Christians was seen as sharing in the suffering of Christ that was further strengthened by the Christian belief in resurrection and the continuing power of the "holy dead". 'Suffering' for Christ (including mortification of the body that was prominent in asceticism) is, thus, an important feature of ecclesiology especially of the early centuries and it is an open issue for further debate whether we can apply the same principles in our ecclesiological reflections in the contemporary Indian context in which Christians are brutalized by the Hindutva forces. We will leave the issue open here as we will have occasion to critically look at it in the later stages of this study. At the moment, we will turn to another important theme, namely, the idea of community that had emerged in the midst of suffering and got established as a widely accepted description of the Church in ecclesiological reflections even to this day.

Idea of Community

The idea of community is an important theme that has provided much substance to the understanding of the Church in the New Testament and beyond. Even if one has to dispute the notion of the Church as having emerged from Jesus, his selection of a small band of disciples and also a wider group of men and women can in no way be disputed and it presupposes that Jesus had an idea of an ongoing 'community' in his mind. If this is taken seriously, then, we can argue that it was this community that had developed into ecclesia in the post-resurrection period. As Donald Guthrie points out, Jesus gathered a *group of people* who were to continue his ministry in this world and the initial band of disciples, in some way, were the representatives of the future 'communities' of the faithful.[59]

The early Christians had a notion of the Church as the true Israel, which finds further expression in the epistles.[60] It appears that the early Christians appropriated this idea as an integral part of their new understanding of the Church. In this regard we need to take two concepts seriously, namely, the idea of the Christian 'community' as the true Israel, and the Kingdom of God. Hans Küng, however, sounds a caution against any tendency to translate the term Israel into the New Testament ecclesia, even though one might find certain close connections between these two ideas.[61] Central to this new perception was the idea of the 'community', which came into being through the new covenant in Jesus Christ who demanded that they live in this relationship and mediate the same to the entire world.

This relationship provided much force to the early Christians' self-understanding and, as a consequence, their existence exhibited certain distinctive behavior patterns. *First*, as noted, within a short while the early Christians' exclusive Jewish cleavages had to give way for a pluralistic cultural situation with the conversion and subsequent influx of the Gentiles into the new fellowship. Of course, this transition came not without its own difficulties; for it required a special vision for Peter, for example, to accept this transition (Acts 10) – a vision that symbolizes the demolition of the purity-pollution ideology and, thereby, breaking up of the rigid barriers that divided the Jewish and Gentile believers. It paved the way for a transition from rigid and exclusive cultural patterns to embrace plurality of cultures. Thus, they came forward to sort out the difficulties that arose from differences and learned to banish racial discriminations within a short span of time. *Second*, the early Christians quickly came to realize the importance of collective way of living, based on the relationship mentioned earlier, and it was Paul, more than anyone else, who expended a great amount of his intellectual energy to expound the Christian collective living in terms of community. It is no exaggeration to say that this is a new development in ecclesiology that had provided greater theological substance for the believers to hold on to their faith and engage in proclaiming the Gospel of the risen Christ in the midst of acute hostility and persecution.

Even though the idea of community does not presuppose an egalitarian way of life, the believers (according to Acts 2:44, 4:32) came forward to share their material resources in common. As scholars opine, the point here is not a common ownership of property or material possessions but a strong sense of concern for each other, which led them to look after the welfare of the underprivileged (Acts 6). Thus, the main emphasis within the community was a sense of responsibility towards each other, especially towards those who were socially deprived, which prompted the early believers to take certain concerted actions when they realized that a good number of the believers were drawn from the marginalized sections of the society. This mode of mutual support was extended between communities (of believers) also, as exemplified by the act of collection made by the Church in Antioch in aid of the Church in Jerusalem (Acts 11: 27ff, 1 Cor. 16: 1ff) as a means of demonstrating the *Gentiles'* concern for their *Jewish* brothers and sisters.[62] This act points to certain crucial principles that could effectively guide the contemporary Indian Church: an act of charity, an act of solidarity, and an act of eschatological spiritual journey, not in isolation but along with other brothers and sisters.

A close look at the development of the Church in the New Testament reveals the fact that the early believers quickly developed a sense of common worship and a practice of common meals in the Christians' homes, especially when the people around them and the state turned hostile towards them. This has to be understood at two levels: (a) sharing of material resources as an expression of their fellowship in Christ and their solidarity with fellow Christians at times of troubles, and (b) as a typical example of viewing their existence, not as disjuncted between spiritual and mundane, but as a permutation of both spiritual and physical well-being of the people. This new image of the Church mirrored the divine-human relationship and the intimate relationship that existed among the believers within the faith 'community' in spite of their cultural differences.

Paul's Understanding of the Church as Community

To be sure, Paul's idea of community is a unique contribution to ecclesiology. There are two ways in which one can look at his idea of community: (a) a doctrinal study of his view, unrelated to the socio-political-cultural milieu, and (b) a contextual outlook, taking into account his interaction with and involvement in the society around him that contributed to the views expressed in his letters. In this study, the latter is taken seriously and it would certainly eliminate any notion of Paul's pristine theological contemplation cut off from the daily life, because it is this aspect that gives more force and creativity to his idea of community. An important consideration is that his different approaches to the idea of community are predicated on what for him is the fundamental reality of the Gospel.[63] In his letters, Paul refers to the Church in two ways: the community of believers in a specific locality, and the Church universal.[64] Of course, it is rather difficult to arrive at any conclusive description of the universal concept of the Church because the universal Church is neither a conglomerate of local communities nor a unified, homogenous monolithic entity, for each ecclesial 'community', in essence, is *the* Church and at the same tine connected with other ecclesial communities.

Paul's understanding of community emerged within the political milieu of Roman colonialism and the dominance of Greek culture. Traditionally, there were two types of community with which people identified themselves: *politeia*, the public life of the city or nation to which they had citizenry bonds, and *oikonōmia*, the immediate family unit to which they belonged. Robert Banks, however, makes an important observation that this sort of twin relationship was meaningful only to free citizens as they alone could meaningfully participate in these institutions. But there were others – the slaves, dependents of various kinds, adults who remained unmarried, and outcasts of the society – who could only exist in those territories without any major participatory roles to play. He further opines that Paul's was a time characterized by a growing trend of the disintegration of these institutions in the face of the increasing power-play among the dominant, leading to an escalating disenchantment among the citizens. It gave rise to at least two developments with lasting impact: *first*, when the wider community failed to engender what the people desired, they tended to look to smaller communities, especially the households, in which they lived and where they could find a greater deal of unity and commonality of life; and *second*, a section of people, when they found their aspirations unfulfilled within this narrow household, shifted their allegiance towards a cosmopolitan order or a universal commonwealth that could encompass different people where the basic divisions that had separated them might be resolved. Two sources can be identified as responsible for this development: (a) the Stoican commonwealth governed by reason; and (b) the theocratic rule headed by the Messiah of Judaism.[65]

Paul employs the idea of community in two ways: community of believers in a specified locality, and the universal Church. In both the cases, we are cautioned not to hasten to transpose the present day structures of the Church upon Paul's idea of community, for it is quite evident from his letters that the structure of the early Church was not as rigid as we have it in the present day Church.[66] What we experience today is that even though every local Church is said to have the same faith in the one Christ, the way this faith is understood, interpreted, schematized and codified in each Church is different from each other and no Church is willing to make any modification in its dogmatic position. Of course, some *allowances* would be made to recognize the *relative* validity of each other's positions (in the context of the ecumenical debates), but there cannot be any one-to-one dogmatic agreement between recalcitrant Churches.[67]

To be sure, *Acts* does not present a universal Church, but scattered house Churches in various localities. This, however, does not negate the concept of a universal Church because each local Church stood for the basic belief that exhibited all the traits of the concept of the one Church under the authority of the same Lord. The early believers demonstrated a remarkable strength in this regard, in which the local Church was regarded not as an organization in the modern sense of the term, but as a living organism, networked into a bond of unity in faith in the one Lord and in the common vision of proclaiming the Gospel in the neighbourhood, prompted not by the ecclesiastical edicts or episcopal pronouncements, but by the Spirit of God, a fact that is made clear by the method of decision-making in the Church, i.e., when decisions had to be made, they were made not in closed-door-high-level-representative-committees, but in the company of the entire believers (Acts 6).

An important feature of the early Church was the form of communities that survived as house Churches, at least for the first couple of centuries when Christians dedicated their homes for the gathering of the believers for worship and fellowship meals. Scholars, however, caution us not to idealize or essentialize the concept of the house Churches. Luke himself was cautious not to place any extra emphasis on the house Churches, even though he emphasized the importance of the households and the hospitality, which played such an important role in the works of Paul (Acts 16:15, 33; 18:18 cf. Acts 2:46, 12:12-13). He emphasizes the city-wide Church, modeled after the *koinonia* of Jerusalem with its sharing of resources almost to the exclusion of any significance of an individual household. This is perhaps because of the problems that cropped up in the table fellowship in the house Churches (1 Cor. 11:17-34).[68] Nevertheless, the house Church mode of Christian expression, in many respects, provided the believers with the vigour and vitality required for the cause of the Gospel of God's Kingdom and a close-knit fellowship of the believers that enabled them to care for each other more personally.[69] It appears that Paul lived this family relationship with his co-workers and communities and he wanted them to live the same way because, in his estimation, the core of the community was in fact the family. Thus the practical necessity of meeting in private homes seems to have been blended with his theological understanding of the Christian community.[70]

Distinctiveness of the Christian Idea of Community

The idea of community as depicted in the New Testament is endowed with certain distinctive features quite different from the Jewish/Hellenistic understanding of the same in the New Testament times. For the members of the Jewish religious organizations (the Pharisees and the Qumran community), life revolved around a *code* as embodied in the Torah.[71] This is particularly so in the Synagogue worships in which the important components are blessings, readings, expositions, confessions and prayers. Similarly, life for the Hellenistic religious assemblies centered primarily on a *cult* with dramatic rituals and mystical experiences. Contrary to these modes of religious expressions, Christian life, according to Paul, centered primarily on the *fellowship (communion)* of believers with God and with one another. This clearly reflects Paul's earlier experience and expressions of reconciliation brought into effect by God in Christ that brings the believers together in communion. Thus, for the Christian communities, the referral and focal point is neither a book nor a rite, neither a code nor a cult, and not even a sacred site, but a set of relationships.[72] This, of course, must not be misconstrued that the book or religious rituals or site became totally out of place and, hence, they can be dispensed with. Certainly, they have great value, since it is the Word of God that brings the community into being, which is engaged in several rituals like worship and administering sacraments. Nevertheless, we need to realize that without the existence of the communion of the people of God, the Word is inexpressive and the rituals become ineffective, and, as such, the communion of the people of God becomes the referral point for the Christian self-understanding.

The above aspect of the Church's existence can be contrasted with the Hindu nationalist situation, which is increasingly becoming fanatic towards the canonized text, rituals, and a sacred site. Consequently, preservation of the culture, rituals, and protection of the holy land as enshrined in the sacred text from the enemies become pivotal for Hindu nationalists. In the process human relationships and well being are almost sacrificed on the altar of an all-embracing, corporatist, and ascriptive Hindu identity. A similar transition also occurred within Christianity in which the Roman Catholicism increasingly followed the cultic path, making the rituals the centre of its activities and Protestantism adhered to the practices of the synagogue, placing the sacred Book and the Lord's Supper (known as the visible Word) at the centre of its activities. But the idea of community with its inherent relationship is a vitally important component in our search for the self-understanding of the Church in our own context.

Kingdom of God and the Church

In addition to the idea of community, the concept of the 'Kingdom of God' is an indispensable theme in ecclesiology. A good number of modern theologians had shown keen interest in the idea of the 'Kingdom of God' as a potential theological theme, especially in the context of the structural injustice. There is a general opinion among scholars that the Kingdom of God and the Church are not one and the same. Obviously, ecclesia cannot usurp the place of the Kingdom of God, but it certainly represents the Kingdom. It does not confine the Kingdom, but it must define and demonstrate what the Kingdom means to the world. Jesus began his ministry heralding the arrival of the Kingdom of God (Mark 1:15) and his teachings on the Kingdom emerged in the context of his mission.[73] Here, one has to admit that there cannot be a one-to-one correspondence between the Kingdom sayings of Jesus and ecclesia sayings of the Scripture. When Jesus sent out his disciples, they were to preach about the Kingdom of God, i.e., the rule of God and not the Church. The Kingdom of God is centered around Jesus and not on the disciples (or the community) – a fact that eliminates all inclinations to conceive of a Kingdom-ecclesia identity.[74] This, however, does not discard the idea of the Kingdom from the idea of the collective of the people of God because this collective, which is commonly described in terms of 'community', is an inevitable component for the realization or visible manifestation of the Kingdom of God.[75]

The fact that God's Kingdom cannot operate in vacuum and it does require a locus or sphere in which human beings are also involved makes it possible to argue that the Church has its basis in the Kingdom of God. As we carefully analyze the Kingdom sayings of Jesus as recorded in the Gospels, we come across a key term "entering" into the Kingdom (Mt. 7:21, Mk. 9:47, Lk. 16:16). If we understand this term metaphorically, then, it implies that the life and ministry of Jesus has opened up a new possibility for humans to "enter" a new way of life, which will be predicated on the will of God or God's rule. In order to understand the link between the idea of the Kingdom of God and that of the Church, we need to further look into the parables of Jesus pertaining to the Kingdom of God (Mt. 13:47f; Mk 4:30-32). These parables clearly illustrate that the Kingdom is an all-embracing phenomenon that affects both good and bad, and at the end of the age the bad will be ejected. Hence, it can be affirmed that all those who belong to the Kingdom or God's rule could be part of the Church, but all those who belong to the visible Church do not necessarily form part of the Kingdom.[76]

The idea of the Kingdom of God became an important item in the theological agenda in modern times.[77] The new trend is the result of some theologians' attempt to establish the role of ethics in the improvement of human society. Albrecht Ritschl was the first one to introduce the idea of Kingdom of God in relation to human ethical behavior. His double foci, i.e., his emphasis on the transcendence of God and an appeal to work for the Kingdom of God, had set a new agenda in theological debates. For him, Christianity hinges on two fundamental categories, namely, the salvific act of God in Christ and the ethical action of the individuals in the Kingdom of God. His critique of the Reformation is that its emphasis on the divine side of salvation is asymmetrical and it needs to be counter-balanced with an emphasis on human side. A strong reaction to his synthesis of the divine and human sides came from Johannes Weiss, who criticized Ritschl of over accentuating the human and presenting a moral Christianity. Weiss argued that Jesus understood the Kingdom of God to be God's future reign and not in any way connected to human behavior.[78]

In the 20th century, two influential theologians, C. H. Dodd and R. Bultmann, continued the discussions on the Kingdom from a liberal Protestant perspective. They attempted to demonstrate that the eschatological character of Jesus' message does not in any way stand as a barrier to understanding it as the foundation of Christian ethics today. Dodd was the first to introduce the concept 'already and not yet', meaning the Kingdom of God has already come in Jesus Christ, but its consummation or final fulfillment is awaited in the future (realized and future eschatology), which became very common in New Testament theology in the later periods. Dodd was convinced that the teachings of Jesus formed the basic guidelines for actual human behavior. For Rudolf Bultmann, the project of demythologization made it possible to preserve the eschatological character of Jesus' message of the Kingdom of God, including its meaning today. He found the whole exercise of Christian life to be a decision, i.e., by hearing the eschatological message of Jesus humans have a 'last chance' to choose for God.[79] Later, there was the social Gospel movement, whose adherents were deeply involved in 'christianizing the social order', and there were others who protested against any confusion of political entities with the coming of the Kingdom of God. After these intense debates, the discourses on the Kingdom of God receded to the background but resurged again in the 1960s with the emergence of the Liberation theology in Latin America.[80]

In any case, it is unlikely that the early followers of Jesus invented the idea of constituting a Church contrary to the will of their master. If it were maintained otherwise, it would lead to the conclusion that the Kingdom sayings of Jesus had only a limited scope that he intended the presence of the Kingdom in a restricted manner to be present only during his earthly ministry.[81] This puts too many constrictions on the Church, making it impossible to draw any connection between Jesus' teachings and the present day Church,[82] and it would call into question the authenticity of the Church. Hence, contrary to this restrictive/reductive approach, I would iterate that even though the Church and the Kingdom of God are not one and the same, the Church came into existence not without the will of Jesus. Evidently, the Church does have certain traits of the Kingdom, sometimes fully revealed and at other times obscured, but despite this weakness the Church has the fundamental task of witnessing to the Kingdom of God, whose full realization, of course, does not belong to the present age.

Non-Conformity to the World

Another important feature of the Church, especially in its early expression, is the attitude of 'renunciation of the self and the world'. Two sources can be identified as having given rise to this attitude: *first,* according to the synoptic accounts, Jesus demanded his disciples and those who intended to follow him to do so by bearing the cross daily by denying the self (Mk 8:34); and *second*, in Romans (12:2), Paul called Christians not to conform to the ways of the world – a principle that might have later come to be linked to martyrdom and then to asceticism. The cult of martyrs often went along with ascetic practices with the characteristic features of self-mortification, extreme austerities, and withdrawal from the world. All these can be summarized into a single concept, i.e., denial – denial of the self and the denial of the world to be in close communion with God (Mk 8:34; Lk. 9:23; Rom 12:2). The underlying idea might have been the notion of good-evil dichotomy in which the flesh is seen as evil and so also the material world. The predominant concern was to save the soul from being ensnared by the evil – a prominent attitude among the ascetics.

Christian asceticism had its origin in the mid-third century, and gradually there emerged a community of monks in the Egyptian desert (*eremos* = desert, hence *eremite* and hermit) who lived a solitary life or in single-sex communities, practicing extreme austerities.[83] In many instances, the hermits drew a large number of people who came to seek counsels concerning their spiritual and day-to-day life. It is extremely important to note that the multitudes who frequented the hermit monks were seeking counsels *not* for their ostentatious lives, but for their lives in the midst of suffering from persecutions.[84] These hermits or monks were known as "Desert Fathers", who were famous for their extreme austerities and spiritual powers of healing and exorcism.[85] Paul has a metaphor of an athlete in 1 Cor. 9:24 – 27 – an image of a spiritual athlete. Athletes, in many instances, abstain from certain food and behavior patterns to keep their bodies fit for the race. Similarly, the spiritual athletes – the ascetics, derived from Greek *askesis*, meaning 'training'[86] – took extreme measures to deny their bodies, fine-tune their souls, and to be in union with the ultimate.

In the philosophical traditions of antiquity, the students were constantly told that possessions are burdensome and would foster greed and ambitions. Hence, the wise needed to cultivate a sense of detachment, reduce needs, and seek after goodness, and not success. In this schema, the most important aspect of human existence was the rational soul, which was seen as the human link to God. Hence, if a human being gets entangled in the web of the desire for the material or mundane things, it would be a terrible distraction of the soul from being in communion with God. If the preoccupations of the body could be minimized, it could be brought under the control of reason. Following this tradition, some ascetics reduced their eating habits, especially meat and wine, as they were regarded to be over-stimulating, and some even abstained from eating because food signified human mortality.[87] These were some of the important spiritual attitudes that had developed in the course of the development of the Church and one cannot claim that they are grounded on the Scripture because Scripture does not provide any clear teachings about these attitudes. Nonetheless, we cannot deny that there are a number of traces of such attitudes in the Scripture. In these attitudes, an important concern was to make a clear distinction between the spiritual and the mundane, ascribing them with higher and lower values respectively and we need to remember that these were the expressions of the believers' concern to be in intimate relationship with their Lord.[88]

Pietistic tendency was predominant among the early Christians, especially in their day-to-day life in which they maintained a high profile of regarding themselves as brothers and sisters on the basis of their common faith in Jesus Christ, which was still astonishing and attractive to the people outside ecclesia. Further, the Christian communities developed their own structures, especially the organized care for the sick, poor, orphans, widows, travelers, strangers, prisoners, needy, and the old, which was made possible by the voluntary gifts under the oversight of the bishop. These images, lifestyles and meaning-constructions had their own impacts on the world as they provided enough force for the shaping of various cultures across the globe. But with the passage of time the Church emerged from its beleaguered status to a favored position, which saw the inroad of certain new elements into the Church's life marking a new transition to be an embodiment of a dominant religion.

Transitions within the Church

The purpose of the preceding discussions on the life journey of the Church, its mission across boundaries and frontiers, and the spiritual/

theological attitudes and life-styles that had developed over a period of time is not to romanticize or essentialize the past glory of the Church, and not even to paint an idealist picture of the Church, but to analyze certain crucial developments in the worldwide Church's life journey, which had acted as effective pointers to a new way of life – a life of intimate relationship. The Church, up to this point, was welcomed by people cutting across borders. But not everything went well with the Church as certain new developments became scandalous to the life of the Church. Some of those developments that had lasting impact on the Church we will see below.

Unity of the Church

Visible unity and *full communion* are important concerns of the ecumenical movement, which assumes unity as a gift that the believers received as the members of the body of Christ, and to be faithful to this gift, Christians must manifest it in their collective life, common witness and service to the world.[89] Of course, the idea of visible unity and full communion are contested issues as to what they really signify. But there exists a consensus among ecumenical theologians that *unity is not uniformity* and the worldwide ecumenical movement appears to have drawn a great deal of its theology from the fundamental Christian faith in the Trinity. It entails that as the Trinity embraces differences in its *perichoretic* relationship, so our faith in the Trinity must provide space for legitimate pluralism of liturgical, dogmatic and administrative practices among Churches without allowing their apostolic faith being imperiled. But the modern ecumenical movement could achieve only very little of its original goal of the visible unity of the Church.

Disunity within the Church is not a modern phenomenon. As early as in the first century, there emerged a conflict between Paul and other disciples with regard to the status of the Gentiles within the Church. At that point, the issue was the role of circumcision and the observance of Torah among the believers. When the Jewish Christians insisted that these symbols must be made mandatory for the Gentiles to become true Christians, Paul came out with a different interpretation vis-à-vis the doctrine of justification (Eph. 2:8-10). In his view, neither the ritual of circumcision nor the observance of the law makes a person acceptable (righteous) before God, rather acceptability comes through Jesus Christ alone, who paid the price by being "cursed" under the terms of the law. The mechanism operated thus: because Jesus Christ, who was righteous and without blemish, had been counted among the sinners, those who were sinners could now be counted among the righteous and be regarded as those who entered into a new covenant with God. This new status of one's being justified before God was not the result of one's own behavior as weighed by the law, but the concomitance of God's free grace (Col. 2:11-12, 1 Cor. 7:19, Gal. 5:6, 6:15 Cf. Acts 15:1-11). This, according to Paul, has opened up new possibilities, both for Jews and Gentiles, to enter into a new relationship under the law of love. Here, it has to be noted that what Paul intended was not to erase the Jewish and Gentile identities, but their being embraced into a new form of communion in Christ as his body.

One may be fascinated and easily enticed by this idea since it appears to be the most appropriate vision of Christian unity in the present context of unprecedented fragmentation, especially within the Church. It might even appear to be an ideal vision of an ecclesia in which culturally and ethnically variegated groups can come together and co-exist within the same fellowship under the headship of Christ with the understanding of Christ as having broken down the wall of separation (Eph. 2:11-16). But the tragic reality is that even Paul, with this ideal vision, could not mend the cracks that occurred within the Church completely. Hence, the task of holding various people groups within one fold without making discriminations and without getting entangled into conflict is a tough one. Now, whether we opt for the Pauline vision or do we attempt to construct new models, one thing is sure, i.e., the identity of the Indian Christians is contingent on the way they could express their unity in Christ even if our choices of forms, modes, and methods might vary.

To be sure, Paul sketched out a useful, if not entirely acceptable, theological basis for the cross-cultural experience that was emerging within the early Church. Early Christians brought with them much of their traditional cultural substances when they joined Christianity. Some elements such as the rituals pertaining to the worship of other gods were rejected and some others, including personal behaviors, sexual norms and moral codes, patterns of family life, economic activities and forms of worship were adopted with certain modifications. In any case, as Irvin and Sunquist opine, the general trend of the early Christian life style could not be seen as totally disjuncted from the past, rather there remained a significant degree of continuity with the multiple pasts as evidenced by the Pentecost experience. The translation of the message of Jesus Christ into various languages on this occasion entailed, in fact, a two-way conversion – the conversion of the Gospel to new and diverse cultures and the conversion of diverse people to faith in the Gospel of Jesus Christ.[90] More discussion on this would follow as the study progresses. Our focus now is on certain theological controversies that had rocked the Church.

Trinitarian/Christological Controversies[91]

With the expansion of Christianity across boundaries, several of its initial features were to give way for more complicated patterns of life, thought and structures. As Christianity negotiated multiple worldviews, cultures and civilizations, different faith persuasions and intellectual patterns, it could not remain constant. Rather, it did affect and allowed itself to be affected by these factors – a phenomenon that gave rise to multiple views and voices pertaining to the central matrix of Christian faith. The first one happened to be the conflicting views on the person of Christ – the central symbol of Christian faith – with lasting impact on the life of the Church. Is it a matter of frustration or a source of courage and confidence? One possible approach might be to accept these controversies as not being aimed at shattering the foundation of the faith of the Church, but as attempts to understand the inexhaustible mystery of Christ intimately related to specific contexts. Nevertheless, we need to remind ourselves that it had resulted in some of the bitterest conflicts in the subsequent periods of Christian history.

We have noted that the early Christians went out as refugees and as outlawed sects. Yet their zeal to proclaim the Gospel of Jesus Christ was vibrant that they set out to win converts in whatever locality they had come to settle in. This zeal to win converts from various ethnic, national, linguistic and cultural groups was not without its own ramifications, for Christianity had to encounter a number of factors such as new philosophical schools, life styles, political situations (both favorable and adverse) and religions, at times appropriating certain traits and at other times rejecting certain others in view of its faith in Jesus Christ. Christianity's encounter with diverse social, political, religious, cultural and intellectual patterns had its first impact on the meaning of Christ. The Church, in fact, was in a dilemma for it had to maintain a monotheistic belief system and, at the same time, account for the person and work of Jesus Christ, after whom it had taken shape and continued to embrace a large number of followers for him.

It is this dilemma that had driven the Church to construct the Trinitarian dogma in which the Church came to firmly establish its understanding of God in terms of God the Father, God the Son, and God the Holy Spirit, interpreted as three persons within a single Godhead with substantial identity (*Homoousia*), and hypostatical differences. A possible inference here can be that the specific understanding of the inner *perichoretic* communion of the three persons of the Trinity might have provided greater strength to affirm the unity of the Church in the midst of diverse views on the person of Christ that potentially threatened to divide the Church. The idea of Christ's co-equality with the one God and plurality of persons within Godhead, however, could not satisfactorily answer any rational scrutiny and it gave rise to a number of competing interpretations among theologians of different schools, bringing them under the banner either of apologists or heretics.[92] It is notable that the notions of *apology* (generally understood as orthodoxy) and *heresy* and the discourses surrounding them had rocked the Church's unity in those early centuries.

Traditionally, heresy was regarded to be "the departure from the faith once delivered to the saints" (Jude 3). The early Christian teachers (apologists) firmly held this view in their writings, which came to be challenged by modern scholarship. Walter Bauer, for instance, calls for a reassessment of this traditional view as he maintains that in many areas of antiquity *heresy* preceded *orthodoxy* in Christian history. Even though his views (expressed in 1934) elicited sharp criticisms, they were reinforced by the Nag Hammadi documents, which point to the fact that as early as in the first and second centuries, there existed diverse interpretations of Jesus and his message. If "heresy" preceded "orthodoxy", at least in some areas, it could well follow that the heretical views can best be termed as alternatives rather than false teachings. The outcome is that our understanding of the New Testament and other early Christian writings is enriched rather than distorted by the reading of the sources that bring to light the so-called heretical voices.[93] In Bauer's view, orthodoxy represented the form of Christianity supported by the majority of Christians in Rome, which came to be firmly established in the second century and became successfully promoted in other areas to the east around 200 CE. Further, for Bauer, the Church at Rome was a Church of Peter and Paul, not influenced by 'heretical' teachers and it was able to extend its influence elsewhere due to its superior organizations and powers. The 'heretical' groups in that region (though in good numbers) were unorganized and could not counter the power and influence of the leaders of the Church at Rome. According to this view, orthodoxy cannot be rendered as the opposite of heresy; rather it must be seen as the triumph over earlier forms of Christianity.[94]

It raises a pertinent question related to the kind of thought world the Christian apologists faced. One strand of argument suggests that the most crucial issue that the early Church faced was neither the Trinitarian issue *per se* nor the person of Christ as it came to be later established in the Councils of Nicaea and Chalcedon, but the notion of incarnation.[95] Another view maintains that the perplexing issue before the Church and the Christian apologists in those early centuries was Christian defiance to persecutions and martyrdom, regarded to be the highest virtue and the highest possible proclamation of the message of Jesus Christ, which eventually came to rock the unity of the Church with the eruption of schisms.[96] While reading the so-called 'heretical' writings, we frequently stumble upon the issues of the humanity and divinity of Jesus as the most debated points. This is particularly so among the Ebionite, Gnostic, Marcionite, Adoptionist, Arian and other similar view points.

The issue of human-divine nature of Jesus is linked to the issue of incarnation and it is the divinity of Jesus that was most scandalous to the Jewish Christian 'heretics' who had been nurtured in the strict monotheistic belief system and steeped in the expectation of the anointed-human-Jewish-Messiah, a view upheld by Trypho in his encounter with Justin Martyr. To quote a brief text from Justin:

> And Trypho said, "Those who affirm him [Christ] to have been a man, and to have been anointed by election, and then to have become Christ, appear to me to speak more plausibly than you [who] hold those opinions which you express. For we all expect that Christ will be a man [born] of men, and that Elijah when he comes will anoint him. But if this man appears to be Christ, He must certainly be known as man [born] of men." [97]

Here Trypho's problem is that he found Justin's Christology overstepping the boundary between God and humanity which is implied in the incarnation – an unacceptable phenomenon from a Jewish point of view indeed.[98] Even within Greek philosophical thought, such difficulty is expressed as illustrated by Celsus' remarks:

> God is good, and beautiful, and blessed, and that in the best and most beautiful degree. But if He comes down among men, He must undergo a change, and a change from good to evil, from virtue to vice, from happiness to misery, and from best to worst. Who, then, would make a choice of such a change? It is the nature of a mortal, indeed, to undergo change and remoulding, but of an immortal to remain the same and unaltered. God, then, could not admit of such a change.[99]
>
> God either really changes Himself, as these assert, into a mortal body, and the impossibility of that has been already declared; or else He does not undergo a change, but only causes the beholders to imagine so, and thus deceives them, and is guilty of falsehood.[100]
>
> O Jews and Christians, no God or son of God either came or will come down (to earth).[101]

These debates point to the emerging trends in theological/ ecclesiological discourses that include 'heretical' thinkers like the Adoptionists and the Docetists. It illustrates that it is against such 'heretical' tendencies that the New Testament writers (like Paul), the early apologists, and the anti-heretical writers were, in most part, reacting. The crucial issue that had been fiercely debated was the nature of incarnation, especially its relation to Christ's suffering, which was so crucial in later Trinitarian and Christological debates. The significance of these controversies leading up to the great Councils at Nicaea and Chalcedon was that they became instrumental and foundational for later dogmatic and systematic theological constructions. Thus, it is likely that there was no uniform theological system during the early centuries of the Christian era. In many respects, the theological terrain of this period bears certain marked semblance of the heterogeneous nature of modern/postmodern worldviews, which normally regard the competing claims not as antithetical, but as multiple answers to the same question. From these complex theological ratiocinations, the Church went through another historical transition with the 'conversion' of Emperor Constantine and subsequent imperial favour.

Imperial Favouritism and the Church

The 'conversion' of Emperor Constantine (ca. 285-337) and the subsequent status of Christianity as an official religion, in many respects, was a new turning point in the life of the Church, especially in terms of its new self-understanding, theological development, style of functioning, and mission. Until then it had been an outlawed sect and suddenly there was a complete metamorphosis that turned Christianity into the most favored religion and the Church into the most privileged institution. It had ushered in specific changes within the life of the Church almost in accordance with the sociological factors of the surrounding world: the small communions became a large organization; the minority turned out to be the majority; the hideout Church was transformed into the State Church; the persecuted became the rulers and eventually persecutors. For better or for worse, the Church came to adapt to the new situation and adopt the new status conferred on it by the empire. Obviously, then, the new Church had to modify its theology in accordance with the new face of the Church.

H. Leitzmann narrates Constantine's conversion as follows:

> Constantine had attuned to the knowledge of Christian truth by the time he engaged in the decisive battle, he asked God to reveal himself and come to his aid. He was given a sign: early in the afternoon *a luminous cross appeared above the sun*, with these words: *In hoc signo Vinces* (with this sign you will conquer). The emperor and all his soldiers contemplated this spectacle with astonishment. The following night Christ appeared to Constantine holding this luminous cross and exhorted him to make an imitation of the celestial sign as means of protection.[102] [Emphases as in the text]

Constantine, like his father Diocletian, was a worshipper of the *sol invictus*. So it is not surprising that he had a vision of the Sun God. But what is surprising is the vision of the cross over the Sun, which had assumed greater theological significance in the subsequent epoch of Christian history – the cross took precedence over the Sun and the Sun soon became the symbol of the risen Christ.[103] The effect of Constantine's conversion is well known. Constantine, and his co-regent, Licinius, granted Christians complete freedom of their religious practices and equality of treatment with the followers of other religions.[104] This transition is not greeted with acclamation by most scholars. Rodney Stark, for instance, terms it as the "curse of Constantine". A most striking metamorphosis in this whole drama is the new portrayal of the image of Jesus that has come to stay permanently in the liturgy, theology, and spirituality of the Church. The carpenter's son from Nazareth became the exalted Jesus, being seated at the right hand of God with all glory and honor; the rugged cross on which he died became a luminous cross; the one who came in the form of a slave, lived as a refugee, resisted the empire, and died as an outcast became the one who fought for the emperor; and the suffering servant became the victorious Lord – a thoroughgoing transformation of Christianity, in which the Church, with breath-taking agility, appropriated, assimilated and assumed the imperial traits that were lavished on it by Constantine and his successors.[105]

Now that the Church had become a powerful institution, the question of essential Christianity becomes crucial for the self-understanding of the Church. There had been great amazement and exuberance among Christians that every persecution aimed at exterminating Christianity had, in fact, turned out to be profitable to the Church and a failure to the empire. It appears that Tertullian was right in his claim that the blood of the martyrs proliferate the number of Christians. As a result, ecclesiology also began to take a different course in consonance with the new changes. Previously, when the Church had made a remarkable break into the world of Gentiles, it gave rise to a Hellenistic paradigm to Christianity, both ecclesiastically and culturally, through the fusion of faith and reason, theology and philosophy, and Church and culture. Now the Church made yet another breakthrough in the political realm "with the combination of the Church and empire".[106]

The Church received the most favored treatment, especially in terms of near-limitless financial resources and imperial favour, changing the very face of the Church. An outlawed sect that had been meeting in humble structures was suddenly housed in magnificent public buildings. St. Peter's Church in Rome built by Constantine, for instance, was modeled on the basilican form used for imperial throne halls in the ancient royal palaces. Its clergy, who were previously recruited from among the believers and modestly sustained by member contributions, suddenly found their jobs enviable with power, status, and wealth. The bishops, who were previously wanted lawbreakers, now became high-ranking officials, equal in status and power with the wealthiest senators in Rome. Thus, with the flamboyant privileges, exemptions, imperial favours, and public status, the office of the ministry became an enviable position, and there was heavy rush to the priesthood of the Church.[107] It is most likely that this was the beginning of clericalism within the Church. *Pastoral ministry*, a service to the people of God, had transformed itself into a *pastoral office*.

According to Paul, ministerial 'offices' (not in the sense of authority) like apostles, prophets, evangelists, and pastors were initiated precisely for the purpose of equipping "the saints for the work of ministry for the building up of the body of Christ" (Eph. 4:11-12). But Constantinian concessions to the Church made the Christian ministerial offices another form of imperial preferment that they soon came to be filled by the descendants of the aristocracy, even circumventing the ecclesial rules. Late in the fourth century, for instance, Auxentius became the bishop of Milan without even having been baptized.[108] However, it is unfair to categorically dump all those who occupied high offices as impious opportunists. In the case of St. Ambrose (ca. 340-397), for instance, it took only a week for him to make a giant leap from Baptism through ordination in the clerical rank and then to his consecration as bishop. Yet he was regarded as a man of faith and principles. Similarly, Pope Gregory I (590-604), despite coming from a papal family, fully deserved to be remembered as Pope Gregory the Great in the history of the Church.

Nevertheless, the overall picture was not very encouraging in which the Church was run by a very worldly, political, luxury-loving, and sometimes notoriously immoral hierarchy. It was this aspect of the Church that became one of the factors that prompted the German Reformer to raise his voice of protest. Eventually, simony became rampant, involving the trading not only of the high offices such as bishophorics, but even local parish placements. This gave rise to another trend of clerical families whose sons and grandsons continued to occupy the holy offices, even up to the papacy for a long period in the history of the Church.[109] The outcome of this trend was that the clergy (leading up to the highest Pontifical office) became callous to the grave needs of the people and concerned more about maintaining and sustaining their enviable positions as clerics – Pastors, Bishops, and Popes. As early as in the Council of Sardica in 341, the Church framed certain rules to be followed in ordaining people into priesthood and then elevating them to the higher offices. But these rules were ignored or conveniently circumvented in order to accommodate favoured persons into the high offices of the Church.

Constantine's opulent favoritism towards Christianity came at the expense of Paganism, which was the State supported religion before. The Pagan temples had been surviving through State funding and by a few rich benefactors. Now, when the state funds were steeply curtailed, Paganism was rapidly collapsing and Christianity became too powerful, especially with the support of the empire and its potent new role in the state politics.[110] Gradually, Christianity became an arrogant religion, and the Christian monks came out in public, intimidating the Pagans and ravaging their temples. Libanus, a Pagan poet, registered a complaint with emperor Theodocius in 390 CE, lamenting:

> You did not order the temples to be closed, but the men in black [Christian monks] attack the temples with stones, poles and iron crowbars, or even their bare hands and feet. Then the roofs are knocked in and the walls leveled to the ground, the statues are overturned and the altars demolished. The temple priests must suffer in silence and die.[111]

This Pagan appeal was viewed as a threat to the stability of the 'Christian state' and the state's policy of religious toleration came to an end. It saw the destruction of the Pagan temples and the confiscation of the Pagan properties[112] – a virtual cleanup measure that saw the near wiping out of Paganism from public expression at least within the city limits of the empire.

A concomitant development within the Church was militarism that surfaced with the crusades, fought under the icon of the cross. To cite a classic example of the Crusades of the middle ages: addressing a huge gathering outside the French city of Clermont (1095) over the recent Muslim persecutions of Christian pilgrims to the Holy Land, Pope Urban II, an eloquent monk, with his crucifix raised high, challenged his belligerent listeners to bathe in the blood of the infidels, thundering:

> It is Christ himself who comes from the tomb and presents you with this cross...Wear it upon your shoulders and your breasts. Let it shine upon your arms and upon your standards. It will be to you the surety of victory or the palm of martyrdom. It will increasingly remind you that Christ died for you, and that it is your duty to die for him".[113]

It has to be noted that militarism is uncharacteristic of Christianity. Neither Jesus nor his early followers advocated armed resistance, perhaps with the exception of Jesus once asking his followers to obtain arms (Lk. 22: 36). However, Jesus soon reversed it when he rebuked his disciple, who struck the slave of the high priest, saying: "all those who take the sword will perish by the sword" (Mt

26: 52). Nevertheless, the Church eventually engaged not only in bloody conflicts but also came out with theological justifications in support of militancy. This perhaps is the darkest side of the life of the Church.

The root of the Crusades goes back to two sources: the first was Constantine's vision of the transformed cross,[114] and the second was Augustine's theology that legitimized the use of force by the lawful authority for just reasons.[115] Since bishops and popes had long been involved in the temporal affairs of the State, they were not averse to the use of force in maintaining discipline and order within their jurisdiction. But the idea of the crusades provided a new theological justification to armed conflicts that made it possible for war to occupy a place at the very heart of the Church's understanding of its task on earth. Bernard of Clairvaux was a prominent Christian theoretician who provided theological justification for the killing of the infidels.[116] This new development, pattern of thought, and ultimately its intellectual rationalization were contributed partly by the conceptual framework that emerged from the synthesis of spiritual and temporal realms. Popes Leo IX, Humburt, Gregory VII, and Urban, all construed these two realms not as separate but as a single whole, united under the spiritual authority of the pope – an authority that was regarded as having flowed from Christ to Peter, from Peter to the apostles, and to the succession of vicars. Accordingly, Pope is the existing Vicar of Christ on earth and so crusade was a holy war under the sign of the victorious cross. It made the western Christians believe that crusade had something *deeply Christian* about it and, hence, it was their *Christian duty* to defend their faith by avenging the enemies of Christ.

Why crusades? Primarily, the rise of Islam had swept Christianity out of several territories and Jerusalem fell to the Muslims. Hence, the reason given for the crusades was to avenge the enemies of Christ and liberate the Holy Land. But there was a hidden agenda, which had to do with the growing deterioration of papal authority. Theoretically speaking, the crucial issue here is the crisis of identity and meaning. It is common knowledge that one's identity – especially superior identity – can be established only when there is an 'other', and only in relation to the 'other' one can assert one's superiority. When this identity crisis is pushed to the extreme, the 'other' is often demonized and identified as the enemy. This principle applies perfectly to the Church of the middle ages. With imperial favor, even though the Church came to establish itself as a strong socio-political reality with enormous power, authority and wealth, there was also a weakening of the Church, and papal authority due to heresies, internal conflicts, contradictions, schisms and various abuses.

In such a situation, the papacy could strategically use the crisis of identity and meaning to establish its primacy through these crusades by easily identifying the Muslims who invaded the Holy Land as the 'others' and the enemies of Christ. The logic, perhaps, is that the stronger the enemy, the stronger is the solidarity of Christians under the supreme Vicar, the pope. It is not very difficult to find identical traits in contemporary religious situation the world over. The Islamic extremists are out there to avenge the 'enemies' of Allah and the contemporary Hindu nationalists in India are charged with the zeal to destroy the 'enemies' of Hinduism. This is a dangerous trait and if this tendency is allowed to flourish, it would lead to human self-destruction. Samuel Huntington tends to categorize this trend as "the clash of civilizations" wherein he contrasts 'Western civilization' with 'Islamic civilization', 'Hindu civilization', and 'Buddhist civilization', and so on. Amartya Sen challenges the notion of 'the clash of civilizations' on the ground that it is a reductionist view of lumping many-sided human beings into certain straitjacketed categories of "civilization-based thinking" and seeking for programmes of "dialogue among civilizations".[117]

Secondly, an important cause of crusades lies in the eleventh century Western Christian understanding of the world and the place of the Holy Land in Christian history. For Western Christianity, Jerusalem is the centre of the history of world salvation. It was sacred to the Christians because Jesus lived there.[118] Would Jesus or his early disciples have entertained any such obsession with Jerusalem or any other site? Before making any judgment, it is important to remind ourselves that Jerusalem rejected and executed Jesus and drove out his early followers; they went out as refugees and preached his Gospel; and the early Church never identified itself as a site based religion, but sustained by its faith in the person of Jesus and a set of relationships among the believers. If that were the case, how and why these new traits found their way into the Church? The crusade was presented to the crusaders as a sort of a pilgrimage to the city of Jerusalem, the holy city of the beginning and the consummation of the history of Christianity. Does this not have striking parallelisms in Hindutva's site based politics today?

Thirdly, crusades were directed not only against the external 'enemies', but also against the 'enemies' of Christ from within the Church, especially those who did not formally subscribe to the universal spiritual authority of the Pope. Hence, crusades were often interpreted as "means of salvation".[119] It raises certain critical questions: Would Jesus, in whose name were the crusades undertaken, have ever approved such bloody acts of his followers, given the fact that his whole message constantly and consistently insisted love, even loving enemies? Was not the cross of the crusaders (which they bore on their chests) a totally transformed cross of the Nazarene's rugged cross – a cross symbolizing self-giving – with legitimizing theological substance? If so, in what way are we going to deconstruct such legitimizing theologies? Without doubt, bloody encounter is uncharacteristic of the Church, which was founded on the sacrifice of the one who came with the proclamation of the message of love for humanity; who taught to 'show the other cheek' and to 'love enemies'; and who endured unjust suffering and death. Without doubt, the crusades represent the dark phase of the Church. Perhaps, the only consolation is that the worldwide Church could come to its senses to realize the futility of such fateful acts. It obviously tells us that it is dangerous for humanity when religion turns violent. It serves no purpose except indulging in heinous crimes against humanity. The religious identities world over – be it fundamentalist Christianity, Islamic extremism, Hindutva or fundamentalist Buddhism – must be told that violence is not the answer to any problem and no one can protect one's religion through violence. In fact, when the Church engaged itself in the crusades, it aimed at using them as means to consolidate its house so that Roman Catholicism could be made a unified, ordered, powerful, and all-encompassing universal phenomenon – a vision of the Church as a single most powerful institution on earth with the pope as its head. But the irony is that instead of unity, the Church ended up in further schisms.[120]

Schisms within the Church

Describing the unity of the body of Christ, the Church, Paul passionately affirms: "There is one body and one Spirit, just as you were called to one hope of your calling, one Lord, one faith, one Baptism, one God and father of all, who is above all and through all and in all" (Eph. 4:4-5). But the Church in its visible manifestation has somehow miserably failed to hold on to unity and preferred a fragmented expression. A number of factors – spiritual/theological, personal, national, social and economic – came to play their role in the events of schism in the Church. In almost all instances of schism, these factors are rationalized by a set of theological arguments. It has been observed that although the Church, in many respects, transcends (or at least claims to transcend) nations, classes, races, and ethnicities, the Church militant has never been able either to suppress or correct the evils of nationalism. On several occasions, the Church stood with the injustices of nationalist systems[121] and only on a few instances did the Church react against such phenomena.

The earliest literary evidence to ecclesial dissension came from Clement shortly after the death of Paul – from his appeal to the Corinthians to refrain from party strife and to hold on to concord and obedience.[122] Novatianism in the Churches in the African province of Carthage exemplifies the role of these elements in schism. Cyprian was baptized in the year 245 or 246 CE. After a short period of service as presbyter, he was consecrated bishop of Carthage in 248. This generated some amount of anger fuelled by jealousy among a group of presbyters. Being on the lookout for reasons to oppose him, they picked up two reasons: (i) when Decian persecution broke out, Cyprian went into hiding, leaving his clergy to administer the Church – a sufficient ground indeed to provoke at least those who underwent torture, which was termed as 'genuine' reaction from the zealous ones; and (ii) when there was a dispute with regard to the readmission of the lapsed, Cyprian himself took a rigid stand against their readmission into communion pending a Council's decision. It has to be noted that it was not any ordinary person, but a towering personality of Cyprian who had to come into conflict with the rigorism of another highly calibered, morally strict presbyter, Novatian, leading to the formation of a 'heretical' Church of the pure (*katharoi*). This drama led to the excommunication of those who challenged Cyprian, resulting in formal schism in which Novatus obtained his own consecration as a rival bishop. Certainly this was not fought on any theological grounds, except for the fact that the 'lapse' was interpreted as an act of betrayal of the Gospel.[123]

The Donatist schism in the 4th century also typifies the influence of almost all the tendencies of schism.[124] It had been incubating ever since Diocletian's persecution in 303. At first, the human 'weakness' to submit in the face of fierce persecution generated disputes with regard to ecclesiastical discipline. After the persecution, the rigorists (those who dared persecution) refused to regard the 'lapsed' as faithful and retorted that the action of the *traditores* (those who handed over the sacred scriptures to be burnt) amounted to the destruction of the holy Word and could never be restored to communion, let alone to offices. The rigorist party stood behind Donatus (a Greek Bishop in Numidia) against the regularly appointed Bishop of Carthage. The rift was not confined to the religious domain, but extended to others – national, social, and economic spheres. In North Africa, there were three social strata: (i) the land owning aristocrats with their Latin identity; (ii) the Punics, who were forced to serve their new Roman overlords in their lands and who had their own Churches and Bishops in Numidia; and (iii) the Berbers, who embraced Christianity when Rome was persecuting Christians and were basically anti-Roman, and now they expressed their solidarity with the branch of Christianity disapproved by Rome, the Donatists.[125]

Understandably, there was an anti-Roman nationalist feeling, especially among the Berbers and Punics in the country regions like Numudia and Maretania. Historians glean a clear division between the urban Catholics and rural Donatists, and their respective allegiance to the empire and the local.[126] The Donatists considered themselves as the legitimate heirs of the true Church that had been reeling under successive waves of persecutions. Besides, their anti-Roman resentment was quite strong. The dispute they had with the Catholics involved several factors and could not be easily resolved through customary judicial proceedings or by ecclesiastical councils. There were 'theological' reasons like that of the rigorism of the left wing and the mild approach of the 'so-called' *traditores* (traitors) and the lapsed. There were also issues of socio-economic importance. The Numidian Bishops, for instance, were closer to the poor and the agricultural workers than the Bishops of Proconsular Africa. The Numidians were also considered to be radicals who indulged in armed resistance against their overlords. These developments left their permanent mark in African Christianity. It has been noted that such tragic division, which so much weakened the African Christianity, could have been averted had a few Christians controlled their baser passions. However, the factors that contributed to the weakening of African Christianity cannot be wholly attributed to personal, national, social, and economic sentiments. The rise of Islam also played its part with its military invasion of Africa. But the Church could not recover its earlier vitality that had been shattered by the Donatist schism and hence could not put a strong resistance against the onslaught of Islam.[127] Had the African Church stood united, it could have averted major casualties when it was threatened from the external factors

Another intense trauma of irreconcilable division that occurred was the East-West schism.[128] The following factors must be noted for the alienation of the East from the West.

i. The linguistic affiliations of the Western and Eastern Churches often led to mutual spiritual and cultural encapsulations as well as misunderstandings that even extended up to theological terminologies. It has been noted that a highly calibered Pope like Gregory the Great could not speak Greek and the Byzantine Patriarchs could not speak Latin, which led them to depend on translators and secretaries for mutual communication.
ii. There was a lack of mutual respect for the differences in cultural and spiritual values between these two. Often the Greeks looked upon the Latins as uneducated and Barbaric, while the Latins viewed the Greeks as arrogant, pernickety and deceitful.

iii. Despite a shared dogma, the Eastern Churches grew with an independent form of Church life, liturgy, theology, worship, piety, Church law, constitution and organization. When the clergies of the East and West met, there was a sense of alienness – Married Eastern clergy and celibate Latin priests – indicative of an unbridgeable cultural gap.

iv. There was strong resentment among the Eastern Churches to accept the growing papal authority. The absolutist, monarchical, centralized and uniform Church that was in the making in the West was not a welcome model of ecclesia for the Easterners. The Eastern model of ecclesia begins not from the universal vicar (of Christ), but from the fellowship of believers (a model that Luther advanced in his ecclesiology), from the local Churches and their bishops. It was not the canon law but the sacraments, liturgy, and symbols of faith that stood at the centre of their Church life, understood in terms of a collegially ordered federal communion of the Churches.

v. The Patriarch of Constantinople came to establish the East's own canonical authority, and a Byzantine Church law. At this point, we must also admit that the Eastern Church understood itself as the Church of 'seven councils' (from Nicaea I in 325 to Nicaea II in 787), in that it preserved the original Church order far more strongly than the West. In matters pertaining to Christian life and Church order, the East had the New Testament as its fundamental guide than its Western counterpart, which mostly adhered to tradition.[129]

vi. The *filioque* clause that was interpolated into the Nicene Creed, which affirms the double procession of the Holy Spirit from the Father and the Son, became cause for a permanent disagreement between the East and the West.

Added to these divisions came the Reformation in the 16th century and it had deeper implications for the life, theology, and mission of the Church the world over.

Summary

With regard to the true image of the Church, it can be affirmed that even though ecclesia has undergone a number of trajectories in its worldwide journey, the essential inner constitution of the Church hinges on the communion of the believers with God and with the fellow believers. It embodies an intimacy that exists between the divine and human. Therefore, if the Church is to express itself as the body of Christ, it has to make its presence known through a set of relationships. The early phase of the life of the Church did demonstrate this relationship transcending narrow particularisms as evidenced by (a) the Church's ability to transcend its exclusiveness to embrace differences as in the Jewish-Gentile Christian encounter; and (b) the enthusiasm of the Church in Antioch (predominantly Gentile Church) to take initiative to financially support the Jerusalem Church (predominantly Jewish Church) in its crisis situation. This cannot be simply dismissed as mere altruism; rather it must be seen as the visible expression of their genuine solidarity with the fellow believers in their crisis, which grew out of their new consciousness of being united in Christ. And the Church continued its worldwide journey with vigour and vitality (despite its many inner weaknesses), providing new hope to a hurt and hurting world.

We shall now move on to investigate Martin Luther's thoughts on the Church, which grew out of his two primary concerns, namely, (a) a passionate desire to be in communion – communion with God and with fellow believers; and (b) to reform the Church of his time, which was in many ways obstructing to a meaningful communion due to some of the serious distortions of its life and theology. The Reformer firmly believed that the reform of the Church would lead to the reform of the society also because the Church was in control of the state. It was a situation in which the religious and temporal realms were so intertwined that the Church could take advantage of the spiritual powers to establish its supremacy over the temporal realm. Luther found that the Church, instead of being rooted in the Gospel of Christ and serving the people, had, in fact, turned out to be an instrument of oppression, especially of the weak and the vulnerable. Our concern in the ensuing chapter is to understand how the Reformer expounded the meaning of ecclesia within the parameters of his theological principle, *unity of the opposites*, which, in fact, provided a new thrust to his theological constructions and to the Reformation movement.

Notes

1 Hans Küng, *Christianity: Essence, History, Future* (New York: Continuum, 1995), p. 1.

2 For a discussion on this issue, see T. K. Oommen, "Religious Nationalism and Democratic Polity in India: Impossibility of Reconciliation" in Mark T. B. Laing, ed., *Nationalism and Hindutva: A Christian Response* – Papers from 10th CMS Conference (Delhi: CMS/UBS/ISPCK, 2005), p. 35-52.

3 For an informative reading on the way contemporary world deals with difference and 'otherness', see Robert Schreiter, *Reconciliation: Mission and Ministry in a Changing World Order* (Maryknoll, New York: Orbis Books, 1992), pp. 50ff.

4 Christopher Duraisingh, "Encountering Difference in a Plural World: A Pentecost Paradigm" in Ian T. Douglas, ed., *Waging Reconciliation: God's Mission in a Time of Globalization and Crisis* (New York: Church Publishing Incorporated, 2002), p. 187.

5 V. D. Savarkar, *Hindutva: Who is a Hindu?*, p. 17. In a provocative and most venomous speech in a rally organized in the aftermath of the killing of Swami Lakshmanananda and in the midst of the brutal killings of Christians, VHP leader Praveen Togadia alleged that it was Christians who killed Swami and, hence, the Church should be banned in Orissa (Source: CNN-IBN, 07 September, 2008).

6 Amartya Sen identifies this sort of disintegration of human relations as parochialism, segregationism, and external/internal isolationism. See *The Argumentative Indian*, pp. 65-86 & 289-349. For further discussion on the role of religious elements in these issues, see Bimal Prasad, *Pathway to India's Partition: The Foundations of Muslim Nationalism* Part I (Delhi: Manohar Publications, 1999).

7 See, for instance, the works such as: W. P. Hares, *History of the Christian Church of the first Six Centuries* (Madras: CLS, 2nd ed. 1975); Kenneth Scott Latourette, *History of Christianity* (London: Eyre and Spottishwoods, 1953); and Dale T. Irvin & Scott W. Sunquist, *History of the World Christian Movement* Vol. I *Earliest Christianity to 1453* (Bangalore: TPI 2004).

8 Hans Küng, *Christianity:Eessence, History, Future*, pp. 1-9.

9 Alister E. McGrath, *An Introduction to Christianity* (Cambridge, USA & Oxford, UK: Blackwell, 1997), pp. xix-xx.

10 Avery Dulles, *Models of the Church* (New York: Random House, Expanded Edition, 2002, 1st 1978).

11 J. Russell Chandran, *The Church in Mission: Some Reflections* (Madras: CLS, 1991), p. 70. See also K. C. Abraham, ed., *Ecumenism in Asia* (Bangalore: ATESEA & BTE-SSC, 1999); Mathai Zachariah, *Beyond Ecumenism: A journey into Light* (Thiruvalla: CSS, 2002); & Samuel Kobia, *Called to One Hope: A New Ecumenical Epoch* (Thiruvalla: CSS, 2007).

12 See Leonardo Boff, *Ecclesiologenesis: Base Communities Reinvent the Church* (Maryknoll, New York: Orbis Books, 1986).

13 Dale T. Irvin and Scott W. Sunquist, *History of the World Christian Movement*, p.vii.

14 See, for instance, Newton Flew, *Jesus and His Church: A study of the Idea of the Ecclesia in the New Testament* (London: Epworth Press, 1938); George Johnston, *The Doctrine of the Church* (London: Oxford University Press, 1943); R. Schnackenburgh, *The Church in the New Testament* (London: Burnes and Oates, 1965); and R. J. Mckelvey, *The New Temple: The Church in the New Testament* (London: Oxford University Press, 1969), pp. 701-731.

15 For an informative reading on the denial of the origin of ecclesia sayings from Jesus, see Eduard Schweizer, *Church Order in the New Testament* (Napervile: Alec R. Allenson, 1961), pp. 20-33.

16 Alfred Loisy, *The Gospel and the Church* (Philadelphia: Fortress Press, 1976), pp. 12-13.

17 For a detailed discussion on this problem, see Donald Guthrie, *New Testament Theology* (England: Inter-Varsity Press, 1981), pp. 701-731.

18 Alfred Loisy, for instance, quips: "Jesus announced the Kingdom of God, but it is the Church that had come". *The Gospel and the Church*, p. 13. To understand some of the serious charges of Westernization and cultural uprootment of the Indian Christians, see E. Stanley Jones, *Christ at the Round Table* (Lucknow: Lucknow Publishing House, Reprint 2007 of 1928), pp. 184-202.

19 Robert Schreiter, *The New Catholicity: Theology between the Global and Local* (Maryknoll, New York: Orbis Books, 1997), pp. 122-127. To understand some of the important transitions that occurred within Christianity, see John Mbiti, "Christianity Tilts to the South: A New Challenge for Christian Ministry and Theological Education" *Indian*

Journal of Theology Vol. 33, Nos. 1-3 (Jan-Sept, 1984), pp. 2ff & Alister E. McGrath, *An Introduction to Christianity*, p. xiv.

20 It is an undeniable fact that it is the Church (Christian missionaries), who carried the torch of education and health care to the remotest parts of India, i.e., to the most neglected and completely peripheralized human populations of the Indian society. This is not a story of the past but even today this is the real but obscured story of the Church in India. The "Niyogi Commission" constituted by the Government of India in 1954 to probe into the missionary activities in the state of Madhya Pradesh (which was otherwise extremely critical and negative about the missionary activities of 'proselytizing') did recognize the pioneering work of missionaries in the field of education and health care. See Sebastian C. H. Kim, "Hindutva, Secular India and the Report of the Christian Missionary Activities Enquiry Committee: 1954-57" in Mark. T. B. Laing, ed., *Nationalism and Hindutva*, p. 123. For a critical view of the Report of the Committee, see M. Hermanns and K. L. Fernandes, *Hinduism and Tribal Culture: An Anthropological Verdict on the Niyogi Report* (Bombay: CAB, 1957); and A. Soares, ed., *Truth Shall Prevail: Reply to Niyogi Committee* (Bombay: CAB, 1957).

21 A more recent text that enumerates the Indian Christian contribution towards nation building in detail is: K. M. George, *Christianity in India through the Centuries* (Secundrabad, India: Authentic Media, 2007), esp. Ch. 5: "The Impact of Indian Christianity on Indian Society", pp. 205-252.

22 Hans Küng, *The Church* (London: Burns & Oates, 1968), p. 6.

23 Hägglund, for instance, identifies a fundamental shift of emphasis in the teachings of the apostolic fathers, especially their emphasis is on what is called *moralism* (also called *nomism* and *legalism*) in comparison with the New Testament. In them, there is strong tendency to stress 'obedience to law' and 'imitation of Christ' as vitally important for salvation. See Bengt Hägglund, *History of Theology*, Tr by Gene J. Lund (Saint Louis: Concordia Publishing House, 3rd Edition, 1968), pp. 16-18.

24 See Juan Luis Segundo, *Grace and Human Condition* (Maryknoll, NY: Orbis Books, 1973), p. 17.

25 For a discussion on the Pelagian controversy, see Rebecca Harden Weaver, *Divine Grace and Human Agency: A study of the Semi-Pelagian Controversy* (Macon: Mercer University Press, 1996).

26 We might not enumerate the various images of the Church as we see in the scripture. What we intend in this section is to highlight those

images of ecclesia that proclaim the new relationship that God has inaugurated in Jesus Christ. For a reading on the various images of the Church readers may consult Paul S. Minear, *Images of the Church in the New Testament* (Louisville, KY: Westminster John Knox Press, 1960). In this volume, Minear identifies as many as ninety-six images of the Church.

27 See Luke Timothy Johnson, "Making Connections: The Material Expression of Friendship in the New Testament" in *Interpretation* (April 2004), pp. 158-171.

28 The theological significance of the expression "people" is that even though they eventually constituted themselves to be a nation, they preferred to understand themselves as a "people" rather than a "nation" because, while the latter had a predominantly political connotation, the former had, at the same time, a sociological-cultural-theological connotation, signifying that they are "the people of Yahweh" (*am Yahwâh*). Frank S. Frick, "People, Peoples" in *Harper's Bible Dictionary*, p. 770.

29 Bernhard W. Anderson, *Understanding the Old Testament* (London: Prentice-Hall, 1966), p. 374.

30 See Jacques Rossel, *The Roots of Western Europe: An Essay on Interpretation of Cultures During the First Nine Centuries A.D.* (Bangalore: ATC, 2001), p. 55.

31 For a detailed discussion on the changing patterns of social units, see Gillian Clark, *Christianity and the Roman Society* (Cambridge, UK: Cambridge University Press, 2004).

32 Studies on the theme "Israel as the People of God" reveal that the terms *edhah* and *qahal*, along with other similar terms such as *am*, *miqra* have the general meaning of gathering, assembly, congregation, convocation etc. Of these, *edhah* and *qahal* are the frequently used terms to refer to the people of Israel, identifying them as a religious/cult community. See B. Jayaraj, "The People of God in the Priestly Source" *The Indian Journal of Theology* Vol. 28, Nos. 3 &4 (July - Dec 1979), pp. 129-130. Biblical scholarship identifies a close connection between the Old Testament "*edahah/qahal* of Yahweh" and the New Testament *ekklesia*. See Mathew Vellanickal, "The Church in the Bible" *The Indian Journal of Theology* Vol. 28, Nos. 3 &4 (July - Dec 1979), pp. 109-115 & M. Mariaselvam, "The Church according to the Prophetic Tradition" *The Indian Journal of Theology* Vol. 28, Nos. 3 &4 (July - Dec 1979), pp. 135-142.

33 Evelyn Monterio, *Church and Culture: Communion in Pluralism* (Delhi: ISPCK, 2004), p. 8. For an analysis of the use of the term *ekklesia* (Church) in the secular Roman world and in Christianity, see Gillian Clark, *Christianity and Roman Society*, pp. 21ff.

34 For a discussion on the use of the term *ekklesia* in Septuagint and its Christian development, see Robert Banks, *Paul's Idea of Community* (Massachusetts: Hendrickson Publishers, 1994), pp. 26-40.

35 A. Mariaselvam, "The Church according to the Prophetic Tradition", p. 137. At this point, we are also cautioned not to privilege the exodus model for the fact that the Israelites, the once enslaved has turned out to be an oppressive force in contemporary history.

36 When God made the covenant with the patriarch (Gen 17), his older name was *Abram* (meaning, "May the divine Father be exalted"); and his new name was *Abraham* ("Father of a multitude"). Bernhard W. Anderson, *Understanding the Old Testament*, p. 387.

37 According to Woodhead, this was a "new ingredient" added to the spiritual melting pot of the time of Jesus by groups who looked to him for authority, which can be seen as the early Christians' use of the genre of Gospel as a way of presenting their own interpretation of Jesus, i.e., "a mode of theological construction than of strict historical record". Linda Woodhead, *An Introduction to Christianity* (Cambridge, UK: Cambridge University Press, 2004), pp. 20f.

38 Also see Pheme Perkins, "Messiah" in *Harper's Bible Dictionary*, p. 630.

39 In a recent study, Paul Barnett asserts with astute certainty that Jesus was identified as the Christ by his followers in his life time itself. In his concluding remarks, he affirms: "Speaking personally, my own long-held belief is that the historical Jesus was the Christ, both in his own mind and eventually also in the minds of the disciples...that he was the Christ is the hypothesis that makes best sense of all the evidence both before and after resurrection." See Paul Barnett, *Finding the Historical Christ*, After Jesus, Vol. 3 (Grand Rapids: Wm B. Eerdmans, 2009), p. 269.

40 Linda Woodhead, *An Introduction to Christianity*, p. 25.

41 Woodhead, for instance, alleges: "To become a Christian was to abandon loyalty to competing institutions and join one of the Christian communities". *An Introduction to Christianity*, p. 25.

42 Daniel Jenkins, *The Strangeness of the Church* (New York: Doubleday, 1955), p. 10.

43 For a more informative reading on this, see Pralay Kanungo, "Hindutva's Fury against Christians in Orissa" *Economic and Political Weekly* (September 13, 2008), pp. 16-19.

44 See Francois Gautier, "What Made Hindus Angry in Karnataka" *The New Indian Express* (October 06, 2008), p. 9.

45 Quoted from Rajashekara, "Saffron Terror" *The New Indian Express* (September 28, 2008), p. 2.

46 See *Dinakaran* (07 October 2008), p. 18.

47 Adolf von Harnack, *Militia Christi: The Christian Religion and the Military in the First Three Centuries*, Tr. by David McInnes Gracie (Philadelphia: Fortress Press, 1981), p. 27.

48 Hindu fanaticism is further transformed into terrorism (e.g., the case related to the 2008 Malegaon bomb blast), which the Home Minister referred to as *Saffron Terror*. See Teesta Setelvad, "Bomb versus Bomb" *The New Indian Express* (Nov. 12, 2008), p. 10. Of course, new evidences of saffron terror are surfacing. (CNN-IBN, 06 Jan 2011).

49 See Paul Tilich, *A History of Christian Thought* (New York: Simon and Schuster, 1968), pp. 1-9. For a detailed discussion on the influence of philosophy on Christian theology see Colin Brown, *Philosophy and the Christian Faith* (Illinois: Inter Varsity Press, 1968).

50 See Roy Bhasker, *Reflections on Meta-Reality: Transcendence, Emancipation and Everyday Life* (New Delhi: Sage Publications, 2002); and Mary C. Grey, *Prophecy and Mysticism: The Heart of Postmodern Church* (Edinburgh: T & T Clark, 1997).

51 S. Painadath, ed., *Jesus and Society: Selected Writings of Sebastian Kappen*, Vol. 1 (Delhi: ISPCK, 2002), pp. 208f.

52 Gillian Clark, *Christianity and Roman Society*, p. 6.

53 Tertullian, *Apology*, 50:13-14, 197 CE.

54 For a discussion on the meaning and motives of martyrdom, see G. Bowersock, *Martyrdom and Rome* (Cambridge: Cambridge University Press, 1995) & L. Alexander, "Foolishness to the Greeks: Jews and Christians in the Public Life of the Empire" in G. Clark and T. Rajak, eds., *Philosophy and Power in the Graeco-Roman World* (Oxford: Oxford University Press, 1995), pp. 229-249.

55 Gillian Clark, *Christianity and Roman Society*, p. 39.

56 J. Perkins, *The Suffering Self: Pain and Narrative Representation in the Early Christian Era* (London: SCM Press, 1995).

57 For an informative reading on martyrdom and a critique for and against such narratives, see Gillian Clark, "Bodies and blood: Martyrdom, Virginity and Resurrection in Late Antiquity" in D. Montserata, ed.,

Changing Bodies, Changing Meaning: Studies on the Human Body in Late Antiquity (London: SCM Press, 1998), pp. 99-115; and M. Tilley, *Donatist Martyr Stories: The Church in Conflict in Roman North Africa* (Liverpool: Liverpool University Press, 1996), pp. 48ff.

58 See Gillian Clark, *Christianity and Roman Society*, p. 49.

59 Donald Guthrie, *New Testament Theology*, p. 712.

60 In the Septuagint, two predominant terms are used to designate the people of God: 'assembly' (*ekklēsia*) and 'synagogue' (*synagogē*). Since the Jews in the first century used the term *synagogē*, the first century Greek-speaking Christians adopted the term *ekklēsia* in order to show that their roots lay in the Old Testament and that they continued to be the Old Testament people of God. (Cf. 1 Pet 2:9 & Ex 19:5-6 and the Christians are called Abraham's descendents – Gal 3:29). See Ernest Best, "Church" in *Harper's Bible Dictionary*, pp. 168-170

61 Hans Küng, *The Church*, p. 115.

62 Cf. K. F. Nickle, *The Collection: A Study in Paul's Strategy* (London: SCM Press, 1966).

63 Paul has three key images in his exposition of the community: the image of the head and the body, the image of the bride, and the image of the building. For a detailed study of the various NT images of the Church, see Paul Sevier Minear, *Images of the Church in the New Testament* (Westminster: John Knox Press, 1960) in which the author examines as many as ninety-six images.

64 Donald Guthrie, *Theology of the New Testament*, p. 742. However, there are other critics who regard that Paul cannot be considered to be the founder of a universal concept of the Church. See Eduard Schweizer, *Church Order in the New Testament*, pp. 105 ff.

65 Robert Banks, *Paul's Idea of Community*, pp. 7ff.

66 Donald Guthrie, *New Testament Theology*, p. 741.

67 This is best illustrated by the 'historic' signing of the document: "Joint Declaration on the Doctrine of Justification" between the Lutheran and Roman Catholic Churches on 31 October 1999 at Augsburg. The Lutheran Church-Missouri Synod (which was not a partner in the signing of the document), for instance, is in no mood to accept the formula "doctrinal disagreement is not necessarily divisive". See the following documents: The full text of "Righteous Before God: An Agreement on the Doctrine of Justification", a document prepared by the Lutheran World Federation (LWF) in consultation with the Pontifical Council for Promoting Christian Unity (PCPCU), released in print form and in a Video film by the LWF, Nov. 1999. See also

The Joint Declaration on the Doctrine of Justification in the Confessional Lutheran Perspective (St. Louis, Missouri: CTCR- LCMS, 1999) & *The Formula of Agreement in Confessional Lutheran Perspective* (St. Louis, Missouri: CTCR, LCMS, 1999).

68 For more discussion, see Vincent Branick, *The House Church in the Writings of Paul* (Wilmington, USA: Michael Glacier, 1989).

69 There is a strong criticism that Paul's conception of the community emerged from his predominant ethical principle of "love-patriarchalism" (*lieberpatriarchalismus*), an integrative ethic, which does not intent to challenge or change the forces that consistently work to foster economic and social stratification nor does it champion a particular social or economic status. Conversely, love-patriarchalism urges Christians to transcend such distinctions within the framework of a religious community, which generates mutual love and respect. See John H. Shütz, "Introduction" in Gerd Theissen, *The Social Settings of Pauline Christianity* (Edinburgh: T & T Clark, 1982), pp.11ff.

70 Robert Banks, *Paul's Idea of Community*, pp. 59ff.

71 For a brief discussion on the use of the Torah in Jewish cultic practices, see Gunther Bornkamm, *Early Christian Experience* (New York: Harper and Row, 1969), especially the section, "On Understanding Worship", pp. 161-179. See also Robert Banks, *Paul's Idea of Community*, pp. 107ff.

72 Robert Banks, *Paul's Idea of Community*, p. 108.

73 Donald Guthrie, *New Testament Theology*, p. 702. For a discussion on the relationship between the kingdom and the Church, see George Eldon Ladd, *The Presence of the Future: Eschatology of Biblical Realism* (Grand Rapids, Michigan: Wm B. Eerdmans, 1974), pp. 239-273, and Hans Küng, *The Church*, pp. 88ff.

74 R. N. Flew, *Jesus and His Church*, p. 22. Flew points out that at least during the first four centuries such a notion was alien to the community of believers.

75 Guthrie points out that in Mt. 16:18f, the ideas of the Church and the Kingdom are mentioned together and their meanings seem to be closely related. Donald Guthrie, *New Testament Theology*, p. 703. Conzelmann, however, argues that Jesus did not found a Church, because Jesus was more concerned about his eschatological vocation and the awareness of that in him does not permit any notion of a present Church. Hans Conzelmann, *Outline of the Theology of the New Testament* (London: SCM Press, 1969), p. 33.

76 Scholars will contest this interpretation as too general to link it up to ecclesia. See Herman. N. Ridderbos, *The Coming of the Kingdom* (Grand Rapids, Michigan: Wm B. Eerdmans, 1997), pp. 346ff.

77 For a brief discussion on this line of thinking see, Kune E. Biezeveld, "The Kingdom of God and the Mission of the Church" in Christine Lienemann-Perrin, Hendrik M. Vroom and Michael Weinrich, eds., *Reformed and Ecumenical: On Being Reformed in Ecumenical Encounters* (Amsterdam - Atlanta: Rodopi, 2000), pp. 42-59.

78 Kune E. Biezeveld, "The Kingdom of God and the Mission of the Church", p. 45.

79 Charles Harold Dodd, *Parables of the Kingdom* (London: Nisbet & Co., 1936); and Rudolf Bultmann, *Theology of the New Testament* (London: SCM Press, 1965).

80 Gustavo Gutierrez, *A Theology of Liberation: History, Politics and Salvation* (London: SCM Press, 1974), pp. 160-231. See also Jon Sobrino, *Jesus the Liberator: A Historical-Theological Reading of Jesus of Nazareth*, Tr. by Paul Burns and Francis McDonagh (Kent: Burns & Oates, 1994), p. 82-110; Jon Sobrino, *Christology at the Crossroads – A Latin American approach*, Tr. by John Drury (Maryknoll, New York: Orbis Books, 1978), pp. 44ff; M. H. Ellis and Otto Maduro, eds., *The Future of Liberation Theology* (Maryknoll, New York: Orbis Books, 1989).

81 Werner Georg Kümmel, *Promise and Fulfillment: The Eschatological Message of Jesus* (London: SCM Press, 1961), pp. 150ff.

82 Hindutva does exactly the same as it demands Christians to discard their Palestinian connections and alleges that the foundation of the Church's mission is built on the fantasy of the later followers of the Church. See Arun Shourie, *Harvesting Our Souls*, pp. 360-370.

83 Gillian Clark, *Christianity and Roman Society*, p. 61. According to Küng, Asceticism/Monasticism originated not within Christianity and not even in Judaism, but an old Indian institution. The Upanishads already laid out certain reasons as to why renunciation can be one of the supreme virtues. Further, central to Buddhism lies monasticism. This means that there were striking similarities between Hindu, Buddhist and Christian spiritualities. See Hans Küng, *Christianity: Essence, History and Future*, pp. 216f.

84 A. Cameron, *Christianity and the Rhetoric of the Empire: the Development of Christian Discourse* (Berkeley, CA: University of California Press, 1991), pp. 79-118.

85 For an informative reading on the Desert Fathers and their life/ministry, see G. Gould, *The Desert Fathers and Monastic community* (Oxford, UK: Oxford University Press, 1993) and Helen Waddell, *Desert Fathers* (London: Constable & Co., 1936).

86 Gillian Clark, *Christianity and Roman Society*, p. 62

87 T. Shaw, *The burden of the Flesh: Fasting and Sexuality in early Christianity* (Minneapolis: University of Minnesota Press, 1998), pp. 58ff.

88 For a discussion on certain other Christian attitudes developed in line with the idea of renunciation, see A. Cameron, *Christianity and the Rhetoric of the Empire* (op. cit.), pp. 79-118. An important point that this volume discusses is Christian attitude to the State, which has certain important features. Christians certainly showed great determination in refusing to worship the emperors, but that had never deterred them from being loyal citizens, perhaps in accordance with Jesus' warrant: "Render unto Caesar what is Caesar's" and also with Paul's directives to obey the temporal authority and pay taxes to the State because even State authorities were God's servants to look after the welfare of the citizens.

89 Joseph L. Mangina, "Ecumenical Theology" in Trevor A. Hart et al., eds., *The Dictionary of Historical Theology*, p. 171.

90 Dale T. Irvin and Scott W. Sunquist, H*istory of the World Christian Movement* Vol. 1, p. 40.

91 Some of the most important source materials pertaining to various controversial teachings and the reactions to those teachings by the Church Fathers are listed below: (1) James M. Robinson, ed., *The Nag Hammadi Library in English* (San Francisco: Harper Collins, 3rd edition, 1988). This is the translation of the fifty-two tractates of the ancient texts, many of them by Gnostic writers, discovered in a cave at Nag Hammadi in Egypt in 1945, which drove the researchers of New Testament, early Christian history and theology to reassess what had been said about the Gnostics and eventually about other 'heretics'. (2) Alexander Roberts and James Donaldson, eds., *The Ante-Nicene Fathers*, 10 Vols. (First Published in 1885-97 and Reprinted by Peabody, Massachusetts: Hendrickson Publishers, 1994). (3) Cyril C. Richardson, ed., *Early Christian Fathers*, Library of Christian Classics 1 (Philadelphia: Westminster Press, 1953). (4) Eusebius, *The History of the Church from Christ to Constantine*, Tr. by G. A. Williamson (Minneapolis: Augsburg Publishing House, 1975). (5) Werner Foerster, ed., *Gnosis: A Selection of Gnostic Texts*, 2 Vols. (Oxford: Clarendon Press, 1972-74). (6) Robert M. Grant, ed., *Gnosticism: A Source Book of*

Heretical Writings from the Early Christian Period (New York: Harper & Brothers, 1961). (7) Irenaeus, *Against Heresies*, Tr. by Dominic J. Unger (New York: Paulist Press, 1992). (8) St. Justin Martyr, *The Fathers of the Church*, Vol. 6, Tr. by Thomas B. Falls (New York: Christian Heritage, 1949). (9) *Tertullian Adversus Marcionem*, 2 Vols., Tr. by Ernest Evans (Oxford: Clarendon Press, 1972).

92 It has been a truism that heretical writings, and ideas have been transmitted to us mainly by those who fought against them. Hence, it will not be fair to lend full credibility of truth to the apologists or to the heretics as they reported the views of their opponents. In such situations, it is customary to lean towards the victors. But we need to assess the accounts of the victors in conjunction with those of the opponents. For a detailed account of this issue, see Arland J. Hultgren and Steven A. Haggmark, eds., *The Earliest Christian Heretics: Readings from Their Opponents* (Minneapolis: Fortress Press, 1996).

93 Arland J. Hultgren and Steven A. Haggmark, eds., *The Earliest Christian Heresies*, p. 7.

94 Walter Bauer, *Orthodoxy and Heresy in Earliest Christianity* (Philadelphia: Fortress Press, 1971, first published 1934), pp. 53, 230-240.

95 Oscar Skarsaune, *Incarnation: Myth or Fact?* (St. Louis, Missouri: Concordia Publishing House, 1991). In this volume, the author deals with this issue in fair detail. See also V. C. Samuel, *The Council of Chalcedon Re-examined: A Historical Theological Survey* (Delhi: ISPCK, 2001), pp. 3-43 wherein the author deals with the events (controversies) leading up to Chalcedon.

96 This view is advanced by Eliaine H. Pagels, "Christology in Dialogue with Gnosticism" in R. F. Berkeley and Sarah A. Edwards, eds., *Christology in Dialogue* (Cleveland: Pilgrim Press, 1993), 79ff.

97 Justin Martyr, "Dialogue with Trypho" in Alexander Roberts and James Donaldson, eds., *The Ante-Nicene Fathers: Translations of the Writings of the Fathers Down to AD. 325*, Vol. 1, p. 219.

98 Oscar Skarsaune, *Incarnation: Myth or Fact?*, p. 47.

99 Origen, *Against Celsus* in *Ante-Nicene Fathers*, Vol. 4, p. 502.

100 Ibid., p. 504. It has to be noted that the divine Christ pulls off at crucifixion in Gnostic Christologies.

101 Ibid., p. 543

102 As cited in Jacques Rossel, *The Roots of Western Europe*, p. 255 from H. Leitzmann, *History of the Ancient Church*.

103 Rodney Stark, *For the Glory of God: How Monotheism let to Reformations, Science, Witch-Hunts, and the End of Slavery* (Princeton and Oxford: Princeton University Press, 2003), pp. 15ff.

104 Through the 'Edict of Milan' (313), see Jacques Rossel, *The Roots of Western Europe*, p. 255.

105 For a detailed account of Constantine's conversion and its aftermath, see Jacques Rossel, *The roots of Western Europe*, pp. 227-285 & Hans Küng, *Christianity*, pp. 176ff.

106 Hans Küng, *Christianity*, p. 176.

107 Richard Fletcher, *The Barbarian Conversion: From Paganism to Christianity* (New York: Henry Holt, 1997), pp. 38ff.

108 Rodney Stark, *For the Glory of God*, p. 34. R. Bainton, *Christendom: A Short History of Christianity and Its Impact on Western Civilization*, Vol. I (New York: Harper & Row, 1966), pp. 124f.

109 Stark lists out about twelve Popes – from Pope Innocent I (401-417) up to Benedict IX (1032-1044) – who occupied this coveted office and who were either sons or grandsons of previous Popes. Rodney Stark, *For the Glory of God*, p. 34. For further discussion on the issue of clericalism within the Church and papacy being ruled by blood-relatives of successive Popes, see Eamon Duffy, *Saints and Sinners: A History of Popes* (New Haven: Yale University Press, 1997); and Nicholas Cheetham, *Keepers of the Keys: A History of Popes from St. Peter to John Paul II* (New York: Charles Scribner's Sons, 1983).

110 R. MacMullen, *Christianizing the Roman Empire* (New Haven: Yale University Press, 1984), pp. 91ff.

111 As cited in Rodney stark, *For the Glory of God*, p. 35. This does not, however, intend to portray the Pagans as a pious group. Far from being pious, they also rioted and reacted violently against the Christianizing project of the Church. In 356, a bishop in Alexandria was murdered and another bishop in Syria was lynched by a Pagan mob, following the destruction of a temple. See R. MacMullen, *Christianizing the Roman Empire*, p. 91.

112 R. MacMullen, *Christianizing the Roman Empire*, p. 101.

113 As cited by Rodney Stark, *For the Glory of God*, pp. 49f. For a detailed account of the campaign and the Crusades, see Christoph Maier, *Preaching the Crusades: Mendicant Friars and the Cross in the Thirteenth Century* (Cambridge: Cambridge University Press, 1994).

114 Dale T. Irvin and Scott W. Sunquist, *History of the World Christian Movement*, Vol. I, p. 395.

115 Hans Küng, *Christianity*, p. 400.

116 Hans Küng, *Christianity*, p. 398.

117 Amatya Sen, *Identity and Violence: The Illusion of Destiny* (London: Penguin Books, 2006), pp. 11f; see also pp. 1-17 & 40-58

118 Dale T. Irvin and Scott W. Sunquist, *History of the World Christian Movement*, Vol. I, p. 395.

119 Hans Küng, *Christianity* (op. cit.), p. 399. For more reading on the crusades in the 12th and 13th centuries, see Küng, *Christianity*, pp. 395-401.

120 For an account of the early schisms, see S. L. Greenslade, *Schism in the Early Church* (London: SCM Press, 1953), pp. 15-34 & 37ff.

121 For a detailed discussion on this issue, see Hans Küng, *Christianity* (op. cit), pp. 398-401; Rodney Stark, *One True God: Historical Consequences of Monotheism* (Princeton: Princeton University Press, 2001), pp 48-67, 246-255; and Robert Chazan, *European Jewry and the First Crusade* (Berkeley, CA: University of California Press, 1986).

122 W Jaeger, *Early Christianity and Greek Paideia* (London: Harvard University Press, 1961), pp. 13-57.

123 S. L. Greenslade, *Schism in the Early Church*, pp. 38ff.

124 See S. L. Greenslade, *Schism in the Early Church*, pp. 38ff & Hans Küng, *Christianity*, pp. 153ff.

125 R. H. Bainton, *Christendom*, pp. 96-97.

126 Jacques Rossel, *Roots of Western Europe*, pp. 286-289.

127 For a detailed discussion on the rise of Islam and its impact on Christianity see Dale T. Irvin and Scott W. Sunquist, *History of the World Christian Movement*, Vol. I, pp. 260-304.

128 For a detailed account of this schism, see Hans Küng, *Christianity*, pp.216-278 and S.L. Greenslade, *Schism in the Early Church*.

129 Hans Küng, *Christianity*, pp. 243-246.

Chapter Four

ECCLESIA IN MARTIN LUTHER'S THOUGHT

Ecclesiological Task

From a biblical vantage point, ecclesia is the "communion of believers" called by Jesus Christ 'out of darkness into his marvelous light in order to proclaim his wonderful deeds in this world'. (1 Peter 2:9). It is a communion held together by the Spirit, informed by the Word, and marked by the proclamation of the Gospel. Church is universal with particular historical expressions and it has an eschatological vision of making the will of God real, i.e., proclaiming God's plan of creating the new humanity and/or the new heaven and the new earth in Jesus Christ (2 Cor. 5:17, Is 65:17-25, Rev 21:1). Its inner characteristic is the communion of believers, which entails that the inner constitution of ecclesia is a new quality of intimate relationship among the members of this communion, an intimacy whose source is the Divine initiative to reconcile the world with God in Christ. This intimacy, I believe, was particularly appealing to the world around the Church's early existence because it served as a credible pointer to a new quality of life in sharp contrast to the life in conflict.[1] If the inner constitution of ecclesia is intimacy, then, its fundamental evangelical mission is to point to this new relationship to a world riddled with fragmentation, conflict, despair, suffering, misery, incertitude, and meaninglessness. In other words, it is the ministry of reconciliation and healing as represented in 2 Cor. 5:17-20, which must be the priority and preoccupation of the Church. This is an important task, especially in the context of Hindutva's anti-other discourse. It requires adequate theological resources, and in this study Martin Luther's thought on the Church has been identified as a helpful resource to accomplish this task. This chapter, then, endeavors to analyse Luther's thoughts on ecclesia.

Opinions vary with regard to the Reformer and his theological articulations. In his diatribe against the Reformer and his theology, Richard Niebhur maintains:

> Honestly and naïvely the peasants of Germany had believed that Luther's appeal to the New Testament was not an appeal to Pauline theology alone but to the ethics of the Sermon on the Mount as well. All too soon they discovered that the new Protestantism they had espoused so heartily *protested less against their masters than against their masters' enemies* and that the new faith dealt with their extreme necessities even less effectively than did the old...From Luther they learned that they could not look to Protestantism for salvation from the dual standard which bade rulers rule in accordance with the code of Old Testament precepts of strict reward and punishment while it required subjects to obey their political and economic masters in the spirit of a Christian and self-sacrificing meekness.[2] [Emphasis added]

Hans Küng, on the other hand, seems to be more positive in his analysis of the Reformation and Reformation theology as he affirms:

> No break since the Gregorian reform of the eleventh century and the breakthrough of the Roman Catholic paradigm in Western Christianity was deeper and more momentous than the Lutheran Reformation. In the sixteenth century Martin Luther initiated a new era: a further paradigm shift for the Church, theology and Christianity generally, away from the Roman Catholic paradigm of the Middle Ages to the Protestant Evangelical paradigm of the Reformation.[3]

In an attempt to understand Luther's theological thought and its contemporary appeal, Klaus Nürnberger, a South African theologian, affirms with great exhilaration:

> Martin Luther is amazing. Immerse yourself in his work and you will not easily get out of it again. It is always tantalizingly fresh, always a direct response to actual issues of life, never stale doctrine, never mental gymnastics. You may be profoundly comforted, radically challenged, deeply offended – but you cannot help being struck. Luther's legacy is a prototype of an existential, experiential, contextual theology. During the conflict-ridden decades of my career as a lecturer of theology in South Africa, I have repeatedly become aware of the extraordinary relevance and power such theology is able to develop under most diverse circumstances.[4]

Luther's thoughts come to us not as an exhaustively worked out theological system and our approach to his thoughts is self-consciously critical because they were ignited by his encounter with the emerging socio-political-religious issues and the influence of other existing philosophical and theological factors.[5] We would commence our enquiry on Luther's thoughts on the Church with his emergence as the Reformer.

Martin Luther, the Reformer

Martin Luther (1483 – 1546),[6] the Augustinian monk, was a devout pastor of the Church and a dedicated student of the Bible. His theology has often been called the theology of the Word of God. In 1510, the vicar-general of the Augustinian priory sent Luther to Rome with an appeal to the pope on certain issues pertaining to the cloister and the journey had historic consequences, for Luther was deeply perturbed by the worst excesses like the callousness, open blasphemy and impiety of the priests even when they celebrated the mass.[7] Such impiety of the clergy and his unhappiness over the life of the Church, however, did not motivate him to leave the Church. Instead, he committed himself to remain within and reform it.

The time of Luther's emergence coincided with the bewildering moments of crisis across Europe and the people looked up to the Church for credible signs of hope to the future. But the medieval

Church appeared to be callous towards the calamities of the masses as it was busy exhibiting and establishing its temporal authority. The reformation movement grew out of Luther's conflict with the papacy's abuses of its privileged position and the initial spark emanated from his frontal attack on the ingenious marketing of indulgences, which was challenged by Luther through his famous *Ninety-five Theses*.[8] The Reformation movement had, in fact, made its deeper impacts on the world, which can perhaps be understood as the impact of the Reformer's career as the member of the university faculty. For his impact was not confined within the enclaves of ecclesia and academia alone. Rather it had become resonant in almost all domains of European life. As Ebeling states:

> In the case of Martin Luther there are special reasons for bearing in mind that the university was the primary place in which his life and work was conducted. The various pictures we have of him: the former monk, the preacher, the writer, the reformer of the Church, the spiritual leader of a popular movement which spread throughout Europe, make it very easy to forget that his work as a university professor was not just incidental to his other work. In fact, the rest of his work was immediately related to his university post, and the obligation this imposed was expressed in his doctorate, a degree which at that time was still rare, and one which was held by very few professors.[9]

The extent of the influence of his career on his thinking can further be illustrated by his own words: "In the course of this teaching, the papacy slipped away from me".[10] This reminiscence, made about fourteen years after the nailing of his ninety-five theses on the door of the All Saints Church at Wittenberg, makes it clear that his academic career as a professor along with his continuous preaching ministry was his starting point and a firm foundation that enabled him to set in motion the revolutionary movement called the Protestant Reformation. As Ebeling further exclaims, it was unprecedented in the history of any university that the work of a scholar, in his study and lecture rooms, made such an impact upon the world and brought about revolutionary changes, not only in the theological realm but also in the secular world! This is one of the most important aspects that drew not only theologians, but also academicians from other disciplines: historians, philosophers, psychologists, philologists, and legal historians to study Luther. It draws us to the middle ages in which Luther lived and engaged in his theological imagination.

Middle Ages

The middle ages exhibited at least four differentiated periods of religious and political significance. (i) *The period of Transition* 600-1000 CE: The year 600 marks the papacy of Gregory the great, in whom we can identify an interest to preserve the old and to receive the new. It was an era marked by a transition from the ancient to the medieval world – a period sometimes called the *dark ages*,[11] especially the 9th and 10th centuries. (ii) *Early Middle Ages* 1000-1200 CE: It was a period of novelty, in which new and original forms of ideas developed which were decisively different from the ancient world and it was a creative period represented by Roman arts. (iii) *High Middle Ages* 1200-1300 CE: It was a period in which all the basic religious and social motifs were developed and configured into the systems of the scholastics, Gothic art, and feudal life. (iv) *Late Middle Ages* 1300-1450 CE: This was a period of the disintegration of the middle ages. Nevertheless, this period set the stage for both Renaissance and Reformation.

Paul Tillich identifies three predominant attitudes of cognitive, intellectual, and theological significance the medieval world had brought to light and set the stage for Reformation: Scholasticism, Mysticism, and Biblicism.

Scholasticism was an attempt to provide a methodological explanation to the content of the Christian faith for the rational minds, which was a determinative intellectual enterprise. The term *scholastic* is derived from the word *school*, which implies that it is a philosophy taught in school. To a large extent, scholasticism remained far removed from ordinary life during the medieval period. Even though the real intention of scholasticism was the theological interpretation of all problems of life, scholastic education was available only to a few upper class people because scholastic literature was produced in Latin, a language known only to the educated upper class.

Mysticism was characterized by a desire to attain personal experience of the divine in every sphere of life. In a rather narrow sense, every scholastic was a mystic, i.e., a person with deep personal experience of what *he* was talking about. The basis of this mystical experience was the unity with the divine through devotion, meditation, prayer and ascetic practices. Beside scholasticism and mysticism, the middle age was characterized by another trend called Biblicism.

Biblicism was strong during this period. It was an attempt to postulate Bible as the norm and criterion for practical Christianity especially for the laity. It enabled many lay people to read the Bible even before Reformation. In most cases these three attitudes were combined in one person. In short, scholasticism was the theology of the middle ages; mysticism was the personal experiential piety; and Biblicism was the critical reaction emerging from the Biblical tradition, penetrating into the other two attitudes and finally culminating into the Reformation.[12]

The publication of the complete works of Aristotle formed a crucial turning point in the intellectual history during the early medieval period. At first there were voices of protest against the use of this metaphysics to explain Christian faith. But this objection was overcome by the realization that there was a great possibility in this system to bring faith and reason in harmony and to construct a comprehensive and systematic intellectual unity conjoining the natural and supernatural. Aquinas worked out a comprehensive system of reality following the logic: "[S]ince grace does not destroy nature, but perfects it, the natural reason must serve faith, in the same way as the natural inclination of the will follows love".[13] Aristotelian concept of knowledge was, thus, firmly established and theology came to be known as rational knowledge with the presumptions that (a) there was no contradiction between philosophy and theology; and (b) Aristotle was indispensable for theology.[14] Luther found this as a 'distortion' of theology for, in his view, it was a deviation from the Scripture and he opposed the theology-philosophy/faith-reason synthesis as he argued:

> It is an error to say that without Aristotle no one can become a theologian. On the contrary, one only becomes a theologian when one does so without Aristotle. The assertion that a theologian who is not a logician is an abominable heretic is itself abominable and heretical...In short, the whole of Aristotle is related to theology as darkness is to light.[15]

Of course, Luther was not alone in this fight against the faith-reason interface. About two hundred years before him William of Ockham protested against Aquinas' vision of faith-reason synthesis. Ockham had two perceptible strands of thought: an emphasis on the influence of a genuine religious feeling in theology that is completely different from philosophy for theology rests on faith within the parameters of the authority of revelation; and an intensified and formalist use of reason that maintained Church doctrine as beyond rational verification, and its authority as resting on a positive source of an otherwise unknowable truth.[16] Being educated in the Ockhamist tradition, Luther regarded himself as a nominalist[17] and was highly critical about Aristotle. In his view, Aristotelian terminology and method of enquiry had obscured the genuine understanding of the Holy Scripture. Accordingly, for him, true wisdom is not the knowledge of an arbitrary object attained by human reason, but something specifically biblical, namely the wisdom of the cross of Christ, i.e. faith in Christ.[18]

Medieval Church

There is a conspicuous absence of any special place for the doctrine of the Church in the systems of medieval theologians. This might perhaps be due to the general perception that the church's existence was self-evident as it was the foundation of all life and not a matter of a special doctrine. Here we need to find an answer to the question: what is the relation of the Church to the Kingdom of God? For in the answer to this question hinges a host of other elements of ecclesiology such as the relation of the Church to the secular power, culture, and politics. The background to this is Augustine's interpretation of the Church.[19] In Augustine, we find much reluctance – a dilemma –

to fully identify or separate the Church and the Kingdom of God because he was aware of the fact that the Church comprised of a mixed body of people – people who formally belonged to the Church but in reality they did not. Nevertheless, the Church attempted to identify itself with the Kingdom of God in terms of its hierarchical graces. Similarly, in Augustine there was also a tendency to identify the state with the kingdom of Satan, partly because he viewed the states as "robber states" – states fashioned after a group of gangsters capable of taking the state into their hands.[20] Augustine's view was influenced greatly by his context when the Roman Empire, and later Germanic-Romanic kingdoms remained domains of non-Christian powers and the substance of ancient culture was not yet replaced by the religious substance of the Church. This situation, however, changed with the expansion of Christianity towards the West. Now the Church became the agent of the cultural substance, the power which determined the individual relations, expressions of art, knowledge, ethics, social relations, human relation to nature, and all other forms of human life.[21] In such a situation one could no longer designate the state as the kingdom of Satan because now the substance of the state was also that of the Church.

In the middle ages, there arose a general discomfiture among the people over the moral-spiritual decadence within the Church. A number of revival movements, namely, the monastic movements, lay movements, and the renaissance humanism of Desiderius Erasmus took shape during this period. They attempted to renew the Church and rescue it from the signs of decadence, purify its abuses, disconnect it from its economic interests, and political powers since the hierarchy of the Church was seen both as feudal lords and exercisers of enormous political power. In this context, Luther found the need for both social and ecclesiastical reforms, and from the prevalent situation he came to the conclusion that the social reform was possible only by way of the reform of the Church.

At the religious front, Luther encountered a sort of a semi-Pelagian tendency that promoted a doctrine of salvation through an anthropocentric schema of merit earning, which was a prominent teaching of the Church. It was in line with the common position of Roman Catholicism that 'truth was identical to what the Church taught, preached, professed, and interpreted'. But Luther countered it with a God-centered salvation through the doctrine of justification.[22] He argued that the fallen humanity must be converted first before they could see or know; they must be liberated from their bondages of self-interests, prejudices, pre-judgments, and presuppositions before they could perceive truth – truth as it draws near and makes itself known to them and not as something discovered by reason. It was an attempt to shift the centrality of the ecclesiastical hierarchy and to postulate Christ at the centre of all theological thinking and human life.

Luther was further influenced by personal piety or mysticism of the medieval times. It was a kind of an insistence on personal transformation, or conversion leading the believer to an intimate union with God in Christ on account of justification. In fact, his discovery of justification addressed two demands: *personal transformation* and *the reform of the Church. First,* justification engendered freedom at the personal realm and brought the moralistic theory of salvation (work righteousness or salvation through meritorious works) to an end. Luther declared that through faith, and faith alone, salvation is made available, which provided much respite to those who lined up to buy indulgences for the abrogation of their personal sins and the sins of those who were suffering in the purgatory. It also sealed the easy path approach to salvation, i.e., by way of indulgences and posited salvation through the hard path, i.e., through penitence and transformation of the whole life of the believer. *Second,* it shook the very foundation of the institutionalized Church of his time as it deprived the Church of its power and the divine legitimation of the Church's clandestine acts. In this way Luther firmly established that in matters concerning the life of the Church and its believers, the supreme authority was not the pope or the canon law, but the people of God under the guidance of the word of God.[23] Luther's call to the German nobility to the reform of the Church was based on the principle that this task was vested with the people as "priests" – the Royal Priesthood of all baptized believers. It implies a radical equality and utter opposition of all discrimination in terms of people's status. It is a revaluation and reclaiming of human dignity and worth, not on the basis of what they possess, produce and consume, but on the basis of what they *are* as human beings. It engenders the honour due to every human person within the Church and elsewhere.

Reformation[24] and Its Impact on the Church

Being a devout monk of the Augustinian order, Luther was keen to live the most austere life as laid out by the priory. But increasingly he came to realize that the Roman Catholic system had indulged in several blatant abuses, such as compulsory celibacy,[25] utter poverty among numerous clergy and the affluence of the few, the encouragement of beggary among the monks (mendicant order), the domination of the canon law over the life of the Church, theology and society, and the terrifying cult of relics. These traits created a tension, which manifested in several enthusiastic-apocalyptic forms, the callousness among the educated people in the cities and despair among the exploited German peasants. There were ominous signs of the brewing up of a crisis situation in the Church and the society. In such a situation the traditional theology of the Church could do precious little to cope with the emergent crisis.[26]

According to Hans Küng, the Reformation was the culmination of "a whole syndrome of manifestations of crisis"[27] that includes: the collapse of the papal rule of the world,[28] the great schism in the Church between East and West, the twofold and then the threefold papacy in Avignon, Rome and Pisa along with the rise of the nation states of France, England and Spain; the failure of the previous councils (Constance, Basel, Florence, Lateran) in bringing about the reforms of the Church; the shift in economy (natural economy to money economy), the invention of printing press, widespread desire for education and the eagerness of the Christians to read the bible; the absolutist centrism of the Curia, its immorality, its exploitative fiscal policy, its stubborn resistance to reform, and finally the huge marketing of indulgences, which was viewed in Germany as the peak of Curial exploitation.[29]

The concept of indulgence is a classic example of theological innovation. It all began with Augustine who in his interpretation of such texts as Maccabees (12:39-45) and 1 Corinthians (3:11-15) declared that no one (except some saints) goes to heaven directly upon his/her death. The condemned go to hell and the remainder to a slightly less painful form of hell in order to do penance until they are purged (hence 'purgatory') of those sins that had not been remissioned by good works during their lifetime. Since, the time in purgatory (which can extend up to thousands or even millions of years) was a substitute for good works, it followed that one's languishing in the purgatory can be minimized by equivalent amount of good works. Meanwhile, someone stumbled upon the idea that works that benefit the Church could count for more value than other varieties. For instance, participation in a crusade was valued as sufficient to total remission from purgatory. This was further modified and proposed that those who pay sufficient money to the Church to hire a crusader might be purged of all sins. In the later periods, the crusades died out, but not the Church's avarice for more funds. Hence, it was declared that those who pay contributions to the Church can earn release from torture for their sins of the past, present and future.

Soon the Church began selling sealed certificates of indulgences, some specifying a period of remission, some others providing dispensations to commit or for having committed various sins.[30] As papacy's financial ambition could not be quenched, an elaborate scheme of indulgence sale network was developed using the traveling monks. In 1476, Pope Sixtus IV conceived of using this network to build up more funds to pay back his debts and to continue the work on the Sistine chapel. So he authorized the sale of indulgences to the living in order to release their loved ones who suffer in the purgatory. One of the attractive slogans claimed that "The moment the money tinkles in the collecting box, a soul flies out of purgatory".[31] The pious, including the prominent ones, like Peter Abelard, John Wyclif, John Huss and Desiderius Erasmus challenged the sale of indulgence. What prompted Luther to act was the massive sale campaign launched in Germany to fund the rebuilding of St. Peter's Basilica in Rome. Johannes Tetzel (1465-1519), a prominent preacher of indulgences, was in charge of the campaign. Here is a typical piece of his sermon:

> [D]o you not hear the voices of your dead parents and other people, screaming and saying, 'Have pity on me, have pity on me...We are suffering severe punishments and pain, from which you could rescue us with a few alms, if you would'."[32]

Luther was infuriated at this heartless commercialization of the divine grace that deceived the innocent. It prompted him to advance his Ninety-five Theses, which he nailed on the door of All Saints Church in Wittenberg on 31 October 1517, a day known as the Reformation day, particularly directed against the practice of indulgence. What irked the Church was that Luther's critique became widely known beyond the Latin-educated elites across the frontiers. Pope Leo X ordered Luther to Rome, but the German Elector Frederick objected to the Pope's order and it was agreed that Luther would appear before Cardinal Cajetan in Augsburg. Luther appeared before him on 07 October 1518 and discovered that the Cardinal had only one agenda, i.e., to order Luther to retract his Ninety-five Theses and not to have any debate. The defiant Luther refused and his friends helped him to escape from Augsburg to Wittenberg.

In 1520, Luther wrote four tracts, popularly known as the Reformation Treatises. The first one was a long sermon addressed to the Churches entitled *On Good Works.*[33] Written in German, the tenor of this tract was more edifying the people than motivating action. In this treatise, Luther dealt with the fundamental question of Christian existence, i.e., the relationship between faith and works. As he conceived: the innermost motive of a Christian is faith and good works are the consequence of this faith. Explaining the Ten Commandments, Luther attempted to demonstrate that faith, i.e., the trusting confidence in God, gives God alone the glory, which is fundamental to Christian existence and good works can and should follow from faith.

The second one was an open letter *To the Christian Nobility of the German Nation Concerning the Reform of the Christian Estate,*[34] urging the temporal powers to avert a popular uprising by intervening to reform the Church that never showed any concern to address the various grievances of the German people against Rome. His contention was that Rome was indulging in sheer exploitation of

Germany. To end such exploitations, Luther proposed to establish a national Church independent of Rome, headed by Bishop of Mainz. He also called for the reduction of mendicant orders, abolition of masses for the dead, abolition of the (discriminatory) canon law, establishing one set of laws and courts for everyone, and marriage of the clergy.

The third tract, *The Babylonian Captivity of the Church*,[35] was addressed to German clergy and scholars, in which Luther proposed a complete revamping of religion. Comparing the thousand-year papal dispensation of the Church with the Babylonian captivity of the Jews, Luther vehemently opposed the doctrines of purgatory and transubstantiation; called for the dissolution of religious orders and an end to the vows of celibacy. He made a virulent attack on the masses for the dead and indulgences, and declared that the Hussites were right in demanding the right for everyone to drink of the Communion cup and not just the priests. Above all, he firmly asserted the authority and centrality of the scripture in matters of faith and life and salvation through faith alone. The fourth one was *A Treatise on Christian Liberty*,[36] which clarified the ethical aspect of salvation by faith. Following the injunction found in Matthew 7:20, Luther affirmed that faith alone makes a person a true Christian and good works follow from faith.

Confronted by such serious criticisms, the Church moved swiftly into action. Luther's writings were officially condemned and he was excommunicated in 1521 by Pope Leo X. In the meantime, he was ordered to appear before the imperial Diet of Worms, in which he was declared an outlaw by the Holy Roman emperor. But his supporters hid him away in the castle of Wartburg. From there he returned to Wittenberg, where he found the amazing support of a large number of clergies, nuns and monks in addition to the popular support. Modern minds might be cynical about the Reformation as an elite movement led by trained theologians and upheld by the nobility. But, as a matter of fact, it was greeted with greater receptivity by the common people.[37] The masses stood in support of Luther because now they could find themselves in closer proximity to a new form of Christianity. Luther remained a man of deep faith, who out of his existential need struggled over the grace of God in the face of human fallenness and found that the fundamental source of comfort to the troubled human conscience is the Gospel alone. From this conviction, he intended to navigate the Church from its deviations to the Gospel of Jesus Christ as the central Reformation principle. Hence, against ecclesiastical traditions, canon laws and papal authorities, Luther set the primacy of scripture (*sola scriptura*); against the numerous saints and mediators between God and humanity, he set the primacy of Christ (*solus Christus*); against the faith-reason synthesis of scholastic theology, he emphasized the centrality of faith (*sola fide*); and against human piety and religious achievements by way of good works, Luther stressed the primacy of justifying grace (*sola gratia*)

Luther's new understanding of the essence of the Gospel, i.e., '*justification by grace alone through faith alone on account of Christ alone*' transformed the existing theological landscape. It provided theology with a new orientation and the Church with a new structure.[38] Within the Reformation tradition, first and foremost, theological terminologies underwent a major change. In his analysis of Aquinas and Luther, Ebeling has illustrated how the basic theological terms are changed in Luther's theology, especially in the light of the new discovery of the Gospel. Medieval theology, following the Greek sapiential tradition, showed greater inclination towards physical and physiological categories: act and potency, form and matter, substance and accident, effective, material, formal and purposive causes, actualization, and growth. But Luther employed personal categories: gracious God and sinful human being, pronouncing righteous, trust, and confidence. Medieval thinking greatly followed the principle of contradiction (then sinners and now righteous, following the Aristotelian categories of static and historical dynamics).[39] But Luther viewed reality dialectically (e.g., *simul iustus et peccator*). He rejected the allegorical method of interpretation advanced by Origen and Augustine and advanced a strict linguistic and grammatical exegesis of the scripture.[40]

Reformation further led to a new understanding of God, humans, Church and sacraments. God is no longer understood in speculative metaphysical categories, but in concrete terms as God *for me* (*pro me*) or *for us* (*pro nobis*), on whose grace alone one may place his/her trust. It provided a new anthropology, not within the framework of nature and grace, but within the dynamics of Law and gospel, letter and spirit, faith and works, and freedom and bondage. It also gave rise to a new understanding of the Church, not as a bureaucratic institution, but as a renewed *communion of the faithful* within the doctrine of the priesthood of all believers, based on the principle of true brother/sisterhood and servanthood. Similarly, the theology of the sacraments underwent a major shift from ritualism (of quasi-magical power) to an understanding of God's promise of forgiveness and signs of trusting faith in a gracious God.

Following the Reformation, a great variety of interests and revolts that were fuming from underneath began to crop up, particularly from the radical groups known as the "enthusiasts".[41] It resulted in riots as early as in 1522, even in Luther's own town of Wittenberg and finally broke out as the Peasant war in 1523.[42] The radical groups appealed to the personal experience of direct revelation of the Spirit over against the papists. It was a political and revolutionary conflagration with an appeal to the Gospel, following the Reformation model. Luther became apprehensive that the Peasants' revolt might compromise his programme of Reformation, and he first called for peace through mediation.[43] But the subsequent horrifying reports of atrocity committed by the Peasants made Luther to react strongly against their agitation, which came in the form a tract entitled: "Against the Robbing and Murdering Hordes of Peasants (1525)".[44] Incidentally, by the time this tract came out in public, the rulers had dealt severely with the agitating Peasants, including the execution of the top leaders like Thomas Münzter. But it served well to provide a clear conscience to the rulers for curbing the revolt with iron hand.

It appears that Luther was trapped in a 'top down' perception of reality at one level (in which the authority must be obeyed even if it is repressive) that he was not ready to arrive at certain radical political and social conclusions from his radical demand for Christian freedom vis-à-vis his new theology of justification. His call to the rulers did stand as sufficient justification of their use of brutal force against the rebellion and the Peasants, the largest social groups in the empire, were once again became the victims of the rulers, which did make a deep dent in Luther's popularity. His invitation to the princes to be the arbiters of the Church also did not go well with his intentions, for they became the 'emergency bishops' and eventually became the lords of the Church. Meanwhile, Lutheran movement spread across frontiers. In the backdrop of these prefatory remarks on the emergence of Luther's thoughts and also the Hindu nationalist discourse, which we had analysed in the previous chapter, we embark on the study of the Reformer's thoughts on the Church.

Ecclesia within Luther's Horizon of Thought

Luther constructed his thoughts on ecclesia through his intense study of the scripture, taking cognizance of the contextual realities around him. He, however, never put those thoughts together in a single volume or treatise as a closed doctrine of the Church. Rather they emerged over a period of time in response to the emergent situations and issues. But, despite the fragmented expression of his thoughts on the Church, there are certain critically important theological components inherent in his articulations, which would explore here.

Theology of the Cross

In his 'Heidelburg Disputation (1518)', Luther describes the essence of true theology as the theology of the cross (*theologia crucis*) and its antithesis as 'theology of glory' (*theologia gloriae*). [45] According to him, the theology of glory knows God from God's works (of creation and its majesties), and the theology of the cross knows God from God's suffering. Here "work" indicates not only God's works, but also the works of humans; and similarly "suffering" refers not only to Christ's suffering, but also to human suffering – a synthesis of the right knowledge of God and the right ethical attitude of humans. For him, natural theology and speculative metaphysics are ways in which humans exalt themselves to the level of God, leading them to express their pride and inflate their 'ego'. But the cross of Christ is not simply a subject matter of theology; rather it is the distinctive mark of theology because cross is the centre that provides perspective to all theological statements,[46] and there is no conceivable dogmatic/ theological subject for which the cross is not a point of reference. This is illustrated by Luther's comment on who may rightly be called a theologian:

> That person does not deserve to be a theologian who looks upon the invisible things of God as if it were clearly perceptible in those things which have actually happened. He deserves to be called a theologian, however, who comprehends the visible and manifest things of God seen through suffering and the cross.[47]

In Luther's view, God demands humans to come to the knowledge of God paradoxically – according to the standard of the cross (in God's sufferings). Here, Luther affirms that the theology of glory leads humans to strike a bargain with God on the basis of their ethical achievements by fulfilling law because:

> It is impossible for a person not to be puffed up by his good works...That wisdom which sees the invisible nature of God in works as perceived by man is completely puffed up, blinded, and hardened.[48]

But the theology of the cross understands human being as the one who has been called to suffer because:

> He, however, who has emptied himself through suffering no longer does works but knows that God works and does all things in him. He neither boasts if he does good works, nor is he disturbed if God does not do good works through him. He knows that it is sufficient if he suffers and is brought low by the cross in order to be annihilated all the more.[49]

Three of the significant insights that strike our attention are: (a) Luther clearly shows that religious intellectualism and moralism are not in consonance with, but in opposition to, the theology of the cross; (b) cross points to the deep correlation between the suffering Christ and the suffering human being; and (c) it means that knowledge of God is not theoretical knowledge, but a matter of existential knowledge, and it occurs in death – the death of Christ – only when we experience Christ's death as our own. There is a close interconnection between Luther's theology of the Church and his theology of the cross, which is evident from his affirmation that the communion of saints is made possible by the principle of love as exemplified by Christ – his *agape*.

Theology of Justification

Whereas the cross provides the perspective for his theology, 'justification'[50] serves as the hermeneutical key to understand all true theological statements in Luther's thinking. As far as the article of justification is concerned, the Reformer is quite emphatic as he affirms: "We must learn therefore diligently the article of justification, as I often admonish you. For all other articles of our faith are comprehended in it; and if that remain[s] sound, then all the rest [will be] sound."[51] To him, a human person is justified wholly for the sake of Christ (*propter Christum*), which means that God does not impute sin on him/her but forgives sin (cf. Ps. 32:1). This means that the righteousness of Christ is imputed to the sinner, which is *alien* to human possession and he/she is considered righteous on account of Christ alone. The righteousness of a Christian is, thus, a *passive* righteousness, which is existentially appropriated by faith alone and not through any meritorious acts on the part of the person. Luther affirms so persistently: "Now it is certain that Christ or the righteousness of Christ is outside of us and foreign to us, which cannot be laid hold of by our works"[52]. "This is spiritual theology, which the philosophers do not understand, since they call righteousness a human quality".[53] "[A] Christian is righteous by faith… that is, he is righteous by the mercy and grace of God. This mercy and grace is not something human; it is not some sort of disposition or quality in the heart. It is divine blessing… Is not this righteousness an alien righteousness?"[54] "To be outside of us means to be beyond our powers. Righteousness is our possession, to be sure, since it was given to us out of mercy. Nevertheless, it is alien to us, because we have not merited it".[55] "The righteousness comes from us is not Christian righteousness. Christian righteousness is just the opposite; it is passive and we receive it; we do nothing for ourselves but allow someone else, namely God, to work in us".[56]

Faith also does not do the act of justifying; rather it lays hold of the promise of grace and relies on the mercy of God. That is why this doctrine is structured: "justification *by* grace *through* faith alone *for* Christ's sake".[57] Otherwise, it will turn out to be righteousness *because of* human faith. Further, justification is not processual; rather it is an instantaneous act of God whereby God declares the sinner free of his/her guilt. From that moment he/she is totally righteous in God's sight because, for Christ's sake, God does not remember his/her sins any more. Thus, justification

> does not take place through works, but by faith alone, without any works, and not piecemeal, but completely at once (*nicht mit Stücken, sondern auf einem Haufen*). The testament, i.e., the Gospel promise, includes everything in itself: justification, salvation, inheritance, and blessing. It is appropriated by faith completely at once, not piecemeal (*ganz auf einem mal, nicht stucklich besessen durch den Glauben*). Truly it is plain, then, that faith alone brings such good things of God, that is, justification and salvation, and makes us instantaneously, not gradually, children and heirs, who then freely do good works of all kinds.[58]

Justifying faith means a sinner becomes a new creation in Christ. This new condition makes the sinner glad in God and brings the slavish toils under law to an end. It leads the justified sinner to a new obedience to God's will and enables him/her to readily serve someone else in love and to suffer "in love and praise of God", which is the ethical fruitfulness of faith in Christ. In his *Preface to Romans* Luther affirms:

> Faith is a divine work in us which changes us and makes us to be born anew of God, John 1[:12-13]. It kills the old Adam and makes us altogether different men, in heart and spirit and mind and powers; and it brings with it the Holy Spirit.... It is impossible for it not to be doing good works incessantly....Faith is a living, daring confidence in God's grace, so sure and certain that the believer would stake his life on it a thousand times. This knowledge and confidence in God's grace makes men glad and bold and happy in dealing with God and with all creatures. And this is the work which the Holy Spirit performs in faith. Because of it, without compulsion, a person is ready to and glad to do good to everyone, to serve everyone, to suffer everything, out of love and praise to God who has shown him this grace.[59]

Two effects of faith are: it appropriates the forgiveness of sins and therewith the imputation of righteousness; and it re-generates a sinner into a new being. Luther's ecclesiology consistently reflects these thoughts. His understanding of community, royal priesthood, sacraments, and Church-State interface are all laced with the theology of the cross and justification.

There is a strong criticism that the doctrine of justification as understood by Luther is not maintainable in concrete human situations as it leads to a kind of an ethical passivity. Paul Rajasekhar refutes this criticism and affirms that Luther advocates neither ethical passivity nor social quietism through this doctrine.[60] Walter Altmann understands this theory as providing solid basis for the freedom of the Christian.[61] But those who criticize this theory point out that this is 'unjustified justification' as it provides greater respite to the perpetrators of inequality and oppression and not to the victims of injustice.[62] It is customary among the Lutherans to identify 'justification' as the evangelical discovery of Luther and uncritically apply it as an all-embracing universal category. However, a close analysis of the way Luther applied 'justification' reveals the fact that he efficiently contextualized this doctrine in order to critique papacy's abuses of its power and exploitation of the poor, which is something similar to what Paul did in his encounter with the Jewish-Gentile Christian conflict within the Church.

Law and Gospel

Luther's theology of justification is reflected in his understanding of Law and Gospel, especially the way he *distinguishes* and *integrates* them. According to him, the Word of God comes to human beings in twofold form – Law and Gospel (and he perceives these two in terms of *opposition in unity*).[63] Law is nothing new; and it was given to humans ever since creation (as written in their hearts by nature – Rom 2:14). Hence, Luther argues that even if God did not give the written law (Decalogue) through Moses, still human beings could have been able to know naturally that they should worship God and love their neighbours. The essential matrix of the Law is God's eternal will for humans and salvation is contingent on fulfilling the will of God to the last letter. In this sense, then, Law represents the divine-human relationship. However, sin (human fall) has altered the whole basis and nature of Law's relationship to human beings as the eternal will of God, which has now become "Law" in its specifically legalistic sense. In this new perception, the function of Law is to convict and that of the Gospel is to comfort the sinner.[64]

Luther's exposition of the Law is quite insightful. According to him, Law assumes a twofold function: *civil function* and *spiritual/theological function*.[65] The civil function of the Law is to obstruct or check flagitious crimes and the cycle of violence in this temporal world, which is predominantly under the reign of the devil. It further promotes peace and order (law and order), which is demonstrated by the functioning of governments and other civil institutions instituted by God.[66] In this sense, then, human beings are capable of fulfilling the Civil Law and produce Civil Justice acceptable to the world independent of any spiritual substance. However, the spiritual-theological function is the true and genuine function of the law, according to Luther.[67] It demands a pure heart, perfect obedience, fear, and love of God. Within this domain the Law originally was an expression of God's love; but now it has turned out to be an instrument of God's wrath and it leads human beings to realize their sinfulness and to repent.[68]

To be sure, the Law is God's own Word and therefore it is spiritual because it is the truth that comes from the Spirit. Yet, at the same time, it has to be distinguished from the other side of God's Word, i.e., God's gift through the Gospel of Jesus Christ. Accordingly, when the Spirit speaks through the Law it convicts the sinners and when the Spirit speaks through the Gospel, it comforts and makes us holy and alive. Thus, the distinction between the Law and the Gospel can be seen as functioning in the opposite directions: the Law places human beings under the wrath and judgment of God, but the Gospel brings grace and life; the Law convicts the sinners and leads them to death, but the Gospel proclaims eternal life through the power of Christ's redemption. Functionally, then, Law and Gospel stand in opposition to each other and they are to be distinguished for our proper understanding but not to be disjuncted.[69] Here, even though Luther finds certain functional distinctions between the Law and the Gospel as standing in opposition to each other, it does not follow that Law and Gospel are in conflict with each other. Rather, they are inseparably bound together and connected with each other.[70] For this reason, Luther urges that both must be preached, because there is *antithesis* and *harmony* between the Law and the Gospel. Thus, for instance, when we proclaim Christ as the redeemer, it is also the proclamation of the Law because redemption presupposes the existence of sin,[71] which is based on the principle that 'whatever shows us what we ought and ought not to do and whatever tells us that we remain in sin is always Law'.[72]

Law and Gospel have different functions, yet they are the functions of the same Word. But faith moves from the Law to the Gospel, which is irreversible because the Gospel is the word of comfort and promise for the guilty. In this sense, then, the Gospel transcends the Law and the Law never transcends the Gospel. Here, faith means placing the Gospel above the Law and holding on to the Gospel as God's promise of accepting the unacceptable. Thus, in its deepest sense, such faith in the Gospel fulfills the Law because it is a Gospel of promise, which closely follows Luther's theology of the cross and justification. It entails that the justified are set at liberty from the demands of the Law and its condemnation and transferred from the domain of Law to the kingdom of Christ. This, then, is the fruit of the Gospel – the liberty from the demands of the Law, the freedom and dignity engendered by justification, which altogether resulted from the cross of Christ – that forms the basis of Luther's theology of the Church.

Meaning of Ecclesia in Luther's Perception

At the outset, we need to recognize two fundamental methodological shifts Luther had made in his reconstruction of ecclesiology: (i) his central theological principle of *distinction and integration* or *unity of the opposites* that enabled him to view reality in dialectical terms (e.g. a sinner and a saint at the same time) and not in oppositional terms (e.g. then a sinner and now a saint), i.e., *opposition in unity*; and (ii) his understanding of the Church as 'the people of God' or 'the communion of saints' over against the Roman perception of the Church as an *objective order* established by God on earth to do God's work. These shifts provided the Reformer with ample scope to critique the existent conceptions of the Church and carry out the programme of Reformation. The Reformer consistently maintained these two components with careful precision throughout his theological thinking, especially his ecclesiological constructions.

With regard to the inner constitution of the Church, there is a fundamental difference between the Roman Catholic and the Reformer's doctrines. According to the Roman Catholicism, the Church has its base on the authority Christ had vested with the apostles and successively transmitted from Peter to the bishop of Rome (called the pope, meaning 'holy Father') who assumed the mantle of the sole legitimate head of the Church universal. Whereas, for Luther, the notion that the Church was founded on the authority of the papal hierarchy was unsustainable because such a doctrine has given rise to the abuse of power, and stood as a hindrance to the proclamation of the Gospel and the growth of the Church. Hence, according to him, the Church has its base on the proclamation of the Gospel, which creates faith in the believers and they constitute the Church.[73]

Luther added Baptism and Lord's Supper also as foundational to the Church. Yet, he understood the sacraments as nothing but the "Visible Word" (*verbum visibile*) because they offer nothing but the Gospel of Christ in different forms. Thus, the unity of the Church, in Luther's view, is contingent not on the uniformity of humanly instituted ceremonies, but on the preaching of the Gospel in its pure understanding and the administration of the sacraments in accordance with God's Word.[74] Rightly approached, Luther's position has immense resources to reconstruct the nature and function of the Church, especially in the context of the internal and external challenges. Based on its core doctrine, the Church must be the most open and accommodating of all institutions since its only prerequisite is the proclamation of the Gospel of God's unconditional, redeeming acceptance of the unacceptable. But unfortunately, this theory is far removed from the life, theology, and function of the contemporary Churches. The Roman Catholic Church considered Luther's position as a dangerous heresy since it replaced the objective order established by God for divine purposes with the subjective interests of the believers.[75]

Luther's theology emerged from his intense study of the Word of God and its existential appropriation. "Where the Word is, there is faith; and where faith is, there is the true Church", affirms Luther.[76] To him, "the Bible is a book of life through which God directly speaks to the human souls."[77] His basic definition of the Church is derived from the biblical concept: "people of God", as found in the Apostle's Creed as the "communion of saints" (*communio sanctorum*), meaning the 'Holy Christian Church'. In this exposition, the main issue is whether the term *communio* indicates a congregation (*Congregatio*), group (*Haufe),* community (*Gemeinde*), gathering (*Sammlung*), and assembly (*Versammlung*), or whether it means participation (*Gemeinschaft*) in the ordinary 16th century use of the term. Here participation means at least two things: (i) an act of common participation with fellow people, and (ii) an act of participation having a common right to something. Now in the former sense *sanctorum* is a subjective genitive, which stands as a masculine noun and in the latter sense, it is an objective genitive, which can mean masculine (referring to the saints, the holy people) or neuter gender (meaning the 'holy objects'). There are two possibilities: (i) *communio sanctorum* can mean participation with other saints, and (ii) it can also mean participation in the benefits of grace. It is most likely that Luther understood *communio* in both ways, and his thinking might have been influenced by the Vulgate text of Romans 12:13 – "communicating", i.e., contributing to the needs of the saints (*necessitatibus sanctorum Communicantes*).

In the Large Catechism, Luther says:

> The Creed calls the holy Christian church a *communio sanctorum*, "a communion of saints"...The word *ecclesia* properly means an assembly. We, however, are accustomed to the term *Kirche*, "church", by which simple folks understand not a group of people but a consecrated house or building. But the house should not be called a church except for the simple reason that the group of people assembles there...Thus the word "church" (*Kirche*) really means nothing else than a common assembly... In our mother tongue therefore it ought to be called "a Christian congregation or assembly", or best and most clearly of all, "a holy Christian people"...This is the sum and substance of this phrase: I believe

> that there is on earth a little holy flock or community of pure saints under one head, Christ. It is called together by the Holy Spirit in one faith, mind and understanding. It possesses a variety of gifts, yet is united without sect or schism. Of this community I also am a part and member, participant and co-partner in all the blessings it possesses. I was brought to it by the Holy Spirit and incorporated into it through the fact that I have heard and still hear God's Word, which is the first step in entering it.[78]

Thus, in Luther's view, we *participate* with the believers in the benefits of nature, and of salvation as well as in their needs. This is a clear expression of the intimacy or the *perichoretic* experience with which the believers are united in Christ and Luther consistently clings to this relationship throughout his delineations of the Church. In fact, he seldom preferred the term Church (*Kirche*) and showed greater inclination to speak of the Church as *communio*, mainly due to the fact that this later expression indicates the nature of ecclesia as an intimately held communion of the faithful participating in the gifts of grace and the mutual sharing of each other's burdens.

At this point the Reformer encountered a crucial hermeneutical issue, i.e., the role of tradition in biblical interpretation and the life and ministry of the Church. At one level he was inclined to denounce the ecclesiastical hierarchy that had indulged in the distortion and abuse of its spiritual power, especially the imposition of unbearable burdens on the innocent believers in the name of traditions; and, at another level, he found the urgent need to safeguard the authentic traditions of the Church from being vitiated by the vested interests. His anti-traditionalist stance, however, did not lead him to a rigid Biblicism. With regard to his stance on infant Baptism, for instance, especially in his argument against the Anabaptists,[79] Luther invoked the common ecclesiastical tradition with the argument that it has been "practiced since the beginning of the Church," and it comes to us "from the apostles and has been preserved ever since their time". This position stems from his theology of history: 'God will not allow a wrong practice to keep going for so long in history'. The precise point, as Luther understands, is that God has subjected all the heresies that arose much later to perish, whereas God preserved the practice of infant Baptism to continue in the Church.[80] But the Reformer could not lend any credence to the papacy's claim to have absolute authority to interpret the scripture, convene a council, and have the final say on matters of faith and life of the believers on the basis of tradition. Here he accepted scripture alone as the norm and authority and, thereby, deprived the professional biblical scholars of the monopoly of interpreting the scripture.

The *Communio sanctorum* is fashioned after the biblical concept of 'people of God' or 'communion' and it is both a hidden reality (*absconditus*) and a visible fellowship (*schietbar*) as we see in 1 Cor. 2:7-15. The true nature of the Church, however, is identified through certain essential signs such as the proclamation of the Word, the proper administration of sacraments and the confession of faith.[81] Even though the true (nature of the) Church is obscured, the empirical Church is visible for the sake of the confession of faith (Rom 10:10). Luther's intention here is not to paint an idealist or perfectionist image of the Church. For, he affirms that the communion of saints is at the same time the communion of sinners. In these delineations, his epistemological foundation is the Word of God and Church's obedience to the Word of God is paramount for him. But, to his dismay, Luther found that the Church, the community/communion of the faithful, of his time had completely drifted away from true obedience to the Word of God.

The Idea of Community/Communion in Luther

There is greater euphoria over the newfound *turn to community* among contemporary thinkers who often adjudge the past as vitiated by individualism.[82] But despite the contemporary thinkers' penchant for the idea of community, they are not unanimous about what they mean by the concept of community.[83] The task of getting a fair grasp of the concept of community further slips away due to the realization that people are members of several communities simultaneously. Over against the present misunderstanding, we need to bear in mind that several thinkers of the past clearly defined what a 'community' – Christian 'community' to be precise – stands for, especially amidst changing realities and circumstances. Martin Luther was certainly one among those thinkers and his theology of the Church is predicated on the idea of communion, a cognate of community.

Theoretically, a community is constituted by a group of people, conscious of a similar frame of reference they share and a common manner of viewing the world.[84] They construct the meaning of the shared space they occupy through (common) symbols like language, rituals, and so on. Almost all communities have a group focus that is operant in their shared living that evokes in them a common identity, which is nurtured by a common task and a kind of solidarity among them.[85] This sort of communitarian life entails that it is contingent on a shared concern to be part of an ongoing process of discerning what constitutes the identity of a particular community. In a community's existence, there is also 'person focus', in which the individual derives his/her identity from the community.[86] Underlying this perception of individual identity formation is the theory that the self is not an autonomous entity, but part of a social reality and, hence, meaning is not a matter of individual concern but it is a matter of interpersonal or relational construction, i.e., self-worth or meaning or identity is a social phenomenon.[87] From this vantage point Luther's concept of *communio sanctorum* is predicated on communitarian values and not on utilitarian individualism. For, in his view, the Church does not come into existence *per se*, rather it is the Word of God, which creates faith in people through the Holy Spirit and it is this faith that results in the formation of the communion of the faithful. It, then, becomes appropriate to examine the important components of his ecclesiology.

Church as the *Communio Sanctorum*

Luther derived his fundamental definition of the Church from the Apostles' Creed, which describes Church as the 'communion of saints'. The idea of 'community/communion (*Gemeinde*) of saints' seems to be so dear to him that he preserved it at the heart of his theology of the Church[88] and his writings on the Church consistently reflect this idea. Even though he found much significance in the expression "one holy Christian Church" in the creed, he preferred the expressions: "Christian Community", "gathering", "holy Christendom", and "holy Christian people of God" to describe the Church and his conception of the Church envisages incorporating all those "who hear the voice of the shepherd". Luther affirms that this communion is "called together by the Holy Spirit through the Gospel".[89] As this communion is gathered together and preserved by the Word, this Word necessarily becomes its decisive mark. Luther, however, adds the sacraments of Baptism and the Lord's Supper as co-constituting the Church together with the Word of God. Thus the unique marks of the Church are the Word of God and the sacraments. Other marks Luther adds to the Church are: the office of the keys, the presence of the ministers and offices in the Church, prayer, public praise of God (worship), and the "shrine of the holy cross", i.e., the inner temptations and outward persecutions.[90]

To explain his concept of the Church, Luther constructed a double thesis: "God's word cannot exist without God's people and God's people cannot exist without God's word". He is quite emphatic that wherever the Word is being preached and people are being drawn to the Word and subsequently to faith in Christ, there exists the true Catholic Church because God's Word cannot remain without effect (Isaiah 55:11). The preaching of the Word has a twin effect: it points forward (as it creates God's people) and it points backward (as proclamation and people's listening to the Word presuppose that people of God are already in existence there). An important aspect of this delineation is the participation (*Gemeinschaft*) of the believers, i.e., *being bound together with*, *participating with someone*, *an act of common participation*, and *having a common right to something*. This, *communio* is constituted by saints (*sanctorum*) – "a holy community" or "a holy people"[91] – a communion in which everything is held in common as he affirms: "I believe that in this community or Christendom all things are held in common".[92]

In Luther's perception, the Church is one and hence catholic because of its faith in the one Gospel of Jesus Christ and, in this sense, he understood the Church not as a disjuncted and new entity, but as a continuity of the old. It existed from the beginning, i.e., from the time of Adam and it will continue to exist until the end of the world, which becomes clear as he argues:

> The Church has always existed; there has always been a people of God from the time of the first person Adam to the very latest infant born even granting that at times the Church has been exceedingly weak and so dispersed that it was manifest nowhere. [93]

The visible manifestation of the Church is made possible by the Word of God and the Sacraments. Within the Church the people are gathered together by the justifying faith, which makes the believers a holy Christian people of God. This has led him to maintain that the Church is the only locus of salvation as he affirms:

> I believe that in this congregation, *and nowhere else*, there is forgiveness of sins; that outside of it, good works, however great they may be or many, are of no avail for the forgiveness of sins; but that within it, no matter how much, how greatly or how often men may sin, nothing can hinder forgiveness of sins, which abides wherever and as long as this one congregation abides. To this congregation Christ gives the keys, and says, in Matthew xviii, 'whatsoever ye shall bind on earth shall be bound in heaven.'[94] [Emphasis added]

Roman Catholicism also has an understanding of *extra ecclesiam nulla salus*. But there is a fundamental difference between the Roman Catholic and Lutheran understandings of this doctrine. Roman Catholicism understands itself as an institution for dispensing salvation through the official hierarchy, which has been authorized by Christ. Hence, it is not possible to gain salvation outside the Church, i.e., the Roman Catholic Church. In contrast, Luther maintained that salvation is contingent on the believers' being exposed to the Gospel, i.e., the message of being accepted by God *in grace,* and the believers' acceptance of this new status of being accepted by God *in faith*. The communion of believers proclaims this message and those who lend an ear to this message in faith become part of this communion. And in this sense there is no salvation outside the Church.[95]

This position, however, fails to surmount a serious problem, especially related to the institutional Church in which this is an obstinate and extreme position, which guarantees the Church to have supreme power to bind or lose – a power to forgive or withhold forgiveness of sins. Even though, Luther proposed this view within the context of his interpretation of the Church as the communion of saints gathered around the Word of God and the Sacraments, the institutionalizing tendency of the Church cannot be overlooked, not only in Luther's time but also at all times in history. Having this position at the centre of its theological fabric, the Church can claim to hold the key despite the deadliest sins of its members (both clergy and laity alike). This is problematic in yet another way in the existential context of the Indian Church, both internally and externally. Internally it perpetuates a sense of pride – doctrinal and ecclesiastical pride – among the members. Externally, it negates the working of God beyond the enclaves of the Church. Two crucial rubrics need to be objectively and seriously thought about in this regard: (i) the question concerning the non-baptized believers in Christ,[96] and (ii) the reality of religious pluralism. Hence an uncritical application of this perception in the present context of the Indian Church will have serious ramifications.

There is a close interconnection between Luther's theology of the Church and his theology of the cross, which is evident from his perception of the Church as both visible and hidden. We need to note that often Luther is erroneously understood as having defined Church in terms of *visible-invisible* Church. But in reality, Luther talks about the *hidden (absconditus)* Church, and not invisible Church. It is visible insofar as it can be recognized by its visible signs; but, at the same time, the Church is also a deeply hidden entity that no one can see or recognize but only grasp and believe. It shares this hiddenness with the entire content of faith and thus with God's revelation in general and with Jesus Christ in particular. The Church in the present age is hidden under many errors and failures and hence, the Church "will not be known by sight, but by faith."[97]

The communion of saints is made possible by the principle of love as exemplified by Christ – his *agape*. The Church appropriates and reflects this love in its existence as a communion and it expresses its love not in vacuum but in the acts of sharing of goods. Luther, however, found a gross distortion of this trend in the Roman Catholic Church in two ways. *First*, Roman Catholicism maintained an essential unity between the earthly Church, the Church in heaven and the Church that is suffering in purgatory. The relationship is expressed by way of certain ritualistic acts such as the veneration of the saints and the use of merits. Consequently, the real sharing has been relegated to the margin. *Second,* Even the minimal practice of sharing in the Church was vitiated by egocentric moralism ('workism' according to Luther).[98]

At this point, Luther commenced his reconstruction of the concept of the Church and he did it in two ways. First, he navigated *Communio sactorum* from the 'other world' and located it on the earth.[99] He could derive the necessary theological resources for such a task from his study of Paul's letters, wherein he discovered that the saints are not a specific group within the community but all its members, i.e., all those who have faith in Jesus Christ. This is in contrast to the earlier prevalent view, which described saints as the "blessed" and the "perfected" ones. Luther emphasized that the saints were to be found not only in heaven but also on earth in flesh and blood and, over against the distinction between *the saints* and *the ordinary Christians,* he advocated a distinction between the saints who had already departed and the saints who are still alive. In consonance with this new perception, Luther shifted the focus of service to the saints from above to below, i.e., to the least of the sisters and brothers.

> Whatever it is that you want to do for the saints, turn your attention away from the dead toward the living. The living saints are your neighbours, the naked, the hungry, the thirsty, [and] the poor people who have wives and children and suffer shame. Direct your help toward them, begin your work here, use your tongue in order to protect them, your coat in order to cover them and to give them honor.[100]

The reason for such an advocacy is that we do not know the life of the departed:

> Let the dear saints rest where they are and [let us] take care of those whom we have with us; for we have enough to take care of [those who are] with ourselves if we are to live as Christians should. Therefore let them be, and God take care of them. We can

> neither know nor understand how they live in the world beyond. That world is quite different from this one.[101]

Roman Catholicism had a doctrine of 'the treasury of the Church', which granted the Church the authority to keep in reserve the merits earned by Christ and the saints and to administer the same through the authority of the 'office of the keys' as a way of enabling the sinners to balance their lack in good works, and penitential sacrifices. Luther vehemently opposed this as he argued that "...no saint has adequately fulfilled God's commandment in this life. Consequently the saints have done absolutely nothing which is superabundant. Therefore they left nothing to be allocated through indulgences".[102] This being the case, it would not be fruitful to use their meritorious achievements to prove the truth of the Gospel, nor can their lives be summarized in a rule and imitated as a legalistic example. Nevertheless, Luther did approve of the treasury of the Church, but with a totally different understanding from that of the medieval theology. The lives of the saints are a treasury not because of the merit they produced but because Christians live, suffer and do everything for each other as members of one body and this mode of existence is fraught with the communitarian values around which the *Communio sanctorum* is and ought to be organized, and not on the merit of the individual persons. Luther argues:

> Therefore this part of the thesis [Thesis 58] is proved, that is, that the merits of the saints cannot act as treasury for us since the saints themselves considered them deficient; unless someone should think that they are a treasure for us, not because they have surplus merits, but because the Church is a communion of saints in which each one works for the other, as members of one another.[103]

Luther's new perception of the saints is based on his theology of justification, which has proved to be a strong counter to the medieval understanding of the saints and their merits, primarily because of the fact that our salvation is contingent on God's free mercy and not on any human merit. Hence, the transfer of merits in the heavenly bank from one account to another has lost its meaning and relevance, and his new interpretation of the treasury of the Church, then, replaced the legalistic meritorious dynamics with dutiful and humble service in love – a service directed not to the saints above but to the saints who live in flesh and blood, which marks the re-discovery of the Church as depicted in the *Book of Acts* (2:42-47). The fundamental difference between the medieval and the Reformer's doctrines of community is that according to medieval doctrine, self-denial becomes authentic as an ascetic achievement that a person produces by him/herself apart from any relationship to fellow humans and this was regarded as a merit that can be transferred or credited to others. Over against this understanding, Luther affirmed self-denial in terms of substitutionary participation in the life situation of others, which is made meaningful only in a person's identification with particular burdens of others as a means to liberate them from those burdens. In the medieval conception, human beings were thought of as a community in which measurable values can be transferred, but in Luther's thought, they were a community of people living together characterized by mutual sharing of burdens.[104]

The *second* point by which Luther reconstructed the concept of *communio* is that the medieval Church demonstrated its inability to perceive ecclesia as a real community as it was dominated by moralistic principles of self-purity and perfection. Moralism is selfish and it does not permit real community of believers to come into existence. The quest for outstanding ecstatic experiences and spiritual achievements brought forth spiritual/religious classes and a kind of stratification, which shattered the very idea of the equality of the members of the body of Christ. This made real communion impossible as some made supercilious claims to act as mediators for the ordinary Christians, tending to the development of a work-righteousness. Luther's response to this issue was assertive and apt:

> Those who trust in their own work righteousness had to establish divisions and differences among Christians. The priests wanted to be better than the laity, and the monks wanted to be better than the parish priests, the virgins wanted to be better than the married people, and those who prayed and fasted often wanted to be better than those who worked, while those who lived austere lives wanted to be more than those who simply lived normal

> lives...So it was that the attention of the simple people was drawn away from the work of faith and the calling which comes to the believer... Finally these people reached the point of wanting to pray for poor Christians and thus despised other conditions of life as of no value at all.[105]

The Gospel, in Luther's view, stands in sharp contrast to this medieval perception in relation to the communion of saints. He was convinced that only the good news of justification could create authentic community of faith and not the self-seeking pietism. Our faith in the Gospel commends salvation totally in the hands of God and liberates us from that selfish concern and frees us to active participation for the welfare of the others. Thus, Luther could affirm that our works are but the ethical response to what God has done to us in Christ and that they are to be aimed solely at serving the fellow-members of the body of Christ. If we are to use our acts of ethics or morality for self-elevation, it would lead to division and dissension.[106] These views, however, do not presuppose that Roman Catholicism does not define the Church as the body of Christ. It does describe the Church as the body of Christ and is also well aware of the fact that the law of the Church is love. But all this is vitiated by human moralism and selfish piety in Luther's view.

The *Communio Sanctorum* originates from Christ's sacrificial love, which is the empirical factor that constitutes the individual members into one body in and/or with Christ and also therefore with each other. In his exposition of Genesis 2:24: "For the two shall be one flesh", Luther defines it in terms of the union of Christ with his bride – the Church – as Paul affirmed in Ephesians 5:31f: "This is a great mystery, and I take it to mean Christ and the Church".[107] In this body the existence of individual believers for selfish motive ceases and it is replaced, not by a mystical union into each other, but by an existential sharing of life in love. Luther here posits faith, hope, love, and other gifts of grace as the common possession of all those who are part of this communion. Here again one can notice that the underlying principle is the twofold meaning of the *Communio*, which we discussed earlier.

> The Church is...the divine, the heavenly, the noblest brotherhood;... the community of saints in which we are brothers and sisters, so closely united that a closer relation cannot be conceived for here we have one Baptism, one sacrament, one food, one gospel, one faith, one spirit, one spiritual body (Eph 4:4f), and each person is a member of the other (Rom 12:5).[108]

Participation in the *Communio Sanctorum*, thus, brings every believer under the conditions of a call and a commitment.[109] In brief, as Luther puts it, "all the goods of Christ and all the saints are my goods; my burden, trouble and sin belong to Christ and all the saints".[110] Thus, in life and death the believer is never alone, for Christ and the Church are always with him/her.[111]

These delineations suggest yet another dimension of the Church, i.e., this communion is never a mere gift of faith but always vested with the task of love.[112] The faith of the communion of believers can never be a mode of passive receptivity but a mode of active love. It is incumbent that each believer takes the burden of Christ and his Church upon him/herself as if it belongs to him/herself. The shame of Christ, the troubles of the Church, the unjust suffering of the innocent, the guilt and shame of the sinner, the needs of the poor – all these one must feel in his/her heart, not with a cheap sympathy but with a commitment to bear the burdens of the neighbours. The Reformer's understanding of the Church obviously tells that it is a communion that is brought into existence not to merely enjoy the benefits of grace but to share the destiny of the suffering humanity. Luther is passionate as he exhorts the believers not to shy away when calamities struck the Church:

> For if the bishops or priests or any persons at all are wicked, and if you were aglow with real love, you would not flee. No, even if you were at the ends of the ocean, you would come running back to them and weep, warn, reprove, and do absolutely everything. And if you followed the teaching of the apostle [Gal. 6:2] you would know that it is not benefits but burdens that you have to bear.[113]

Does this not raise certain pertinent questions concerning our response to the unjust suffering of Christians in Kandhamal in Orissa and the recent attacks on the Churches in other parts of the country? Does this not point to the Church's response to the suffering of the vulnerable? These delineations proffer certain definite pointers to discern the true nature of ecclesia, which would become more lucid as we analyse Luther's explication of the doctrine of the Priesthood of all believers and its relation to the Church.

'The Priesthood of all Believers'

One of the most significant contributions of Luther is his rediscovery of the symbol of the priesthood – the universal priesthood of all baptized believers. This must be seen as one of the guiding principles of the Church's (at least the Protestant Church) life in this world, which is one of Luther's profound spiritual legacies.

> For a priest, especially in the New Testament, was not made but was born. He was created, not ordained. He was born not indeed of flesh, but through a birth of the Spirit, in the washing of regeneration [John 3:6f.; Titus 3:5f.]. Indeed all Christians are priests, and all priests are Christians...The Scriptures of God... assert, 'You are a priest forever after the order of Melchizedek' [Ps. 110:4]. Christ himself was neither shorn nor anointed with oil in order to become a priest.[114]

> Christ has been made the first priest of the New Testament...He made all his apostles and his disciples priests.[115]

Here Christ is seen as the model – as the great high priest who performed his high priestly acts not as an authoritative office but as the function of a servant as evidenced by his washing of the disciples' feet and his death on the cross. The Church is founded on Christ's priesthood and its inner constitution is the priesthood of all believers. They share in Christ's priestly office as brothers, and sisters of Christ through Baptism, Regeneration, and the Anointing of the Holy Spirit. By definition, priesthood means the believers standing before God, praying for others, interceding and sacrificing oneself to God and proclaiming the Word to one another and to the world.[116]

Luther's delineation of the 'priesthood of all believers' carries with it deeper implications for our Christian existence both in the Church and in the society today. It is more so in the Indian context where human life is stratified and discriminated over several social phenomena like that of the caste system and the emergence of Hindu chauvinism that violently ostracizes and/or annihilates the 'other'. In such a context, the idea of 'royal priesthood' sharply penetrates deep into all such established hegemonies and demands to reconstruct the entire spectrum of our religious doctrines and social structures in order to discern the reality of the equality of all people of God in the religious and social domains. At the social domain in India, for instance, the hierarchical caste system had driven the untouchables (*avarṇās* as designated by Vedic Hinduism and *Dalits* in the contemporary times) out of the boundaries of the Hindu religious system and thereby sealed all the possibilities of their salvation.[117] Here, the Biblical principle of royal priesthood not only embraces the marginalized within its 'sacred' boundaries, but also affirms their status as priests (a status reserved exclusively for the priestly class in the Hindu religious system). Thus, the doctrine of 'royal priesthood' proffers a new principle and framework for the marginalized to affirm their identity and dignity. In Luther's view, this equality of the believers in the sight of God is one of the essential marks of Christians that makes them distinctive from the rest of humanity, for they are a priestly generation, a royal priesthood.[118] Along with the *priesthood*, yet another important component in the Reformer's exposition of ecclesia is the doctrine of the Sacraments, which we would explore next.

Sacraments

The Roman Catholic Church can rightly be called the greatest sacramental institution in world history. This is no exaggeration for in the medieval Church sacraments indicated all kinds of things. It could indicate the deeds of Christ, his sufferings, the cross, the gospels, the oil, the holy relics, the biblical symbols, the symbolic character of Church building, and all the activities in the Church. In short, sacrament was something in which the people experienced the presence of the divine. Sacraments are the continuation of the fundamental sacramental reality of God's manifestation in Christ. Any object or act becomes sacramental if a transcendental substance is infused into it. An important characteristic of sacrament is its power of healing. The theory behind it is that against the wounds inflicted by the original and actual sins God established the sacraments as remedies.[119]

Until the 12th century there were a number of sacraments and sacramental activities in the medieval Church. In due course the number of sacraments came to be limited to seven with specific significations and effects: Baptism, Eucharist, Penance, Confirmation, Ordination, Marriage, and Extreme unction. Baptism and Eucharist are effective in extricating original and venial sins respectively. Penance is important for personal piety and for the removal of mortal sins. Confirmation and extreme unction are supportive sacraments in the life of believers in which the former makes a person a soldier for Christ, and the latter removes whatever is left over of one's sins before his/her death. Ordination introduces one into the clergy and gives *him* the authority to administer all the other sacraments in addition to the preaching of the word. Marriage acts as the controlling factor of natural life and leads to the natural vocation of life as man and wife. The general perception of sacraments is that they are the visible and sensuous signs instituted by God in which, under the cover of a visible substance or act, the power of God hiddenly works. The decisive point in the medieval Church with regard to the sacraments is that they are effective in us *ex opere operato*, i.e., effective by their very performance and not by any virtue on the part of the participant.[120] This minimum theory, however, tends to regard the sacraments as an objective event of quasi-magical character, which was one of the major issues the Reformers were most critical about. According to them, the most essential characteristic of a sacrament is the Word of promise attached to a sign, instituted by God.[121] In Luther's ecclesiology, only two events (or symbols) are established as sacraments: Baptism and Eucharist.

Sacrament of Baptism

Baptism[122] is considered to be one of the central symbols of Christian life and witness and it is generally accepted among Christians that Baptism originated from Jesus Christ, which Luther also affirms in his theological reflections. Nevertheless, Modern scholars express considerable suspicion about the notion that the command to baptize did really originate from Jesus himself. *First*, there is no authentic evidence to suggest that Jesus did the priestly function of baptizing anyone except the fact that he subjected himself to be baptized by John, which was a Baptism of penitence. *Second*, Jesus and his disciples were not involved in baptizing according to the Synoptic Gospels. Only John (4:2) suggests that Jesus and the disciples were engaged in acts of baptizing. Other references related to Baptism are Mark 16:15-16, Matthew 28:19, and John 3:5.

Scholars are of the opinion that these texts cannot be taken as authentic words of Jesus since these words are likely to have emerged from a tradition or practice of the primitive community of believers. Apart from these references, there is none other to attribute the institution of Baptism to Jesus. However, there are evidences to suggest that the early Church began to baptize very shortly after Easter. Even Bultmann opines that Baptism was in practice from the very inception of the Church. The problem before us to solve is to reconcile two realities: on the one hand, the authentic evidences to prove Jesus' command or institution of Baptism are sparse; and, on the other hand, there is verifiable evidence that from the very beginning of its inception the Church engaged itself in baptizing the believers.

The root of Baptism goes back to Jewish (not Hellenistic) cultic practices and the Gospels themselves point to the Baptism of John as the prototype. Moreover, scholars, including the most critical ones, agree on the fact that Jesus was baptized by John – a fact that attaches more authenticity to Baptism in the Church. This can be seen as a sign of Jesus' approval of the practice of Baptism of repentance for the forgiveness of sins. The new community of believers subjected themselves to the baptismal rite in memory of Jesus, who himself approved and accepted Baptism. Easter, then, gave a totally new meaning to it. Although, Baptism was initially practiced for repentance and forgiveness of sins, now it has assumed a new meaning of turning to Christ, for God has given the promised salvation through Christ and has created an eschatological community with the bestowal of the Holy Spirit. This, then, distinguishes the Baptism of the Christian community and that of John or even the Jewish practice.[123]

Of course, Baptism is one of the central symbols of Christian faith and life. But there is every chance that this symbol of faith may fall into an obstinate legalistic practice if we fail to understand the true nature and purpose of this symbol. Therefore, any contemporary discussion on Baptism must of necessity take into account the theological and sociological elements that are inherent in it. Sociologically, it is an act of initiation of a person into the covenant community; and theologically, it is a gateway to the believers' adoption as God's children. Baptism in Christianity is some-thing similar to circumcision in Judaism.[124] Christian baptismal practice retains the sense of ritual purification (1 Peter 3:21) and the notion of adoption of humans by God as God's children.

However, in our social context, Baptism is viewed as a barrier for many who would otherwise like to be in communion with the body of Christ. It is also seen as a bond that uproots people from their cultural roots and transplants, and confines them in another culture. If it is so, Can Baptism be regarded as an essential symbol or as an *adiaphoron*? How can we approach and minister to a host of people who remain outside the official Church, yet with strong faith in Christ without undergoing the ritual of Baptism? After his intense study on the issue of non-baptized believers in Christ, Herbert Hoefer comes to the following conclusion regarding Baptism. When one takes a clear stand that the Lord commanded Baptism, he/she needs to be reminded that the intention of Jesus is not to make it a legalistic principle to cast unbearable burdens on people, rather it is to renew and uplift the Gospel. But with semantic changes, especially in the process of institutionalization and doctrinal piety, it is possible that Baptism could have become a source of pride, self-righteousness, social exclusion, spiritual apathy, communalism, moralism, and legalism.[125] Such trajectories necessitate a rethinking of the theology and practice of Baptism perhaps because, in such a situation, the very words of promise of life may turn out to be a curse and death (cf. Rom 6:8-13). Here, Hoefer tries to understand the role of Baptism in the light of justification and sanctification. The principle of justification, as found in the scripture and also as interpreted by Luther, makes it clear that justification is solely by grace through faith, and not through anything which we do to be worthy to merit grace. Paul posits faith and Baptism side by side as ways to 'put on Christ' and become children of God (Gal 3:26-27) by way of sanctification. In this sense, then, the gift of justifying grace is given outside Baptism and not contingent on it.[126]

Luther seems to be firm on his belief that Christian Baptism originates from Christ himself as he refers to Matthew 28:19 and Mark 16:16 in his *Large Catechism* as the words of command and institution and demands that no doubt or apprehension must be cast on the origin of Baptism. "You should not doubt...that Baptism is of divine origin, not something devised or invented by men".[127] This indicates that it communicates everything that is implied in human salvation. In Luther's own words:

> In Baptism...every Christian has enough to study and practice all his life. Christians always have enough to do to believe firmly what Baptism promises and brings – victory over death and the devil, forgiveness of sin, God's grace, the entire Christ and the Holy Spirit with his gifts. In short, the blessings of Baptism are so boundless that if our timid nature considers them, it may well doubt whether they could all be true. ...Now, here in Baptism there is brought, free of charge, to every person's door...a treasure and medicine that swallows up death and keeps all people alive. Thus, we must regard Baptism and put it to use in such a way that we may draw strength and comfort from it when our sins or conscience oppress us and say: 'But I am baptized! And if I have been baptized, I have the promise that I shall be saved and have eternal life, both in soul and body'.[128]

Luther further asserts that Baptism "effects forgiveness of sins, delivers the believers from death and devil, and grants eternal salvation to all who believe". He consistently emphasizes these aspects in his writings related to Baptism in which the believer is granted not simply partial grace, but the entirety of grace: "the entire Christ and the Holy Spirit with his gifts".[129] A Christian carries all these gifts throughout in his/her new life because "the truth of promise once made to us remains unchanged; it waits to receive us with open arms when we repent".[130]

The act of Baptism in Luther's view is not a human act but an act of God. Hence, he would argue, "To be baptized in God's name is to be baptized not by men, but by God himself. Although it is performed by human hands, it is nevertheless truly God's own act".[131] The acts of immersion in water and being raised again from water in the baptismal rite are identified with the death of the old being and the renewal of the new being. This has occurred once and for all in a 'sacramental' way in the act of Baptism. In Baptism, then, God makes a covenant and gives us the assurance of forgiveness of sins by subjecting our sinful self to death and creating us anew. In turn a Christian enters into a covenant with God "to submit himself into the sacrament of Baptism, to participate in God's gracious work in him by fighting against sin and killing it until he himself dies".[132] Looking at Baptism from the above perspective, it serves as an effective means to combat all that is devilish because under the cover of the water God bestows God's power upon the believer and creates him/her anew by sanctifying, purifying, and vivifying both his/her body and soul. By this act, then, God intends to use the human creatures as effective instruments to fulfill God's work on earth.[133] This is an important point that Luther frequently emphasized in his lectures on Genesis.[134] Luther uses two analogies to illustrate that God's power indwells in the external element of water in Baptism:

> When you grab an iron rod that has been lying in the forge and is glowing, you are not grabbing merely the rod but fire as well even though you only see the iron rod not fire...Likewise, you should recognize that Baptism has been incorporated into God's name and is permeated with it, so that it is one essence with it.[135]
> Likewise, a delicious drink that is made for a sick person is made with water but also has tasty spices and sugar mixed in it, so that it does not taste like water anymore. In the same way this is a much more delicious water, which has been sweetened with God's name, has become completely divine, even though you see nothing but water before your eyes.[136]

In this way Luther challenged the ritualism and moralism that were so entrenched in medieval piety. He rejected various forms of monastic practices that were claimed to be holier ways of life. It was even claimed that entering a monastery itself was a second Baptism, which Luther vehemently opposed.[137] Similarly, Duns Scotus had maintained that there was a magical power in the baptismal water itself.[138] Over against this tendency, Luther urged his hearers to hold simply on to the Word of God, which alone acts in all that Baptism brings in – purification from sin, deliverance from death, and new birth – through the power of God the Father, Son and Holy Spirit and not the element, i.e., water.[139]

Luther's theology of Baptism had to face a major challenge from the Anabaptists with regard to infant Baptism, which prompted him to base his theology of Baptism on adequate foundations. In defense of his conviction about infant Baptism, Luther had to depend heavily on the age-old tradition of the Church.[140] He showed no reluctance in admitting that there is no clear scriptural reference that could support infant Baptism. Nevertheless, the scripture does not speak against infant Baptism either and he could glean several indirect references such as Matthew 19, Mark 10, and Luke 18, where Christ is found inviting children to him and saying that they are the heirs of the Kingdom of God. Further, in the great commission (Matthew 28:18-20), Jesus commands his disciples to baptize all nations in which there is no expressed discrimination against children. And it is logical then to infer that children are included in and not excluded from Baptism. The validity of Christ's command to baptize, which apparently corresponds to the apostolic practice of Baptism, is the expression of the universalism of the Gospel, which makes a decísive point for Luther. This means that the Anabaptists, who opposed infant Baptism, were in want of solid foundation to prove their objection.

When human religiosity/spirituality leads to strong pietistic predispositions, it gives rise to a common tendency among humanity to attribute certain amount of supernatural power to anything they consider to be from above. A host of such objects as the baptismal water, the wafer and wine used in the Eucharist, and so on are regarded to be holy in the ordinary lives of the people. These objects are normally regarded as talismans – as having some magical power, and hence venerable. In this context, it will be resourceful to look at Luther's understanding of the sacraments. His basic understanding of the sacraments is that they only *represent* a sign of God's promise offered through God's word, which is existentially appropriated in our life as real through true faith. In the absence of these two empirical factors – God's promise and our faith – the sacramental elements contribute nothing to our salvation.[141] With assiduous consistency, Luther explains this factor in his writings, especially in his polemical writings against the Roman sacramentalism, to drive home this truth into the minds of his readers. Luther affirms:

> The very first thing necessary, then is faith, in these words [the words of institution] and signs, man must be fully and whole heartedly believe that [what] he [Jesus] says and signifies is true.[142]
>
> Since every sacrament contains a divine word and promise in which God offers and pledges his grace, it is truly not enough just to put away the obstacles as they [Rome] call it, but there must be an unwavering, unshaken faith in the heart which receives the promise and sign...[143]
>
> Hence to seek the efficacy of the sacrament apart from the promise and without faith is to labor in vain and to find condemnation.[144]

Thus it can be summed up that neither the act of Baptism nor the external element (water) is efficacious but only the word of promise of God that is effective. Similarly, neither the baptizer nor the baptized is important but God is everything in Baptism, according to Luther. Three important principles can be deduced from Luther's treatment of Baptism: (a) its close interrelation to the cross of Christ,[145] (b) its efficacy on all human beings irrespective of their age,[146] and (c) its work of gathering the believers as a communion or body of Christ.[147]

Sacrament of the Lord's Supper

In Luther's perception, the Eucharist is one of the most essential symbols that points to and builds up the Church as the communion of saints. "The Eucharist is the sacrament of love" and in the making of bread the individual grains of wheat lose their individual shape and form, and disappear in the flour to become one loaf. Similarly the grapes lose their individual existence in becoming wine. And while we eat and drink the same bread and wine, we, as individual believers are transformed into one body, which is the communion of saints, a process in which the individual identity dissipates and they obtain a collective identity as the body of Christ.[148] The sacrament of the mass, then, points to love as the underlying principle of Christian life and witness.[149] Of course, the idea that the 'Eucharist is a symbol of love' appears often in the ancient teachers of faith and later theologians of the Church like Cyprian, Augustine and Aquinas, but with only scant reference to the fact that in the Eucharistic situation the many become one. But what is most important in Luther's interpretation is the idea that the grains of wheat and the grapes lose their own form, just as Christ has taken our form and we take Christ's form and that of the others. It is a mark of "true brotherhood" in Luther's understanding.[150] Close in heels with this perception of the *Communio* Luther emphasizes the twofold significance of the Eucharist: *it guarantees the partaker of the priestly sacrifice of Christ for his/her sake*; and *it demands a priestly sacrifice of the believer for the sake of others.*[151]

Thus, being a communion that is built on the sacrifice of Christ, the Christians of the *Communio sanctorum* cannot have the luxury of complacency and satisfaction to the extent of forgetting their duty. Rather it demands their commitment to the Church and fellow believers, especially in their need as explained by Luther himself:

> When you have partaken of this sacrament, therefore, or desire to partake of it, you must in turn share the misfortune of the community...Your heart must go out in love and learn that this is a sacrament of love. As love and support are given you, you in turn must render love and support to Christ and his needy ones.[152]

Over against the individualistic perception of the Eucharist by the medieval Church, Luther argues that individual or egocentric gains are out of the purview of the Lord's Supper because the basis as well as the fruit of the Eucharist is love. Here, Luther seems to be making a comparison between the primitive Christian Lord's Supper and the distorted and individualistically celebrated sacrament of the mass that was common in his time. His new exposition reminds the communion of believers that the Lord's Supper that was in practice in the primitive Church was the confession and sign which enabled the Christians to recognize each other and which resulted in persecution and death,[153] a clear pointer to his theology of the cross, which is a central symbol of the Christian Church, the communion of saints.

These thoughts had, however, been relegated to the background once Luther confronted the issue of the real presence of the body and blood of Christ in the Eucharistic bread and wine, especially the doctrines of *transubstantiation* and *consubstantiation.* In the medieval doctrine of *transubstantiation* (promulgated by the Fourth Lateran Council, 1215 CE), the Church taught that the substance of the elements – the bread and the wine – was changed into the substance of Christ's body and blood, while the accidents of the elements remained unchanged in the celebration of the mass.[154] Over against this teaching, Luther advanced the doctrine of the real presence. Here, we need to look at the historical development of this doctrine distinguishing two phases of its development: (a) pre 1524 – when Luther was opposing Roman sacramentalism (that taught the mass as a *sacrifice offered to God*) and trying to establish the meaning of the sacrament of the Lord's Supper *as a gift of God*; and (b) post 1524 – when he was wrestling against the Enthusiasts and trying to oppose all symbolic interpretations in order to establish *the bodily presence of the body and blood of Christ* in the bread and wine used in the Eucharist.

In his new exposition of the doctrine of the Eucharist the major modification he made was to discard the doctrine of transubstantiation and to substitute it with the theory of consubstantiation. It proposes that the sacrament is held together by two rudiments – *the promise of forgiveness* and *faith.* "For without promise there is nothing to believe, while without faith, the promise remains without effect; for it is established and fulfilled through faith".[155] The entire power of the mass rests on the words of Christ because through his words he says that the remission of sins is bestowed on all those who believe that his body is broken and his blood shed for them. In the mass, Christ affixed his body and blood as a memorial sign of this great promise when he said, "Do this in remembrance of me". This makes it clear that in every promise of God two essential factors are offered to us – the word and the sign – in order that we may grasp the Word to be the promise (testament or covenant) and the sign to be the sacrament.

> Thus in the mass, the word of Christ is the testament, and the bread and wine are the sacrament.[156]
> [T]he mass is...the gift and promise of God, offered to all men by the hand of the priest. It is certain, therefore, that the mass is not a work which may be communicated, but it is the object...of faith, for the strengthening and nourishing of the personal faith of each individual.[157]

This is the position Luther maintained over against the Roman belief of the mass as a "sacrifice offered to God".

Luther realized that the Church had confused the doctrine of transubstantiation (pertaining to the miracle of real presence) erroneously with an article of faith, which was incompatible with the scriptural teaching of the Lord's Supper. What made him so scornful was the fact that this theory was based on the philosophical metaphysics of Aristotle.[158] Luther found this as a captivity of the sacrament and he employed analogical method to retrieve the meaning of the sacrament with his theory of real presence, which directly links up to Christology, i.e., the deity dwells in the complete and untransformed human nature.[159] The Eucharist, in his view, bears the twofold sign of the *Communio* – the Christian is assured that Christ and his saints are interceding for him/her, and in turn he/she is obligated to work and intercede for the benefit of Christ and his people. This is the true mark of the sacrament, which, in fact is a sacrament of love that finds its expression in the *Communio sanctorum.* In his "A Treatise on the New Testament, that is, the Holy Mass", Luther insists on the importance of the words of Jesus. "Everything depends...on the words of this sacrament. These are the words of Christ".[160] It demands humans to grasp the promise – the promise of the forgiveness of sins – in simple faith because Christ, by his death, has established this promise in an irrevocable manner. This is a new development in the later phase of Luther's thinking with regard to the doctrine of the real presence.

For his doctrine of real presence, Luther derived his basic source from Paul's interpretation of the Eucharist in his first letter to the Corinthians chapters 10 and 11. Here, he argues that the words of institution must be understood and followed as they read without ascribing any tropological meaning. This corresponds to his general principle of scriptural interpretation – every text of the scripture must be understood according to its simple literal meaning as he suggests: "In Scripture we should let the words retain their natural force, just as they read, and give no other interpretation unless a clear article of faith compels us otherwise".[161] With regard to the words of institution of the Lord's Supper, Luther is rather passionate in his commitment to adhere to the literal sense of those words. In the year 1528 Luther made a memorable statement in his "Confession Concerning Christ's Supper", expressing his passionate commitment to preserve the literal sense of the words of institution of the Lord's Supper. It also reflects his perception of God-human relationship, the relationship between divine truth and human reason, and the relationship between God's word and human faith. To quote him:

> First, when we are dealing with the works and words of God, reason and all human wisdom must submit to being taken captive, as St. Paul teaches in II Corinthians 10 [:5]. They must allow themselves to be blinded and led, directed, and instructed, lest we presume to sit in judgment over God's words. We shall surely lose out when we try to judge his words as Psalm 51 [:4] testifies. Second, if we surrender to him and confess that we do not comprehend his words and works, we should be satisfied. We should speak of his works simply using his words as he pronounced them for us and prescribed that we speak them after him; and we should not presume to use our words as if they were better than his. For we surely go wrong unless we simply repeat his words after him as he pronounces them for us, just as a child repeats the creed or the Lord's Prayer after his father. Here we need to walk in the dark with our eyes closed, and simply cling to the word and follow. For since we are confronted by God's word, "This is my body" – distinct, clear, common, definite words, which certainly are no trope, either in scripture or in any language – we must embrace them with faith, and allow our reason to be blinded and taken

> captive. So, not as hairsplitting sophistry dictates but as God says them for us, we must repeat these words after him and hold to them.[162]

God's unambiguous Words must, thus, be obeyed unconditionally, according to Luther, whether we understand or not as to how Christ's body and blood are present in the bread and wine. Luther iterates that the *how* of the real presence is to be hidden from our reason.[163] This reflects his general tendency to posit reason as antithetical and incompatible to faith. For, in his view, if reason is allowed to function autonomously, it will impinge upon the realm of faith and shatter its very foundation because "if it [reason] disapproves this one, it also disapproves all articles. For God's Word is always folly to reason, I Corinthians 1[:8]."[164] Therefore, in religious matters rational argument must give way to simple faith and an unconditional and absolute obedience to the Word of God, because if we allow rational objections to one article of faith, it will lead to a train of such objections.[165]

The real presence, that is, *the bodily presence of the true body and blood of Christ in the bread and wine*, occurs in the community celebration of the Eucharist. In this celebration, the celebrant who acts "as the mouth of all of us", performs and speaks (or sings) Christ's own words of institution. Within this whole exercise of celebration, the decisive element is the words: "This is my body" and "This is my blood" and through the power of these words, Christ's body and blood are present. All that matters for us in the Eucharist is our faith and if anyone partakes of it without faith he/she becomes unworthy. In such instances, it works as poison and brings about death and judgment. In this sense, the Eucharistic situation is an occasion in which grace draws and places a person for a decision – a decision either for life or for death.

There is a close interconnection between Luther's Christology and his theology of real presence. In his Christology the interrelation between the divine and human natures of Christ finds an extensive place. This was given birth by the Christological concept of *perichoresis* (the mutual indwelling of the divine and human natures in the person of Christ). The Reformer radicalized this idea using another existent concept, namely, the concept of the *communicatio idiomatum* (communication of attributes). The outcome of his opinion on the communication of attributes later led him in two different directions. The *first* one is the omnipresence of the body of Christ, which emanates from the idea that the attributes of Christ's human nature participate in the divine attribute of ubiquity or omnipresence. This concept gave much force to Luther's understanding of the 'real presence' of the body and blood of Christ *with*, *in* and *under* the sacramental elements and it has deep soteriological value to Luther. The *second* one is the idea of the suffering God. To Luther the *communicatio idiomatum* is not a one way path in which only the human attributes take part in the divine attributes, rather it also implies that the divinity is involved in humanity and the inevitable outcome is the idea of God undergoing the human destiny and suffering. Even though Luther did not develop the theory of the "suffering God" as developed by the 19th and 20th century theology, this thought was already present in Luther's thinking. This is evidenced from his concept of the "cross from eternity"[166] and one cannot deny Luther's influence on theologians who took the notion of the *pain of God* in their theological reflections.[167]

Luther, however, shifted his focus from the religious/social interpretation of the Lord's Supper to the metaphysical-judicial-forensic interpretation once he had to face the opposition of his attackers (the Enthusiasts and Roman Church), almost restricting and impoverishing the Sacrament of its deeper meaning, which has its own ramifications. *First*, As Paul Althaus affirms:

> There can be no question that this development restricted and impoverished the doctrine of the sacrament of the Lord's Supper and the celebration of this meal in the Lutheran Church compared with its fullness among primitive Christians.... As celebrated in our Church, it is certainly the high point of the individual Christian life; but is not equally the community's life of sharing as the body of Christ. In this respect Luther's earliest writings (the treatise of 1519) stand far above all those that follow. We today must once again take up his (earlier) thoughts.[168]

Second, the doctrine of justification and that of the Eucharist have also become a vexing issue and a stumbling block in the way of ecumenical dialogues. In the ecumenical dialogues between the Indian Churches during the previous decades, the Lutheran theologians, for instance, were bent upon consensus on the dogmatic issues over against the others.[169] *Third*, unintended by the Reformer though, his thoughts had led at least a section of the Church organized around his name to hold on to doctrinal rigidity/primacy over all other aspects of Christian spirituality. The negative attitude of the Confessional Lutheran Churches towards the historic signing of the document: "Joint Declaration on the Doctrine of Justification" (JDDJ) by the Lutheran and the Roman Catholic Churches at Augsburg on the Reformation Day, 1999, for instance, is based purely on doctrinal issues. In response to the JDDJ, Robert Preus writes:

> First, any attempt at rapprochement between Lutheran Churches and Rome might well begin with a serious attempt to find consensus on the article of justification. Second, to establish true and meaningful consensus on the doctrine of justification will involve serious study of the topics of sin, Law, Gospel, redemption, repentance, Church, Sacraments, eschatology, and all the articles of faith which are integral to and interrelated with the entire body of doctrine.[170]

Luther's understanding of the Eucharist, especially his earlier interpretation, in fact, transcends such narrow developments and brings out an important insight, namely, the sacrament as symbolizing "true brotherhood",[171] which needs to be further elaborated, interpreted, and critically evaluated. In one of his sermons at the Wittenberg Church, Luther charged the Christians as follows:

> You are willing to take all of God's goods in the sacrament, but you are not willing to pour them out again in love. Nobody extends a helping hand to another, nobody seriously considers the other person, but everyone looks out for himself and his own gain, insists on his own way, and lets everything else go.[172]

Luther considers this tendency amounts to be blasphemy as he asserts: "What terrible blasphemy against God that we all take the sacrament and want to be good Christians, but none of us is willing to stoop down and serve our neighbour".[173] It is unfortunate that the contemporary Church has either lost or willfully obscured Luther's earlier interpretation of the Lord's Supper. For the Church to be contextually appropriate, it has to unearth such spiritual/theological resources, so that it can render an authentic Christian voice in the contemporary Hindu nationalist situation in India. The foregoing discussion on the Sacraments points to another important element in ecclesiology, i.e., (office of the) ministry.

Public Ministry

As Luther understands, the office of the ministry is one of the visible signs or manifestations of the Church in this world and he expounded the office of the ministry based on the principle of servanthood in opposition to the non-personal materialistic interpretation of the saints in scholastic theology and the related theory of merit formulated in the 13th century.[174] Here 'merit' (*Verdienst*) is replaced with service (*Dienst*) and Luther underscores our Christian responsibility to bear the burdens of others following the example of Christ. It obviously suggests that the reality of the Christian communion (not the notion of religious individualism) forms the basis or locus of Luther's conception of ministry.[175]

The communion of saints, with the visible signs, is the historical reality in and through which God works in the world and provides the premise where this communion shares the *royal priesthood* with Christ. Following this principle, Luther explained the priesthood as a "holy order" for the Church universal instituted by God through the authority of the Word.[176] The theory of the universal priesthood of all believers as developed by Luther can thus be seen as one of the most fertile, significant, and radical doctrines in the history of Christian thought. Much of its inherent meaning and implications, however, have either been lost or befogged over the elapse of time in the institutionalized Church.

The office of the ministry is founded on the principle of the priesthood and its credibility and validity is contingent on the principle of servanthood. In this sense, every Christian is a servant-priest (1 Cor. 4:1), vested with the responsibility of true service and stewardship. Thus, parish priests are *not* a special class of people, as often been presumed and interpreted; rather they are on equal footing with every other believer, with only a functional difference. The hierarchical structure of ecclesia, according to Luther, is not a Christian idea but an idea found its way into Jewish culture from Pagan cultic symbols, and Christianity inherited it from these sources.[177] Thus the consecration of priests is not a sacrament of the holy order but a liturgical function of the local Church – a rite – through which a believer is *called* to the public office of the ministry *in the stead of* the communion of the faithful as a whole.

This call to the public ministry does not presuppose any license to the arbitrary exercise of self-ordination, as it would create chaos in the Church and would amount to disobedience to God. It is God's will that "nothing be done as a result of one's own choice or decision, but everything as a consequence of a *command* (*befehl*) or a *call (Beruf)*".[178] The fundamental duties of a priest are, among others, the preaching of the Word and administering the Sacraments in their proper form as commanded by God. These specific activities cannot be and shall not be done by everyone, for to do so is to create "shameful confusion".[179]

> For the whole group cannot do this but must either themselves order someone or permit someone to do it. Otherwise what would be the result if everyone wanted to preach or to administer the sacrament and no one would give in to anyone else? One individual must be appointed and he must do the preaching.[180]

In this light, one can arrive at the conclusion that the office of the ministry is a temporal arrangement made by the people of God in order to maintain order and discipline and to avoid inner confusion within the communion. It can also be maintained that Luther could not accept ordination as a sacrament because it is only a temporal arrangement by the people of God and it does not fall within the parameters of the basic principles of a Sacrament. The necessity of such an arrangement, however, is not denied as it is derived from the scripture. Paul, for instance, affirms that God has given specific gifts to individual believers and appointed them to different tasks for the common good (Eph 4:8-11, 1 Cor. 12:7).[181]

The office of the ministry is one of the key doctrines that has generated much heat and dust within ecumenical deliberations and still remains unresolved even among the Protestant Churches. It raises a fundamental question: Is the office of the public ministry established by divine will and command or is it a product of temporal arrangement by the people of God for social expediency?[182] Lutheranism, however, invested a strong dose of divine authority on the ordained ministry mainly for reasons of institutional validity as demonstrated by the claims of ordained ministry as the gift of the Spirit.[183] But, behind his derivations of the ordained ministry, Luther had certain important purposes: to challenge the papal abuse of power, to break down the walls that separated the clergy and laity, to put the Church back on a strong Biblical footing, and to orient the Church to the service of the Gospel of Christ. Hence, even though he does not discard the role of the Spirit in upholding the office of the ministry, he, nevertheless, posits ordination as a rite exercised by the Church. In this process, Luther attempts to bring two apparently antithetical derivations of the office of the ministry – the *call* and the *command* – in a framework of synthesis, and he finds no inner contradiction in this method. We can identify two lines of thinking operant in Luther in the development of this doctrine: *the call* is dependent on Luther's understanding of the universal priesthood of all believers and as such it is a mediated office; and *the command* is gleaned directly from its establishment by Christ without seeking recourse to the universal priesthood, and hence, it is an unmediated office.

Here, we should be able to identify the two different lines of discourse that had given rise to the development of the doctrine of the office of the ministry in Roman Catholic and Lutheran traditions. In the former, the Bishops who are in the line of apostolic succession, and who are under the authority of the Pope, appoint and ordain the lower clergy. The Priests must be male celibates and they must subject themselves to their superiors up to the Canon law. Thus, they have a special status derived from the Bishops conferred by ordination. Logically, then, there can be no equality of status between clergy and laity – the laity is below that of the entire hierarchy. They are required to obey and uphold this elaborate hierarchical system, because it is believed that the structure is anchored in divine law with the underlying notion that it is perfect and, hence, eternally valid and immutable. It has given rise to a rigid establishment of a Church structure, which is as rigid as a rock.

Conversely, Luther came to the understanding of the ordained ministry in response to his conflicts with the Papists and the Enthusiasts through his dialectic of God's internal and external rules by means of God's Word as Law and Gospel, on the one hand, and through the institutions and structures of the society respectively, on the other. What is basic in Luther's understanding is the preaching of the Word and the administration of the Sacraments. The ordained minister is a representative and the servant of the Church, while the Church as a whole is set apart to be the servant and representative of God in the world. It does not ascribe any special status to the clergy apart from a functional difference.[184]

Luther made a distinction between the ministry of the members of the Church for one another and the public ministry (for the whole community), i.e., to exercise the office at times of emergency and to exercise the same in public: "For it is one thing to exercise the right publicly; another to use it in times of emergency. Publicly one may not exercise a right without the consent of the whole body or of the Church. In times of emergency each may use it as he deems best".[185] Thus, to Luther, the office of the public ministry is established for the sake of order (even though it has important ministries of the Word and Sacraments) within the congregation in line with what Paul commands in 1 Cor. 14:40, "all things should be done decently and in order". By the act of calling an individual to public ministry, the congregation delegates the authority it possesses to the person called for the purpose. Only then *he* exercises his office in accordance with the call and on behalf of the congregation. As the authority of the Word and Sacraments has been vested with the entire congregation, no individual member should dare presume to exercise it on arbitrary authority. On the contrary, the pastor is the one who "teaches and preaches in the *stead of* and on the *commission of* the rest".[186]

In summary, it can be concluded that Luther found the principle of the universal priesthood engendered by justification and upheld by servanthood as the foundation of the office of the ministry in the Church. These concepts have both spiritual and social consequences. Spiritually, they signify the privilege (the liberation from the burdens of sin) and the communion that the believers enjoy with God in Christ. It entails that, before God, hierarchy or discrimination withers away in order to give way for the equality of all believers. Socially, these symbols engender the freedom and dignity, which is the most essential component to have any meaningful relationship within the society. They undercut all notions or intentions of ostracism because no one is excluded from the purview of the saving grace of God. Thus, what constitutes ecclesia is essentially the intimate relationship – "true brotherhood" – that exists among the believers. This ecclesia exists to build relationships (communion) across all boundaries. We will return to these insights in the ensuing chapters of this study. For the moment, we shall turn to the Reformer's interpretation of the Church-State relationship.

Church and State – Two Realms of God's Activity

The meaning of the term *State* at this stage is highly misleading if we transpose the modern notion of the *secular state* to Luther's time because medieval Europe never had the notion of a nation state as we have it today. What Luther dealt with in his writings was two distinctive but inseparably interrelated entities: the *temporal* and *spiritual* authorities. The medieval society exhibited a great deal of ambiguity with regard to the relationship between these two realms. At one level, they were clearly distinguished and disjuncted as antithetical or polar opposites. Ecclesia, at this level, was viewed as belonging to the spiritual realm and the temporal world was viewed as evil with the predominant spiritual metaphor of denial of the world, which was seen as an important prerequisite for a true spiritual or pietistic or religious life. At another level, the Church and State were viewed as identical entities, a fact that was attested by the Church's readiness to adopt a structure completely identical to that of the temporal realm.[187] The medieval Church was itself owned huge lands and it exercised enormous political powers. It was also infected with worldliness, moral decadence and corruption, extending even up to the monastic orders. Luther came to experience these existential realities himself when he entered the Augustinian cloister, known for its disciplined austerities.

In this milieu of complex Church-State interface, Luther viewed them dialectically rather than as separate, autonomous or opposite entities,[188] following his method of the *unity of the opposites*. For him, reality is not *split* into segments of damnation and salvation, but rather characterized by a *conflict* between salvation and damnation, good and evil, and so on. This perception has prompted him to appreciate even all aesthetics, including the family life, as God's gifts for the service of humanity. For, at times, Luther spoke of God's rule in terms of "three orders" – the home, the state and the Church.[189] In this process he constructed his key thesis: *Christians live in two kingdoms simultaneously* – the kingdom of God and the kingdom of the World – in consonance with his central theological principle, i.e., the unity of the opposites. We need to be cautious not to fall into the easy trap of misrepresenting Luther concerning his theology of the two kingdoms. As mentioned, sometimes Luther spoke about three orders and at other instances he talked about God's rule in two kingdoms. A major point to bear in mind is the different implications of the phrase "two kingdoms" in Luther's usage: the two kingdoms can denote the hostile kingdoms of God and the devil; and it can also refer to the two Governments (spiritual and temporal authorities) that God had established precisely to frustrate Satan's designs.[190] A notable point is that in these delineations, Luther's was not philosophical but practical.

Luther's theology of two kingdoms was informed by biblical principles. The New Testament makes a distinction between the spiritual and temporal authorities without dichotomizing them because ultimately God is in control of both the realms (John 19:10-11). Nevertheless, there is considerable ambivalence in this perception of the relationship between the Church and the state. On the one hand, even the pagan civil Government is God's instrument in order to enhance the life of its citizens and hence it must be respected and obeyed (Rom 13:1-7 especially v 4, Matt 22:15-22). But, on the other hand, the New Testament draws clear boundaries between human obedience to spiritual and temporal authorities (Acts 4:18-20, 5:27-29). The Scripture demands absolute loyalty to God when Christians are in a compelling situation to make a choice between their loyalty to the Spiritual and Civil Authorities. Thus, the basic Christian attitude towards the civil authority must be respectful obedience and positive cooperation as it is God who established it. But Christians must be ultimately loyal to God than the civil authority when there is a demanding situation, which is a direct inference from Matthew 10: 28.

In his interpretation of the Church-State interface, Luther followed his basic principle of the *unity of the opposites* with careful precision and maintained that Christians live in both the realms simultaneously and that these two realms must be clearly distinguished without being disjuncted.[191] He explained the purpose of the temporal authority, its proper limits, and the appropriate Christian response to it in his tract: "Temporal authority: To what extent It Should Be Obeyed (1523)".[192] His distinction of the two Kingdoms is based on his understanding of two kinds of human justice – Christian/spiritual and civil justice – in which, the former is rooted in faith and the latter is rooted in human morality.[193] The civil authority, as seen by Luther, is not something to be despised but to be honoured as it is established by God for order and for human well being. The civil Government, in the strict analysis, reflects God's gracious concern for the creation. This is a new perception indeed, which finds God's activity beyond the rigid boundaries of the Church, and God is seen as the Lord of both Church and State. Each entity, however, is governed by different means: Law and Gospel respectively. Accordingly, there are two kinds of justice (righteousness) – Christian or spiritual justice (rooted in faith created by the Holy Spirit), and civil righteousness (based on human rationality). Thus, human beings are righteous in relation to God only by faith; but they may be righteous in the civil sense by way of upholding the law of the society. Christian justice is grounded in the Gospel, which works faith in the Christians through the Holy Spirit, whereas civil justice judges according to the measure of one's obedience to the law.[194]

In this way, Luther preserves an equilibrium between Christian and civil justice, which leads to the question of resisting evil, and in his theology, the issue of resistance or non-resistance of evil is held in a tension. Only the situation will decide as to what an appropriate Christian response to violence is. Luther argues:

> In this way, the two propositions are brought into harmony with one another: at one and the same time you satisfy God's kingdom inwardly and the kingdom of the World outwardly. You suffer evil and injustice, and yet at the same time you punish evil and injustice; you do not resist evil, and at the same time, you do resist it. In the one case, you consider yourself and what is yours; in the other, you consider your neighbor and what is his. In what concerns you and yours, you govern yourself by the gospel and suffer injustice toward yourself as a true Christian; in what concerns the person or property of others, you govern yourself according to love and tolerate no injustice towards your neighbor. The gospel does not forbid this; in fact, in other places it actually commands it.[195]

This is one of the most crucial issues that generates much heat in the debates concerning the liberation of the marginalized. The question is whether violent resistance is justifiable in the struggle for justice and there are protagonists of both the viewpoints. Luther's critics identify his engagement with the Peasant War, especially his advocacy to use (brutal) force to deal with the rebels, as the dark spot in his career. His reaction, however, is not arbitrary rather it has its roots in his understanding of violence as he emphatically stated:

> For rebellion is not just simple murder; it is like a great fire, which attacks and devastates a whole land. Thus rebellion brings with it a land filled with murder and bloodshed; it creates widows and orphans, and turns everything upside down, like the worst disaster. Therefore let everyone who can, *smite*, *slay*, and *stab*, secretly or openly, remembering that nothing can be more poisonous, hurtful, or devilish than the rebel. It is just as when one must kill a mad dog; if you do not strike him, he will strike you, and a whole land with you.[196]

The issue, nevertheless, is not so simple to deal with. As is well known, history offers us with numerous instances in which the principle of non-violence provided the strong foundation for great personalities to fight against evil. In his struggle against the British, for instance, Gandhi used the weapon of non-violence. A more recent example is the Truth and Reconciliation Commission in South Africa.[197] Similarly, Jesus denounced armed resistance and no civilized society will advocate violence as a means of retribution (more discussion on this to follow in the ensuing chapter). Coming back to the Reformer, while his *theological reasons* are fully justified, his *final verdict* became absurd for the simple reason that in order to quench one type of violence Luther advocated another type and it happened to be against the oppressed, which is viewed with utmost seriousness. Hence, we need to consistently maintain a distinction between these two aspects of his writings in our research.

For Luther, there is a clear distinction between the principles that govern the Church and the State: the former is ruled by faith and love, and the latter is governed by reason and justice. As far as civil justice is concerned, Luther was aware that human rationality is capable of finding a good set of positive laws and upright customs to serve society – no matter how many or few Christians lived in it.[198] Thus, Luther viewed natural law as capable of providing human reason all that is needed for civil justice and, therefore, it must be grounded in the law and human reason rather than in the Gospel and faith. But at the same time, he was well aware of the ill effects of civil authority, especially when it pertains to matters of faith and religiosity. It prompted him to make a distinction between the exercise of authority appropriate to the Church and that of the State.

> We want to make this so clear that everyone will grasp it, and our fine gentlemen, the princes and bishops, will see what fools they are when they seek to coerce the people with their laws and commandments into believing this and that...[199]
> Again you say, 'The temporal power is not forcing men to believe; it is simply seeing to it externally that no one deceives the people by false doctrine; how could heretics otherwise be restrained?' Answer: This the bishops should do; it is a function entrusted to them and not to the princes. Heresy can never be restrained by

> force. One will have to tackle the problem in some other way, for heresy must be opposed and dealt with otherwise than with sword. Here God's word must do the fighting. If it does not succeed, certainly the temporal power will succeed either, even if it were to drench the world in blood. Heresy is a spiritual matter which you cannot hack to pieces with iron.[200]

Thus, within the Reformer's delineations, the temporal authority and the spiritual authority are preserved in a dialectical tension without letting them to be dichotomized or homogenized. The Church and the State are the two realms of God's activity for the benefit of God's people. This distinction emerged with a definite purpose of challenging and resisting the corruption of the Church, which had assumed political power and used the same for selfish ends. It enabled him to condemn the passage of indulgence with an incisive argument that the forgiveness of sins is a free gift of God appropriated through faith and not to be traded for economic advantage. It also added strength to his critique of the ecclesiastical structure, which had given rise to a manifestly concrete system of exploitation.[201]

Summary

Luther's ecclesiology is a communion ecclesiology, which is held together by God's redeeming love and the communion of the believers with Jesus Christ and with fellow believers. The theological principle that animated his ecclesiological discourse is his method of the *unity of the opposites*, which had enabled him to critique the existing structure and style of function of ecclesia and reconstruct the theology of the Church in order to make the Church respond to the crisis situation of his own time. It certainly marks a paradigm shift of viewing reality in dialectical terms over against the medieval 'synthetic' approach. This major shift was aimed at re-inscribing the Gospel at the centre of ecclesial life and to make it available to the public. David V. N. Bagchi, for instance, understands that during the Reformation period, "theology has moved out of the lecture hall and into the public domain to an extent rarely paralleled in the history of Christianity".[202]

Scholars and researchers generally regard Reformer's *theology of the cross* and *doctrine of justification* as the two central elements that navigate the entire spectrum of his theology, in which the former provided the perspective and the latter played the key hermeneutical role in his theological constructions.[203] The Reformer employed these critical elements not arbitrarily, but self-consciously, i.e., for the purpose of bringing together ostensibly antithetical categories into a vital dialogical relationship with a clear focus on human existential condition. Hence, for instance, when he deals with the sinful condition of human beings and their salvation, he invokes the symbols of *justification* and *cross*. In this procedure, he first makes a *distinction* between God's righteousness and human sinfulness. But what is the meeting point of these two opposite categories? It is at this point, Luther turns to the cross and discovers that God meets human beings in their sinfulness on the cross of Christ and *imputes* Christ's righteousness on them, *declaring* them righteous on account of Christ. It is very important not to miss out the terms "impute" and "declare", which clearly explain Luther's way of thinking that human beings neither merited this righteousness through fulfilling their moral obligations nor are they *made* righteous to be complete autonomous selves; rather they are both saints and sinners at the same time. It further enabled him to view reality in terms of a set of dualism of opposites, and the method of distinction between the opposites has become a regular feature of his theology.

But if we stop at this point, then we would end up in misreading Luther of dichotomizing reality into separate realms or domains, as done by many scholars and critics in the past. As a matter of fact, the method of distinction forms only one part of the Reformer's way of thinking; and to stop with it would provide only partial understanding of the Reformer's theology. He does not stop with distinguishing; rather he moves further to integrate them in a balanced manner. Therefore, a full grasp of the Reformer's theology is possible only when we allow both distinction and integration to come together. To be sure, *distinction* and *integration* serve as two sides of the same coin in his theology. Thus, for instance, in the preface to his Commentary on Galatians (1535), the Reformer asserted:

> This is our theology, by which we preach a precise distinction between two kinds of righteousness, the active and passive, so that morality and faith, works and grace, secular society and religion may not be *confused*. Both are necessary, but both must be kept within their limits. [Emphasis added][204]

It is quite unfortunate that only the principle of distinction has prominently captivated the attention of many scholars. It has led many critics to hurl virulent attacks on him, particularly related to his doctrine of the Church-State relationship. Further, it also led up to the gross misuse of it in the history of Germany in the 20th century when even many well-meaning Lutheran theologians made a preferential option to side with Hitler's National Socialism.

But the Reformer's central theological principle has two sides: *distinction* and *integration*. In this regard, Luther's own position is that human beings exist in two dependent and interdependent domains, intrinsically and essentially, characterized by two interrelated domains of relationship, which may be explained in terms of vertical and horizontal spheres. In Robert Kolb's words, "the vertical relationship is delineated with God both above us (because he is the lord and author of the life of his children) and beneath us (because he is the loving Father who lifts us up and cuddles us to himself in Christ). The horizontal relationship has bound us to the rest of creation as people who are held accountable for exercising God-given responsibilities toward other creatures in an adult manner, human but also animal, mineral, and vegetable".[205]

An important point to note in this way of Luther's thinking is that he posits human ethical activities as a consequential movement, and not a causal movement. That is to say that good works towards our fellow humans and to the creation as a whole can proceed only from a good person (justified sinner). Paul Tillich's maxim, "religious reservation" and "religious obligation", i.e., 'because we receive from above in grace we give freely' clearly brings out the depth of meaning inherent in Luther's method of distinction and integration.[206] The apt Biblical illustration to make this point clear is Jesus' own saying: "...every good tree bears good fruit, but the bad tree bears bad fruit. A good tree cannot bear bad fruits, nor can a bad tree bear good fruit...Thus you will know them by their fruits" (Mt 7:17-20). The 'good tree' is none other than the one who is justified on account of Christ and good fruits can come forth only from those who are good. The Reformer's thoughts on the Church clearly exhibit the operation of this principle right through. It is our task now to critically evaluate the Reformer's thoughts on the Church and see the appropriate ways in which we can enter into dialogue with those thoughts in our own reflections on ecclesia in the contemporary context of Hindu nationalism.

Notes

1 To have a glimpse of the conflicting socio-political reality in which Christianity emerged, see Gillian Clark, *Christianity and the Roman Society* (op. cit.).

2 H. Richard Niebhur, *The Social Sources of Denominationalism* (New York: Meridian Books, 4th Printing, 1960), pp. 34-35.

3 Hans Küng, *Christianity*, p. 524.

4 Klaus Nürnberger, *Martin Luther's Message for Us Today*, p. 2.

5 The philosophical-theological factors include: Platonism and Neo-Platonism, Stoicism, Renaissance Humanism, Mysticism, Nominalism, and Medieval Scholasticism. Since the scope of this study does not permit us to delve deep into these important factors, we would mention certain important texts that deal with them in detail for the benefit of the readers. (i) Heiko A. Oberman, *Luther: Man Between God and the Devil* (New York: Image Books, 1992), (ii) Gerhard Ebeling, *Luther: An Introduction to His Thought* (London: Collins, 1970), (iii) Paul Tillich, *The Protestant Era*, Tr. by James Luther Adam (Chicago: Phoenix Books, 1963), (iv) Etienne Gilson, *History of Christian Philosophy in the Middle Ages* (London: Sheed and Ward, 1955), (v) Colin Brown, *Philosophy & the Christian Faith* (Illinois: Inter Varsity Press, 1968), (vi) Paul Tillich, *A History of Christian Thought* (New York: Harper & Row, 1968), (vii) Sem Dresden, *Humanism in the Renaissance*, Tr. from Dutch by Margaret King (London: World University Library, 1968), (viii) Martin C. D'Arcy, *Humanism and Christianity* (New York: An Nal Book, 1969), (ix) Carl E. Braaten, "Introduction" in Paul Tillich, *Perspectives on 19th and 20th Century Protestant Theology* (New York: Harper and Row Publishers, 1967), (x) Andrew Louth, "Dionysius the Areopagite" in T. A. Hart, ed., *The Dictionary of*

Historical Theology (Grand Rapid, Michigan: Wm B Eerdmans, 2000), (xi) A.N.S. Lane, "Bernard of Clairvaux (1090/1-1153)" in *The Dictionary of Historical Theology*, (xii) Richard Cross, "Nominalism" in *The Dictionary of Historical Theology*, (xiii) Bengt Hägglund, *History of Theology*, Tr. By Gene J. Lund Saint Louis: Concordia Publishing House, 1968), (xiv) Gordon Leff, *Medieval Thought: From Augustine to Ockham* (Middlesex: Penguin, 1958), (xv) Alexander Broadie, "Duns Scotus and William Ockham" in G. R. Evans, ed., *The Medieval Theologians* (Oxford: Blackwell, 2001), pp. 250-265, (xvi) "Apology to the Augsburg Confession", in *Book of Concord*, ed. By Theodore G. Tappert (Philadelphia: Fortress Press, 1959), pp. 187-232, (xvii) Jacques Rossel, *The Roots of Western Europe: An Essay on Interpretation of Cultures during the First Nine Centuries A. D.* (Bangalore: ATC, 2nd edition, 2001), and (xviii) Martin Luther, "The Disputation against Scholastic Theology" (1517), *LW* 31, pp. 3-16; *WA* 1, pp. 221-228.

6 For biographical details of Luther, the following works can be consulted: Roland H. Bainton, *Here I Stand: A Life of Martin Luther* (Nashville: Abingdon Press, 1959); James M. Kittleson, *Luther the Reformer* (Minneapolis: Augsburg Publishing House, 1986). For a brief biography, see Robert Kolb, *Luther's Way of Thinking: Introductory Essays* (Trivandrum: Luther Academy India, 2006), pp. 1-36.

7 This must not be dismissed as a retroactive rationalizing, for it was the typical response of devout pilgrims who visited Rome during that time. Erasmus (also an Augustinian monk), from his visit to Rome five years before Luther, reported: "[W]ith my own ears I heard the most loathsome blasphemies against Christ and His Apostles. Many acquaintances of mine have heard priests of the curia uttering disgusting words so loudly, even during mass, that all around them could hear". There is a further report that ten years later Ignatius of Loyola (1491-1556), the founder of the Jesuits Order, was advised not to go to Rome, lest his faith be shattered by "its stupendous depravity". As cited in Heiko A. Oberman, *Luther: Man Between God and the Devil*, p. 149.

8 *L W* 31, pp. 17-34; *WA* 1, pp. 233-238.

9 Gerhard Ebeling, *Luther: An Introduction to His Thought*, p. 15.

10 *LW* 12, p. 32; *WA* 30, p. 3.

11 Of course, it was not an age of complete intellectual blackout. Nevertheless, the collapse of the Roman Empire was accompanied by a kind of slackness in intellectual activity and whose renewal came

to pass only in the 11th century. See Colin Brown, *Philosophy & the Christian Faith*, p. 17.

12 See Paul Tillich, *A History of Christian Thought*, pp. 135ff.

13 As quoted by Gerhard Ebeling, *Luther: An Introduction to His Thought*, p. 84.

14 Ebeling, *Luther: An Introduction to His Thought*, p. 85.

15 As quoted by Gerhard Ebeling, *Luther: An Introduction to His Thought*, p. 89. See also Luther's tract on: "The Disputation against Scholastic Theology" (1517) for his arguments against Aristotle and scholastic theology in *LW* 31, pp. 3-16.

16 Ebeling, *Luther: An Introduction to His Thought*, pp. 85-86.

17 Richard Cross, "Nominalism" in *The Dictionary of Historical Theology*, p. 401.

18 Gerhard Ebeling, *Luther: An Introduction to His Thought*, p. 87. For Luther, reason must surrender itself to faith. *LW* 34, p. 216.

19 St. Augustine, *The City of God*, ed. by R. V. Tasker (London: J. M. Dent & Sons, 1957).

20 Paul Tillich, *A History of Christian Thought*, pp. 149f.

21 Jacques Rossel, *The Roots of Western Europe*, p. 624.

22 According to Luther, "it will be far too safe to ascribe too much to God than to man". As cited in James Atkinson, *Rome and Reformation Today: How Luther speaks to the New Situation* (Oxford: Latimer House, 1982), pp. 10-11. See also Bengt Hagglund, *History of Theology*, pp. 75-85.

23 Walter Altmann, *Luther and Liberation*, pp. 11ff.

24 See the following works that deal with the history of Reformation(s): Roland H. Bainton, *Here I Stand: A Life of Martin Luther*; Owen Chadwick, *The Reformation* (London: Penguin Books, 1972); Will Durant, *The Reformation* (New York: Simon and Schuster, 1957); G. R. Elton, ed., *Renaissance and Reformation: 1300-1648* (New York: Macmillan, 6th Printing, 1966); G. R. Elton, *Reform and Reformation, England 1517-1559* (Oxford: Blackwell, 1999); James M. Kittelson, *Luther the Reformer* (Minneapolis: Augsburg Publishing House, 1986); and Heiko A. Oberman, *Luther: Man Between God and the Devil*.

25 Luther advanced five reasons against monastic vows: the vows are contrary to the Word of God, contrary to faith, contrary to evangelical liberty, opposed to God's commandments, and opposed to reason. See Michael von Brück, "In Search of an Authentic Christian Life-Style: Luther and Monasticism" *Bangalore Theological Forum* Vol. XV, No. 3 (Sept-Dec, 1983), pp. 218-236.

26 Hans Küng, *Christianity*, p. 529.

27 Hans Küng, *Christianity*, p. 528.

28 For an informative reading on the origin of papacy, Apostolic Succession, Claims of papal primacy, and opposition to the claim of papal primacy, See Quentin F. Wesselschmidt, "The Beginnings of the Papacy in the Early Church" *Concordia Journal* Vol. 29, No. 4 (October 2003), pp. 374-391.

29 Hans Küng, *Christianity*, p. 528f.

30 Rodney Stark, *For the Glory of God*, pp. 80ff.

31 Owen Chadwick, *The Reformation*, p. 42.

32 Heiko A. Oberman, *Luther: Man Between God and the Devil*, p. 188.

33 *LW* 44, pp. 21-114; *WA* 6, pp. 202-276.

34 *LW* 44, pp. 123-217; *WA* 6, pp. 404-469. At the core of this tract there is a strong German (nationalist?) sentiment against the papal exploitation of the poor Germans (more discussion on this issue follows in the ensuing chapter).

35 *LW* 36, pp. 11-126; *WA* 6, pp. 497-573.

36 *LW* 31, pp. 333-377 (esp. 343-377); *WA* 7, pp. 49-73.

37 Rodney Stark, *For the Glory of God*, p. 85.

38 See S. Pfürtner, "The Paradigms of Thomas Aquinas and Martin Luther: Did Luther's Message of Justification Mean a Paradigm Change?" in Hans Küng and David Tracy, eds., *Paradigm Change in Theology* (Edinburgh: T & T Clark, 1989), pp. 130-160.

39 Carl R. Trueman and R. Scott Clark, eds., *Protestant Scholasticism: Essays in Reassessment* (Great Britain: Paternoster, 2005), "Introduction", p. xiii. Also see David C. Steinmetz, *Luther in Context* (Grand Rapids, Michigan: Baker Press, 1995).

40 Gerhard Ebeling, *Luther: An Introduction to His Thought* (op. cit).

41 For a quick reading of Enthusiasts see W. T. Whitley, "Enthusiasts (Religious)" in James Hastings, ed., *Encyclopedia of Religion and Ethics* Vol. 5 (New York: Charles Scribner's Sons, nd.), pp. 317-321.

42 The Peasants' war has provided Luther's critics with a strong weapon to attack him. For a brief discussion on the Pesant's war, see Hans Küng, *The Church*, pp. 193-197. An excellent analysis of the Reformer's response to the Peasants' war can be found in Lloyd B. Volkmar, *Luther's Response to Violence: Why the Reformer Hurled His Harsh 'No!' Against the Peasants* (New York: Vantage Press, 1974). In fact Luther was arbitrating between the Peasants and the Princes in order to find an amicable solution to the grievances of the Peasants. To understand the 12 demands of the Peasants see LW 46, pp. 8-16; to see Luther's response to those twelve demands see "Admonition to Peace. A Reply

to the Twelve Articles of the Peasants in Swabia", *LW* 46, pp. 17-43; *WA* 18, pp. 291-334.

43 See Ibid.

44 Ibid., pp. 47-61.

45 Theses 19 & 24: *LW* 31, pp. 52ff; *WA* 1, pp. 353-374.

46 Walther von Loewenich, *Luther's Theology of the Cross* (Belfast: Christian Journals Limited, 1976), p. 18; and also Paul Althaus, *The Theology of Martin Luther*, Tr. by Robert C. Schultz. (Philadelphia: Fortress Press, 1966), p. 25.

47 Thesis 19: *LW* 31, p. 52; *WA* 1, p. 354.

48 Thesis 21: *LW* 31, p. 53; *WA* 1, p. 354.

49 Thesis 24: *LW* 31, p. 55; *WA* 1, p. 355.

50 For a detailed discussion on the development of the theory of justification, see F. Edward Cranz, *An Essay on the Development of Luther's Thought on justice, Law, and Society* Issued as an extra number of the *Harvard Theological Review* (Cambridge: Harvard University Press, 1959); Sarnivaara Uuras, *Luther Discovers the Gospel: New Light upon Luther's Way from Medieval Catholicism to Evangelical Faith* (St. Louis, Missouri: Concordia Publishing House, 1951); and Paul Althaus, *The Theology of Marin Luther*, pp. 118-129 & 224-286.

51 As quoted by Frank D. Macchia, "Justification by New Creation: The Holy Spirit and the Doctrine by which the Church Stands or Falls", *Theology Today* Vol.58, No.2 (July 2001), p. 202. "This is the highest article of our faith, and if one should abandon it as the Jews do or pervert it like the papists, the Church cannot stand nor can God maintain His glory which consists in this that He might be merciful and that He desires to pardon sins for His Son's sake and to save. If this doctrine is overthrown or disappears, then all knowledge of truth is lost at the same time. If this doctrine flourishes, then all good things flourish: religion, true worship, the glory of God, the right knowledge of all conditions of life and of all things". As quoted by Robert Preus in *Justification and Rome*, p.17

52 Disputation I, 27: *LW* 34, p. 153; *WA* 39 ^{I}, p. 83.

53 *LW* 34, p. 169; *WA* 39 ^{I}, p. 99.

54 *L W* 12, p. 328; *WA* 40, p. 353.

55 *LW* 34, p. 178; *WA* 39^{I}, p. 109

56 *LW* 26, p. 4; *WA* 40^{I}, p. 41.

57 Robert Preus, *Justification and Rome*, p. 27.

58 As cited by Uuras Saarnivaara, *Luther Discovers the Gospel*, p. 10.

59 *LW* 35, p. 370f; *WA* DB7, p. 10.

60 Paul Rajashekar, "Luther's Doctrine of Justification and Christian Social Responsibility in India" *Bangalore Theological Forum* Vol. XV, No. 3 (September - December, 1983), pp. 197-217. Also see Alister E. McGrath, *Justification by Faith* (Grand Rapids, Michigan: Zondervan, 1998).

61 See, Walter Altman, *Luther and Liberation*, pp. 1-9.

62 See Andrew Sung Park, *The Wounded Heart of God: The Asian Concept of Han and the Christian Concept of Sin* (Nashville: Abingdon Press, 1993), "Unjustifiable Justification by Faith", pp. 87 – 98.

63 See Paul Althaus, *The Theology of Martin Luther*, pp. 251ff.

64 Cf. *LW* 22, pp. 139-147; also see *LW* 26, p. 274-276; *WA* 40, pp. 428-431. .

65 *LW* 26, pp. 274, 308f; *WA* 40, pp. 428f, 478ff.

66 *LW* 26, p. 39; *WA* 40, pp. 92-94, *LW* 45, pp. 89f; 11, p. 250.

67 *LW* 20, pp. 274-276; *WA* 40, p. 428-432.

68 *LW* 32, p. 224; *WA* 8, p. 103.

69 Luther affirms: "When the Holy Spirit is God in his nature, he is the author of law, without whom the law does not convict anyone of sin. When, however, he is that gift which is given us through Christ, he is the one who makes us alive and sanctifies us." *WA* 39^{I}, p. 391. He further maintains: "The law and the Gospel neither can nor should be separated; just as repentance and the forgiveness of sins should not be separated. For they are so closely bound together and involved in each other." *WA* 39^{I}, p. 416. Also see LW 35, p. 162f.

70 *LW* 22, pp. 145-148; *WA* 46, pp. 538ff.

71 "Thus even when we say that Christ is set before us as an example, or as the Redeemer, we teach the law. And this is a true preaching of the law. For if he comes to you as your Redeemer and Savior, you must have sinned; redemption itself presupposes sin." *WA* 39^{I}, p. 464.

72 "The proclamation of the law...reveals sin...but this can be done even by showing the benefits of Christ who had to suffer such great things for your sins. It is all the same whether this is done by preaching the benefits of Christ or the law; ...it is all law." *WA* 39^{I}, 535.

73 Klaus Nürnberger, *Martin Luther's Message for Us Today*, p. 130.

74 *Book of Concord,* p. 85.

75 Klaus Nürnberger, *Martin Luther's Message for Us Today*, p. 130.

76 E. W. Gritsch, "Introduction" in *Luther's Works* Vol.39 (Philadelphia: Fortress Press, 1970) p. xii.

77 As quoted by J. G. F. Collison, "Issues in the History of Biblical Hermeneutics: A Protestant Perspective" in Frederick S. Downs and

Eric J. Lott, eds., *What is God Factor? Sermons and Writings of Frank Collison* (Delhi: ISPCK, 1999), p. 80.

78 See Martin Luther, "Large Catechism" in *The Book of Concord*, pp. 416-417.

79 See Cornelius J. Dyck, "Anabaptism" in Mircea Eliade, ed., *Encyclopedia of Religion*, Vol. 1 (New York: Macmillan Publishing Company, 1987), pp. 247-249.

80 According Luther, the preservation of infant Baptism in the Church in all places and all ages is a miracle and the work of God and as such it must be preserved "for where we see the work of God, we should yield and believe in the same way as when we hear his word, unless the plain scripture tells us otherwise." *LW* 40, p.241; *WA* 26, p. 155.

81 E. W. Gritsch, "Introduction" in *Luther's Works* Vol. 39, p. xiii.

82 Is individualism to be completely denounced? There are critics who maintain that we need to distinguish between crass (absolute/downright/utilitarian) individualism and positive individualism. See David S. Smith, "Luther's Contribution to Positive Individualism", *Concordia Journal* Vol. 22, No.3, (July 1996), pp. 263-278.

83 Stanley J. Grenz, "Ecclesiology", p. 253 (More discussion on the idea of community in chapter VI).

84 Peter L. Berger, *Invitation to Sociology: A Humanistic Perspective* (New York: Doubleday, 1963), pp. 63f.

85 Arthur J. Dyke, *Rethinking Rights and Responsibilities: The Moral Bonds of Community* (Cleveland, OH: Pilgrim Press, 1992), pp. 126f. Also Derek L. Philips, *Looking Backward: A Critical Appraisal of Communitarian Thought* (Princeton, CA: Princeton University Press, 1993), pp. 17f.

86 For a more detailed discussion on individual identity, see Michael Sandel, *Liberalism and the Limits of Justice* (Cambridge, UK: Cambridge University Press, 1998).

87 G. Herbert Mead, *Mind, Self and Society* (Chicago: University of Chicago Press, 1962), pp.118-164.

88 Cf. *WA* 2, pp. 190, 415; *WA* 6, p. 606; *WA* 11, p. 53, *WA* 31^{I}, pp. 92, 189; *WA* 50, p. 624; *LW* 51, p. 166, & *Book Concord*, pp. 416f.

89 Martin Luther, "Small Catechism" in *The Book of Concord*, p. 345.

90 *LW*, 41, pp. 148-168; *WA* 50, pp. 639-649.

91 *WA* 50, pp. 624ff.

92 *WA* 7, 219.

93 *LW* 13, p. 88; *WA* 40^{III}, p. 505.

94 Hugh Thompson Kerr, ed., *A Compend of Luther's Theology*, p. 124 (*LW* 37, p. 368).

95 Klaus Nürnberger, *Martin Luther's Message for Us Today*, p. 133.

96 See Herbert E. Hoefer, *Churchless Christianity* (Madras: Gurukul, 1991), especially pp. 149-188.

97 *L W* 35, pp. 410.

98 Paul Althaus, *The Theology of Martin Luther,* pp. 297ff.

99 Paul Althaus, *The Theology of Martin Luther*, p. 298.

100 As cited in Paul Althaus, *The Theology of Martin Luther,* p. 299 from *WA* 10^{III}, pp. 407f.

101 As cited in Paul Althaus, *The Theology of Martin Luther*, p. 298 from WA 17^{II}, p. 255

102 *LW*, 31, p. 213; *WA* 1, pp. 605ff. See also the entire section, pp. 212-228.

103 *LW* 31, p. 215f; *WA* 1, p. 607.

104 *Paul Althaus, The Theology of Martin Luther* p. 302.

105 As cited in Paul Althaus, *Theology of Martin Luther*, p. 303 from *WA* 17^{II}, p. 33.

106 Luther affirms: "[I]f there is anything in us it is not our own; it is a gift of God. But if it is a gift of God, then it is entirely a debt we owe to love, that is, to the law of Christ. If it is a debt owed to love, then I must serve others with it. Thus my learning is not my own; it belonged to the unlearned and it is a debt I owe to them. My chastity is not my own; it belongs to those who commit sins of the flesh, and I am obligated to serve them through it by offering it to God for them by sustaining and excusing them, and thus, with my responsibility veiling their shame before God and men.... Thus my wisdom belongs to the foolish, my power to the oppressed. Thus my wealth belongs to the poor, my righteousness to the sinners." *LW* 27, p. 303: *WA* 2, p. 602.

107 *LW*, 31, p. 190; *WA* 1, p. 593.

108 *LW*, 35, p. 70.

109 See Paul Althaus, *The Theology of Martin Luther*, p. 306. Luther makes a clear distinction between these two aspects in "The Blessed Sacrament of the Holy and True Body of Christ and the Brotherhoods" *L W*, 32, pp. 52ff; *WA* 2, pp. 742ff.

110 *L W*, 31, pp. 190.

111 Cf. *WA* 50, p. 241, *Book of Concord*, p. 310.

112 Paul Althaus, *The Theology of Martin Luther*, pp. 306f. See also *LW* 35, pp. 55-61 & 72; *WA* 2, pp. 745-750 & 757.

113 *LW* 27, p. 392; *WA* 2, p. 605.

114 *LW* 40, p.19; *WA* 12, p. 183.
115 *LW* 40, p. 20; *WA* 12, p. 184.
116 Luther lists out seven priestly functions: (i) to preach the word of God, (ii) to baptize, (iii) to celebrate the sacrament of the altar, (iv) to administer the office of the keys, (v) to pray for others, (vi) to sacrifice (self), (vii) to judge doctrine and to distinguish spirits. *LW* 40, pp. 21-32; *WA* 12, p. 180ff.
117 See Kancha Ilaiah, *Why I am Not a Hindu: A Sudra Critique of Hindutva Philosophy, Culture and Political Economy* (Delhi: Batkal & Sen 2001).
118 *LW* 27, p. 394; *WA* 2, p. 606.
119 Paul Tillich, *A History of Christian Thought*, p. 155.
120 Paul Tillich, *A History of Christian Thought*, pp. 156ff.
121 *LW* 36, pp. 65 & 124; *WA* 6, pp. 532 & 572.
122 The following are the basic sources to understand Luther's theology of Baptism: "The Holy and Blessed Sacrament of Baptism" - 1519 (*LW* 35, pp. 29-43; *WA* 2, pp. 727-737); "The Babylonian Captivity of the Church" - 1520 (*LW* 36, pp. 11-126; *WA* 6, pp. 497-573); and the *Small and Large Catechisms*, in *Book of Concord*, pp. 348f & 436-446; *WA* 30^{I}, pp. 308-313 & pp. 212-222.
123 See Hans Kung, *The Church*, pp. 203ff.
124 Jerome H. Neyrey, "Baptism" in *Harper's Bible Dictionary*, pp. 92f.
125 Herbert E. Hoefer, *Churchless Christianity*, pp. 160ff.
126 Ibid., pp. 160-168.
127 *BC*, p. 437.
128 *BC*, p. 458.
129 *Small Catechism, BC*, p. 442
130 *L W* 35, p. 38; *WA* 2, p. 736.
131 *BC*, p. 437.
132 *LW*, 35, p.38; *WA* 2, p. 737.
133 *LW* 12, pp. 81ff; *WA* 40, pp. 273ff.
134 Robert Kolb, *Luther's Way of Thinking*, p. 113.
135 *LW* 12, p. 537; *WA* 37, p. 642.
136 *LW* 12, pp. 73ff; *WA* 37, pp. 22f.
137 "Babylonian Captivity" *LW* 36, pp. 74ff; *WA* 46, pp. 557ff.
138 Robert Kolb, *Luther's Way of Thinking*, p. 125.
139 *WA* 46, pp. 8-24 & 30-169; *Book of Concord*, p. 320.
140 See Luther's tract: "Concerning Rebaptism", *LW* 40, pp. 229-262; *WA* 26, pp. 144-174 (Luther advances six reasons: see *LW* 40, pp. 254-258) & "Large Catechism" in *Book of Concord*, pp. 442ff.

141 It is here the principle of *adiaphora* comes into force. When the Jewish Christians coerced their Hellenistic counterparts to undergo circumcision, Paul intervened and made a distinction between essentials and non-essentials to salvation and he adjudged circumcision as an *adiaphoron*, i.e., non-essential to salvation (Gal 5:6). See Herbert Hoefer, *Churchless Christianity*, pp. 160-182.

142 *LW* 32, p.15; *WA* 7, p. 315

143 *LW* 32, p.15; *WA* 7, p. 315

144 *LW* 36, p.67; WA 6, p. 552.

145 Luther draws a parallel between Christ's death and resurrection and that of the believers who are drawn to Christ in Baptism based on Rom. 6 & Col. 2. See *WA* 46, pp. 14-18 & 31-37.

146 See *BC*, pp. 463-464. Also see Jaroslav Pelikan, "Luther's Defense of Infant Baptism" in Carl S. Meyer, ed., *Luther for an Ecumenical Age* (Saint Louis: CPH, 1967), pp. 200-218.

147 Luther would firmly argue that the Church of Christ would cease to exist in this world if it is not gathered through Baptism. *WA* 27, pp. 29-45.

148 See Luther's tracts: "The Blessed Sacrament of the Holy and True Body of Christ and the Brotherhoods - 1519 (*LW* 35, pp. 49-73; *WA* 2, pp. 742-758) & "A Treatise on the New Testament, that is, the Holy Mass" - 1520 (*LW* 35, pp. 79-111; *WA* 6, pp. 353-378). Apart from the original sources (*WA* & *LW*), two helpful secondary sources in English to understand Luther's theology of the Lord's Supper are: Hermann Sasse, *This Is My Body: Luther's Contention for the Real Presence in the Sacrament of the Altar* (Minneapolis: Augsburg Publishing House, 1959), pp. 233-272; and Jaroslav Pelikan, *Luther the Expositor: Introduction to the Reformer's Exegetical Writings* (St. Louis: Concordia Publishing House, 1959), pp. 137-260.

149 *LW* 35, p. 58; *WA* 2, p. 751f.

150 See Paul Althaus, *The Theology of Martin Luther*, p. 319.

151 *LW* 35, pp. 51-53; *WA* 2, pp. 745-747.

152 *LW* 35, p. 54; *WA* 2, p. 745.

153 *LW* 35, p. 57; *WA* 2, p. 748.

154 See the editor's notes in Martin Luther, "The Babylonian Captivity of the Church" in *Three Treatises* (Philadelphia: Muhlenberg Press, 1947) p. 137. Also see Edward J. Gratsch, *Aquinas' Summa: An Introduction and Interpretation* (Bangalore: TPI, 1990), p. 252.

155 See "The Babylonian Captivity of the Church", *LW* 36, pp. 28ff; *WA* 6, pp. 508ff.

156 *LW* 36, p. 151; *WA* 6, p. 508
157 *LW* 36, p. 161; *WA* 6, p. 521.
158 See *LW* 36, p. 62 (n. 118). In one of his theories, Aristotle maintains: "An affirmative proposition demands the agreement of the subject and the predicate". The logical outcome of this theory in theology is obvious – when Jesus said, "This is my body", the subject of this proposition (*This*) cannot correspond to and be identical with the bread, but it must be identical with the body of Christ.
159 Luther understands the real presence in correlation to his Christology, as he affirms: "Thus what is true in regard to Christ is also true in regard to the sacrament". *LW* 36, p. 35; *WA* 6, p. 511.
160 *LW* 35, p. 88; *WA* 6, p. 362.
161 *LW* 37, p. 270; *WA* 26, p. 375. Luther's principle of the literal interpretation is indicative of the fact that when Luther speaks about the word of God, it has a different meaning than the canonized scripture. The word of God, according to Luther, is not identical with the scripture, but rather, the word of God is to be found in the scripture, which is known as the principle of "canon within canon".
162 *LW* 37, p. 296; *WA 26,* p. 398.
163 *LW* 40, p. 216; *WA* 18, p. 106.
164 *LW* 37, p. 53; *WA* 23, p.103.
165 This is contrary to Enlightenment rationality. See Kant, "What is Enlightenment" in Peter Gay, ed., *The Enlightenment: A Comprehensive Anthology* (New York: Simon Schuster, 1973), pp. 384ff.
166 See Klass Zwanepol, "A Human God: Some Remarks on Luther's Christology" *Concordia Journal* Vol. 30, Nos. 1 & 2 (January-April 2004), pp. 40-53.
167 For instance, Kazoh Kitamori, *The Theology of the Pain of God* (London: SCM Press, 1966).
168 Paul Althaus, *The Theology of Martin Luther*, p. 322.
169 B. H. Jackayya, "The Place of Augsburg Confession in the Ecumenical Dialogues in India" in Herbert Hoefer, ed., *The Augsburg Confession and Ecumenism in India* (Madras: Gurukul, 1980.), p. 7.
170 Robert Preus, *Justification and Rome* (Saint Louis: Concordia Academic Press, 1997.), p. 13.
171 *LW* 35, p. 70; *WA* 2, p. 747.
172 *LW* 51, p. 96; *WA* 10 ^{III}, p. 57.
173 *WA* 12, p. 470
174 See the explanation of the 58th of the 95 theses in *LW* 31, pp. 212-228.

175 LW 36, p. 116; WA 6, p. 566. The following are the important original sources to understand Luther's theology of the office of the ministry based on the universal priesthood and the principle of servanthood: "An Open letter to the Christian Nobility" (op.cit.), "The Babylonian Captivity of the Church" (op.cit.), "Concerning the Ministry" (*LW* 40, pp. 7-44; *WA* 12, pp. 169-195), "That a Christian Assembly or Congregation Has the Right and Power to Judge All Teachings and to Call, Appoint, and Dismiss Teachers, Established and Proved from Scripture" - 1523 (*LW* 39, pp. 305-314; *WA* 11, pp. 408-416), and "The Private Mass and the Consecration of Priests" (*LW* 38, pp. 141-214; *WA* 38, pp. 195-256).

176 *LW* 37, p. 364; *WA* 26, p. 499.

177 *LW* 40, p. 35; *WA* 12, pp. 22ff.

178 *LW* 13, p. 65.

179 *LW* 40, p. 34.

180 *WA* 50, p. 633.

181 For further reading, see Werner Elert, *The Structure of Lutheranism* (St. Louis, Missouri: Concordia Publishing House, 1962), pp. 1f & 344ff.

182 For a discussion on these issues, see John Johnson, "The Office of the Pastoral Ministry: Scriptural and Confessional Considerations" in Jerald C. Jorez and Paul T. McCain, eds., *Church and Ministry* (St. Louis, Missouri: LCMS, 1998), pp. 77-99 and also the two responses to this presentation by Kurt Marquart & William Diekelman, pp. 100-122; David S. Yeago, "The Office of the Keys: On Disappearance of Discipline in Protestant Modernity" & Carl E. Braaten, " The Special Ministry of the Ordained" in Carl E. Braaten and Robert W. Jenson, eds., *Marks of the Body of Christ* (Grand Rapids, Michigan: Wm B. Eerdmans, 1999), pp. 95-122 & 123-136.

183 John Johnson, "The Office of the Pastoral Ministry", p. 83. It is worth noting that the author, while acknowledging that Jesus does not say *expressis verbis*: "Let there be pastors", comes to the final conclusion that ordained ministry is a gift of the Spirit.

184 For a detailed discussion on the concept of the office of the ministry in Roman Catholicism and Luther, see Klaus Nürnberger, *Martin Luther's Message for Us Today*, pp. 152-188.

185 *LW* 40, p. 34.

186 *LW* 40, p. 34.

187 Walter Altman, *Luther and Liberation*, p. 6.

188 It is here that many critics misread Luther as having divided the two realms into two autonomous realms. See *Render Unto Caesar*, p. 18; & Paul Tillich, *A History of Christian Thought*, p. 187.
189 *Render Unto Caesar*, p. 34.
190 John R. Stephenson, "The two Governments and the Two Kingdoms in Luther's Thought" *Scottish Journal of Theology* Vol. 34, No. 4 (August 1981), pp. 321ff.
191 William H. Lazareth, *Luther on the Christian Home: An Application of the Social Ethics of the Reformation* (Philadelphia: Muhlenberg Press, 1960), pp. 102ff.
192 *LW* 45, pp. 75-129; *WA* 11, pp. 245-280.
193 See Ibid. For further discussion, see Holsten Fagerberg, *A New Look at the Lutheran Confessions (1529-1537)*, Tr. by Gene J. Lund (St. Louis, Missouri: CPH, 1972), pp. 102-111.
194 See *WA* 54, p. 186; *LW* 34, p. 337 cf. *WA* 40 [I], pp.40-41; *LW* 26, pp. 4-5.
195 *LW* 45, p. 96; *WA* 11, p. 202.
196 "Against the Robbing and Murdering Peasants", *LW* 46, p. 50.
197 See Desmond Tutu, *No Future without Forgiveness* (London: Rider, 1999). For a critique of the TRC in South Africa, see Kay Carmichael, *Sin and Forgiveness: New Responses in a Changing World* (Aldershot, England: Ashgate, 2003); Richard Holloway, *On Forgiveness: How Can We Forgive the Unforgivable?* (Edinburgh: Canongate Books, 2003) and Richard A. Wilson, *The Politics of Truth and Reconciliation in South Africa: Legitimizing the Post-Apartheid State* (Cambridge, UK: Cambridge University Press, 2001).
198 Robert Kolb, "Christian Civic Responsibility in an Age of Judgment" *Concordia Journal* Vol. 19, No. 1 (January 1993), p. 20.
199 *LW* 45, p. 105.
200 *LW* 45, p. 114. This has a lot to do with 'Christ and Culture' discourse. See Richard Niebhur, *Christ and Culture* (London: Faber and Faber, 1951), pp. 58-228. The difference between Neibhur and Luther is: Neibhur holds the symbols of justification and sanctification, faith and obedience on equal footing with each other.' Whereas Luther holds justification and faith as the central symbols and the Lutherans would argue that Neibhur confuses law and gospel. See *Render unto Caesar*, p. 36f.
201 *LW* 36, pp. 27-163; *WA* 6, pp. 465-597.
202 See "Reformation" in *The Dictionary of Historical Theology*, p. 466.

203 See the following works: Bernard Lhose, *Martin Luther's Theology: Its Systematic and Historic Development* (Minneapolis: University of Minnesota Press, 1999) and Heinrich Holze, ed., *The Church as Communion: Lutheran Contributions to Ecclesiology* (Geneva: LWF, 1997).

204 *LW* 26, p. 7; *WA* 40, p. 45.

205 Robert Kolb, "Luther on the Two Kinds of Righteousness: Reflections on His Two-Dimensional definition of Humanity at the Heart of His Theology", in *Luther's Way of Thinking*, pp. 67f.

206 Paul Tillich, *A History of Christian Thought*, p. 186.

Chapter Five

A CRITIQUE OF LUTHER'S THOUGHTS ON THE CHURCH

The Critical Task

> When Lutheranism achieves its goal of reforming the Church, it goes out of business as a confessional movement. Otherwise it lingers on as a sect.[1]
>
> Most of the time, I find Luther's writings fascinating; once in a while, they are also irritating. If he still can have this impact after five centuries and across oceans, in the midst of different cultures, and in radically different Church situations, what must Luther's impact have been in his own time?[2]

Luther lived in a turbulent era characterized by dramatic changes in the social, economic, political, religious, and moral domains of human life. As a result, much of what he uttered and did was in response to the metamorphoses that were taking place around him. This aspect of his life and thought had, in fact, given rise to divergent images of himself. He was seen as a 'prophet' – the uncompromising defender of pure doctrine – by the seventeenth century Lutheranism; and pietism found in him the one who attained peace with God through the Word of God and faith.[3] The enlightenment acclaimed Luther as the "liberator from narrow mindedness", which the dogmatic authoritarianism of the Church had established so firmly.[4]

Eric Erikson, the well-known psychiatrist, analyzed Luther on the basis of his relationship with his father.[5] And the post-Tridentine Roman Catholicism found Luther the devil personified.[6] The question before us now is how to assess Luther and his theological thoughts, especially his understanding of the Church because Luther still remains alive amidst us today, not simply because we form part of his theological and historical legacy but because there is so much of his influence, both direct and indirect, that underlies different Church bodies and the modern world as a whole.

In a sense, Luther's ecclesiology is "offensive", i.e., a theology of protest, not in the ordinary sense of rebelliousness but in the sense of a *pro-test*, meaning 'in favor of certain higher values'.[7] This interpretation is justifiable because, as Protestants, we are not simply the protesters, but a communion of believers standing in solidarity with a host of other believers for the service of the Gospel of Christ insofar as this Gospel reconciles the fragmented and fractured humanity into a bond of common humanhood, consistently proclaiming that in Christ God has shattered the wall of separation, ended hostility and made peace by accepting the unacceptable (Eph 2:16, Col 1:20ff). The idea of *God's acceptance of the unacceptable* is made prominent by Luther with his doctrine of justification. Studies on conversion in India show that this *feeling of being accepted* is so strongly etched in the consciousness of the converts to Christianity, which prompts them to come to a firm conviction that they are not only accepted through the grace of Christ but also completely transformed to a new way of life to accept others as Christ had accepted them.[8]

Luther's basic interest was to re-inscribe the Gospel at the centre of Christian life, and his theology of the Church characteristically exhibits his commitment to proclaim the Gospel, challenging new situations as he found the Gospel foundational to Christian life, praxis and identity. Luther never intended to found a new Church; rather, his primary objective was to make reforms within the Church he belonged to, namely, the Roman Catholic Church. Robert McAfee Brown, for instance, is quite emphatic that the Reformers were neither inventing a new Church nor were they intending to break away from the Church, but they were trying to revive the 'old' religion as found in the New Testament and make it once again normative for Christianity and the Church.[9] This is one of the reasons why the Reformer never attempted to carve out a neat structure for a new Church. What is intended in this study is not a description of his ecclesiology as a dogmatic system; rather we are concerned about his thoughts insofar as they have the potential to lead us to a process of critical and creative reflection on ecclesia related to the context of Hindu nationalism in India – a context that reminds us of Carl E. Braaten's two crises that have serious consequences for the life and well-being of humanity, namely, *the crisis of meaning and identity* and *the crisis of human misery*.[10]

This situation poses a challenge to the hermeneutic of the Church's mission to show what relevance the Church has in the midst of these human maladies. Hence, the task of ecclesiology is to show primarily that the Church stands for the healing of a fractured, fragmented and hurting world because the God whom we believe reconciled the world to God's self in Jesus Christ,[11] and entrusted the Church with the ministry of reconciliation. It becomes the hope for a new world – a hope that envisions a world free of all hostilities and hatred. If this is not what the Indian Church stands for, it immediately becomes obsolescent. This vision of the Church is important as we search for the meaning of the Church in the context of Hindu nationalism in India.

With the above task at hand, I attempt to assess Martin Luther's thoughts on the Church without privileging him or his thoughts. It is a search for certain viable theological insights that would help envision a relevant theology of the Church in the contemporary Indian context, more specifically related to the Hindu nationalist situation in order to provide an adequate theological basis for what the people of God do in the Church, namely, their corporate worship, preaching, caring for each other and those in the wider society, their family and social life, and their engagement in the world, especially their struggle for justice, peace and amity. Hence, in this chapter, we would evaluate the important ecclesiological themes that Luther had dealt with, highlighting their prospective and problematic aspects and offer a brief definition of Luther's basic theological principle – *unity of the opposites* or *distinction* and *integration* – that would facilitate our own reflections on the Church.

Approaching Luther's Ecclesiological Constructions

No system of human thoughts can be absolutised with impunity and Luther's ecclesiology is no exception. One of the major limitations that any study on Luther's ecclesiology has to face is the fragmented and scattered pieces of his writings on the Church over a period of about three decades. Another problem is the literary dimension because most of his thoughts on the Church emerged through his polemical writings, aggressive critiques, and emphatic answers to his enemies. These pieces of his writings contain a number of valuable insights; a few areas have serious ramifications; there are some areas that are not given adequate weightage in his thinking; and there are points wherein one can find a sort of a disjunction between his theological reasons and historical judgments. For the most part, in the treatment of the Reformer's thoughts on ecclesia, my concentration will be on the theological side of the Reformer.

The history of the Church exhibits numerous trajectories in terms of its existential situation, theological constructions/reconstructions, and missiological orientation. The primitive Church existed in a hostile environment (at least for the first three centuries) in which Christians were subjected to intermittent violence and often intense persecution. This occurred despite the fact that the Roman state exercised religious tolerance. Within the Empire, the imperial policy unhesitatingly upheld side by side the rational (enlightened) and the religious (superstitious) ways of life of its citizens. For the ordinary citizens, all the prevalent religious practices within the Roman world were equally true; for the philosophers, they were equally false; and for the magistrates, they were equally useful for objectively arbitrating between communities.[12]

A notable point in the life and mission of the Church during this early phase was that amidst intense persecution, the believers were tenacious enough to proclaim the new life God had engendered in Christ to the entire humanity. But with the collapse of the Roman Empire, the Church usurped civil power and exercised enormous influence upon European civilization. Augustine's exploration of the functions and relations of Church and state was the foundation of most medieval and modern political discourses in the Western world. He was the inspiration of both the Holy Roman Empire and much of the papal claims of Gregory VII and Innocent II. For him, history is controlled by God and it is moving towards a goal beyond time through the interaction of the earthly and heavenly communities, which are founded respectively upon self love and the love of God to which correspond in some measure the state and the Church.[13] During the middle ages, the Church was preoccupied with rebuilding its legal and ecclesiastical structures. The bloody battles between the emperors and kings over territorial ownership became handy to successive popes to use their spiritual authority to tame hostile rulers, especially with the whip of excommunication. It was a situation in which the Church was leading the state and such a privileged status paved the way for the entry of several ills into the Church, and Luther emerged as the Reformer in this milieu.

Two fundamental limitations Luther encountered in his theological constructions were the emerging challenges from various fronts and the limitation of time to carefully articulate his views in a more polished and cohesive manner. He was never at ease ever since he challenged the Church, not as an outsider but as an insider, and until his death he could not find tranquility. Hence, his articulations were mostly related to the immediate situation and often times he had to modify them in view of newer challenges. It was an extremely critical situation and all those developments had impacted his thoughts. Here we need to note that the present reality in which the Church exists is entirely different from Luther's context. His thoughts emerged from and in response to the Roman Church's privileged position and dominant tendencies. But today, we engage in ecclesiological reflections in India where, on the one hand, the Church has to adhere to the law of the land, and it has to exist and engage in its mission in a hostile environment created by Hindutva's hate-filled fascist ideology, particularly directed against religious minorities (Muslims and Christians), on the other.[14] Here, the Church has to take cognizance of the fact that Hindu nationalism is an attempt to re-establish the dominance of Brahminic Hinduism over the multiple social, cultural, and religious persuasions of India. Critics wonder at the way the ancient institution of Brahminic hierarchy continues to exercise its stronghold on Indian population over against the evolutionary conception of human history, which anticipated the disappearance of caste discriminations with the advent of modernisation, secularisation and modern education.[15] It is from this context that we attempt to understand the meaning of ecclesia in critical interaction with Luther's thoughts on the Church.

Even though Luther had initiated renewed discussions on the Church and intensified the same in due course, he never explained his understanding of the Church in a single book, dogmatic system or treatise, "*de ecclesia*".[16] Nevertheless, he constructed the meaning of the Church based on certain Biblical/theological categories: theology of the cross, doctrine of justification, Word and Sacraments, ministry, priesthood and servanthood, and Church-state relationship. In his theological imaginations, he consistently worked with a set of opposite categories within the framework of a dialogical relationship – a method of the *unity of the opposites* or *distinction and integration.* Recapturing this feature of Luther's thinking, Gerhard Ebeling affirms:

> Luther's thought always contains an antithesis, tension between strongly opposed but related polarities: theology and philosophy, the letter and the spirit, the law and the gospel, the double use of the law, person and works, faith and love, the Kingdom of Christ and the Kingdom of the world, man as Christian and man in the world, freedom and bondage, God hidden and God revealed.[17]

In his "Heidelberg Disputation" (1518), Luther affirms:

> [I]n John 14 [:8], where Philip spoke according to the theology of glory, 'Show us the Father', Christ straightaway set aside his flighty thoughts about seeing God elsewhere and led him to himself, saying, 'Philip, he who has seen me has seen the Father'. For this reason true theology and recognition of God are in the crucified Christ.[18]

In this affirmation, Luther confesses that God meets the estranged, rebellious humans not in the ostentatious ivory chambers of the princes and lords, but in the gallows, in the shadows cast by death. It is a paradigm shift in the history of Christian thought, which brings the otherwise opposite categories – God and humans, life and death, salvation and sin – together on the cross of Christ. Is it not a new conceptual framework to reflect on God-human relationship?[19] Further, the kind of freedom that we find in the field of Biblical interpretation, the emergence of various Church bodies and their global missions, and the numerous strands of theological discourse, without doubt, are the outcome of Luther's breakthrough.[20] His understanding of the Church as *communio sanctorum* makes yet another shift of emphasis, critiquing the existing order of the Church.

Luther's breakthrough is also not without its own problems. In our quest for the visible unity of the Church today, for instance, his breakthrough poses a real challenge. Quite unintended by him, the Churches of the Protestant tradition came to obstinately establish their own structures, making it almost impossible to broach into – a transition from the Catholic institutionalism to a kind of Protestant institutionalism. The Protestants either failed to recognize or completely obscured the fact that the Reformer's attempt was to break the constellation and abuse of power by the hierarchy and to motivate the Church to direct its resources to care for God's people in their everyday life and not to fragment the Church, far less to create a new Church after his name. In his disputation with Luther in the year 1518, for instance, Cardinal Cajetan condensed Luther's entire arguments in one sentence: "What you say means founding a new Church". Luther's definite response to him was that he never intended to break with the Catholic Church, which he accepted and held life-long as the true, apostolic and Catholic Church.[21]

Luther has been virulently attacked on several fronts: his engagement with the princes and peasants, his doctrine of the two kingdoms and his anti-Jewish writings are a few of them. Critics expressed their utter contempt against the Reformer for his 'failure' to recognize the masses as the subjects of the reform of the Church and his 'alliance' with the princes. In light of the contemporary intellectual discourses, it is judged as a methodological flaw and the Reformer is seen as an offender. He has been castigated for his 'offense' of divorcing human existence into spiritual and temporal realms, which allegedly involved a double standard and led to ethical passivity in the public realm. His anti-Jewish writings form yet another serious impediment.[22] Therefore, in the eyes of the critics and detractors, Luther and his thoughts are irrelevant today. However, most of the views advanced by his detractors did not seem to comport with what the Reformer actually stood for and I believe that Luther's thoughts still have valuable insights for our reflections on the Church in the 21st century and we will begin our discussion from Luther's engagement with the princes and peasants.

Luther's Tryst with the Princes and the Peasants

In a postmodern and/or postcolonial situation, any inclination to privilege the powerful will elicit sharp reactions. Of course, such reactions are not baseless because the devastating effects of the colonial power and authority still linger on in the erstwhile colonies.[23] Further, once authority becomes institutionalized, its power and scope becomes unlimited. But despite all the criticisms and polemics with regard to power and authority, it is inevitable to deal with this phenomenon in our daily life because it is there everywhere around us. Undeniably, Luther is one of the prominent figures in history who had dealt with the issue of power quite extensively. Here, it must not go without mention that for him the ultimate source of power and authority is none other than God as enshrined in the Word of God and his delineations characteristically revolve around this conviction.

As a Reformation formula, Luther proposed that the supreme authority in the reform of the Church was neither Pope nor Canon Law but the people of God under the guidance of the Word of God. His call to the German nobility for the reform of the Church was based on the principle that this task was vested with the people as priests – the *royal priesthood* of all baptized believers. This was done with a specific purpose, which can be understood and appreciated only if we revisit his extensive tract "*To the German Nobility*". Although the fundamental thrust of Reformation was religious, other interests came to coalesce with it: social, economic and political. This tract, which was prepared with the assistance of the Saxon court officials, clearly reflects the grievances of the entire German people that had a history of about a millennium.[24] Luther also firmly believed that the reform of the society was possible only through the reform of the Church, because the Church was holding the spiritual and temporal power to which the territorial princes also had to toe in. Therefore, when he called the princes to act, he insisted that their involvement was to redeem the poor Germans from the tyranny of the papacy. From the beginning to the end of this treatise, Luther expresses his anguish and anger over the way Rome had indulged in exploiting the German people. His thoughts in this regard are so powerful and it would be worth quoting a few of them.

> In fact, some have estimated that more than three hundred thousand gulden a year find their way from Germany to Rome. This money serves no use or purpose. We get nothing for it except scorn and contempt. And we still go on wondering why princes and nobles, cities and endowments, land and people grow poor. We ought to marvel that we have anything left to eat.[25]
>
> O noble princes and Lords, how long will you leave your lands and your people naked and exposed to such ravening wolves?[26]
>
> The temporal authority is *under obligation* to protect the innocent and prevent injustice, as Paul teaches in Romans 13, and Peter in I Peter 2:[14].[27]
>
> We have the title, but they have the land and the city. They have always abused our simplicity to serve their own arrogant and tyrannical designs.[28]
>
> We carry the title of the empire, but the pope who has its wealth, honour, body, life, soul, and all that we possess. This is how they deceive the Germans.[29]
>
> Thus we Germans have been taught our German (meaning, "we Germans have been tricked"). While we supposed we were going to be masters, we became in fact slaves to the most deceitful tyrants of all time. We have the name, the title and the insignia of the empire, but the pope has its treasures, authority, rights, and liberties. The pope gobbles the kernel, while we are left playing with the husk.[30]

These texts reflect his concern for the emancipation of the victims of structural injustice and Luther believed that the German nobility had the responsibility, both spiritually (as baptized believers) and temporally (as they had the administrative powers and skills), to commit themselves to the cause of the Church and society. This discourse drives home the most important point that the problem of the poor is not 'their' problem, but it is 'our' problem to be collectively dealt with, so that both the Church and the society would emerge out of their captivity.

Luther's revolutionary ideas drew different classes of people to him. His doctrine of justification received great reception as a symbol of liberation. His doctrine of 'the priesthood of all believers' was appealing to the peasants and nobles alike, even though the central teaching of this doctrine was not social egalitarianism but spiritual equality of all believers by virtue of a common divine calling. In his teachings on economic reforms,[31] Luther touched upon all classes of people – peasants, lords, princes, tradesmen, craftsmen, and statesmen – and his primary concern was to call their consciences to unselfishly seek to fulfill their responsibility to achieve the goal of justice and equity for all so that God's will might prevail in the social realm as well. In fact, these interpretations penetrated deep into the established and inert systems of the Church and society that had been preserving an intractable *status quo* and perpetuating an unbridgeable chasm between the higher and lower human beings. In such a situation, Luther made a valorous attempt to theologically integrate the seemingly opposite categories for the common good.

However, we also recognize the pervasiveness of some ambiguity in Luther's view of authority. (a) Luther appears to be indecisive with regard to the cumulative power of hierarchy, resulting in a kind of truncated judgment about the papacy on the one hand and the princes on the other. Ironically, while he found the power of papacy hazardous, he could attest the power of the princes to deliver justice to the victims, which proved to be a mistaken notion. (b) Along with most of the medieval thinkers, the Reformer also held a positivistic theory of the state authority. In addition to this positivism, he also maintained a *double standard* – tolerance/obedience for civilians and repression for state authority – that had serious repercussions, especially to the survival of the peasants. (c) In his harsh tract against the peasant mutiny, Luther called the princes to curb the peasant mutiny by violent repression and his position on violence was taken to legitimise the brutality with which the territorial princes and lords curbed the rebellion. It necessitates explaining briefly the way Luther understood law.

The expression 'double standard' (see point 'b' above) is not intended to castigate Luther. Rather it points to his attempt to understand the implications of law, especially when it is applied in governance and more specifically the relationship between the state and the citizens. As propounded by the Reformer, while the state is entitled to use the law to maintain order and peace for the good of the citizens, the citizens are restrained to take law into their hands, which closely corresponds to the modern state-citizen relationship.[32] Law, according to Luther, has two dimensions: Natural law and Christian law or law of love. What is the extra substance that makes Christian law different from Natural law? Addressing the Peasants, Luther declared: "Suffering! suffering! Cross! cross! This and nothing else is the Christian law!"[33] Two sources that provided the essential substance to Luther's concept of Christian law are: the Sermon on the Mount and the Cross of Christ. Christian law, thus, demands Christians to be ready to suffer following the model of Christ.[34] Going by the spirit of this position, the victims are left with no other choice to resist but to submit and suffer. However, while taking cognizance of the serious problems involved in this theological position, we need to bear in mind that this is addressed to a specific situation, i.e., the peasants' preparedness to engage in bloody battle by taking law into their hands. It was his attempt to pacify the agitated peasants and settle the issue peacefully and Luther does not valorize this as a universally applicable principle. It is certainly a dark spot in the Reformer's career and he cannot be absolved completely. Two undesirable consequences are: the princes, whom Luther invited to be the arbiters of the Church in an emergency situation, assumed themselves the role of the custodians of the Church; and Luther gave the princes, whom he had earlier castigated for their injustice to the peasants, a 'good conscience' for curbing the mutiny ruthlessly. These factors, however, need to be critically assessed to see if Luther's positions were consistent with his overall deliberations on the Church.

Reformation paved the way to unsettle old structures, authorities and certainties on a large scale, giving rise to a kind of insecurity, both social and religious, which put the people in a difficult situation to subscribe to any authority. It necessitated developing new patterns of community life and reorganizing the Church structure, which were massive tasks. There were not too many people with competence to undertake these immediate responsibilities. In this circumstance, Luther invited the princes to use their *gifts* to serve the Church. Here again, his distinction between spiritual authority (God's rule on the right with the Word) and the political/institutional authority (God's rule on the left with human reason) came into play very strongly and he tried to synthesize both for the benefit of the Church and society. According to him, both belonged to God, and therefore, there was no reason why the princes could not look after the affairs of the Church. The irony, however, is that while the Reformer had disputed the right of the bishops and pope (spiritual leaders) to exercise secular authority, he gave his consent to the political leaders to become the heads of the Church in the place of the bishops and the pope, though in administrative matters alone.[35] It, however, proved to be a formidable support to the nobility to espouse the Church for their selfish ends and led to a situation in which the feudal lords came to decide which Church tradition their subjects must adhere to. In several territories and countries, the Church became an organ of the state with little spiritual and theological substance to back up such developments – quite unintended or unforeseen by the Reformer – and it ended up in a disjunction between his theological reasons and final outcome.

Similarly, any investigator who deals with Luther's encounter with the peasants would be perplexed with the troubling question: what had prompted the Reformer, who had so passionately advocated the peasants' cause and God's loving kindness, suddenly turned against their agitation so savagely in his harsh tract? Admittedly, there is no ready-made answer to this question. One possible (but not undisputable) answer is that this is a typical instance of the disjunction between his theological reasons and historical judgments. In this case, for the most part, his theological reasons were genuine, but his historical judgments turned out to be lumbering. Luther proposed the method of arbitration to both the peasants and the rulers. In all earnest, he believed that his counsel would be heeded and the bloody encounter would be averted. He exhorted the princes, priests, monks, and bishops to consider the peasant revolt as God's judgment and have genuine introspection to see the ways in which they had wronged the peasants:

> We have no one on earth to thank for the disastrous rebellion, except you princes and lords, and especially you blind bishops and mad priests and monks, whose hearts are hardened...You do not cease to rant and rave against the holy Gospel, even though you know that it is true that you cannot refute it. In addition, as temporal rulers, you do nothing but cheat and rob the people so that you may lead a life of luxury and extravagance. The poor common people cannot bear it any longer. The sword is already at your throats, but you think [that] you sit so firm in the saddle that no one can unhorse you. This false security and stubborn perversity will break your necks...I have often told you before to beware of the saying in Psalm 107[:40], '*Effundit contemptum super principes*' ('He pours out contempt upon princes'). You however, keep asking for trouble and want to be hit over the head. And no warning and exhortation will keep you from getting what you want. Well, then, since you are the cause of this wrath of God, it will undoubtedly come upon you, unless you mend ways in time... For the peasants are banding together, and, unless our repentance moves God to prevent it, this must result in the ruin, destruction, and isolation of Germany by cruel murder and bloodshed.[36]

We have already noted his exhortation to the clergy and the nobles to redress the peasants' grievances.[37] Luther never uttered a word against the peasants until he personally witnessed the devastations caused by the mob violence and the magnitude of suffering inflicted on both sides. In Luther's view, the peasants and their leaders indulged in this unlawful act, and they were acting on the behest of the devil.[38] Luther made a sharp distinction between simple murder and organized riot and he equated the latter to "a great fire, which attacks and devastates a whole land. Thus, rebellion brings with it a land filled with murder and bloodshed; it makes widows and orphans, and turns everything upside down, like a worst disaster".[39] More than the entire text of the harsh tract, three harsh words earned him the notoriety that lingers on to the present day: "Therefore let everyone who can, *smite*, *slay* and *stab*, secretly or openly, remembering that nothing can be more poisonous, hurtful, or devilish than a rebel" [emphases added].[40] Nonetheless, in spite of those hurtful words, he still appealed to the princes to extend opportunity to the poor peasants, who had been dragged into this situation, to repent; and they were to be punished only if they remained adamant.[41] But the peasants, who were under the fatal grips of emotion promoted by the rhetorics of the fiery preachers, would not heed to the counsel of reason or Gospel and their war ended up in abysmal calamity.

Luther advanced three reasons for his call to the princes to curb the peasants' mutiny. (i) The peasants broke their oath of loyalty to the authorities – a punishable offense with outlawing the culprits in Germanic legal provisions. (ii) They plunged the country into chaos and destruction by committing murders, which left many women as widows and children as orphans, plundering, and burning monasteries. (iii) They used the Gospel to cover up this sin, claiming that they did this as Christians and forcing others to follow. This, in his view, was a serious offence against the holy name of God.[42] It would be preposterous, however, to presume that Luther took shelter under the Princes because he was neither a coward to take shelter under the patronizing support of the princess to safeguard the reform movement, nor was he a political broker to play the card of an opportunist. As Lloyd B. Volkmar observed, "There was also a possibility that the peasants might win, in which event his own life would be forfeit. The most tempting course...[in such a situation] would have been to throw his support behind the peasants".[43] But Luther pushed his personal interests to the fringes to boldly stand for his convictions. There is an important lesson for us, which the Reformer foresaw, i.e., how dangerous it is to drag religion for political causes.

Luther's stance on mob violence was in line with the tradition of resisting violence. Violence, according to this tradition, is the usurpation of power by the people who have 'no legitimate right to power' and who use violence to disrupt and destroy the peaceful existence of others in the society for their self interest. It impels us to critically look at the issue of violence, especially in the contemporary context of pervasive communal riots, terrorism, and people resorting to violence for redressal. The important question before us is: can we advocate violence of this nature even if the cause is legitimate? Before hastening to say 'yes' or 'no' we need to take into account the following factors. The Reformer faced such a situation and his response was an emphatic 'no' to mob violence and a 'yes' to state authority to deal with the rioting mobs in accordance with the law.[44] Gadamer has a useful insight in this regard as he asserts: "The law is always imperfect, not because it is imperfect in itself, but because, in comparison with the ordered world of law, human reality is necessarily imperfect and hence does not allow of any simple application of the former".[45]

It is common knowledge that in our democratic situation (people's rule), citizens are restrained from taking law into their hands, but the state's authority to enforce law has been accepted, though not without criticism. The general conception is that whereas the state's enforcement of law is guided by reason, the mob violence is emotively motivated and, hence, it lacks rational judgment. In this sense, the state enjoys the privilege of the general acceptance and it is entitled to enforce law, not arbitrarily, but to contain flagitious crimes and maintain peace and order. Even though law has its own imperfection, as Gadamer points out, it has a normative appeal. Law also contains a chasm between its generalization and the particular situation in which it is applied.[46] We subscribe to the rule of law, not because law is perfect, but because it is lesser evil than lawlessness. Over and above all, in any violent conflict the worst affected are the poor, the weak and the defenseless. In such conflictual situations, law must be allowed to take its own course. Therefore, whether we advocate or castigate mob violence, we need to be critical. The Reformer consistently stood firm on his convictions against violence until his death as is made clear by the fact that he never regretted for his stance or retracted his utterances against mob violence. But he appears to be a villain in the eyes of his critics who castigate him based on his harsh tract, without taking into account the other two related tracts, which I have mentioned before and also the circumstances

– his lived experience as a pastor, his mediation between the peasants and the lords with a sincere hope to diffuse the tension and restore the legitimate appeals of the peasants and as a personal witness to the rampages – that led him to come out harshly against violence.[47]

The preceding critical observations lead us to take a look at the issue of violence in the contemporary context from a Christian point of view. This is particularly significant in view of the issue of 'just violence' advocated by certain strands of social and theological discourse.[48] The term violence encompasses a wide range of meaning and implication and it is beyond the scope of this study to deal with it in its entirety. What concerns us here is the violence on communal lines through "the insertion of religious symbols into mobilization for politics" that inflicts great pain and suffering to the people.[49] As Larson aptly described, the agony of contemporary India is over religion – a fact that has been attested by several of the recent studies.[50] It has often been pointed out that an important factor that perpetuates communal conflicts is human captivity to the past.[51] Within the Indian context (and also elsewhere) it is mostly the right wing middle class that has become intolerant with no compunction for fellow humans who become victims to religiously motivated violence. As Ravider Kaur argues, "Perhaps, realization of the victim's secondary status is what the perpetrators aim at, since the sentiment of 'teach them a lesson' often accompanies the actual violence".[52] On the political/ bureaucratic level, there is a usual cliché that explains away violence as 'spontaneous outburst of emotions' or the handiwork of a few 'anti-social elements'. But such simple categorisations proved to be deplorable, given the fact that many of the violent riots witnessed the participation of large crowds, gruesome massacre of the minority communities, the dubious role of the state machinery and the transformation of the minority communities into second-class citizens. Thus, it becomes imperative to renegotiate our usual notions of violence from a Christian point of view.

Martin Luther stood consistently firm on his stand against organised violence, because as a disciple of Jesus Christ he could not act otherwise. His stance on violence is still relevant today in our own context in the twenty-first century. The ideology of "holy war" is the key to understand the contemporary phenomenon of organised violence fuelled by religion. Turning to the Old Testament, the number of armed conflicts between nations, especially those involving Israel, were legitimised as divinely sanctioned, although, the specific expression *holy war* is not mentioned (Joshua 8:1, Judges 4:14- 15, 2 Kings 3:18). The notion of God as the 'great warrior' certainly causes numerous problems for theologians and ethicists and yet the view of war as a "necessary evil" is not absent in human thinking.[53] Islam promotes the ideology of "jihad" (holy war).[54] Hinduism also has the concept of "*dharmayudh*" in *Mahabharath* and *Ramayan*, i.e., God fighting to destroy the forces of evil and to protect the innocent. The root of the problem lies in the ancient legal systems that had promoted the ideology of "tit-for-tat" (e.g. an eye for an eye in the OT) or "pay back in the same coin" (e.g. Savarkar). The most dangerous phenomenon that causes great concern today is the application of the ideologies of "holy war" and "pay back in the same coin" in modern terrorist activities across the globe and in communal riots in India.

It is unfortunate that contemporary human religiosity is riddled with the irony of preaching love at the idealistic level and perpetuating hatred and bloody conflicts in actuality. It is something similar to what Christopher Duraisingh calls the "twin forces – one of intense integration and the other of divisive fragmentation".[55] It is regrettable that in a globalised context we encounter a tendency to identify differences with divisiveness. As a consequence, the dominant usually view the differently 'other' as the enemy to be ostracised. It leads to violent reactions denying the sanctity of life. Therefore, we need to hold on to all the available resources that can guide our emotional, intellectual and spiritual senses in the path of non-violence.

Now the crucial question before us today is: can the Church legitimise organised violence? Within the Christian tradition, we can discern an apparent contradiction between the teachings of Jesus and later theology. Jesus, a born Jew having been brought up within the Jewish tradition and its legal system, made a radical reversal of the Jewish law with his teachings of "showing the other cheek" instead of "tit-for-tat". But the post resurrection Christian theology quickly turned around to legitimise the violent death of Jesus as an atoning sacrifice. Perhaps two 'strange' instances in Jesus' life – the cleansing of the temple (Mt 21:12, Mk 11:15- 17, Lk. 19:45 – 46) and Jesus urging his disciples to procure arms in the wake of his impending arrest (Lk. 22: 36) might be cited as examples of Jesus' approval of violence. But, in the instance of the temple cleansing, there is hardly any evidence that Jesus physically assaulted the vendors and money-changers. In a similar way, even though he urged the disciples to obtain some arms (having been troubled by the possibility of his arrest), and even though his disciples did procure some, Jesus rebuked Peter when he struck the servant of the chief priest during his arrest (John 18: 10-11). Although the Christian tradition emerged from the Jewish religious tradition, it has appropriated its Master's teachings and even in the midst of unjust repression and persecution, demonstrated utter restraint, at least for the first three centuries. Thus, violence is alien to Christianity and if Christianity indulged in violence, it was not in consonance with its essential nature.

Many modern critics castigate the Reformer for his invitation to the princes and his failure to recognise the common people as effective agents of the reform of the Church and society, even though he regarded the authority of reform being vested with the people. In fact, such criticisms spring from the newly emergent perspectives brought forth by the postmodern situation. This cannot be an appropriate approach to Luther's thoughts because it would amount essentialising modern worldviews and extrapolating our context upon Luther's, completely ignoring the fact that he lived in an entirely different milieu. To be fair, Luther's engagement with the princes and the peasants and his utterances related to the whole event must be evaluated in the light of his own context, the crisis situation he faced, and the criteria he had set for his involvement in the Church and society. Any attempt to use modern perspectives or criteria to evaluate Luther's thought will yield only a truncated picture. More than anyone else the Reformer knew his context; he knew the utter powerlessness of the poor; and he was also well aware that it would be disastrous for them to engage in any violent mutiny. As a matter of fact, Luther had every chance to use the disgruntled peasants as an easy springboard to fame by mobilising them and become a popular hero among the peasants and a champion of the oppressed in the eyes of the critics, both then and now. But he did not indulge in such cheap political gymnastics as we witness in modern secular and religious realms. Rather he exhorted the princes to fight for the people's liberation for he believed that they had the responsibility and administrative skills to do so on account of their political power and spiritual obligation.

To sum up, viewing from the perspective of modern critics, Luther's call to the German nobility would appear to be his toeing in with the princes and lords. His positivistic approach to state authority has been severely criticised as infusing more substance to the repressive state. Some even tend to trivialise the reform movement itself by saying that Luther aligned with the princes against the peasants for fear of his reform project being jeopardised. These are far from truth and, as noted earlier, Luther was not a coward to take shelter under the patronization of the princes. Till his last breath Luther never regretted for his stance, not because of his arrogance but because he was convinced about his stance on his engagement with the peasants and princes. Luther speaks of the natural law as a 'Golden Rule' and it must be observed to preserve peace and order.[56] Explaining the fifth commandment, he maintains: "...neither God nor the government is included in this commandment, yet their right to take human life is not abrogated... Therefore what is forbidden here applies to private individuals, not to governments".[57] As noted before, Luther establishes a double standard – tolerance for the civilians and repression for the authorities:

> [T]he rule in the Kingdom of Christ is the toleration of everything, forgiveness, and the recompense of evil with good. On the other hand, in the realm of the emperor, there should be no tolerance shown toward any injustice, but rather a defense against wrong and punishment of it, and an effort to maintain the right, according to what each one's office or station may require.[58]

Thus, in the strict analysis, we can conclude that the Reformer's stance was not against the peasants but against violence.[59]

Here, one needs to bear in mind the fact that with all the awareness campaigns, critical thinking, legal provisions and grass-root movements, the notion of "people's power" is only an emergent phenomenon and it would take a long time for it to come to fruition. Luther's conscience did not allow him to sacrifice the poor peasants who lived in miserable conditions with limited, or no freedom. Most of the critics attacked Luther based on his tract, "Against the Robbing and Murdering Hordes of Peasants" (1525),[60] which was written in response to the violent mutiny by the agitating peasants. This cannot provide any ground for a fair assessment of the situation in which Luther came out with this tract. In order to have a fair assessment we need to read the two other tracts he wrote in connection with the peasants' agitation: "Admonition to Peace: A Reply to Twelve Articles of the Peasants of Swabia" (1525);[61] and "An Open Letter on the Harsh Book against the Peasants" (1525).[62] In fact, Luther was arbitrating between the peasants and the princes pertaining to the legitimate demands of the former. But the long suffering of the peasants made them impatient and the evangelical radicals added fuel to the fire, resulting in the premature revolt of the peasants. Yet another fact that has always been downplayed was that even before the Reformer could make known his treatise against the peasants, the princes dealt with them severely and Luther's tract helped them legitimise their actions.[63] It would be fair, I believe, to conclude this discussion at this point and allow the readers to come to an assessment of the Reformer's stance on the peasant agitation and mob violence. Our attention is drawn now to review his theology of 'justification', which is vital for his ecclesiological thoughts.

Hermeneutical Significance of 'Justification' in Luther's Thought

The doctrine of justification is an important Biblical symbol and it played a central role in the Reformer's theological thinking and Christian praxis. It was this doctrine that provided the fundamental hermeneutical key to him to enter into the world of the Scripture and unearth its wealth of meaning that proffered a new theological thrust to challenge the stronghold of the Church over the ordinary people and engendered the necessary impetus to the reform movement itself. No wonder, the Reformer was inclined to hold on to this doctrine throughout his theological thinking and articulations. Rightly understood it was his attempt to contextualize this doctrine, which provided a counter consciousness to him in his fight against the papacy that had been abusing its privileged position as an 'objective order' for its selfish ends by imposing unbearable burdens on the poor believers. Justification came to collide head on with the papacy when it promoted the sale of indulgences, which was nothing but a spurious way to fill up its coffers. In this context, Luther's teaching that righteousness (justification) was a 'free gift of God's grace alone that could be appropriated by faith alone' had made a great appeal to the people. In this whole exercise, Luther took seriously Paul's interpretation of justification in his encounter with the Jewish Christian legalism vis-à-vis its insistence on circumcision as an essential precondition for the Gentile believers to be part of the Christian communion.

A careful analysis of the 'doctrine justification' brings to light three stages of its development. *First*, in its origin in Genesis 15:6, its structure was like a cause and effect formula: "And he [Abram] believed the Lord; and the Lord reckoned it to him as righteousness". This righteousness or justification is not pronounced in the context of sin or moral disaster and it is attributed as the corollary of faith, which has strong traits of legalism. *Second*, in the New Testament, Paul's affirmation is notable: "For by grace you have been saved through faith, and this is not your own doing; it is the gift of God – not the result of works, so that no one may boast" (Eph. 2:8-9); "having been justified by grace..." (Titus 3:7). The point of departure here is Paul's removal of the legalism by reconstructing the original form with the element of grace. Once again, the notable point is Paul's contextualization of this doctrine not as a remedy for sin but as a counter to Jewish legalism, especially the Jewish Christian insistence on the ritual of circumcision as a pre-requisite for the Gentiles to be embraced into the body of Christ. *Third*, in the reform process, the Reformer redefined it with another strategic element – *on account of Christ* – and, thereby, discarded the mediatory role Roman Catholicism claimed to play between God and humans, especially in the context of the massive sale of indulgences. Hence, with regard to this doctrine, the intention of Luther (even his attempt to establish it so strongly at the heart of his theology), I believe, is not to make it a remedy to every single sin or human moral/ethical disasters, but to place it as a counter to the Church's claim to play the mediatory role of dispensing with grace. According to the Reformer, it is Jesus Christ, and not the Church, who is the mediator of justification – a truly liberative symbol indeed.

The discovery of the doctrine of justification led Luther to a broad understanding of God-human relationship that had critical contextual implications and we will take a quick look at some of the vital insights that emerged from his delineations.

i. Luther's primary existential concern was to find a merciful God, i.e., a God who does not condemn but graciously accepts humans in the midst of their sinfulness. The medieval teaching posited the Church as the mediator between God and the people, which proved to be a heavy burden to ordinary believers, more particularly to the poor, because of the heavy monetary implications. But the new perception of justification gave great respite to them.
ii. Justification ends the hostility between God and humans and brings them in a relationship of communion, which restores the freedom and dignity every human person is entitled to.
iii. It implies a radical equality of all believers and an utter antagonism against all discriminations of people in terms of their status. Within the ambit of justification, people are valued not on the basis of what they possess, produce and consume, but on the basis of what they *are* as justified sinners.
iv. The doctrines of *justification* and *priesthood of all believers* radicalize the usual tendency to value humans in terms of more and lesser perfect beings or hierarchy of believers, and promote a new model of ecclesia, not as a hierarchical and institutionalized system but as a communion of people congregated around and under the Word of God, sharing the benefits of grace and each other's burdens. Two important contextual implications of the doctrine of justification are notable at this point: *first*, in the context of Hindutva's attempt to reinscribe the Vedic Hindu structures of society under the pretext of a 'strong Hindu nation', Luther's

thoughts sharply undercut any tendency to discriminate humans on the basis of caste hierarchy; and, *second*, the 'untouchables' are no longer outside the boundaries of the canonised texts but they are the very subjects of God's dealing with humans – a part of the royal priesthood.

v. With the justifying grace being imparted freely, the believers are free of all captivity and they are called in turn to free others who are in captivity.[64]

vi. The Reformer unearthed this symbol in the context of the Church's hegemony over the life of the people and it was an effective symbol of liberation for those who were gasping under the yoke of the ecclesiastical powers. As an alternative or counter-model, Luther proclaimed that, in the act of justification by grace through faith on account of Christ, God meets humans (in the cross) and endows them with freedom, dignity and fellowship with God (in spite of their sinfulness); and as a consequence (because of the new freedom, i.e. justification), in a state of freedom, the justified sinners meet others with their responsibilities towards them. In his treatise, "On the Freedom of the Christian"(1520), Luther deals with two essential aspects: *freedom in relation to God in faith* and *radical commitment to the neighbours in love.* Luther asserts again:

> God's blessings must flow from one person to another and be shared by all, so that each cares for his neighbour as he cares for himself...that I with my own faith and righteousness must stand in for my neighbour before God, covering his sins, taking them upon me and acting as though they were my own, just as Christ has done for us. Look, this is the essence of love if it is truly love... A Christian does not live in himself, but in Christ and in his neighbour, in Christ through faith and in neighbour through love. Through faith he moves beyond himself into God; through love he moves beyond himself to the neighbour.[65]

In this discourse, the Reformer makes a clear *distinction* between sinfulness and righteousness, but he finds the *integration* of the sinners within the communion of God by grace. No wonder, the Reformer laid exorbitant emphasis on this doctrine and we cannot overlook or downplay these vital insights in our ecclesiological reflections today without impoverishing the Church.

Nonetheless, the whole application of this doctrine in many of the contemporary theological expositions, especially by Lutherans, raises certain vital questions. True it is that the Reformer discovered the Gospel of God's acceptance of the unacceptable in Jesus Christ, which he particularly expounded in and through the doctrine of justification. But should he place such exorbitant emphasis on this doctrine? Despite the fact that Luther contextualised this doctrine for a specific purpose, did he not essentialise and universalise this symbol as is evident by the deep entrenchment of this doctrine in his entire theological writings? Did not Luther contribute to the gross misuse of this doctrine in legitimising or, at least, providing a clear conscience to the perpetrators of injustice than providing respite to the victims in the course of its interpretations? In what way can we solve the exegetical problem of his excessive emphasis on justification and relatively lesser stress on the other two vital symbols – sanctification and reconciliation – that are crucial for our engagement in ecclesiological debates in the contemporary context, precisely because of the fact that these two symbols contain rich theological resources as much as justification?

The legacy of the Reformer's excessive emphasis on justification is quite conspicuous among the Lutherans. Lutheranism often posits formal subscription to its own doctrinal formulation as a precondition for anyone to be part of its fellowship. As Nürnberger observes, it implies not a simple confession of its formula, rather the incorporation of their particular (legal) formulation into the constitution of the communion that intends entering into fellowship with them – a veritable obstacle in ecumenical dialogues. Many Lutheran Churches have incorporated the confessional writings (*Book of Concord*) into their constitutions, leading them to abstain from pulpit or Eucharistic fellowship with other denominations, and even with other Lutherans having a slightly different viewpoint. The irony is that the acceptance of the doctrine of God's unconditional acceptance of the unacceptable becomes the condition for being accepted into their fellowship. The problem lies in the failure among Lutheran theologians to take pains to reinterpret the "legal formulation" of the 'justification of the sinner by grace through faith', which led it easily to slip into a precondition for accepting others into the communion – a veritable transformation of the "open door of the Gospel" into the "gatekeeper" of a new legalism.[66] Thus, the concept of freedom of the believers, the openness of the Gospel that receives the wretched, the unlimited scope of communion, and above all the very act of breaking up of the rigid structure, which Luther promoted passionately could not somehow get into the theological matrix of Lutheranism. Instead, Lutherans quickly turned around and formulated them into another impenetrable legal system, completely ignoring the fact that the Reformer was utterly scornful about any legalism in whatever form.

Similarly, the way some of the Lutheran communions handle this doctrine gives the impression that this doctrine has been designed to justify anyone who chant the name of Christ in faith, irrespective of the nature of one's sin – a gross misrepresentation and underestimation of sin and a destruction of all that the Reformer taught indeed. This is what Bonhoefer described as *cheap grace* and this is the subtle way an essentially liberative symbol has come to be made out into a dominant symbol. Understood this way, medieval papacy with all its heinous sins stands vindicated; the feudal lords who oppressed the peasants are justified; the Nazi regime is absolved; and all the authoritarian rulers, the states, the authorities and individuals who invest their faith in Christ can emerge stainless despite their grave sins. This, however, is not what the Reformer taught or stood for. But then, how can we solve the issue of his essentialising of this doctrine whose pervasiveness is explicit throughout his theological discourses? Two important observations need to be made here. (i) Luther did not produce a dogmatic system to be universally applicable. Rather his thoughts on ecclesia emerged in response to different situations, for which justification provided a strong counter ideology and it fitted in well with his entire works. Therefore, there is no reason to suspect him to be pro-dominant because, fundamentally when he applied justification in his theological constructions, it was a symbol of liberation, not to the princes, lords and the privileged priesthood, but to the poor. (ii) What happened in later theologies was that the symbol of 'justification' that was essentialised by Luther in his context was uprooted and applied, rather than reinterpreted, in contexts that are totally different. Therefore, the problem lies neither with Luther nor with the doctrine of justification, but with its application in later Lutheran traditions.

As Altmann understands, it was the Reformer's contextualisation of this doctrine in a historical situation and a "liberating discovery of the Gospel", which has been subjected to "mere doctrinal reproduction" by later Lutheranism.[67] One of the fundamental issues that emerged from the doctrine of 'justification' is its purported 'individual' appeal. Many critics, both then and now, subscribe to the view that it is too individualistic that has the potential to provide a clear conscience to the perpetrators of exploitation and oppression and not to the victims. Unfortunately, these critics somehow downplay the fact that the Reformer came out with the theory of justification in the historical context of the Church's continuous exploitation of the people in the name of penitential practices and the mediatory role it claimed to possess in imparting graces, which led to the undesirable practice of the sale of indulgences. Now, if we take a close look at Luther's position from this vantage point, it gives us a startling revelation, i.e., when indulgences were on sale, it had a dreadful effect on the conscience of the poor than the rich because the poor could not afford to pay sufficiently neither for themselves nor for their dear ones who were 'supposed to be' suffering in the purgatory. In such a context, the theory of justification was a great boon to the vulnerable.

The discovery of the doctrine of justification turned out to be a turning point in the whole reform movement and the Reformer, in view of the prevailing situation, laid excessive emphasis on this doctrine like what Paul did in his encounter with the Judaisers. But unfortunately, it had led successive generations of Lutherans to chant this doctrine uncritically almost like a magical hermeneutical key to unlock the entire wealth of Biblical meaning for all times and all situations.[68] They would reiterate 'justification' as the only true doctrine for authentic Christian faith and praxis, and reject any attempt to regard it to be one among the many even if assigned a central role.[69] That is the reason why LCMS and its partner Churches abstained from signing the 'Joint Declaration on the Doctrine of Justification' (JDDJ) at Augsburg in 1999. Both Lutheran and Roman Catholic traditions believe in this doctrine, but the fundamental point of departure is that while Luther insisted on unmediated justification, Roman Catholicism insisted on the justification mediated by the Church.[70]

In its meticulous attempts to establish this doctrine at the centre of ecclesial life and practices, confessional Lutheranism has overlooked the fact that the Reformer, while taking justification seriously, had ascribed relatively lesser importance to two important Biblical symbols – sanctification and reconciliation – though he did not discard them from his theological constructions. In the present situation, a relevant theology of the Church must take into account sanctification and reconciliation, especially in view of the internal conflicts within the different communions, inter-Church conflicts and the Church's encounter with plurality of faith persuasions. Justification, however, plays the central role in Luther's understanding of the Church as *communio sanctorum*, as ecclesia is the community of the faithful congregated by virtue of the justifying grace of God. Our attention is now drawn to Luther's explication of *communio* in contradistinction to contemporary discourses on community.

Idea of Community in Luther and Contemporary Discourses

The term 'community' plays an important role in contemporary theological, sociological and political reflections, since modern society is constrained to deal with certain fundamental questions related to their existence in the wake of the loss of traditional community and the emergence of new forms of society.[71] In relation to society, modernity refers to the emergent modes of social organisations or mobilisations. Secularisation, Industrialisation, Bureaucratisation and Democratisation are some of the modes of discourse that embody the Enlightenment ideals of rationality, individual autonomy, and development. As David Harvey puts it, as a cultural and social phenomenon, modernity was "a secular movement that sought the demystification and desacralisation of knowledge and social organisation in order to liberate human beings from their chains".[72] The thrust of modernity was a kind of triumphalistic instrumentation of a universal rationality with its concern for more production of material goods. The recent critical thinking that came to be known as postmodernism generally rejects universalism of rationality, individual autonomy, and the newfound consumerist culture.[73]

More than anyone else, it was Luther who re-invented the idea of community and re-inscribed it in his ecclesiological discussions. His specific use of the expression "communion of saints" has the implicit meaning of community constituted by the people of God. Thus, with regard to ecclesiology, the fundamental difference between medieval Catholicism and Protestantism is their respective emphasis: while Catholicism placed its emphasis on the structure of the Church, the Reformer placed his stress on the people of God. A notable point is that even though Luther was highly critical and polemical about the entire Roman Catholic system, he never condemned the Church and never hesitated to accept that the true Church is present even within the Roman Catholic Church insofar as the Word is preached and the Sacraments are administered. What he challenged was the premises, both theological and administrative, on which medieval Catholicism established itself that had paved the way for the corruption of the entire system.

Roman Catholicism posited the Church as having been built on the authority Christ had given to the particular office, i.e., the office of the apostles, based on Mt. 16:18. Therefore, no 'communion' can properly be called 'Church' if it is not based on the authority of this hierarchy. Luther rejected it as something spurious since it obstructed the proclamation of the Gospel and put unbearable burdens on the ordinary people. His point of departure was the centrality of the Gospel of Christ as the point of reference for ecclesial life and practice over against the hierarchical structure of Roman Catholicism.[74] The pertinent issue is: whether the structure exists for the welfare of the Gospel and of the communion of saints or vice versa. Luther took the unambiguous stance that the structure is for the service of the Gospel and for the welfare of the people and it cannot be otherwise. Undoubtedly, this position critiques any phenomenon that intends to promote the pre-eminence of structures over people, which includes Hindutva's notion of "nation first and citizens next".

Luther is often criticised as the father of modern individualism and existentialism, for Luther emphasised the dignity, freedom and responsibility of the individual. But we need to remember that Western individualism emerged with Enlightenment and not with the Reformation and both had completely different ideas. As against Enlightenment (which affirmed the emergence of the individual from his/her self-imposed non-age), in Luther we find a definite rejection of egocentrism, for according to him, spiritual emancipation does not provide room for the subjective elevation of the believer. Luther had nothing to do with individual autonomy and self-indulgence as he taught that it is sin, which is characterized by 'turning backward into oneself'.[75]

Luther's understanding of the Church as the 'communion of saints' is founded on the principles of freedom, love, sharing, equality and service, for in the communion everyone participates with one another and also with the benefits of grace. It implies that, for a collective and harmonious existence, we require communitarian thinking (without slipping into parochial communalism), subscribing to certain basic and sustainable values. With the idea of *Communio*, Luther negates egocentric, individualistic, utilitarian and rationalistic way of life, and promotes a more egalitarian, participatory and mutually sustainable way of life. If we push this perception of 'mutually-dependent-lifestyle' of the *communio* further, it is possible to develop a relevant theological principle to re-construe the interdependence of humans and nature for a harmonious existence of the entire creation under the divine, which is the central thrust of Luther's principle of *distinction* and *integration* or *unity of the opposites* – a principle that first understands and clearly defines the proper limits of the variegated components involved in the web of the relations between the creator and the created, and then unites them into a communion that could guide our common journey towards the ultimate goal, which we can call the "fullness of life for all".

Luther's concept of *communio* challenges Hindu nationalism and it also critiques our euphoria over the 'rediscovery of community' in the wake of the emergent discourses on contemporary societies. The fundamental difference between Luther's application of the term *communio* and its usage in modern discourses must be noted here. Postmodern situation marked the breakup of normativity and the emergence of plurality of centers, and the new social discourses lay their stress on community over against individuals.[76] This is a welcome sign indeed in the context of the overwhelming social imbalances and human contradictions. Nonetheless, our reaction against the old structures and euphoria over the newfound wisdom tend us to the other extreme of essentialising whatever alternatives that are made available before us, often without realising their potential to make us captives within their own ghettos. This is illustrated by the very fact that even the new reasoning could hardly escape the tragic consequence of the emergent particularised 'centers' re-forming themselves into different ghettos of identity politics at various levels – local, communal, regional, and national. Hindu nationalism is a typical example of this new trend of re-formulation of a homogenous community, which is relentless in its attempts to project India as a strong monolithic Hindu nation with certain ideologically constructed geographical, religious, cultural, social, and political boundaries. The most hazardous part of this entire exercise is its claim that those who subscribe to be within these boundaries alone can find a rightful place within this space and 'others' cannot have a rightful place.[77]

To be sure, Luther's reconstruction of ecclesia as 'communion of saints' does have the traits of community, as 'community' is a derivative of the term 'communion'. But the fundamental difference lies in his emphasis. Unlike contemporary community and Hindu nationalist discourses, his emphasis is on the people as against the imagined structures. Rightly understood, his is a 'communion ecclesiology'. Here is a brilliant text in which Luther envisions his 'communion ecclesiology':

> This is the communion of saints, in which we glory. And whose heart will not be lifted up, even in the midst of great evils, when he believes that...the blessings of all the saints are his blessings, and that his evil is also theirs! For this is the sweet and pleasant picture that Apostle Paul depicts in Galatians 6:2, 'Bear one another's burdens, and so fulfill the law of Christ.' Is it not a blessing to be in such a company in which, 'where one member suffers, all the members

> suffer with it; or one member be honoured, all the members rejoice with it'?...Others bear my burden, and their strength becomes my own. The Church's faith supports my fearfulness, the chastity of others bears the temptation of my flesh...And so truly I can glory in the blessings of others as though they were my own; and they are my own when I find joy and pleasure in them. Even if I am base and vile; yet they, whom I love and admire, are fair and beautiful. And by my love I make not only their blessings, but also their very selves my own; so that by their honour my shame is made honourable, by their abundance my poverty is filled, by their merits my sins are healed. Who, then, could despair in his sins? Who would not rejoice in his pains? For...he bears them not alone, but is assisted by so many holy sons of God, yes, even by Christ Himself. So great a thing is the communion of saints, and the Church of Christ...When we, therefore, feel pain, when we suffer, when we die, let us...firmly believe and be sure that it is not we, or we alone, but that Christ and the Church are in pain, are suffering, are dying with us...we set out upon the way of pain and death attended by the whole Church, and the Church bears the brunt of it all.[78]

This passage is part of a treatise Luther wrote to encourage his prince, Frederick, who fell seriously ill. That is the reason why he lists out the 'benefits' of being part of this communion, and not of the 'costs' of being part of it. If these are the benefits of being in the communion, the costs of being in the communion work the other way round.

It is quite apparent from the above text that Luther's concern is not about the solitary individual who is preoccupied with his/her own worldly well being. Rather, he is more concerned about the communion of saints, wherein everyone is equally free and equally responsible. It is this freedom and responsibility that made the Reformation possible. In this sense, the Church of the Reformation is totally different from the traditional communal model or medieval feudal pattern where the individuals have to strictly adhere to the established structures and dare not overstep their assigned places in the predetermined order.[79] When Luther challenged Roman Catholicism, his purpose was not to carve out another structure but to reform the existing structures for the welfare of the people for he believed that the reform of the society was possible through the reform of the Church.[80]

Both medieval Catholicism and contemporary Hindu nationalism exhibit certain analogous traits. With its fundamental understanding of the Church as an objective order established by God, medieval Catholicism demanded absolute subjection of all human beings, cutting across territorial boundaries, to the Church for their ultimate destiny, i.e., salvation. Similarly, Hindutva demands absolute subjection of all the citizens, irrespective of their cultural, ethnic and religious differences, to the ideologically constructed and politically motivated 'Hindu identity' for their very existence. In both the cases, the faceless structures get prominence over the citizens. Luther's re-discovery of the 'communion of saints' challenged the medieval Church by placing the saints before the Church, and this preferential option for the people of God over the imagined structures undercuts Hindutva's attempts to posit the nation before the citizens, and for this reason, the 'communion of saints' stands as an alternative or new consciousness to Hindutva's baleful attempts to enforce an all-embracing Hindu identity on all the citizens of this country.

Medieval Catholicism and Luther upheld the theory of *extra ecclesiam nulla salus*. In this, medieval Catholicism made it mandatory for every human person to subject him/herself to the objective order of the Church for salvation, for the Church was seen as the custodian of divine grace. Similarly, Hindutva is quite emphatic that one's inclusion as an Indian is contingent on his/her absolute loyalty to the land as the holy land and it is this loyalty to the nation that would determine his/her identity. In other words, one may be a Hindu, Christian, Muslim, or a follower of any other faith, or no faith in the private realm, but he/she must be subjected to the overarching Hindu identity in the public domain. In effect, both medieval Catholicism and contemporary Hindu nationalism would exclude those who do not formally subscribe to the imagined structures. Luther's doctrine of 'no salvation outside the Church' offers a different meaning. In his exposition, the 'communion of saints' comes into existence through faith in Christ. Here, faith does not imply one's formal subscription to a particular rite, creed or the institutionalised structure. It is common knowledge that there are scores of admirers and faithful followers of Jesus across the globe who remain(ed) outside the boundaries of the Church.[81] According to the principle of *adiaphora*, the rituals and structures become superfluous if they stand in the way of genuine faith-formation through the hearing of the Word. Thus, the Reformer's position has enough space for inclusiveness and it opens up new possibilities for our continuing ecclesial reflections, more specifically for building communion transcending the rigid boundaries of the Church.[82]

As understood by Luther, the Church comes into being through the proclamation of the Gospel, which creates faith in those who lend an ear to it and they are embraced into the communion. Faith is not the creation of any human effort, but it is the work of the Spirit through the Word.[83] It raises an important question whether the communion/community is only for the baptised or can it be inclusive of others also in Luther? It is rather difficult to derive a direct answer from the Reformer to this crucial issue because (a) the Reformer neither confronted the issue of religious pluralism, or multicultural context as we encounter today nor was he addressing issues of religious and cultural pluralism; and (b) his fundamental concern was his own Church's deviation from the Gospel and the consequent distortions. Nonetheless, it is not completely out of place to look for certain satisfactory clues from him that could lead us to discern inclusiveness in his delineations. Here we need to ask certain fundamental practical-theological questions to the Reformer: What is fundamental for a person to be embraced within the communion – certain legal rites or the Gospel of God's acceptance of the unacceptable? In other words, Which one, the Law or the Gospel, takes precedence in faith formation? The Reformer's ready response would be Gospel and Gospel alone. He would further affirm that the justifying grace is given to those who have faith in the Gospel of Christ and not contingent on any legalistic practice – be it the membership in a particular local communion, Baptism, the Lord's Supper and so on.[84] Leaving aside the question of inclusiveness in Luther's theology for the moment, we will move on to another debatable doctrine, the two-kingdom theory.

Luther on Two Realms of God's Activity

Luther's two-kingdom theory came under fire and, as we have noted, critics and detractors went to the extent of attacking Luther of abetting Nazism in Germany. But such insinuations have been denounced as unfounded by a number of theologians. Paul Tillich, who had vehemently opposed this criticism,[85] however, viewed that Luther's explication of the Church-State relationship was the most complicated one, and his distinction between spiritual and secular authority had long standing ramifications. But the problem was neither with the doctrine nor with the Reformer's intentions, rather in the way did the theory come to be grossly misunderstood and uncritically applied by Lutherans in particular historical situation, especially when religion and state were in a coalition course. The fulcrum of the issue here is religion-state interface and it requires critical questions about how directly and how substantially the Church should address the state. In the 20th century, however, the two-kingdom theory came to be distorted and applied uncritically by the Church in Germany with disastrous consequences.

When Germany became unified in 1871, the Protestant Churches found themselves in a position of assisting the State to rebuild a stable German society, preserving its cultural heritages intact. But their reconstructive project faced a major setback with the defeat of imperial Germany in 1918, which contributed to a major crisis situation for the Church in Germany. Recapturing the spirit of this crisis, Reinhard Möller, the president of the Conference of German Protestant Churches, remarked:

> We can do nothing else here but bear solemn witness to what rich blessings have issued from the previous close relations between state and Church upon both state and Church, and through both of these upon the people and the fatherland. Moreover, we can do nothing else here but in deep grief bear solemn witness how the Churches of our fatherland owe a deep debt of gratitude to the rulers who have been their patrons.[86]

Many German people found themselves in an uncomfortable situation, especially with the emergence of new ideologies that forged a synthesis between religion and culture and Christianity and morality.[87] German Protestants saw the creation of the 'secular' Weimer Republic as paving the way for an impending catastrophic moral decadence.[88] In their reaction against this development, many of them supported the restoration of a more traditional German State under a sovereign leader (*Fuehrer*), and eventually Adolf Hitler emerged as an authoritarian leader. The most unfortunate situation was that even many eminent theologians welcomed and supported the rise of Hitler, since they saw in Hitler the restoration of traditional German culture.[89]

When Hitler came to power in 1933 he consolidated the Protestant Churches and established them into a Reich Church.[90] Many of the 'German Christians' of these Churches promoted a kind of christianised Nazi ideology for which Luther's two-kingdom theory with his positivist doctrine of the state came in handy. The crucial element in the intellectuals' support of Hitler is that they found in him the restoration of the traditional German culture. But then they miserably failed to see the evils of Nazism as we see it from the consequences of war and holocaust. In the words of Wilhelm Stapel:

> The totalitarian state controls all law, all morality. The Church has all that concerns the kingdom of heaven...Law and order in the Church are subordinate to the State. What must be conceded to the Church is that its members should be able to gather undisturbed in the name of Jesus Christ, that the Gospel should be properly preached and the sacraments correctly administered. Even how that happens, and under what order and law is a secular matter... Does that mean that the state not only can but 'may' do with the Church what it wishes, and the Church may not say a word to rebel? Certainly the state can do that. It can appoint bishops when it likes, and as many as it likes. It can establish community boundaries as it likes. It can transcend the Landeskirchen and organize a Reich Church to suit itself... In short, it can exercise the most rabid control over the Landeskirchen.[91]

Such developments provoked strong and spirited reaction from eminent Lutheran theologians like Dietrich Bonhoeffer and Hermann Sasse, who saw more clearly than many the danger of the Nazi *Fuehrer* principle and radical theories. In this Church-State alliance, even though the alliance partners were aware of their potential to resist each other, they avoided any direct confrontation. Nazi regime did not interfere with the Church's ministry, which gave greater contentment to many German Protestants, who ignored the ominous signs of an impending catastrophe.[92] Their traditional view of the Church and State also failed miserably to provide them with any basis to oppose the civil government even when it was repressive. The two-kingdom principle had, thus, become the rationalisation for looking the other way even when the State became demonic.

Barth's criticism of German Lutheranism was harsh but largely justified as he poignantly stated:

> To a certain extent, Lutheranism has provided a breathing space for German paganism, and has allotted it – with its separation of creation and law from the Gospel – something like a sacral precinct. It is possible for the German pagan to use the Lutheran doctrine of the authority of the state as a Christian justification for National Socialism, and it is possible for the German Christian to feel himself invited by the same doctrine to a recognition of National Socialism. Both have in fact occurred.[93]

Lutheran theologians later came to acknowledge that the two-kingdom theory of Luther must not be applied the way the German Lutherans did, as they confessed:

> True, we have struggled for many years in the name of Jesus Christ against a spirit which found its terrible expression in the National Socialist regime of violence, but we accuse ourselves for not witnessing more courageously, for not praying more faithfully, for believing more joyously, and for not loving more ardently.[94]

After World War II, most Lutherans came to realize the true intent of the Reformer in constructing the two-kingdom theory. They acknowledged that what Luther intended was to demonstrate God's twofold rule of the world through Law and Gospel and not to disjunct them into two differentiated realms of secular and sacred.[95] This acute criticism against Luther's two-kingdom theory notwithstanding, properly understood, it is a potential insight for us to derive appropriate principles in our ongoing theological discourses.[96] It provides us with a new hermeneutic of integration of apparently opposite categories within a framework of a dialogical relationship.

It necessitates an in-depth analysis of the doctrine itself in order to see whether the doctrine itself is a hazardous one or whether it is a helpful one for our ongoing reflections on the Church, more specifically the Church's life and ministry in the context of Hindutva's renewed efforts to overlap religion and state vis-à-vis Hindu nationalism. It needs to be noted that the so-called shortened expression "doctrine of the two kingdoms" was not from Luther, but from the Luther scholarship of late 19th and 20th centuries.[97] When the German Lutherans sought to apply this doctrine in their engagement with National Socialism, they lifted it out of its context and applied it to suit their non-interventionist attitude towards the state in sharp contrast to what Luther intended. This doctrine was neither intended to lock up Christians within the spiritual domain nor was it aimed at preventing them from exercising their social responsibilities. Certainly it does not teach Christians to remain quiet when the State turns out to be authoritarian and repressive. Rather, in constructing this theory, the primary purpose of the Reformer was to prevent the use of religion for narrow political goals and economic ambitions. Two clear illustrations of the above evaluation of this doctrine can be cited here: (i) the Reformation movement itself emerged in reaction to the Church's misuse of its spiritual authority to usurp political power; and (ii) even when the major segment of the German Lutherans, more specifically well meaning theologians, aligned with Hitler, there were young Lutheran theologians like Dietrich Bonhoeffer and Herman Sasse who could derive great influence from Luther to resist the Nazi dispensation and become martyrs for the Gospel of Christ.[98]

There was tremendous turmoil in the wake of Luther's open attack on the Church and the empire. A number of temporal officers volunteered to lend their support to the reform movement. Luther was constrained to respond to their concern and he wrote the treatise: "Temporal Authority: To what Extent It Should be Obeyed" (1523).[99] Here, Luther came out with his understanding of temporal authority, its proper limits and a possible Christian response to it. The notable points are: (a) Civil government does not come into existence arbitrarily, rather it is founded by God and it reflects God's gracious concern for the enhancement of human life in a fallen world. (b) It is not to be condemned as something antithetical to God; rather it has to be positively approached as God's gracious concern for God's creation. (c) God is the Lord of both temporal and Spiritual realms, although governed by different means – Law and Gospel respectively. (d) Christians can at no point imagine that they are alienated from the temporal realm and trans-located in the spiritual realm. Rather they live in both the realms *simultaneously*, which clearly tells that what Luther propounded in terms of the two-kingdom theory is a distinction of the two realms and not a disjunction or divorce of one from the other.[100]

Obviously, there is a tinge of positivism in Luther's understanding of the temporal authority, which was not typical of Luther alone. Rather it was the prevailing notion of his time with regard to the temporal authority.[101] Luther never promoted any idea of state authoritarianism or Christian quietism. On the contrary, he was emphatic in his assertions that the state must exercise its powers with responsibility for the good of the citizens. Thus, the two-kingdom doctrine neither provides any space for Christians to shun away from their social/political responsibilities nor does it provide any scope for social quietism. Rightly understood, it is a doctrine that makes clear distinctions between the Gospel of God's reign that encompasses the entire humanity and the temporal authority that normally operates through rational means. If we fail to make such clear and conscious distinction, it would lead to confusion and dangerous overlapping of religion and politics or the temporal and the spiritual, which is disastrous, as it was evident in the Nazi regime in the past and becoming evident in our own experience of Hindu nationalism in India. Here, one needs only to recall the christianisation of the Roman Empire that followed Constantine's conversion. In this christianising process, the 'pagan cultures' became the first and worst casualty. As Robert Markus recounts, Christians, who had formerly been a threatened minority, emerged to redefine their identity in a changed context of religious respectability in which their "faith became a source of privilege, prestige and power".[102] Christians are not alone in this drive to take pride in identity based on religious faith. Islam has already established itself as a strong political force in many parts of the world. It is the turn of the Hindutva now to re-construe Hinduism as a strong political force. I am inclined to believe that Luther's voice is capable of representing an alternate consciousness in contrast to the religiously coloured political goals of Hindutva that can inflict great injury to the common people.

In Luther's doctrine of the two kingdoms, we can find the configuration of his principle of *distinction and integration* or *the unity of the opposites* in full force and it would be unfair to make him accountable for divorcing the temporal and the spiritual into two autonomous realms because there is no such autonomous thing in his thinking. Rather, in the context of the Church's power over temporal authority across territories and its abuse of this power that made the life of the people miserable, he was in a compelling situation to clearly define their proper limits and show how these two domains can function together for the benefit of the people and not for the powerful alone. Surely, his was a more balanced stance since he saw farther than many others the danger of invoking religion for political goals.

Contemporary Indian situation is something similar. With the invocation of nationalism, Indian politics came to be coloured with the negative aspects of religion and such a synthesis took its heavy toll during partition and, in the present day India, it continues to demand its price up till today in the form of Hindu nationalism. Admittedly, the Reformation movement could not remain within the confines of religion alone, as other interests – social, economic, political, and nationalist (in a limited sense) – came to coalesce with it.[103] In his treatise "To the German Nobility", Luther broke three "walls" that protected papal theocracy, namely, (i) the hierarchical division of the society into spiritual and secular classes ascribing a lower status to the latter, (ii) the pretension that Pope alone was the authentic interpreter of the Scripture, and (iii) the canonized proposition that the Pope alone is authorized to convene a council and that its decisions were valid only with his sanction. Luther's concern was to make Christians aware of their obligation to fulfill unselfishly the God-given responsibilities towards the goals of justice and equality for all people, so that the will of God would prevail in all spheres of life and all will benefit.[104] As Robert Kolb observes, the two-kingdom doctrine clearly defines the two spheres of human existence in dependence and interdependence, and he further stretches it to mean our vertical and horizontal relationships in which the vertical integrates us to God in Christ and the horizontal binds us to the rest of creation.[105] This is a vital insight for our ongoing reflections on the Church.

Two-kingdom doctrine was not intended to promote a culture of silence among the believers by locking them up into their spiritual realm. The Reformer had other important objectives: (i) it was a strategic move to break the unique monopoly of power that the papacy used and abused over the lives of the people; and (ii) it was an attempt to address the issue of perpetual injustice meted out to the poor masses by the Church in favour of the priestly class and the lords. Does not this doctrine critique and challenge Hindu nationalism, which is nothing but religion's resurgence to usurp temporal power for the benefit of a few at the expense of the 'others'? Does not this doctrine challenge Hindutva's violent and reactionary mode of discourse that promotes the principle of "paying back in the same coin", which enmeshes those identified as the 'others' in a crisis of identity and meaning and enhances human misery? The most important point to note here is that Hindu nationalism emerged as an elite middle class ideology.[106] It aims at creating a unitary nation with an all-encompassing culture on the basis of a particular (Hindu) religious ideology.[107] It envisages transforming the heterogeneous public culture into a sovereign, disciplined national culture rooted in what is claimed to be the superior ancient 'Hindu' past.[108] It invokes the emotional attachment to the territories of India (since it is the *punyabhoo*), which tends to generate an anti-minority syndrome, raising skepticism about the loyalty of the religious minorities towards this land.[109] In this milieu, the two-kingdom doctrine must, in fact, be preserved at the heart of ecclesiology in India today.

To sum up, our discussion has unearthed at least three vital insights: Luther's method of the *distinction and integration* of seemingly opposite categories, i.e., the *unity of the opposites*, his *communion ecclesiology*, and his emphasis on the *people of God* over the structures. His 'communion' model must guard us from any temptation to essentialise the 'human' element, for when Luther posited 'communion of saints' as an alternative to the preeminence of structures, his purpose was not to glorify the individual human component, which is an Enlightenment and capitalist aberration, but to postulate people of God (saints) within the communion with freedom and responsibility. Viewing from a postmodern perspective,[110] it will not be an exaggeration to call Luther a 'pioneering postmodernist', since it was he who had opened up the vistas of critical reasoning by breaking up the constellation of power around papacy by his intellectual/ theological discourses and direct praxis. The ecclesial dimension of Luther's thoughts, thus, exhibits certain influential and creative insights that are capable of stimulating our ongoing reflections on ecclesia in a new key, which is enhanced by his theological principle, especially in our encounter with Hindu nationalism. Here, we will briefly explore the efficacy of these and the other components we have identified from Luther's thoughts on the Church.

Unity of the Opposites or Distinction and Integration

Most Luther studies have come to the conclusion that his theology of the cross and theory of justification are central to his theological thinking, which provided perspective and hermeneutical clue respectively to his thoughts. And most of the critical scholars picked up only one side of his method, i.e., *distinction*, in order to castigate him. They have somehow overlooked the other important side of his theological principle, i.e., *integration*. In other words, his central theological principle is *distinction and integration*, which is also known as the *unity of the opposites*. It is an important feature of Luther's way of thinking in which, in the first place, he would distinguish the various components that come into play in his theological thinking, especially those categories that would stand as opposite poles, in order to integrate those seemingly antagonistic and irreconcilable elements. It is best exemplified by the meeting of the divine and the human on the cross, mediated by God's grace through justification. This was crucial in the context of Rome's exploitation of the German people, especially the poor and the weak, on the one hand, and their struggle for survival and liberation from the misery under the feudal system, on the other.[111] A close parallel can be garnered from the struggle of the Indian Christians to affirm their identity and meaning on the one hand, and the struggle of the Subaltern people for emancipation from the misery perpetrated by Vedic Hinduism and the legacy of which is furthered by Hindutva, on the other. Luther's reconstruction of the communion of the saints becomes more sensible and relevant to the Hindu nationalist situation only when we understand the Church from within the framework of *distinction and integration* or *unity of the opposites.*

As the world in which we live is preoccupied with making distinctions between different particularities, aiming at erecting rigid boundaries between the *self* and the *other* in which the other is normally regarded as an outsider or alien or, even worse, an enemy, any proposal for *integration* or *unity of the opposites* will not be a welcome sign. It will also be criticized from another vantage point, i.e., the idea of integration as having the potential to slip into a homogenizing discourse. This is particularly so with the new phenomenon called globalization, and within India, the Hindu nationalism. Both have similar agenda of homogenization of cultures. Whereas globalization envisions a global village, Hindu nationalism attempts to construe a Hindu nation. Hence, we need to be cautious in using Luther's principle of the *unity of the opposites* or *distinction and integration.* What I propose here is not homogenization, but a move away *from* different particularities encamped as opposites in tension *towards* a dialogical relationship without annihilating one for the sake of the other. In other words, it is my passion to work with the principle: 'differences are not necessarily divisive'. It is a discourse in which we self-consciously make *distinctions* of the different particularities that we encounter in the public domain and *integrate* or *embrace* or *unite* the different particularities in a spirit of a mutual relationship, which is life affirming and life enhancing. In the context of the Church it is a discourse that is premised on the perception of ecclesia as a spiritual body of Christ with a tangible communitarian form. As Louis S. Mudge understands, this is a "counter consciousness" with a special openness to the Word of God.[112]

Distinction and integration or *unity of the opposites* presupposes that the various components of any social unit posses within themselves an inner capability to cohere in some determinate fashion with all their differences.[113] As Donald L. Lovine explains, in the field of social sciences the common assumption among theorists is that socio-cultural systems are typified by an "inner coherence and unity" that are essential to their nature, and in modern times, integration is viewed as a "quality of culture that is never perfect but never absent".[114] In nationalist discourses like that of India, the principle on which integration is posited is "unity in diversity". To a great extent it does hold together the diverse social, cultural, linguistic, and ethnic units within India, but not without its own pains, perils, and agonies. Another apt example of this type of unity comes from the ecumenical movement, which obviously tells that any organic unity of the fragmented communities is only a remote possibility. That is the reason why Oscar Cullmann suggests a new model of unity, which he terms as "unity *through* diversity", working out various possibilities within this model.[115] The underlying objective of forging integration in any context is community or social mobilization and the inevitable outcome of such mobilization is a kind of an identity politics, both internal and external.

At the social/political domain the notion of integration works predominantly with certain systems, which might not address the issue of human fragmentation and the consequent crises situation. In other words, the systems preempt the people and relegate them to the periphery with an authority to hold and regulate them together in a community. To be more precise, the existing modes of social or national integration place the systems before the people, which ultimately end up in ascribed/enforced unity. In the final analysis, they demand strict adherence or loyalty to the system, paying only secondary importance to people. Here, we need to take into account the fact that within the integrated wholes, each individual segment or unit would look for the early next occasion to *re-member* its own obscured and/or erased identity and thereby its own preeminence over the 'other'. This applies to every single unit within the social systems, including family and individuals. My intention here is not to negate human search for identity; but to oppose any identity formation that sets out to annihilate the 'other' in order to foster a unified dominant system of classification in terms of civilization, nation, religion, culture, or community; and to uphold the identity formation of the oppressed that provides a sense of belonging and a source of empowerment to their very survival. Also we need to recognise that there are voices that suggest the need for multiple identities in our social relationships. Amartya Sen's voice, for instance, is apt as he points out that "we are *diversely different*" and affirms:

> The hope of harmony in the contemporary world lies to a great extent in a clearer understanding of the plurality of human identity, and in the appreciation that they cut across each other and work against a sharp separation along one single hardened line of impenetrable division.[116]

My own multi-civilisational approach in this study (see chapter two) is premised on the recognition of the richness and beauty of multiplicity which, I believe, is God's design and gift that must be preserved.

Unfortunately, contemporary community formation through social mobilization, for the most part, exhibits a hard-line of classification that diminishes the possibility of mutual interaction and interrelation. When such a hard-line community is formed through social mobilisation, its particularism immediately tends to create an 'other' either to define its own identity or as a means to identify an 'enemy'. That is exactly what happens within the social texture of contemporary India. Hindutva attempts to create a mono-civilisational nation based on Vedic Hinduism through social/political mobilisation. In the process, it imposes an ascribed/enforced identity on the 'unified' selves and demands those who inhabit or intend to live within the geographical space called *India* to be unconditionally loyal to the nation by placing the nation before the selves. It is Hindutva's clever instrumentation of the nationalistic and patriotic doctrines within its own definition of what a nation is. In this whole exercise, Hindutva could create definite enemies (in the garb of anti-nationals and/or cultural aliens) out of those who do not conform to its designs *vis-à-vis* Christians and Muslims.[117]

Integration in the general sense, thus, connotes a sort of an uneasy coalescence of the various units involved in community mobilization, predominantly characterized by identity politics, leading to the creation of animosity within and enemies without. It necessitates that we redefine 'integration' in clear terms in order to apply it as a veritable theological principle in our reflections on ecclesia in the present context. Amartya Sen's proposal for "multiple identities"[118] might be a helpful resource here. Sen contends that community mobilization through the creation of uniform identity becomes problematic in the context of the coexistence of variegated peoples. This is evident, for instance, in the process of the formation of *India* as a nation and it is more so in the context of Hindu nationalism, wherein various minority communities feel that they are *assimilated* within the imagined or ascribed identity against their will. As Sen convincingly puts it:

> [I]dentity can be a source of richness and warmth as well as of violence and terror, and it would make little sense to treat identity as a general evil. Rather, we have to draw on the understanding that the force of a bellicose identity can be challenged by the power of *competing** identities. These can, of course, include the broad commonality of our shared humanity, but also many other identities that everyone simultaneously has. This leads to other ways of classifying people, which can restrain the exploitation of a specifically aggressive use of one particular categorization.[119]

The idea of 'multiple identities' has Biblical basis also, especially Paul's affirmation in 1 Cor. 9: 19-22, wherein he asserts that he had "become all things to all people". It offers a clue for the present task of re-construing the life and mission of the Church. Paul affirms that his identity is not contingent on his being a 'Christian', but on his being in solidarity with the people he encountered, and thereby he could guard his identity from being locked up in an *insider-outsider* (Christian/non-Christian) discourse. This certainly challenges Hindutva's dangerous exercise of ascribing a corporatist identity based on 'who an Indian is'. In a conflicting situation like the one created by Hindutva, this kind of 'identification' tends to get rigidified and the corollary is that the 'other' becomes an outsider, enemy, and anti-national liable to be ostracized. This applies to religions, cultures, ethnicities and nations. The crucial point is: whereas *rigid identities* tend to create conflicts and violence since they are engaged in an exercise of cultural, social, political, and religious ostracism in the name of safeguarding the imagined systems, *multiple identities* transcend these ideologically constructed systems to see the humans (people of God created in God's own image) behind these 'imagined categories'. In this process, any ascription of identity gets blurred and it provides greater possibilities for mutual coexistence and interdependence of people in any given space. It minimises frictions and tensions in a context of multiplicity of cultures and faith persuasions.

There are two clear positive effects of this proposal. *First,* it critiques the formation of particularised identities through community mobilisation as they end up in a kind of an identity politics leading to hostility and violence. Admittedly, this proposal would be challenged by the marginalised communities and those who stand for their cause as a serious threat to their ongoing struggle for liberation. I, however, like to argue it the other way round. It is in fact the identity politics that stands in the way of the true liberation of the marginalised because the very tendency to place the particular (mostly enforced) identity first and the people next leads to a virtual loss of the human face and the beginning of the process of dehumanisation. Here, a person belonging to a particular community is forced to identify him/herself as (as for example in the case of India) an "Indian" first and as a person next. The very term "Indian" (or any other particular expression that denotes a cultural, ethnic or religious identity) is ideologically loaded, historically constructed and externally imposed. It immediately creates an enemy in the 'other' and gets locked up in perpetual conflicting situation. A crucial problem that has escaped the attention of those who champion the cause of the identity politics is that when one segment of human population is enforced under perpetual misery, the other segment regards it as "their" problem and not as the problem of humanity as a whole.[120] In the present scenario, is the collective consciousness of the 'high caste' able to perceive the struggles of the 'untouchables' as our problem? Is the rich able to realize that the problem of the poor is our problem?

Are men able to take up the issue of women's subordination as our problem? The answer to all these questions is an emphatic 'no'. What is the alternative then? Over against these anomalies, my proposal for integration, which is derived from Luther's theological principle of '*distinction and integration*' or *unity of the opposites* allows more freedom and scope for 'people' to affirm their 'identities' in and through 'communion' in which there is greater mutuality and no hostility.

The preceding discussion, then, leads us to the *Second* positive effect of my new proposal. At the very outset, it proposes to place 'people' before the imagined structures. In other words, before being an *Indian*, before being a *Brahmin*, before being a *Dalit*, before being a *Woman*, before being a *Christian* or *Hindu* or *Muslim*, one is a human person. It unambiguously affirms humanhood first and the particularised identity next with the possibility of the blurring of the rigid boundary between persons, communities, ethnicities, nationalities and religions, which must be welcomed without any reservation for the real emancipation of the victims of human made structures. My proposal of the *distinction and integration* as a veritable theological principle has this connotation. Here differences do exist and they are acknowledged without getting tightly interlocked into some sort of narrow particularisms to destroy the 'other'; rather differences are transcended to unveil the human face behind them to toil for the common good of all. The primary emphasis of this model is on 'people' who have faces, and the faceless, but monstrous human made structures get behind people.

Both the Bible and Luther's thoughts, especially his reconstruction of the theology of the Church, provide us with ample sources to envision an ecclesia based on the above model. From a Biblical point of view, such expressions as "people of God", "covenant community", "royal priesthood" and so on obviously suggest that God deals with 'people' and not with structures, and when John declared, "God so loved the world..." (3:16), he unambiguously meant that God loved humans and not the structures. Similarly, when Paul affirmed that he became everything to everyone, he was able to push his being a *Jew*, a *Pharisee* and a *Christian* to the fringes, so that he could see in the 'other' not a *non-Jew*, a *non-Pharisee,* and a *non-Christian*, but a human person who is in need of salvation. It was this attitude that enabled him to break the boundaries of his particularist identity and integrate himself humanely with the 'other' to become 'everything to everyone'. Can we transcend narrow particularisms to re-vision the sanctity of life?

Moving on to Luther's thoughts on the Church, it is quite conspicuous that he made a methodical shift giving primacy to the Gospel and the people of God. His entire theological and ecclesiological reconstructions characteristically exhibit this shift. When he moved away from the medieval theology of glory to his theology of the cross, his emphasis was on the integration of the divine and the human on the cross of Jesus Christ, and not on the structures of the Church. His doctrine of justification further strengthened this position as it engendered freedom and dignity every human person is entitled to before God. His interpretation of the Sacraments was an attempt to reconstruct the Roman sacramentalism, which was an objective, quantitative and magical giving of grace, to mean that the sacramental activity denotes the 'communion' of the believers with God and with one another. The doctrine of the 'priesthood of all believers' together with the doctrine of justification was his passionate attempt to break the hierarchy of the Church to envision the equality of all before God.

Luther was totally disturbed when he found that medieval Catholicism, with its hierarchical structures centered in Rome, indulged in exploiting the poor and his new interpretation of the Church as the "communion of saints" was an effort to reconstruct ecclesia by placing the "saints" in the front relegating the institutional structures to the periphery. His two-kingdom doctrine was not an attempt to divorce the secular from the sacred, rather an attempt to redefine their proper limits, so that they might refrain from constant power struggle and engage themselves in a healthy relationship of mutual correction for the sake of the people. Two important contributions of Luther in this regard need to be noted here. *First,* Luther's expression *communion of saints* is often misread to mean *community* of saints (which amounts to replace one structure with another). Rather, what Luther meant was not a new structure called community, but a radically new communion of saints, called into this fellowship to bear witness to the saving love of God and sharing humanely each other's joys and burdens. *Second*, this is a communion model, which seeks to address the issues of the crises of identity and meaning, and the alleviation of human misery from a new perspective. Here, one's identity is not derived "over against the other" (which is typical of the expressions *non-Christian*, *non-Indian* etc), but in solidarity with all others – not "I-Thou" or "I-It" model but an "inclusive *we*" model. Understood in proper perspective, this model views the entire cosmos as the body of Christ and everyone finds his/her identity and meaning in relation to the fellow humans and the entire creation. It further provides scope for a new approach to dispelling misery, for, in this model, one's suffering is not viewed as 'his/her' problem alone, but as 'our' problem to be collectively dealt with.

The main intent of Luther's principle of integrating seemingly opposite categories is to realize true humanhood or brother/sisterhood that has been robbed off by the existent religious and social structures. He could find this in God's act of reconciliation, mediated through Christ, which became the basis for his theological discourses. A similar trend of theological thinking can be seen in M.M. Thomas who consistently argued for the realization of true humanhood and peoplehood. Arguing for a new paradigm for development, he suggests that 'we should work for a people-oriented state'. Thomas further argues for a new framework – a 'communion' framework, which he extends further to a secular communion.[121]

A frequently asked question in Luther studies is: are not Luther's thoughts too individualistic? The answer is a "yes" and a "no". Contemporary social theories and discourses expended almost their entire resources towards re-discovering 'community', adjudging the individual element as a 'bad category', as it ends up in individualism. In his brilliant essay, David S. Smith has recaptured the role of the individual in transforming the society. He finds two kinds of individualism, namely, positive individualism and crass or abject individualism. According to him, crass individualism turns in on "self-solipsism", which leads to gaining advantage for the self alone as the only motivation of life; self becomes God and self-centered faith becomes its theological foundation.[122] Robert Bellah terms this as "utilitarian individualism".[123] This is not what the Bible means when it alludes to 'individual', and Luther also rejects abject individualism. Conversely, they point to positive individualism. When Luther stressed the justification of the individual sinner, it does not imply that he/she is an autonomous self, totally cut off from the rest, seeking to fulfill his/her ambitions alone. Rather, it has two social tasks: (i) it promotes positive individualism, which affirms individual freedom only in reference to the communion of saints and makes him/her accountable to the rest; and (ii) enables the individual demand the same accountability towards him/her from the structures.[124]

Luther's principle of the *unity of the opposites* provides at least three clear directions for our ongoing reflections on the Church. *First*, it critiques the popular notion of integration, which involves community mobilization through ideologically constructed and imposed identities on humans by creating rigid boundaries between communities, often ensnaring them within the enclaves of narrow particularism. *Second*, it enables us to critique and challenge Hindu nationalism, which, in the name of national integration, attempts to impose a corporatist identity on the variegated human communities, creating a kind of an identity politics from within and an enemy from without. Here the predominant concern is the sovereignty and security of the imagined space called India and not the citizens who inhabit this space. Luther's principle undercuts this tendency. When medieval Catholicism projected the hierarchy of the Church above the ordinary believers, Luther emphasized placing the people of God before the structures of the Church, for according to Luther, national welfare is not protecting a land, but protecting the lives of the vulnerable people.[125] *Third*, as against Hindutva's homogenous identity, Luther's principle promotes multiple identities, providing sufficient scope for mutual interaction between human communities without assimilation or erasing of differences. It resists any tendency to stratify humans as higher and lower humans; it enhances the possibilities for mutual coexistence and amity; it urges those who are in the dominant position to accept the suffering of their fellow humans not as 'their' problem, but as 'our' problem; and thereby provides a new perspective for human liberation – a shift from "their struggle" to "our collective struggle" and, after all, it is human blessedness that is at the heart of all our endeavours.

Summary

Having reviewed Luther's thoughts on the Church, we need to ask whether we are able to garner adequate insights to proceed further in our reflections on ecclesia in the context of Hindu nationalism. At the outset, we reject any attempt to find a simplistic one-to-one correspondence of Luther's thoughts on the Church to the present day context. But the Reformer's theological principle of the *unity of the opposites* or *distinction and integration*, posited on a dialogical relationship of various (often opposing) categories without confusing or separating them, provides us with a strong case, opening up new possibilities for ecclesiological reflections in a world that either makes distinction in oppositional terms or indulges in systemic integration of variegated categories through assimilation into an ascriptive mould. Hindu nationalism is such an intransigent ascriptive movement, in which there is no space for different particularities to affirm their identities. According to Hindutva, for instance, the only way to be an Indian is to unconditionally subscribe to the all-embracing Hindu identity and if someone is unwilling to accept this totalising identity, he/she has to remain a definite 'other', an alien and, worse even, an enemy to be ostracised or annihilated.

In such a context, the principle of *distinction and integration* offers ample space for variegated categories to come together to be in communion through mutual interaction and intersection in a spirit of communion for harmonious living under the Divine. It is a theological situation of mutual indwelling as inspired by the truth and plenitude of the Trinity. Here, we do make distinctions, not to 'bench mark' and pitch different categories against each other, rather to embrace different categories and celebrate differences as a way of affirming the sanctity of life. It is our task to theologically grapple with this fertile theological principle in our journey towards an ecclesiology in the context of Hindu nationalism in India. This, however, is proposed not as the only way of doing ecclesiology in this context, but as a feasible, helpful and relevant way of doing it.

Notes

1 Carl E. Braaten, *Principles of Lutheran Theology* (Philadelphia: Fortress Press, 1983), p. xi.

2 Walter Altmann, *Luther and Liberation* , p. viii.

3 See Walter Altmann, *Luther and Liberation*, p. 133.

4 See Franz Lau, *Luther*, Tr. by Robert H. Fischer (Philadelphia: Westminster Press, 1963), pp. 13ff.

5 Eric H. Erikson, *Young Man Luther: A Study in Psychoanalysis and History* (New York: Norton, 1958).

6 See Walter Altman, *Luther and Liberation*, p. 134.

7 Here I am following the interpretation of Walter Altmann, *Luther and Liberation*, pp. 136ff.

8 See Andrew Wingate, *The Church and Conversion: A Study of Recent Conversions to and from Christianity in the Tamil Area of South India* (Delhi: ISPCK, 1997), pp. 89f.

9 Robert M. Brown, *The Significance of the Church* (Philadelphia: The Westminster Press, nd), pp. 21-22.

10 Carl E. Braaten, *The Apostolic Imperative: Nature and Aim of the Church's Mission and Ministry* (Minneapolis: Augsburg Publishing House, 1985), p. 7.

11 Carl E. Braaten, *The Apostolic Imperative*, p. 8.

12 See Gibbon, *A History of the Christian Church*. ed., by Williston Walter et al. (New York: Charles Scribner's Sons, 1985) pp. 25-26.

13 Wainwright, "Augustine" in M. D. Law, ed., *Chambers Encyclopedia*, Vol. I (London: George Newnes, 1959), pp. 774-775.

14 As early as in 1938, *Hindu Outlook* stated that V. D. Savarkar legitimized the occupation of the "Sudetenland" by Adolf Hitler. See *Hindu Outlook* Vol. 12 (Oct. 1938), p. 13. See also Godwin Shiri, 'Revisiting Ayodhya – The Role of Myths in Aggravating Communalism" in Samson Prabhakar, ed., *Inter-Play of Religion, Politics and Communalism in India* (Bangalore: BTESSC/SATHRI, 2004), pp. 13-25.

15 For a startling reading on the way this institution continues to survive with its hegemony, more particularly by availing the same tools that are promoted against it by modernity see M. N. Srinivas, *Caste: Its Twentieth Century Avatar* (Delhi: Viking, 1996).

16 Markus Wriedt, "Luther on Call and Ordination: A Look at Luther and Ministry" *Concordia Journal*, Vol. 28, No. 3 (July 2002), p. 255 (254-269).

17 Gerhard Ebeling, *Luther: An Introduction to His Thought*, p. 25.

18 *LW* 31, p. 53; *WA* 1, p. 362.

19 For further readings on Luther's theology of the cross and its meaningfulness, see the following works: Walther von Loewenich, *Luther's Theology of the Cross*, tr. Herbert J. A. Bouman (Minneapolis: Augsburg publishing House, 1976); Philip S. Watson, *Let God be God! An Interpretation of the Theology of Martin Luther* (Philadelphia: Muhlenberg Press, 1947); Dennis Ngien, *The Suffering of God According to Martin Luther's 'Theologia Crucis'* (New York: Peter Lang, 1995); Gerhard O. Forde, *On Being a Theologian of the Cross: Reflections on Luther's Heidelberg Disputation, 1518* (Grand Rapids: Wm B. Eerdmans, 1997).

20 For a critique of these changing trends, see Max Weber, *The Protestant Ethic and the Spirit of Capitalism*; Harvey Cox, *Fire from Heaven* (Massachusetts: Addison Wesley Publishing, 1995); Kenneth D. Gill, "Charismatic mission" in A. Scott Moreau, ed., *Evangelical Dictionary of World Missions* (Grand Rapids: Bakkar Book House, 2000), pp. 173-175; Lawrence O. Richards, *A Practical Theology of Spirituality* (Grand Rapids, Michigan: Academic Books, 1987).

21 See Markus Wriedt, "Luther on Call and Ordination: A Look at Luther and Ministry", p. 256.

22 This is a serious impediment that confronts anyone who intends to engage with Luther's thoughts. Critics often draw direct links between Luther's anti-Jewish polemic and the Nazi 'Final Solution' (Auschwitz) in the 20th century. There are others who dismiss this criticism pointing to the fact that Luther's concern was purely religious and never racial. My inclination also is to believe that Luther's polemic against the Jews was *not because of what they were but because of what they did*, i.e., *their resistance to the good news of Christ.* Nonetheless, there is a common view even among the most conservative Lutheran traditions that those writings are unchristian (e.g., Lutheran Church-Missouri Synod). In this study I am not dealing with this issue in detail for want of space and I leave it to the judgment of the readers. To those who incline to have a detailed understanding, I suggest the text: Martin Luther, *Von den Juden und Ihren Lügen* (*On the Jews and Their Lies* – 1543), Tr. by Martin H. Bertram *LW* 47 (Philadelphia: Fortress Press, 1971), pp. 137-306; *WA* 53, pp. 417-552. Also see the following works: Robert Michael, *Holy Hatred: Christianity, Antisemitism, and the Holocaust* (New York: Palgrave Macmillan, 2006); Ronald Berger, *Fathoming the Holocaust: A Social Problems Approach* (New York: Aldine De Gruyter, 2002); Mark U. Edwards Jr., *Luther's Last Battles: Politics and Polemics,*

1531-46 (Ithaca, NY: Cornell University Press, 1983); and Gordon Rupp, *Martin Luther and the Jews* (London: The Council of Christians and Jews, 1972).

23 For a good deal of discussion on how colonialism in India produced certain repertoires of authority and sovereignty, see Thomas Blom Hansen, "Sovereigns Beyond the State: On Legality and Public Authority in India" in Ravinder Kaur, ed., *Religion, Violence and Political Mobilization in South Asia* (New Delhi, Thousand Oaks, CA & London: Sage Publications, 2005), pp. 109-144.

24 James Atkinson, "Introduction to Luther's *To the Christian Nobility of the German Nation Concerning the Reform of the Christian Estate, 1520*" in *Selected Writings of Martin Luther*, ed. by T. G. Tappert & Tr. by C. M. Jacob, Vol. 1 (Philadelphia: Fortress Press, 1967), p. 256.

25 Luther, "To the German Nobility...", *LW* 44, p. 143.

26 Ibid., p. 148.

27 Ibid., p. 157.

28 Ibid., p. 208.

29 Ibid., p. 209

30 Ibid., p. 210.

31 Some of the important sources to understand the Reformer's teachings on economic reforms are: "To the Christian Nobility...", "The Long Sermon on Usury" – 1520 (*LW* 45, pp. 273-308; *WA* 6, pp. 36-60), and "Trade and Usury" – 1524 (*LW* 45, pp. 245-310; *WA* 15, pp. 293-322).

32 For a discussion on Luther's interpretation of law and its pros and cons, see Paul Althaus, *The Ethics of Martin Luther*, Tr. by Robert Schultz (Philadelphia: Fortress Press, 1972), pp. 25-35.

33 *LW* 46, p. 29; *WA* 18, p. 310.

34 Paul Althus, *The Ethics of Martin Luther*, p. 33.

35 See "To the Christian Nobility..." *LW* 44 (op. cit.)

36 *LW* 46, pp. 19-20; *WA* 18, p. 298.

37 See above, footnote No. 36. Cf. *LW* 46, pp. 42f.

38 Klaus Nurnberger, *Martin Luther's Message for Us Today*, p. 263.

39 "Against the Robbing and Murdering Hordes of Peasants", *LW* 46, pp. 47-55; *WA* 18, pp. 357-361.

40 Ibid.

41 *LW* 46, p. 52; *WA* 18, p. 359.

42 *LW* 46, pp. 49-55; *WA* 18, pp. 357-361.

43 Lloyd B. Volkmar, *Luther's Response to Violence*, p. 160.

44 Cf. *LW* 21, pp. 113ff; *WA* 32, pp. 394ff.
45 Hans-Georg Gadamer, *Truth and Method* (New York: Crossroad, 1975), p. 284.
46 Ibid., p. 284; Cf. pp. 471ff.
47 See Lloyd B. Volkmar, *Luther's Response to Violence*, pp. 140-173.
48 For a brief discussion on the issue of "just war" see David Wollenburg, "Is There a God-Pleasing purpose to War? An Introduction to *Just* War Concept" *Concordia Journal*, Vol.29, No. 1(January 2003), pp. 65-69. The author concludes this brief essay with the words: "For me, the ultimate answer comes from our Savior Himself, 'Peace I leave with you…I do not give as the world gives…I have told you now before it happens, so that when it does happen you will believe' (John 14:27 & 29, NIV)". See p. 69.
49 Francis Robinson, "Foreword" in Ravinder Kaur, ed., *Religion, Violence…*, p. 7.
50 Ravinder Kaur, "Mythology of communal Violence: An Introduction" in Ravinder Kaur, ed., *Religion, Violence…*, pp. 19-45. Also see the other six essays in this volume.
51 B. G. Verghese, "Prisoners of the Past" *The New Indian Express* (Tuesday, June 24, 2008).
52 Ravinder Kaur, "Mythology of Communal Violence", p. 20.
53 See Gerald M. Mattingly, "War", in *Harper's Bible Dictionary*, p. 1119.
54 K. M. Panicker, *Gandhi on Pluralism and Communalism*, pp.122ff.
55 Christopher Duraisingh, "Encountering Difference in a Plural World: A Pentecost Paradigm for Mission" in Ian T. Douglas, ed., *Waging Reconciliation: God's Mission in a Time of Globalization and crisis* (New York: Church Publishing Incorporated, 2002), p. 176.
56 *LW* 46, p. 27; *WA* 18, p. 307.
57 *BC*, p. 389; *WA* 30^{I}, p. 157.
58 *LW* 21, p. 113; *WA* 32, p. 394.
59 *LW* 44, p. 113; *WA* 6, p. 217/ *LW* 44, p. 79; *WA* 6, p. 249/*LW* 30, pp. 158-59; *WA* 14, p. 23.
60 *LW* 46, pp. 47-55; *WA* 18, pp. 357-361.
61 *LW* 46, pp. 5-43; *WA* 18, pp. 291-334.
62 *LW* 47, pp. 59-85; *WA* 18, pp. 384-401.
63 For a detailed discussion on this issue, see Lloyd B. volkmar, *Luther's Response to Violence* (op. cit.); Robert M. Bigler, *The Politics of German Protestantism: The Rise of the Protestant Church Elite in Prussia, 1815-1848* (Berkeley, CA: University of California Press, 1972);

and Robert Wuthnow, *Communities of Discourse: Ideology and Social Structure in the Reformation, the Enlightenment, and European Socialism* (Cambridge: Harvard University Press, 1989).

64 In the treatise on "The Fourteen Consolation" (1520), Luther affirms: "It would truly be just as difficult for us to believe that in Christ such great blessings have been bestowed upon us [unworthy creatures] ... I am a sinner, but I am borne by his righteousness which is given to me. I am unclean, but his holiness is my sanctification...I deserve condemnation, but I am set free by his redemption...Such a great thing is faith, such blessings does it bring us, such glorious sons of God does it make us! We cannot be sons without also inheriting our Father's blessings" *LW* 42, p. 164; *WA* 6, p. 132.

65 *LW* 31, p. 371; *WA* 7, p. 263.

66 Klaus Nürnberger, *Martin Luther's Message for Us Today*, p. 147.

67 Walter Altmann, "Justification in a Context of Exclusion" in *Justification in World's Context*, p.117.

68 The doctrine of 'justification' has been so interiorized that some of the Lutheran confessional families seem to be too insecure if this doctrine is challenged. See Robert Preus, *Justification and Rome*, which is a response to the Lutheran-Roman Catholic 'Joint Declaration on the Doctrine of Justification' (JDDJ) from the Lutheran Church-Missouri Synod (LCMS). For an informative reading on the reasons advanced by the LCMS for its disagreement with the JDDJ, see the document "The Joint Declaration on the Doctrine of justification in Confessional Lutheran Perspective" (St. Louis: LCMS, 1999).

69 Robert Preus, *Justification and Rome*, p. 17.

70 Klaus Nürnberbger, *Martin Luther's Message for Us Today*, p. 133.

71 See, Wolfgang Grieve, "Communion, Community, Society", pp. 14f.

72 David Harvey, *The Condition of Postmodernity* (Oxford: Basil Blackwell, 1990), p. 13.

73 Kevin J. Vanhoozer, "Theology and the Condition of Postmodernity: A Report on Knowledge (of God)" in *Cambridge Companion to Postmodern Theology*, p. 7.

74 Klaus Nürnberger, *Martin Luther's Message for Us Today*, p. 130.

75 See Klaus Nürnberger, *Martin Luther's Message for Us Today*, pp. 137-141.

76 Due to the ill effects of the kind of universalism and extreme individualism fostered by Enlightenment modernity, critics turned their attention to community and collective consciousness. It is a move away from Cartesian "turn to the subject" or inward looking to outward

looking. See Nicholas Lash, *Theology on the Way to Emmaus* (London: SCM Press, 1986), p. 143. In the postmodern climate, the individual must finally find his/her place only in reference to the community, and in theological terms, in the Kingdom of God or under the rule of God. See David Fergusson, *Community, Liberalism and Christian Ethics* (Cambridge, UK: Cambridge University Press, 1998), pp. 157ff. It would be too naïve to take an uncritical stance on postmodernist approaches. As Paul Lakeland aptly describes, postmodern sensibility is "characterized by cheerful ahistoricity, contented rootlessness, guiltless consumerism and low expectations of the future". Paul Lakeland, *Postmodernity: Christian Identity in a Fragmented Age* (Minneapolis: Fortress Press, 1997), p. xiii.

77 Savarkar dreamt of a flourishing Hindu nation, which is racially and culturally uniform – a nation whose history goes as far back as some five thousand years to the Vedic age. See V. D. Savarkar, *Hindu Sangathan: Its Ideology and Immediate Programme* (Bombay: Hindu Vivek Kendra, 1940), p. 48. According to M. S. Golwalker: "Hindustan lived a life of unchallenged glory and power for thousands of years and spread its spiritual and cultural effulgence over vast areas of the globe – right from Mexico to Japan" M. S. Golwalker, *Bunch of Thoughts* (Bangalore: Sahitya Sindhu, Reprint, 1996), p. 161.

78 Martin Luther, "Fourteen of Consolations" (1520). As quoted by Klaus Nürnberger from *LW* 42, pp. 162f; *WA* 2, p. 690 in *Martin Luther's Message for Us Today*, pp. 140f.

79 Klaus Nürnberger, *Martin Luther's Message for Us Today*, p. 141.

80 "To the German Nobility..." *LW* 44, pp. 115-217; *WA* 6, pp. 404-469. There are notable points in this long treatise: (i) a strong German (national?) sentiment, even though nationalism as a concept had not emerged during his time; (ii) the positivist doctrine of the state that was prevalent in his time and Luther's call to the princes and nobles to exercise their authority not for their self aggrandisement but for the liberation of the people; and (iii) Luther's reluctance to mobilise the poor peasants and put them in the forefront of a violent protest (as done by the evangelicals) as he knew their utter powerlessness and the power of the feudal lords. Even Friedrich Engels who projected Münzter as the champion of the peasants' cause did acknowledge that it was premature for him to engage in such an agitation. See Friedrich Engels, *The Peasants' War in Germany*, Tr. by Moissaye J. Olgin (London: George Allen & Unwin, 1926), p. 80

81 For a discussion, see M. M. Thomas, "The Church - The Fellowship of the Baptised and the Unbaptised" in *Church's Mission and Postmodern Humanism*, pp. 155-161.

82 Moltmann proposes 'friendship building' to be an important mission of the Church, transcending its boundaries. See Jürgen Moltmann, *The Church in the Power of the Spirit* (New York: Harper & Row, 1977), "In the Friendship of Jesus", pp. 114-120.

83 See Klaus Nürnberger, *Luther's Message for Us Today*, p. 130.

84 For a discussion, see Herbert Hoefer, *Churchless Christianity* (op. cit.), pp. 149-177.

85 To understand Tillich's critique of Luther's ecclesiology, the following texts may be consulted. Paul Tillich, *A History of Christian Thought; Perspectives on 19th and 20th Century Protestant Theology* (New York: Harper and Row Publishers, 1967); *The Protestant Era*, Tr. by James Luther Adam (Chicago: Phoenix Books, 1963); *The Courage to Be* (New Haven: Yale University Press, 5th printing, 1954); and Carl E. Braaten, "Preface: Paul Tillich and the Classical Christian Tradition" in Paul Tillich, *Perspectives on Nineteenth and Twentieth Century Protestant Theology*.

86 As quoted in Klaus Scholder, *The Churches and the Third Reich*, Vol. 1, *Preliminary History and the Times of Illusion 1918-1934*, Tr. by John Bowden (Philadelphia: Fortress Press, 1988), p. 4.

87 Klaus Scholder, *The Churches and the Third Reich*, p. 37.

88 Robert P. Ericksen, *Theologians under Hitler: Gerhard Kittel, Paul Althaus and Emmanuel Hirsch* (New Haven: Yale University Press, 1985), p. 26.

89 Robert P. Ericksen, *Theologians under Hitler*, pp. 117f.

90 For a detailed discussion on these developments, see Eberhard Bethge und Martin Greschat, eds., *Der Holocaust und die Protestanten* (Frankfurt: Athanaum, 1998).

91 As quoted in Klaus Scholder, *The Church and the Third Reich*, pp. 422f from Wilhelm Stapel, *Die Kirche Christi und der Staat Hitlers* (Hamburg, 1933), pp. 65f.

92 Klaus Scholder, *A Requiem for Hitler and Other New Perspectives on the German Church Struggle*, Tr. by John Bowden (London: SCM Press, 1989), pp. 116-139.

93 Quoted in William Lazareth, "The Twentieth Century Recovery of Lutheran Political Responsibility" in Harold Lasswell and Harlan Cleveland, eds., *The Ethic of Power: The Interplay of Religion, Philosophy, and Politics* (New York: Harper and Brothers, 1962), p. 127 from Karl

Barth, *Eine Schweizer Stimme, 1938-1944* (Zollikon-Zürich, 1945), p. 113.

94 Stewart Herman, *The Rebirth of the German Church* (New York: Harper and Row, 1946), pp. 128f.

95 William Lazareth, "The Twentieth Century Recovery of Lutheran Political Responsibility", p. 130.

96 Carl E. Braaten, for instance, made a brave attempt to construct a theology of human rights based on the two-kingdom theory. See *Principles of Lutheran Theology*, "Two-Kingdom Principle", pp. 134ff.

97 *Render unto Caesar... and Unto God...*, p. 34. As we have observed in the previous chapter, in the strict analysis, the Reformer's understanding of God's reign is rather discursive and fluid, not static. See John R. Stephenson, "The Two Governments and the Two Kingdoms in Luther's Thought" (op. cit.)

98 According to Bonhoeffer, it was divine providence that raised Martin Luther. To have a glimpse of Luther's influence on Bonhoeffer, see Dietrich Bonhoeffer, *The cost of Discipleship* (Thiruvalla: Suvartha Bhavan, Indian Print, 2001), pp. 39-47.

99 *LW* 45, pp. 75-129; *WA* 11, pp. 245-280.

100 For further discussion, see William H. Lazareth, *Luther on the Christian Home: An Application of the Social Ethics of the Reformation* (Philadelphia: Muhlenberg Press, 1960), pp. 102ff.

101 Lloyd B. Volkmar, *Luther's Response to Violence*, p. 80.

102 For an informative reading and a critique of this mode of Christianising, see, Robert Markus, *The End of Ancient Christianity* (New York: Cambridge University Press, 5th Print, 1997).

103 At this point various groups identified their interests with Luther – the powerless burghers, the middle class and the peasants. Further, Luther's doctrine of the 'Priesthood of all believers' appealed to the peasants and nobles alike. But all of them misconstrued it: the knights took it as a support to their revolt against the emperor; the peasants considered it as a vindication of their continued struggle to claim their civil rights. See Lloyd B. Volkmar, *Luther's Response to Violence*, pp. 100-114.

104 See Walther I. Brandt, *Introduction to Luther's Trade and Usury, 1524* in *Selected Writings of Martin Luther*, Vol. III (Philadelphia: Fortress Press, 1967), p. 79.

105 Robert Kolb, "Luther on the Two Kinds of Righteousness: Reflections on His Two-Dimensional Definition of Humanity at the Heart of His Theology" in *Luther's Way of Thinking* (op. cit.), p. 67.

106 Mark Juergensmayer, *Religious Nationalism Confronts the Secular State* (Delhi: OUP, 1994), p. 6.
107 C. V. Mathew, *The Saffron Mission* (Delhi: ISPCK, 1999), pp. 286-288.
108 T. B. Hansen, *The Saffron Wave: Democracy and Hindu Nationalism in Modern India* (op. cit.), p. 4.
109 Yogendra K. Malik and V. B. Singh, *Hindu Nationalists in India: The Rise of Bharatiya Janata Party* (op. cit.), p. 22.
110 Postmodern critics are involved in the "reassessment of dominant ideas across the human sciences" George E. Marcus and Michael M. J. Fischer, *Anthropology as Cultural Critique: An Experimental Moment in the Human Sciences* (Chicago: University of Chicago Press, 2nd edition, 1999), p. 7.
111 This might elicit sharp criticism as Luther's attempt to identify and pitch 'Germans' against 'Rome' in sharp contrast to his principle of integration. Here, it is important to note that the Reformer did not attempt to identify Germans over against Romans. Had he done so, it might have acted as a clear drawing of rigid boundaries or marks of opposing ethnic identities. On the contrary, Luther's polemic was against the papal theocracy – papal power which interfaced the spiritual and secular under one headship with an authoritative system of canon law in which the Roman Pontiff, the Vice-regent of God on earth, held a unique monopoly over medieval people, not only in Rome, but also across boundaries. Luther's specific mention of "Germans" is to be understood as an immediate reaction to the exploitation of papacy to which he was a personal witness. Further, it is worth remembering that, as a Christian, he had cherished his being part of the Roman Catholic Church. Lloyd B. Volkmar, *Luther's Response to Violence*, pp. 33-62.
112 Lewis S. Mudge, *Rethinking the Beloved Community: Ecclesiology, Hermeneutics, Social Theory* (Geneva: WCC, 2000), pp. 63-75.
113 Unity, especially involving seemingly opposite and asymmetrical categories, is a struggle, which is evident in the formation of India as a 'nation' with its "poly-ethnic-nation-states". For a brief discussion see G. Aloysius, *Nationalism without a Nation in India*, pp. 10-14. This is also true in the global multi-faith context, which exhorts humanity to live with this reality. For a discussion, see Andrew Wingate, *Celebrating Difference, Staying Faithful*, pp. 1-38 & T. Swami Raju, *Christian Responses to Plurality of Religion* (Bangalore: BTESSC/SATHRI, 2006).

114 Some of the theories of integration are: configurational or thematic integration, connective integration, logical integration, adaptative or functional integration, and regulative integration. For further reading see Donald L. Lovine, "Cultural Integration" in David L. Sills, ed., *International Encyclopedia of the Social Sciences* Vol. 7 (New York: The Macmillan Company & The Fortress Free Press, 1972), pp. 374-376. Also see Robert Cooley Angell, "Social Integration" ibid., pp. 380-386.

115 See Oscar Cullmann, *Unity through Diversity*. For him, unity cannot be uniformity or enforced unity: "*una sancta*" not "*uniformitas sancta*" (p. 31); even when there is separation, it is separation without hostility or harmonious separation (p. 32); the possibility and impossibility of structural solution (p. 35); and cooperative work in some areas of common concern (p. 37).

116 Amartya Sen, *Identity and Violence: The Illusion of Destiny*, pp. xiii-xiv.

117 Eric Lott, *Religious Faith, Human Identity*, p. 300.

118 Amartya Sen, *Identity and Violence*, Chapter 2 "Making Sense of Identity", pp. 18-39.

119 Amartya Sen, *Identity and Violence* [emphasis as in the text], p. 4. [*The term *competing* is used here not in the usual sense of "winning by defeating others", but in its Latin original sense of *com* - 'together' + *petere* - 'aim at, seek'. See Judy Pearsall, ed., *Concise Oxford Dictionary* (Delhi: Oxford University Press, 10th edition, 7th impression, 2001), p. 291.]

120 See Vivekananda's emphatic assertion: "you are responsible for your suffering". Swami Vivekananda, *The Complete Works of Swami Vivekananda* Vol. II (Calcutta: Advaita Ashrama, 1963), pp. 224-225.

121 M. M. Thomas, "Search for a New Ideology of Struggle for Justice with Eco-Justice" in M. M. Thomas, *Church's Mission and Postmodern Humanism – Collection of Essays & Talks* (Tiruvalla: CSS & ISPCK, 1996), pp. 78-85. See also "The Quest for a Human Community in a Religiously Pluralist World – What Does It mean for the Being and Doing of the Church?", pp. 146-154. Cf. Hogg, *The Christian Message to the Hindu*, in Eric Sharpe, ed., *The Theology of A. G. Hogg* (Madras: CLS, 1971), pp. 223-254.

122 David S. Smith, "Luther's Contribution to Positive Individualism", pp. 263-278.

123 Robert Bellah, *Habits of the Heart: Individualism and Commitment in American Life*, p. 46.

124 David S. Smith, "Luther's Contribution to Positive Individualism", p. 278.

125 "To the German Nobility..." *LW* 44, pp. 115-217; *WA* 6, pp. 404-469.

Chapter Six

CHURCH – THE PERICHORETIC COMMUNION OF THE PEOPLE OF GOD

Church in Context

> The Church is not simply an institution. She is a "mode of existence," *a way of being*. The mystery of the Church, even in its institutional dimension, is deeply bound to the being of man, to the being of the world and to the very being of God.[1]
>
> We have drawn many boundary lines around us, which prompt us to keep our isolationist tendency at its highest pitch. We need to break free from these ghettos and widen the horizon of solidarity.[2] [Translation of the Tamil text by the author]

The Church exists in India in an unfavourable situation created by Hindu nationalism that often hurts. In this situation, we seek to decipher the meaning of the Church in a new key: as an instrument of a new *humane* consciousness; as an *interlocutor* and builder of new *communion* amidst hostilities and isolationism; and as a *reconciler*, heralding the hope God offers to the entire world in Jesus Christ amidst miseries and injuries. In this endeavour of ecclesiological imagination, we are enriched by Luther's thoughts on the Church. As noted before, the principle of the *unity of the opposites* or *distinction and integration* potentially navigated Luther's theological/ ecclesiological constructions. The Church, in Luther's view, represents the integration of the people of God with God in Christ and with one another in a spirit of (a *perichoretic*) communion. The integrating factors are the *Word of God* that proclaims the message of God's initiative to the healing and reconciliation of the fallen world in Jesus Christ and *the Sacraments* that constantly remind the believers of the 'new union' that God has made possible for them to be in fellowship with God and with one another. That is why the Reformer regarded these two – the Word and the Sacraments – as the external marks of the Church.[3] Obviously, it is his attempt to reinscribe those essential components at the centre of the life and ministry of the Church.

Scripture is the basic source of Luther's theology.[4] The core of the Biblical perception of reality is the idea of the good-evil dichotomy and the constant struggle between God (seen as light) and Satan (the forces of darkness personified). According to the Biblical worldview, in this perennial conflict, humanity is the worst casualty because Satan could easily entice and trap humanity into captivity and thereby vitiate the entire creation of God. As the story further unfolds in the New Testament, God brings this cosmic struggle to an end in Christ, and thereby, engenders salvation or eternal life to the fallen humanity and the entire creation. The life and mission of the early Church appropriated the message of this antithesis between God and the fallen world and the Christ event as playing the essential mediatory role in this whole cosmic drama. As summarized by evangelist John, "God so loved the world that He gave His only begotten Son that whosoever believes in Him will not perish, but have eternal life" (3:16). It indicates Christ's work of bringing together the two antithetical categories, God and the world, in communion because 'eternal life' here means "being in communion with God" and as a foretaste, therefore, with fellow human beings.

Having appropriated this central message of eternal life, the early Church exhibited a particular lifestyle, i.e., not to conform to the ways of the world but to be transformed by the Gospel, to put on Christ to be the new creation (Rom. 12:2; 2 Cor. 5:17), and to engage in the ministry of proclaiming the Gospel of reconciliation. As a result of this understanding of their being in communion with God on account of Jesus Christ, the early Christians within a short span of time broke themselves free from the narrow boundaries they had erected around them and zealously proclaimed the universal salvific will of God in Christ (Acts 10:1- 48). They derived this specific mode of behavior from the model of Jesus who renounced the ways of the world and yet gave his entire self for the reconciliation and renewal of the world. It is a principle of enduring evil and engaging in the ministry of reconciliation in faith commitment to their Lord even in the midst of acute hostility and intense persecution.

Both the Biblical story and the life of the early Church had their primary focus on human existence, especially their estranged state of existence from the creator on account of the evil designs of the demonic forces;[5] and they continue to look forward in hope to the day when this hostility would be ended and the original relationship restored. Luther, being a Biblical theologian and a devout pastor of the Church, was well aware of this dualism of the opposites and the cosmic struggle to be united with the Creator, which provided him with the necessary tools to derive his principle of the *unity of the opposites*[6] in his theological renditions. It is our task now to see if Luther's thoughts could provide us with sufficient insights to engage in ecclesiological reflection and reconstruction in the contemporary context of Hindu nationalism.

Church is commonly understood as the 'community of believers'.[7] Community discourse is also more akin to the contemporary cry to 'turn to the community', especially in the postmodern situation.[8] *Community* discourse ought to be a welcome move indeed in the globalized context in which the competitive self is glorified and the 'other' despised. A nagging question, however, is whether *community* discourse can adequately define the Church in the contemporary situation, both at the local and the global level. This is so vital because our experience tells that 'community' becomes exclusive, ostracizing and hardly embracing, especially those identified as the 'other'. In India, community life has been vitiated by identity politics and narrow communalism that led to some of the bloodiest conflicts causing great trauma and agony to the nation as a whole and to the vulnerable sections in particular. It implies that there are certain serious impediments in construing ecclesia as a community. Hence, we will make a quick survey of the predominant models on which community is constructed that would facilitate us to meaningfully reflect upon the Church closely attuned to our concrete situation.

Models of Community

Frank G. Kirkpatrick sketches three widely known models of community. (i) *Atomistic/contractarian model*, which is like that of independent atoms coming together in an "enforced relationship". (ii) *Organic/functional model*, which is like interdependent organs acting together within a larger organism. (iii) *Mutual/personal model*, which functions in a mode of mutuality with distinct individual persons finding their "fulfillment in and through living for each other in loving fellowship".[9]

Atomistic/Contractarian Model

This model has had the most vital influence upon the past two hundred years of the history of European and American cultures. It was given its theoretical formulation by Thomas Hobbes (1588-1679)[10] and John Locke (1632-1704).[11] This model attempts to understand society and/or community in terms of an association in which individual entities come together based on a contract and it is more akin to an organisational unity. This notion of community is posited on the agreement of individual members, more specifically for political association. As R. Nisbet understands, the mathematical mind of Thomas Hobbes could regard only individuals as the conceivable and real entities in a social organization; and the only forms of social relationship he could recognise as valid "are those geometrically rigorous logic can establish as arising from the very nature of man, *individual* man, with his instincts and his reason".[12] It is a reductionist approach that conceives reality as essentially composed of distinct atomistic specks of matter. In this model, the fundamental features that characterise human beings are self-interest and hostility towards each other. Why, then, do they enter into relationship or contract, so to say? Hobbes' answer is: because of the fear of annihilation. This theory has the greatest influence on the development of the market society, ushered in by capitalism with special stress on individual progress that has promptly been exported to the rest of the world through essentializing the strictly isolationist categories.

In Locke, however, there is a shift of emphasis from individual to sociability as a natural instinct inherent in humans prior to the creation of civil society. In his analysis, humans live as collectives guided by reason and they intend to live without an authoritative superior on earth to judge between them. They live under a common natural law in "one community" and precisely because of this they are distinct from other creatures. Within this civil unit, humans are in a state of "perfect freedom to order their actions and utilize their possessions and persons as they think fit, within the bounds of the law of nature, without asking or depending upon the will of any other man".[13] What, then, is sociability in Locke's exposition of community? Sociability occurs with the freedom of being equal individuals – autonomous, equal, and free persons. Here, even the Christian concept of *agape* is understood as to occur between equals.[14] This sort of community construction allows sufficient space for the preservation of the individual selves and only when this is accomplished can humans look to others' welfare – a principle that affirms the right to ownership of property and entitlement of the fruit of one's labor – the very tendencies that led to the industrial and capitalist society tinged with a utilitarian mindset and consumerist culture aided by liberal social reasoning.

We can note two fundamental characteristics of this model of community formation, namely, atomism and dualism. When these categories are applied to human life, they manifest themselves in human relationships constructed upon power and dominance, which gives rise to the primacy of individual rights and possessions.[15] This discourse perpetuates the subservience of the vulnerable to the powerful and ushers in an inclination towards self-interest and individualism. To conclude, we would identify two important effects of atomism. (i) The dualism between 'the private individual and the public order', in which human subjectivity with all its emotional aspects are confined to the private realm and in the public domain, only cold and calculated rationality is pressed into service. (ii) The corollary of this dualism is the elimination of religion from the public order, which is identified with emotions or sentiments, and hence, it cannot have any influence on the real world.[16] Atomism, especially its discourse on individual autonomy, has its own impact on (Christian) religion, for it has reinvigorated and reinforced the notions of individual spirituality and individual salvation.

Organic/Functional Model

The realization that human aspirations cannot be fulfilled by cold rationality and mathematical calculations necessitated an alternative that could aid human collective living. It was Hegel who provided the fundamental theoretical tools for the organic model of community. Hegel's primary concern, as Kirkpatrick recaptures, was to discern reality as the unity of the whole, attained through the self-development of the Absolute, which is the Spirit. His emphasis on the unity of the whole piloted him to discern the inter-relatedness of reality, in which the Absolute takes into itself every entity without annihilating its individuality. This notion of unity provides the basis for Hegel's understanding of freedom and the individual's relation to the state. True unity or unity of the whole is achieved only when reality overcomes duality, and only at this stage of the annihilation of the duality of the subject-object structure that the individual finds his/her freedom.[17] Thus, in Hegel's view, true freedom is possible not by the autonomy of the self, but by the identification of the self with the Absolute. If we apply this principle to the citizen-state relationship, it leads to the moral and metaphysical supremacy of the larger, the State, and the self is reduced to *nothing* without its reference to the Absolute (State). As Charles Taylor understands, Hegel's political theory shifts "the centre of gravity...from the individual on to the community, which is seen as the locus of a life or subjectivity".[18] This view has been criticised as totalitarian. But Hegel tried to clear such skepticisms through the metaphor of the 'organism' and 'organs'. As the organism does not stand in opposition to the organs, so also the State does not stand over against the citizens. The weak spot of this conception is that since the State is the 'substance' of the citizen and the citizen finds his/her fulfillment only in subjection to the State, he/she becomes a mere pawn of the State. The real problem of this conception is that it paves the way for the emergence of totalitarianism and authoritarianism of the State.[19]

Hegel's organic model of community came under severe attack from Karl Marx. Although Marx appropriated Hegel's organic model, he showed keen interest in the functionality of the various parts that constitute the organism, which signifies the internal relations. In this conception, the identity or difference between the individual entities is characterised by the functional similarity or difference. In other words, the mutual relation between two co-inhering entities is understood in terms of reciprocity. Marx worked primarily with the notion of organic model in mind in his explication of society,[20] and, in his view, human beings are "social beings".[21] The fundamental difference between Hegel and Marx is that whereas the former is too preoccupied with the State or the absolute, i.e., the substance, the latter placed his emphasis on human beings and their functional relationships within the state polity. Within a strict organic scheme as in the Hegelian-Marxian perception, opines Kirkpatrick:

> [T]he insistence upon the self-fulfillment of each individual organ sorts poorly with the insistence upon the identity of each with others, distinguished only by functional differences...Persons ultimately achieve self-fulfillment only by learning that they are organically interrelated with everything else in a single organic whole.[22]

Two difficulties are apparent in this form of organic perception of human community. (i) Because of its keen inclination to discard the obstacles to self-determination, and self-fulfillment caused by atomistic egoism, it fails to explore the final goal that an individual can choose on the basis of his/her new freedom and sense of fulfillment. (ii) It does not tell what space it provides to persons for their relationships of love and mutuality. It raises the important issue of the space available within this model for individual difference and self-identity.[23]

Another prominent metaphysician who contributed extensively towards organic understanding of community in the twentieth century was Alfred North Whitehead with his process metaphysics.[24] It is a system that rejects one of the most important features of traditional metaphysics, i.e., dualism, and stresses the organic unity of entities, which, in his own words, is "the philosophy of organism".[25] It is an attempt to reconcile singularity and plurality, i.e., to synthesize the plurality of the cosmic reality in unity – envisioning the unity of the *flux* and the *permanence* in a coherent whole. The cosmos, according to this perception, is not a disjuncted and unrelated reality, but one interconnected whole, in which there is no ultimate dualism or "bifurcation".[26] This metaphysics denies two basic abstractions of modern thought: the Newtonian theory of "simple location of material bodies" and the "Cartesian separation of mind from matter".[27] The core of the coherence of the whole in Whitehead's metaphysics is the "presumption that there is only one genus of actual entities".[28]

Whitehead advances three elements – Creativity, multiplicity and singularity – in order to do justice to the *flux* and the *permanence* through the principle of coherence. Reality is characterized by stability and change, and the task of metaphysics is to bring them together without annihilating one for the sake of the other. Unity and diversity are the basic cosmic realities, which are called "actual occasions" that include everything in the universe – from God to the smallest speck. There is nothing called autonomous existence, whether it is ascribed to God, or to particular entities (nations, things, persons). Rather entities are understood together as "requiring each other".[29] Every entity is an "occasion" of becoming. They are ephemeral experiences or processes of feeling or enjoyment, completely interconnected with all else, either dependent on them for their self-becoming or available to the ensuing ones for their enjoyment. Thus, the cosmos is a "concrescence" of multiplicity of entities growing together into a single unified whole. "Concrescence", according to Whitehead, is the principle of creativity, in which the world is engaged in a process of "self-realization", i.e., "growing out of the previous processes and each new one adding a novel unity...to the world".[30] It is an organic process governed by a teleology that encompasses the becoming and the actual occasion of every entity.

It, then, leads us to the idea of community. "The community of actual things is an organism...[which] is an incompletion in process of production",[31] in which "a person is a society of occasions". A society "is an interconnected set of occasions...exhibiting a common characteristic exemplified in each occasion within the nexus and dependent upon its exemplication in the previous occasions".[32] However, what is missing in Whitehead is the everyday experience of mutuality, the ongoing relationship between persons who affect and are affected by each other. One of the brightest spots of his metaphysics is his rejection of dualism. But it needs to be further investigated as to whether this is a sufficient model of a community that can provide enough space for mutuality that is so essential in any love relationship devoid of evil, suffering, injustice, and oppression among human beings.

Mutual/Personal Model

Our age is characterised by the liberal emphasis on individual autonomy, which poses a real problem for interpersonal relations. As Stanley Hauerwas commented, "We have made 'freedom of the individual' an end in itself and have ignored the fact that most of us do not have the slightest idea of what we should do with our freedom. Indeed, the idealists among us are reduced to fighting for the 'freedom' or 'right' of others to realize their self-interests more fully".[33] Contemporary society, perhaps more than ever before, has to deal with the problem of mutual distrust that tends to view 'others' as strangers, infidels or enemies who are out there to usurp what "we" deserve. Mutual/personal model of community is an attempt to overcome this particular problem.

No one who deals with community can ignore the Jewish Philosopher Martin Buber's "*Ich und Du*" model, which is a stream of thinking that takes human interpersonal relationship as the fundamental criterion to perceive the essential human nature and the construction of community.[34] Kirkpatrick garners certain vital insights from Buber: his emphasis on the primacy of relationship and not on individual persons; his conviction that only in a community of mutual relations can *I-Thou* relation be fulfilled; his emphasis on God's indispensable role in community formation, as unity with God and community among the creatures belong together; his insight of an intentionally inclusive community; and his understanding of community as a co-operative venture.[35] Buber, however, appears to be rallying around the organic model of community.

An important feature of Buber's theory is "setting-at-a-distance" as a pre-requisite for inter-personal relationship. Who, then, is a person who is essentially weaved into the web of relationship? The fundamental assumption is that a "person" is imbibed with rationality – a thinking organism – that potentially distinguishes human person from the rest of the organisms. Rene Descartes' famous axiom: "I think, therefore I am" is an example of this way of knowing persons. It implies that this sort of understanding once again falls back into the essentialisation of ego, the "I". Another difficulty is that, even though the mutual/personal model proposes inter-personal relationship and cooperative venture as the most essential features of community formation, especially within the "I-Thou" framework, it does not guarantee that human beings would not indulge in objectifying the 'other'. This, I believe, is what happens in contemporary communities, including the Church.

Community in Indian Context – Ascriptive Movement

Indian society is a collective of variegated communities and Indian consciousness is essentially communal. It means that individual autonomy is not essentially Indian; rather it is the corollary of modern progressive worldview.[36] However, it does not imply that the traditional community dynamism in India was an ideal one. Vedic Hinduism, for instance, constructed a society comprising of variegated communities based on caste system and locked up people within those ascribed communities with their boundaries so rigidly demarcated and mystified that any sort of overstepping or border-crossing elicited serious consequences. It furthered a kind of an 'ingrown and defensive syndrome',[37] making them mostly closed communities. This was one of the ways by which Hinduism attempted to preserve its dominance over the people of this subcontinent. It raises an important question as to whether people's conversion to Christianity could break this obsessive mindset. In fact, the Christian ideal of 'new creation in Christ' must have empowered Christians to break free from the ghettos of caste discriminations. But it has painfully been acknowledged that even Christian theology could not engender sufficient force to break the ingrown and defensive syndrome,[38] which some of the Indian Christian thinkers called as "the *quam* mentality", i.e., an exclusive, attitude, and affinity towards one's own community.[39]

Indian Christian consciousness is triply determined. *First*, an Indian Christian's identity is largely constructed around the particular Church body to which he/she is affiliated with an identity tag as Roman Catholic, Lutheran, and Pentecostal and so on. It is something similar to the *samudāyam-consciousness*[40] that is so widespread among Christians. In addition to this, different Church traditions fostered their own denominational, confessional or sectarian consciousness, and made it mandatory for people to adhere to the rites and dogmas associated with them to be fully included into those traditions.[41] *Second*, the Indian State identifies all professing Christians as 'Christian', irrespective of their denominational, confessional or sectarian boundaries, which is another level of identity formation. Thus, in the public domain, a professing Christian is a 'Christian' irrespective of his/her confessional affiliations. *Third*, even though people belonging to different caste identities are embraced within particular Church bodies, allowing some space for certain amount of border-crossing among people belonging to different ethno-cultural affiliations, still the struggle is on to break the caste consciousness that the Christians inherited from their social location. All these factors come to intersect in the formation of Indian Christian consciousness.[42]

In the light of what is stated above, two observations are in place here: (i) Indian consciousness is essentially communitarian and not individualistic. But this community consciousness is mostly rigidified and inward looking that inter-community relations at the deeper level is a matter of serious concern because at every level the dividing lines are kept alive and active with optimum rigidity and volatility in the name of safeguarding the honour and sanctity of particular communities or identities that even the tiny provocations can spark off bitterest communal conflicts. This volatile situation has come to be exploited by certain religionists who constantly look out for opportunities to teach the 'other' or 'outsider' a fitting lesson because the 'other' is seen as an intruder who disturbs the comforts of the 'insider'. This is what is called communalism in India,[43] where it implies an "activist expression of such sentiments especially when they are contrapuntally positioned against a hated, or negativised, 'other'".[44] Without doubt, Hindutva's contemporary activist discourse and ascriptive movement fall within this category. (ii) In this context, the multi-layered identity of the Indian Christians must be able to provide them with sufficient basis for their mutual relationship. However, the deeply entrenched *community consciousness* often times takes precedence over their Christian identity that, in many instances, it hampers Christian endeavours to be in solidarity with fellow humans, both within the Church and the wider society, which calls for a re-thinking of our usual penchant for 'community' as an alternative to individualism that is characteristic of modernity.

To conclude this discussion, we need to bear in mind certain crucial factors that animate community formation, more specifically in India. (i) Community formation occurs through certain formalised and essentialised elements (e.g. caste, language, region and so on). The most insidious aspect of this mode of community formation is that mostly (if not entirely) rigid boundaries are erected around each community along those essentialised elements, leading to identify those outside the boundaries as 'others' or ostracised as enemies; and even in some instances when the 'other' is welcomed, he/she is welcomed not as part of the community but as a guest who can have no identity or sense of belonging. (ii) Two crucial effects of such rigid community formation are apparent: (a) such a community derives its identity over against the 'other', normally with a view to establish its supremacy over the 'other'; and (b) it creates conflictual situation between communities when this supremacy syndrome is challenged.[45] (iii) Even though the notion of community has the merit of reorienting humans towards collective consciousness from their self-centeredness, it has the serious limitation of a kind of a narrow particularism that could easily enmesh humans into parochialism with little room for openness and responsible living, which is dangerous in the contemporary context. (iv) In light of the above discussion, to construe ecclesia as a community is theologically inadequate because of the inherent limitations of the notion of community such as hierarchical structures, ascriptive identities, (consequent) identity politics and rigid boundaries, which are the hard realities surrounding community-construction. It entails that we need to evolve more viable modes of discourse that would make sense in the context in which we engage in ecclesiological reflections.

Existent Modes of Discourse on the Church

One of the oldest descriptions of the Church is the 'body of Christ', generally understood as the communion of believers (Col. 1:24; Eph. 2:16, 22-3), patterned after a living organism (organic model) with the assumption of the organic unity of the believers in Christ (1 Cor. 6:15). This Church, according to the Nicene Creed, is "one, holy, catholic and apostolic".[46] Medieval theologians, however, ascribed these adjectives to the institutional Church centered in Rome.[47] From a Roman Catholic perspective, *unity* implied the subordination of all believers to the one spiritual authority and magisterium of the Roman Church; *catholicity* came to be understood as the one Church that expanded all over the world that strictly shared its creed, mode of worship, patterns of life, and the system of canon law; *holiness* concentrated on the life of the visible community of the faithful with special focus on the sanctity of the means that fostered holiness, namely, the sacramental system and the moral guidance of an infallible magisterium; and *apostolicity* referred to the legitimate succession of the clergy and their approval by Rome.[48] The Church, especially the hierarchical structure of the Church, is understood as the mediator of the heavenly graces to the ordinary believers. An important posture of the Church within this mode appears to be constituted by a set of beliefs[49] and, more importantly, it is the institutionalised Church that is authorised to determine and supply the kind of beliefs that its members are required to adhere to in order to be included into the Church.

The Church is also understood as particularised communities of believers whose epistemology is derived from people's experience.[50] Summarising the ecclesiological views expressed in the documents of the Federation of the Asian Bishops' Conference (1970-2000), James Thoppil suggests that the purpose of the Asian Church must be to "build up a local Church, which is indigenous, self-supporting, self sufficient and self-propagating".[51] Can this proposal for an 'indigenous local' Church be appropriated as a credible alternative to the Church that has been deeply rooted in its western connections with regard to its theology, missions and even monetary aids? There are at least two difficulties we need to overcome if we have to accept this as a viable model of the Church. *First*, in the strict analysis, a Church of this type would look like an autonomous entity. *Second*, going by the current human tendency to exclude the 'other', a 'self-sufficient' local Church would also foster a kind of an exclusivism that would deny space for the mutual interaction between variegated communities of people. Exclusivism further promotes a kind of suspicion about the 'other' and ultimately leads to hostility against the 'other'. In an ecclesial context in which people from different backgrounds come together, and which has to combat the kind of alienation fostered by Hindu nationalism, autonomy and exclusivism will have dangerous consequences.

Another approach – cultural-linguistic or post-liberal model – takes the doctrine of the Church seriously not as propositional truths, nor as expressive symbols, but as "commonly authoritative rules of discourse, attitude and action".[52] In this approach, the doctrines of and about the Church would be viewed not as unsurpassable truths about the mechanism of the inner constitution and outward expression of ecclesia. Church, in this approach, would mean both a social and metaphysical community of believers, depending on the situation in which it is employed. It identifies the Church as a "marked" community, i.e., "the embodiment of the Biblical narrative of God at work establishing community...and it constitutes the community of reference for its members". It takes the Reformation impulse on the Word and Sacraments seriously and concludes that "the Church is the community gathered around the Word and Sacrament". Here, the Biblical story acts effectively as the 'constitutive narrative' – a shared story belonging to all who in every place gather around the Word and Sacraments, and in this sense the Church is local and at the same time universal because the constitutive narrative of the Church is neither the invention nor the exclusive possession of any one congregation. Rather, while embodying itself in the local assembly, it also transcends all local congregations to unite each local gathering with all other congregations of the faithful.[53]

These discourses on the Church are attempts to locate and understand ecclesia in specific situations and mostly they tend to construct the theological substance of the Church around the idea of community. However, I find that there is further scope for us to transcend these modes and evolve alternative modes of discourse on ecclesia that can speak authentically and meaningfully to the given context and enable the members of 'body of Christ' to live as true Christians and engage in the ministry of the Church. Hence, bearing in mind the problems, limitations, difficulties, and nuances inherent in construing the Church in terms of community, I would like to propose a modified *communion ecclesiology*, i.e., ecclesia as the *perichoretic communion of the people of God*, as a relevant expression of the Church in the contemporary Hindu nationalist situation in India.

Significance of *Perichoretic* Communion

This discourse purposes to understand the nature and function of ecclesia in relation to the diverse religious, social, political, and cultural realities of India, bearing in mind Hindutva's attempts to hijack these diverse realities in order to construe India comprehensively as a Hindu nation, ascribing secondary status to Christians. It aims at enabling the Christians to come to a clear understanding of the meaning of their being Christians and affirm their identity as *Christians* in a hostile situation. It is a theological discourse on the Church that would empower Christians to engage in the ministry of healing and reconciliation that God in Christ had mandated. Therefore, the current discourse transcends the usual construal of the Church patterned after the community model and envisions a *perichoretic* communion of the people of God as the viable model of the Indian Church. It is a Church that embraces differences as an opportunity to rejoice and not as an occasion to exclude the 'other'.

My own personal conviction in this study is that in the context of Hindu nationalism's ascriptive uniformisation of cultures, communities and even religious persuasions and the visible manifestation of its hostility towards the 'others', a *communion ecclesiology* – a vision of the Church as the *perichoretic communion of the people of God* – is a theologically viable and existentially appropriate mode of reflection on the Church. It is the ontology of the Church that embodies the principle of *perichoresis*, i.e., the mutual indwelling of persons in a spirit of communion, following the prototypical Trinitarian communion of the Godhead in Christian theology, which is also a prominent feature of Luther's theological thinking. This way of construing the Church not only enlightens and inspires but also provides space for mutual conversation across boundaries in a spirit of communion that engenders reasons for hope and encouragement,[54] for it points to the "possibility of human *community* across all that divides humans".[55] If this is true, then, the primary purpose of the Church's existence in a diversified world, as Philip Potter puts it, is "to cooperate with God in making the *oikoumene* an *oikos*, a home, a family of men and women of varied gifts, cultures and possibilities, where openness, trust, love, and justice reign".[56] In the contemporary context, it entails that there must be a concerted effort that would exhort humanity as a whole, not just the 'bona fide' members, to grow together, rather than engaging in self-destruction and the destruction of the 'other'.

In the recent times, there has been a great deal of interest among theologians (Roman Catholic, Orthodox, Protestant and Free Church) to re-construe ecclesia in terms of its *communion*.[57] The ecumenical movement held ecclesiological discussions within the framework of inter-Church fellowship, more specifically related to Eucharistic and altar fellowship that falls within the principles of communion, which I try to propose.[58] Here, it has to be pointed out that that it was the Reformer, more than anyone else, who retrieved the communion aspect of the Church and posited it as a new consciousness over against the predominant emphasis on the centrality of the hierarchical structure of medieval Catholicism. The fundamental expression of communion is found in book of Acts 2:42-47, an aspect that was metaphorically interpreted by Paul as "the body of Christ" (1 Cor. 12:12-31; Eph. 1:22; Col. 1:24). Therefore, communion ecclesiology is not a novelty or an innovation; rather it has been prominent ever since the Church came into being.[59] Luther described it as *Communio sanctorum* and our task is to cull out the meaning of his description and reconstruct it to be a relevant model of ecclesia.

As Luther understands, Church is the 'communion of saints' that comes into being not through any human efforts but by the

Word (through the Spirit). It demonstrates the fact that a believer is embraced into the body of Christ as he/she is; and not after having been sanitized of all sins, [60] which is indicative of one of Luther's predominant concerns, i.e., the union of the sinful humanity with the divine. This concern finds its expression in his Christological reconstruction also, which is evident from two notable elements: (a) his understanding of *genus tapeinoticon*: the doctrine that God shared the weakness, suffering, and humiliation of Jesus; and (b) *deipassionism* – the deity of Christ, on account of incarnation and its personal unity with humanity, enters into the uttermost depth of its suffering. Without doubt, these are powerful expressions of his passionate quest for the integration of humanity with the divine – the mutual indwelling of the divine and the human – which, in an ecclesial context, implies that more than anything else the Church epitomizes this *perichoretic* relationship in this broken world.

Perichoretic communion indicates a *network of mutually dependent relationships*, which transcends narrow particularisms and embraces multiplicity and differences and its unique feature is the extension of its scope beyond the boundaries of the Church even to reach out to those who hatch hatred against the Church. It is a way of actualising the *perichoretic* principle[61] as we find in (a) *the divine Trinity*, (b) *the incarnation of the divinity in the Christ event*, and (c) *the unity of the opposites*, around which the Reformer constructed the meaning of the Church. This is certainly different from a community, which normally exists through intra-community relationship and hence, mostly (if not entirely) hinges on uniformity or homogeneity. In a community, one can be assimilated – say for instance in the case of an inter-caste marriage – by undergoing certain commonly held rituals, but can never be embraced unconditionally. As Jean Vanier understands, community is a homogenous group, which is composed of families who share more or less the same root, speak the same language with almost the same accent; follow the same rites and traditions; exhibit the same behavior patterns and accept the same authority. In such a community, there is an apparent solidarity among people mainly because of the above reasons and also to protect the group from external threats.[62] In the Indian context, community discourse inevitably turns towards the caste system and to construe ecclesia as a community would appear to be a caste-like community, which is undesirable. Obviously, these factors etch themselves deeply in human consciousness when they live in a community.

On the contrary, a *perichoretic* communion is characterized not by homogeneity, but by heterogeneity. D. M. Doyle argues that communion is an inclusive vision of human existence that functions from the "points of connection" with variegated groups of people,[63] which can rightly be described as mutual acceptance and co-inherence. It epitomizes human interdependence as it represents the way of mutually responsible living that preserves the sanctity of life.[64] In such an existence, the *perichoretic* relationship is available not only to those who are knit together as *insiders* but also to the alien, the stranger and the disenfranchised, which is the panacea for the healing of the wounds caused by mutual hatred and a cause for greater harmony, peace and amity among people. Delivering the inaugural address at the "India Today Conclave 2009", the Tibetan Spiritual leader, Dalai Lama, observed that violence is a mental attitude, which is dangerous at the practical level; once it is let loose, it becomes unpredictable because it goes out of control; and it has to be addressed by dealing with human mind. He further observed that twenty-first century is a century of dialogue.[65] *Perichoretic* experience is a potential ground for dialogue for it demystifies boundaries and encourages border-crossing.[66] As John S. Dunne described, it is a stupendous experience of *passing over* to the other and *coming back* with fresh insights,[67] a virtual *unity of the opposites* indeed.

While investing our faith in *perichoretic* communion, we also acknowledge its inherent problems. It is possible that this notion might melt down into an imprecise *fellow-feeling* or a substance-less *agree-to-disagree* mode or into an eschatological or mystical ideal without any historical form or force.[68] The temptation here might be to depend too much on this model as a cover for inherent tensions.[69] This model has a universal connotation and might legitimately be castigated as neutral, since 'particularity' is the privileged category in current intellectual/theological deliberations. It also raises a serious question as to what it means to be in a *perichoretic* relationship with a fascist or extremist group or even with Hindutva ideologues. Of course, there are no ready-made answers to these questions and it is a matter of ongoing discussion. But these difficulties, however, do not diminish my optimism about my proposal because it provides ample scope to bring diverse cultural expressions for responsible and harmonious human living. Hence, I would invite all my readers to join me in this journey with the optimism that it has the potency to provide us with adequate theological/spiritual substance to come to a clear self-understanding as human persons created in the image of the one God and called to a life in a spirit of *perichoretic* intimacy and never mutual hatred and self-destruction. For the Indian Christians, this, I believe, is a potentially empowering source to affirm their identity as Christians and continue to engage in their mission amidst Hindutva's suspicion, hatred and hostility.

By virtue of its being "called out of darkness into His marvelous light", ecclesia is existentially dead to the world, and therefore, separated from it, which according to Paul is dying to the world and living for Christ (Romans 6:1-4), and to put on Christ to be a new creation (Rom. 13:14; 2 Cor. 5:17; Eph. 4:22-24). Similarly, the presence of the Church and its ministry in this world is the foretaste of the kingdom of God. In this sense, the Church's ontology becomes closely tied up with Trinity and in and through its ministry, the Church relates fully with the world. As Zizioulas understands, the 'ministry of the Word' "is not to be understood in terms of the Church's 'addressing' the world, but in terms of her being involved in the world with com-passion, since the Word of God is not to be isolated from his *incarnation*".[70] Thus, if the Trinitarian understanding of God represents the inner relationship of the persons of the Trinity; if the *Logos*, one of the persons of the Trinity, became enfleshed; and if the Church is the body of the enfleshed Word, then the Church as the communion of the faithful has to represent the *Trinitarian-perichoretic-communion-in-relationship* to the world. Significantly, the Reformer's view of human religiosity is a constant quest to be in communion – communion with God and with fellow humans – and not to be in vicious circles of individualism or narrow particularism.

Key Components of the *Perichoretic* Communion

This is an ecclesiology that seriously engages itself with wide-ranging approaches in order to be fully local and fully catholic at the same time. The conception of ecclesia as a *perichoretic* communion is a process, a vision and a call to a higher theological domain. It transcends the merely juridical and institutional postures of the Church by emphasising the mystical, the sacramental, and the historical dimensions of the Church. It is a new vision of a *Christ-centered-mutually-sustaining communion of the people of God* – both within and without. This, I believe, is one of the most viable and relevant approaches to ecclesiological thought in a world that is overwhelmed by fragmentation, hostility and hatred, and human impulse to annihilate the 'other' with impunity.

An important problem contemporary theology faces is that theology is subjected to the standardization of discourse in the academy and consequently certain modes of Christian speech are excluded as redundant or as irrelevant. For the most part, modern theological discourses are not strictly governed by Christian doctrines because they are regarded as inadequate to make sense to concrete situations. It all began with the liberal school of modernity that had shaken the doctrinal foundations of the Church,[71] which was further schematised by the liberationist strand of theology,[72] and postmodernity clearly established it with its notion of the breaking up of the epistemological foundationalism.[73] In the recent times, in our theological debates, we often come across naïve expressions like "outdated" and "archaic", mostly referring to the traditional Christian doctrines. Why have doctrines declined to have their impact in contemporary theological discourses? The answer is quite complex and widely ramified that involves some of the most basic mutations in the rise of modern culture. In this regard, Paul Ricour refers to a twofold process: "deregionalisation" and "radicalisation", which provide us with a clue to understand the decline of doctrines in the history of Christian thought.[74] Our inclination, however, is far from essentialising those doctrines, rather to reconstruct some of the Christian doctrines that served as *regulae fidei* in the course of the Church's struggle with controversial teachings and conflicting situations. And our attention is drawn to one of the oldest expressions of ecclesia: Church as the "communion of saints".

"The Communion of Saints"

Sunday after Sunday, Churches worldwide affirm: "We believe in the communion of saints". Do these words remain as mere rhetoric without the force to give any visible, tangible or historical form to this affirmation in an overwhelmingly integrating and at the same time alarmingly fragmenting world? Does this 'communion of saints' have anything to offer to the contemporary world? Given the prevailing global trend of alarming fragmentation and isolationism with exorbitant stress on the competitive self, the future of humanity, I believe, is contingent on developing a human communion with some measure of mutual co-inherence. Hence, to re-vision ecclesia as a *perichoretic* communion is enlightening and inspiring, as it is a broad and inclusive vision of the Church – a Church that consistently stands for closer intimacy, foreshadowing, and embodying its fundamental faith affirmation in God whose truth and plenitude is Trinity in unity. Ecclesia, in this sense, is an occasion – an event – that fosters mutuality and intimacy[75] that would enable us to realise a more humane society in the contemporary situation. Leonardo Boff, for instance, believed:

> We are not condemned to live alone, cut off from one another; we are called to live together and to enter into the communion of the Trinity. Society is not ultimately set in its unjust and unequal relationships, but summoned to transform itself in the light of the open and egalitarian relationships that obtain in the communion of the Trinity, the goal of social and historical progress. If the Trinity is good news, then it is so particularly for the oppressed and those condemned to solitude.[76]

Being the *perichoretic communion of the people of God*, ecclesia engineers mutuality across boundaries and, hence, the Church is not confined to its visible historical expressions like its structures and various activities: these expressions are part of the Church, but the Church is more than all these.[77] As described by Luther, the Church is not the centralised structure in Rome headed by the pope. Rather it is the communion of the faithful, having Christ as its head. It means that the Church has a double foci – it is 'a people of God' created by the Spirit and, at the same time, it exists in this world with particular expression as a human enterprise.[78] It lives in history through the redemptive work of God in Christ empowered by the Spirit, which alone makes the Church unique. Luther delineates this unique aspect of the Church in terms of communion with God and with fellow humans and participation with the benefits of grace. This 'communion' traces its roots to the fundamental Christian faith in the Trinity, which provides us with an apt model of *perichoretic* communion, which can rightly be understood as a *network of mutually responsive and responsible relationships*.

Trinitarian Foundation of Church

To reflect theologically upon the Church is also an endeavour to simultaneously reflect upon the Trinity because of the fact that the truth and plenitude of the Trinity form the foundation of the Church. In other words, there is no historical expression of the Church as *perichoretic* communion without the communion of the Trinity. As McGlasson opines, this does not imply a simple repetition of the past, even though the present Church is extremely indebted to the early teachers of faith, the Reformers and the modern architects of theology. Rather, our rootedness in the faith of the early teachers must motivate us to seek to constantly listen to the voice of God in Christ in the power of the Spirit. [79] The earliest epistolary and liturgical history of the Trinity is rather imprecise.[80] It is generally accepted that the Trinitarian language to understand God emerged from the Church's experience, which was an attempt to understand the mystery of God.[81] As Robert Jenson argues, the Trinitarian language emerged in response to the fundamental Christian question: "Who is God?", and the answer to this question came to be constructed from the central historical event of Christian faith in relation to the incarnation. Thus, the New Testament answer to the question, according to Jenson, is "the one who raised Jesus from the dead", which clearly traces its root to the Exodus event and affirms: 'the one who rescued Israel from the Egyptian bondage is the one who raised Jesus from the dead'.[82]

The logical possibility, then, is that the Trinitarian language is a post-resurrection faith affirmation that attempted to answer the serious questions related to the divinity of the Son. In this sense, then, it came to be firmly established that a Christian is the one who affirms God as "Father, Son and Holy Spirit" in unity. Christian faith is, thus, founded on Trinity in unity, in which the unity of God is expressed in God's one "substance" or "essence" (*substantia*/*ousia*) and God's Trinity or diversity is expressed in terms of "persons" (*hypostases*). This inner relationship or *perichoresis* of the Trinity stands as the epitome of communion in which there is the plenitude of equality and harmony of will and purpose between the three persons of the one Godhead. It would be helpful to revisit the doctrine of the Trinity, paying attention to the way the Reformer attempted to understand it from the historical creedal statements.[83]

According to Luther, the historical creedal formulations (Apostles', Nicene and Athanasian Creeds) confess God the Holy Trinity as: "the Father, Son, and Holy Spirit, three distinct persons in one divine essence and nature [Matthew 28:19], are one God, who has created heaven and earth [1Corinthians 8:6]. The Father is begotten of no one; the Son is begotten of the Father [John 1:14]; the Holy Spirit proceeds from the Father and the Son [John 15:26]". The Christian faith, as enshrined in the creedal statements (*Athanasian Creed* to be precise), thus, adheres to and professes the central affirmation that God is at once 'Trinity in Unity' and 'Unity in Trinity'. More precisely, the Godhead, while one undivided and indivisible substance, is at the same time three persons. As J. N. D. Kelley maintains, this is a paradox, in that the threeness (plurality) of the persons does not in any way contravene the oneness of the substance, and conversely, the oneness of the substance does not in any way violate the real distinction of the persons. Obviously, the early teachers of faith did not employ any modern scientific theories to prove the truth and plenitude of the Trinity.[84] For easy reference, the relevant portion of the *Athanasian Creed* is quoted below:

> "[3]Now this is the Catholic faith, that we worship God in Trinity and Trinity in unity, [4]without either confounding the persons or dividing the substance. [5]For the Father's person is one, the Son's

> another, the Holy Spirit's another; [6]but the Godhead of the Father, the Son and the Holy Spirit is one, their glory is equal, their majesty coeternal. [7]Such as the Father is, such is the Son, such also the Holy Spirit. [8]The Father is increate, the Son increate, the Holy Spirit increate. [9]The Father is infinite, the Son infinite, the Holy Spirit infinite. [10]The Father is eternal, the Son eternal, the Holy Spirit eternal. [11]Yet there are not three eternals, but one eternal; [12]just as there are not three increates or three infinites, but one increate and one infinite. [13]In the same way the Father is almighty, the Son almighty, the Holy Spirit almighty; [14]yet there are not three almighties, but one almighty. [15]Thus the Father is God, the Son God, the Holy Spirit God; [16]yet there are not three Gods, but there is one God. [17]Thus the Father is Lord, the Son Lord and the Holy Spirit Lord; [18]and yet there are not three Lords, but there is one Lord. [19]Because just as we are obliged by Christian truth to acknowledge each person separately both God and Lord, [20]so we are forbidden by the Catholic religion to speak of three Gods or Lords. [21]The Father is from none, not made nor created, nor begotten. [22]The Son is from the Father alone, not made nor created but begotten. [23]The Holy Spirit is from the Father and the Son, not made nor created nor begotten but proceeding…[25]And in this trinity there is nothing before or after, nothing greater or less [26]but all three persons are coeternal with each other and coequal. [27]Thus in all things, as has been stated above, both Trinity in unity and unity in Trinity must be worshipped. [28]So he who desire [sic] to be saved should think thus of the Trinity…[42]This is the Catholic faith. Unless a man believes it faithfully and steadfastly, he will not be able to be saved".[85]

These doctrinal debates emerged from the living context of the Church, a fact that speaks volumes for our reflections on the Church today. It is important to take note of the two strong warnings that this creed puts forward: a warning against confounding or annihilating the distinction between the 'three persons'; and a warning against dividing or splitting asunder the 'one indivisible substance or essence'.[86] The lucid description of the various attributes applicable to the Godhead and to the three persons[87] is a notable point in this brilliant creedal statement. It certainly signals a warning against any tendency to assimilate or erase differences on the one hand, and, at the same time, a warning also against putting asunder or discriminating people in the name of caste, class, race, gender and ethnicity within the ecclesial communion on earth.

The fundamental Trinitarian problem is that of difference and union, which can technically be called 'divine relations'.[88] The central Christian affirmation is that the three persons possess or share the same substance or essence, i.e., they are identical in substance and essence; but they differ in their relation between each other "as a result of their different modes of origin within the divine substance they are",[89] and this is the one and the only way they differ. Yet, despite their differences of origins within the same divine substance, none of them is prior to or greater than the other; they are real and permanent; and they are coequal and coeternal.[90] The inference is that the difference of the three persons in no way vitiates the harmony of the will, purpose and function of the Trinity. Thus, the fundamental doctrine is that the persons in the Godhead stand in a unique relationship to each other by virtue of the mode of origin of each person in the same substance of the Godhead, and it is this relation that constitutes them distinct persons. This relation between the persons in the Trinity is called *perichoresis*, which is an apt model for us to emulate in our ecclesial communion. The Trinity never engages in ostracism and the corresponding insight is that ecclesia is an occasion to embrace and celebrate differences; perpetuate intimacy; and live in harmony.

Our inclination to hold on to the *perichoretic* communion of the Trinity, however, is not intended to idealise or mystify the Trinity as a super structure. It is painfully acknowledged here that the very attempt by the Church to understand the relation between the three persons of the Trinity also became the root cause of the division between the Western and Eastern Churches. After the late 4th century, it had commonly been agreed upon between the East and West the doctrine of Trinity in unity and unity in Trinity. The Cappadocian theologians provided almost the final form to this doctrine of the Trinity, which was mediated to the West by Hilary of Poitiers, Ambrose of Milan and, more particularly, Augustine of Hippo.[91] However, the *filioque* clause of the Trinitarian formula created great strife in the life of the Church. The description of the Father as ingenerate, the Son as begotten and the Holy Spirit as proceeding was common place; but the controversy that rocked the Church stemmed from the 'double procession' of the Spirit 'from the Father and the Son'.[92] In all probability, 'the double procession' of the Spirit was Augustine's solution as a way to find a conceivable relation or bond between the Father and the Son and as a way to explain the hypostatic union between them, for in Augustine's logic, "the Holy Spirit is a certain ineffable communion of the Father and the Son" and is therefore hypostatically what the Father and the Son are in common.[93] His solution presupposes that the Spirit proceeds from the Father and the Son. The Eastern Church, however, regarded this as the original sin of the Latin theology.[94] The above difficulty notwithstanding, the Trinitarian doctrine offers a new way of understanding persons in relationship, both within the Church and in the society.

The place of the Trinitarian doctrine in theological articulations is, nevertheless, a contentious issue. In 1628, the French philosopher René Descartes tried to come out with an irrefutable proof of the existence of God using his philosophical method on an invitation from the Roman Cardinal Berulle.[95] He constructed a God who had no trace of a Trinitarian God; and an image of Jesus that is not what we believe as the incarnate, crucified and risen Jesus, but a remote and vague figure (without any trace of what we believe as one of the persons of the blessed Trinity) that has no actual place in a scientific world. As Leslie Newbigin understands, it is a Unitarian deity, which in public discourse gave rise to two crucial human attitudes: individualism and asymmetrical power relations.[96] He maintains that if God, the ultimate reality, is a single sovereign deity, then it is natural for humans also to claim such sovereignty and autonomy in their earthly existence.[97] It is an attitude that conceives 'person' in terms of private individuals – self-contained entities or hypostases. Further, with the emergence of newer pluralistic theologies of religion, 'the Trinitarian and Christological foundations of the universal mission of the Gospel' are crumbling down.[98] In Braaten's view, these are theologies normally given rise to by the centres of non-confessional academic study of religion.[99]

Similarly, Karl Rhaner laments that the Trinitarian axiom has almost become dysfunctional in theology and Christian life.

According to him, "Christians are, in their practical life, almost mere 'monotheists'. We must be willing to admit that, should the doctrine of the Trinity have to be dropped as false, the major part of the religious literature could well remain unchanged".[100] In modern Protestant theology, the doctrine of Trinity has almost been peripheralised. Immanuel Kant, for instance, declared: "From the doctrine of the Trinity, taken literally, nothing whatsoever can be gained for practical purposes, even if one believed that one comprehended it – and less still if one is conscious that it surpasses all our concepts".[101] Braaten, on the other hand, argues that the pluralist theologians are the ones who are astute in their advocacy for 'theocentrism' – a religious paradigm that "opts for a theocentricity at the expense of the Christological origin of the doctrine of Trinity". Over against the 'strictly monotheistic-theocentrism', Braaten reminds us about two fundamental points: (i) "The doctrine of Trinity is the theological framework for Christology and ecclesiology, for the event of salvation and the Gospel mission"; and (ii) "The Church will not be able to discern the missionary significance of God's revelation in Jesus Christ 'except within the framework of a fully and explicitly Trinitarian doctrine of God'".[102]

In the recent times, however, there arose a renewed interest among theologians towards the Trinitarian theology, which is a welcome sign because our faith in the Trinity has the potencies to dispel isolationism and lead to a new *perichoretic* consciousness in human social intercourse. The term *perichoresis* is an apt expression of the communion of the three persons of the Trinity, which points to the mutual indwelling or the 'co-inhering interpenetration' of the three persons of the Trinity. In this sense, the oneness of the Trinity is not only the oneness of origin but also of one will and one activity.[103] The prelude of the fourth Gospel demonstrates that the 'Word' that was with God from all eternity had an equal role to play along with the Father in the creative process (Jn. 1:3); the Genesis account of creation offers ample evidence to the work of the Spirit also in creation, if the life-giving breath of God (Gen. 2:7) is taken as the *ruah* who proceeds from the Father. In the same manner, the reconciliatory-recreative work was not an isolated work of the Son. Rather both the Father and the Spirit are at work with the Son. Ambrose's exegesis of the text: "With thee is the fountain of life" (Ps 36:9), alludes to the involvement of the Son and the Spirit in creation. The conclusion Ambrose arrives at is that the Spirit, as much as the Father and the Son, is the fountain of life.[104]

If we take the above interpretation of the Trinity seriously, then, mention has to be made here about a difficulty and a real problem that the contemporary theological expression – Creator, Redeemer and Sustainer – poses in understanding the very truth, plenitude and harmony of the Trinity. The Trinitarian language of Creator, Redeemer and Sustainer is the functional expression of the three persons of the Trinity that emerged in the context of the feminist/womanist critique of the masculine language of the Trinity. Of course, in the context of women's struggle for liberation, we need to acknowledge the serious limitations of the masculine Trinitarian language. Nonetheless, the ascription of three distinct functions to the three persons of the Trinity vis-à-vis creation, redemption and sustenance in contemporary theology seriously vitiates the original purpose of the Trinitarian language. It does not mean the same thing as the personal language of the Trinity does and it splits asunder the substance or essence of the Trinity, which has serious implications for ecclesiology, and hence it is incompatible to the real understanding of the Trinity.

Trinity signifies neither an exclusive community nor an impenetrable corporatist identity, but a *perichoretic* communion that embraces plurality and celebrates multiple identities.[105] This is an appropriate interpretation of the term *perichoresis* in the present context. Some of the crucial references to the sayings of Jesus as recorded in the New Testament amply illustrate this point. If we have reasons to believe that these writings emerged from the life of the Church,[106] then we must be studious enough to discern the fact that these references to the *perichoresis* of the Father, the Son and the Spirit, provided the basic theological substance to the conception of the Church as one.[107] It is the richness of this Trinitarian experience that had inspired and provided the theological substance to the Church to embody itself as the *perichoretic* communion of believers by the work of the Spirit through the Word. For the early believers, their lived experience was one of acceptance and embrace of even the most ungodly and unacceptable (Rom 5:10), which was the result of the new life engendered by Christ. In this sense, the incarnation can be understood as the extension of and an invitation to the divine communion offered by God to the entire humanity, which is explicitly spelt out by Paul as an event in and through which "God in Christ was reconciling the world to himself" (2 Cor. 5:18-20) – an integration of the otherwise irreconcilable and antagonistic categories into communion for a life of peace and harmony (Eph 2:14-17). As Paul further explains, we are not simply the passive recipients of this new life to live in self-contentment, rather "ambassadors for Christ, since God is making his appeal through us" (2 Cor. 5:20).

Thus, in its proper spirit, the fundamental evangelical mission of the Church is to continue the ministry of reconciliation, i.e., to be in communion with God and to build up communion with the 'other', transcending borders, which is the uniqueness of the Church. It is in light of the above that we need to understand the brilliance of the Reformer's exposition of God's acceptance of the infidels, not the worthy, which he propounded with great zeal through his doctrine of justification. Hence, the criticism that Luther individualised this doctrine is unfounded. A decisive question Luther encountered was as to how human beings can continue to stand before God. And the decisive answer is 'through justification'. It would be instructive to see how the Reformer expresses the importance of this doctrine in the *Smalcald Articles*:

> Nothing in this article can be given up or compromised... [because] on this article rests all that we teach and practice against the pope, the devil, and the world. Therefore we must be quite certain and have no doubts about it. Otherwise all is lost, and the pope, the devil and all our adversaries will gain the victory.[108]

Church as an Extended Divine Communion

My conviction in this entire study is that the Church of Jesus Christ is being founded on the principle of *interwoven relationships*, which I tried to recapitulate as the *perichoretic communion* in the context of human contradictions and asymmetries that put too many obstacles for them to live in loving trustful or mutually responsible relationship.

It is a painful reality that human existence today is hardly governed by the principle of this sort of relationship but instead by a kind of a social *setting-at-a-distance* syndrome or *atomism*. It is also too disheartening that (certain aspects of) religions perpetuate the above syndrome and have turned out to be the deadly enemies of humanity.

But Christian faith understands and affirms that the creator God, the Being of beings, offered God's self-disclosure in and through the incarnation in an historic human being, Jesus of Nazareth. This affirmation came to be developed into the Trinitarian formula as an elucidation of the mystery of God. Luther stressed the sublime "threeness" and "oneness" of the Trinity in which every person is the entire deity and yet no one person of the Trinity exists as deity without the other two.[109] He, however, acknowledges the inadequacy of human language and concepts to describe the depth of the Trinitarian mystery because the Scripture does not expressly speak of 'Trinity'. Nonetheless, the Scripture does bear witness to the Trinity,[110] and, in his view, the three persons can in no way be theologically differentiated from each other by anything else than their mutual relationship to one another as Father, Son and Holy Spirit. Undeniably, the Trinitarian theology, especially the idea of *perichoresis*, forms the strong foundation of ecclesiology in all ages. As far as the visible expression of this *perichoretic* relationship is concerned, the Church must actualize this *perichoresis*, i.e., co-inhering interpenetration, at two levels: intra and inter ecclesial communion and extra ecclesial communion.

Intra and Inter Ecclesial Communion

Communio sanctorum in the Reformer's rendering is characterized by two visible marks, namely, the proclamation of the Word and the administration of the Sacraments. He further, interprets the Sacraments as nothing but the visible Word. Therefore, it would be beneficial here to explore further the significance of the Sacraments, more specifically the Eucharist, in fostering communion among the believers within ecclesia, for in the celebration of the Holy Communion, there is a synthesis of the Divine, the Human and the material elements in the context of a human collective, even though this central Christian symbol has been subjected to controversial doctrinal debates.

The celebration of the Lord's Supper exhibits different designations among different Church traditions. The Roman Catholicism understands it as the "mass", the "Holy communion" or as the "Eucharist". The terms 'Eucharist' (thanksgiving) and Holy Communion are also current in Protestant Churches, more specifically in ecumenical deliberations.[111] The Orthodox Church speaks of "the divine liturgy" and uses the term *synaxis*, meaning "union" or gathering of the faithful.[112] There are still more designations of the Eucharist. By means of the problematic and misplaced focus on the elements of bread and wine, almost all Church traditions miserably failed to grasp two important aspects of the Holy Communion: (i) the invitation to "take, eat and drink", and (ii) the symbolic act of "taking, breaking and sharing".[113] Luther also shares this guilt of misplaced emphasis in his later expositions as he takes Augustine's position ("When the word comes to the element, there is a sacrament") as authentic.[114] We need to realize that the Sacrament becomes complete only in the synthesis of the Word, the elements, the symbolic act, and the gathering of the faithful.[115]

If we can circumvent or transcend or even peel off the serious doctrinal debates between theologians and Church traditions, especially over the mechanism of Christ's presence in the bread and wine of the Eucharist, we can glean a vital insight that the Sacrament of the altar is an invitation from the Lord to be part of a feast that has both social and spiritual significations. The Reformer's delineations of the sacraments, especially those thoughts prior to 1524, are rampant with ideas that impressively symbolise communion. Some of the interpretations of the Eucharist and the insights that came from the Reformer's pen are stimulating. (a) He understands and affirms the Lord's Supper as the proper Sacrament of the Church that stands at the centre of its life and witness, solemnly guaranteeing the love of Christ, the lifeblood of the Church. It is this love that cements the believers together as a communion. (b) Falsifying the criticism that the Reformer's thoughts are too individualistic, in his exposition of the lord's Supper, he brings out an illuminating imagery through which he equates the believers' eating and drinking of the body and blood of Christ as their 'eating and drinking of each other'[116] in and through their sharing of goods and troubles in love. To quote him:

> To receive this Sacrament in bread and wine, then, is nothing else than to receive a sure sign of this fellowship and incorporation with Christ and all saints.... This fellowship consists in this, that all the spiritual possessions of Christ and his saints are shared with and become the common property of him who receives this sacrament. Again all sufferings and sins also become common property; and thus love engenders love in return and [mutual love] unites.[117]

(c) Luther's interpretation of the Eucharist hinges on a single point – Christ's self-giving presence in the communion and its continued effect of building up communion. It represents a vital conception of the Church that demands the Church *to become Christ for others* that the Church may become a true Church, as we find in Matthew 25:40: "Truly I say to you, as you did it to one of these least of my brethren, you did it to me". The indwelling presence of Christ is, thus, experienced in the Church in its loving service to the disenfranchised.[118]

The *perichoretic* communion finds its further expression in God's creative-recreative activity, because this activity demonstrates God's intimate relationship to the world, which is a continuity of the communion of God's being as Trinity. Further, Christ's work of new creation points to the fact that it is God's intention not to allow God's creation to decay and destruction; rather to renew the fallen creation, wherein God embraces the unworthy to be in communion with God. In Luther's understanding, God's activity is incessant and the very existence of the creatures is contingent on God's continuous and uninterrupted creative activity. Luther writes:

> He [God] has not created the world as though he were a carpenter: building a house that he could walk away from when finished and let it stand the way it is. On the contrary, he remains with and preserves everything he has made. Otherwise it would neither hold up nor endure.[119]

God's continuous preservation of the creation even at every tiny spot of space and time demonstrates not only God's intimate relationship to the creation but also God's ongoing activity of new creation.[120] Here, Luther extends his understanding of *perichoresis* to our existence as creatures. In his fascinating interpretation of the Lord's Supper, Luther proclaims that God's nature is wholly and completely present in all creatures more deeply and inwardly and yet without being circumscribed nowhere in any single being, so that God actually embraces all and is in all.[121] In this sense, then, the Church that proclaims the Gospel, does it not by its own, but it is the mask through which God carries out this task.[122] The important point here is the language of embrace and harmony of the divine, which is but the manifestation of the divine communion, and it is this communion that must be the true mark of the Church in any context.

What, then, is the tangible form of the *perichoretic* communion we can envision and forge between the members of the body of Christ that would sustain the believers in an ambience of intimacy? As Joseph Cardinal Ratzinger puts it:

> ...ultimately there is only one *basic ecclesiology*, which certainly can be approached and worked out in different ways, depending on which of the various aspects are stressed or highlighted. Nevertheless, every exposition must always take into account the harmony of various essential elements of an ecclesiology which intends to be catholic.[123]

An important aspect of contemporary theological reasoning is to place exorbitant stress on the 'inculturated faith expressions' of various *communities* of believers with more emphasis is being placed on social location, ethnicity, and gender in order to re-appropriate, reconstruct and re-articulate multiple and distinctive versions of ecclesial vision.[124] As a matter of fact, all theologies emerge from specific social locations, whether they explicitly affirm that factor or not. True ecclesiology, however, appeals not only to the local but also to the Church universal, since it is a way of being inclusive in a world characterised by hatred, hostility, isolationism, and ostracism

– a broad and inclusive category that provides space for a wide range of legitimate approaches.

This mode of ecclesia-talk focuses on mutual relationship – the relationship among the persons of the Trinity, among human beings and God, among the saints 'within' the Church, and between persons within ecclesia and the wider world. It is in the relationship of the *perichoretic* experience that the body of Christ attains its fullness. When we talk about relationship, it is not any vague relationship, but the relationship of love inspired by the love relationship that God has shared with humanity in Jesus Christ, which had found its tangible expression in the life of the immediate disciples of Jesus and in the early expressions of the Church. The reason for emphasizing this aspect of ecclesiology is that it avoids the overly institutional considerations of the Church and places its focus on the *people of God* who long for veritable signposts to live in harmony amidst all that perpetuates fragmentation and mutual hostility in the contemporary world. The primary emphasis here is 'love' – love that shares the destiny of the suffering humanity – that forms the core of Christian revelation and continues to make intimate connections between God and human beings, which Luther affirms so passionately in his description of ecclesia as the *communio sanctorum*.

The core of the Trinitarian *perichoresis* is the intimacy that exists between the Father, the Son and the Holy Spirit. It is reflected in all the symbols of Christian faith. Therefore, over against the merely juridical and/or institutional description of the Church, communion ecclesiology places its emphasis on relationship. Interconnection is at the heart of this way of understanding ecclesia, which is governed by the principles of love, acceptance, forgiveness, commitment, and intimacy that form the very fabric of the Church. This *perichoretic* communion, as we have seen, is an inclusive vision. Does it mean or imply that no one can ever be excluded? No, what is intended here is not a kind of a grand canopy that includes all categories irrespective of their ideologies that govern them. For instance, as Doyle aptly puts it, in the case of those who engage in willful or deliberate opposition to loving inclusivity and fullness of life for all, "the only reason to exclude someone (or some viewpoints) would ultimately be for their own lack of inclusivity".[125] This must not be called ostracism of people or view-points, but it must be seen as a genuine acknowledgement that certain people/viewpoints (e.g. Hindutva) marginalise themselves and insist on excluding others from any form of communion.

Communion ecclesiology refers to the reality of the Church that consistently witnesses to the presence and activity of God within the Church and in the context of everyday life of the people.[126] As the Reformer understands, the presence of God within the Church is testified by the proclamation of the Word and the administration of the Sacraments; and God's presence in the world is testified by the ongoing works of the Church in and for the world. Luther's explication of the two realms of God's activity, generally understood as the two-kingdom theory, offers a helpful insight for us to have a grasp of God's presence in both the realms equally. The Reformer brilliantly places his emphasis on understanding the spiritual and temporal realms as God's active domains with the intended purpose of engendering goodness to the people. Rightly understood, this is the sacramental reality of the Church, i.e., in and through the life of the Church God makes known God's purpose of the renewal of the world. In this sense, then, the evangelical mission of the Church in the contemporary situation is to foster the *perichoretic* relationship among people transcending all that perpetuates divisions.

Perichoresis involves the integration or re-assemblage of the fragmented, the dispersed, the disenfranchised, and the ostracised without in any way suppressing or erasing plurality or differences. In ecclesiological discussions it is commonplace to allude to the Pentecost experience as a reversal of the confusion and dispersion represented by the Tower of Babel (Genesis 11:1 – 9 & Acts 2:1 – 11). Along with many patristic writers, Luther understands Babel as the shattering of a single language and Pentecost as symbolising the integration of variegated groups (linguistic, cultural, ethnic, and national groups) in communion through the power of the Holy Spirit.[127] Luther maintains:

> Therefore it is a great blessing and an outstanding miracle of the New Testament that by means of various languages the Holy Spirit on the day of Pentecost ***brought men of all nations into the one***

> ***body of the one head, Christ*** (Acts 2). ***Christ joins and unites all into one faith through the Gospel, even though the different languages remain;*** **and** ***he tears down the wall*** (Eph. 2:14), not only ***reconciling us to God*** through his death and speaking to us in a new language but also ***bringing about outward harmony***, so that different flocks are brought together under one shepherd and are gathered into one fold (John 10:16). This is Christ's blessing; and since it is common to all ***differences in outward life causes no offense.***[128] [Emphases added]

These are brilliant and most relevant insights and the fundamental question is: how can we translate these insights into the practical expression of the Church in our own situation? As Tillard understands, three essential elements of the Church are perceptibly present in Pentecost: the Holy Spirit, the apostolic witness and the communion, which closely correspond to the Church's holiness, apostolicity and oneness. Here, it becomes obvious that this mode of ecclesiological reasoning opposes those attempts that reduce the Church to a human made organization.[129] Properly understood, this way of reading the Pentecost lends support and scope to conceive of a Church in oneness that is made manifest in diverse cultures because the Spirit-filled congregation at Pentecost is at the same time the universal and the particular expressions of the one Church of Jesus Christ.

We have already noted that the Reformer had tried with his heart, soul and mind not to fragment the Church. As a matter fact, even when he realised that his parting with the Roman Catholic Church was inevitable, he showed no inclination to construct an alternative protestant structure of ecclesia. This was partly because of his anti-authoritarian perception of the Church and partly because of his anticipation for a rapprochement with his mother Church. That is the reason why he never condemned the Roman Catholic Church in spite of his virulent attack on the papacy and its abuses. Further, he never hesitated to affirm that the true Church was found even within the visible expression of the Church of his time because of the very fact that the Word was preached and the Sacraments were administered in that Church. To the very end of his life, the

Reformer did not give up the hope that the Roman Catholic Church would reform itself and become an instrument for the renewal of the world, for he firmly believed that the Church is one, which is held together by its faith in the Trinity as he affirms: "This is my faith; for so all Christians believe and so the Holy Scriptures teach us".[130] It is historical contingency, however, that the divisions came to stay, resulting in some of the bitterest controversies in the subsequent times in the history of the Christian Church. Today, the cry for communion of the fragmented 'Body of Christ' can be heard among most Christians across the globe. It raises a fundamental question as to how can we realise true communion within the body of Christ transcending the current divided expressions of the Church, which is not just an academic interest but, above all, an existential necessity for the Christians, especially in India.

There is a widespread interest among theologians, both past and present, to re-vision ecclesia in terms of communion. A more developed protestant version of communion ecclesiology can be found in Friedrich Schleiermacher.[131] For him, the unity of the Church forms one of the pivotal and pervasive themes of theology. As summarised by Doyle,[132] there are at least four clear concerns that stand out in his theology of the Church: (i) Church as essentially a "fellowship or communion with God through Jesus Christ" that Christians share among themselves.[133] (ii) The reality of ecclesia is the collective life brought about by Jesus, characterised by a religious intimacy between Jesus and his followers that grows through the spread of like relationships.[134] (iii) The Church is an intrinsic dimension of revelation, not an added extra.[135] (iv) The Lord's Supper is the highest representation of Church unity, bringing together fellowship with Christ and fellowship among believers. The image that aptly describes ecclesia is that of the Body of Christ.[136]

A more recent version of communion ecclesiology has come from the Free Church tradition.[137] Miroslav Volf, for instance, affirms that in the Trinity we can find a model of what the Church ought to be in the world. His main emphasis is on the "complimentarity of relationality and individual personhood". Volf does acknowledge those areas of his own ecclesial tradition that lends credence to individualism while criticising the demise of the individual within the 'mainline' Church traditions and in modern rationality.[138] His primary emphasis is on the local assembly of confessing believers in which Christ is found present *par excellence*. To him, the universal Church is only an eschatological reality. Unlike Schleiermacher, who conceived of the Church as an organic unity (the body of Christ) that leads to an Episcopal structure, Volf, while accepting the body metaphor, argues that this is a metaphor that does not refer to a physical or organic reality. What, then, are the essential interconnections between different Church bodies? Volf's answer is that such connections can be realised from the very gathering of the confessing Christians to bear witness to Christ and their openness towards other Churches that do the same thing. With regard to the ministry of the Church, Volf proposes a ministry based not on monarchical model, but directly on Trinitarian model, which undercuts the notion of the primacy of the episcopacies of the 'mainline' Churches, including the papacy of Roman Catholicism.

To conclude our discussion on inter-Church relationship, we would take a look at two mutually complimentary positions. *First*, as Archbishop John Quinn argued:

> In considering the papal office and the call to Christian unity, we have to confront the challenging truth that it is not permitted to defer unity until there is a pope who can fulfill everyone's expectations or agenda. We cannot hold unity hostage until there is a perfect pope in a perfect Church. Christian unity will require sacrifice. But it cannot mean that all the sacrifices must be made by those who want full communion with the Catholic Church while the Catholic Church herself makes no significant sacrifices.[139]

Of course, the visible unity of the Church is still a long way off. Yet there are credible pointers that could be deciphered from the various ecclesiological deliberations that are taking place across the globe. *Second*, Volf places a powerful argument as to why the Churches of Episcopal tradition must accept the full ecclesiality of Free Churches:

> Today…exclusivity is no longer credible. I am thinking less of the sociological fact that exclusive positions in modern societies are

> unpersuasive than of the observation that the dynamic life and the orthodox faith of the many, quickly proliferating Free Churches make it difficult to deny them full ecclesiality. Let me illustrate this difficulty by referring to a situation that, although doubtless atypical, must nonetheless be the touchstone of any ecclesiology precisely because it is a borderline case. Should, for example, a Catholic or Orthodox diocese whose members are inclined more to superstition than to faith and who identify with the Church more for nationalistic reasons – should a diocese be viewed as a Church, while a Baptist congregation that has preserved its faith through the crucible of persecution *not* be considered such? Would not understanding of ecclesiality that leads to such a conclusion take us to the brink of absurdity? Equally untenable is the early, though still widespread, Free Church position that denies ecclesiality to Episcopal Churches.[140]

What we require today is a shared vision that would embrace differing positions, viewpoints and ways of life without discriminating one for or over the other. It is a vision of an ecclesia that makes its presence in history in and through its mission of building this mutual relationship inspired by the plenitude of God's being 'Trinity in unity and unity in Trinity'. It is this Church, which is truly one, holy, catholic and apostolic. It is a vision of a *perichoretic* communion – a re-visioning of the Church that exists visibly through the mutual indwelling of the people of God throughout the world. In this vision of the Church, various forms of ministerial offices (institutional structures) assume significance only insofar as they stand for and commit themselves to this *perichoresis*. The moment they become inclined towards exclusivism or isolationism, they become obsolescent. This is a vision of ecclesia that goes back to its Master's mandate that proclaims: "For where two or three are gathered in my name, I am there among them" (Mt. 18:20).

In Luther's reconstruction of *communio sanctorum*, the people of God take precedence over the rigidly established structures and true *perichoresis* can happen only with the people of God and not with the structures, be it the office of the pastor, bishop, pope, or councils. The structures are not denied or dumped as redundant; rather they are valued only if they stand in the service of the Gospel.

In the contemporary context, the central thrust of this service can be understood as building *perichoretic* communion across boundaries. This is the evangelical mission of the Church, which is the basis for all activities of the Church in and for the world. If this is true of ecclesia, then, we can declare with great conviction that truly our age is an age of dialogue – dialogue that accepts all constituents as equal partners. It applies to all realms of our life – our life within the Church, in the society and the relationship between Church and the society.

Extra Ecclesial Communion

It is a challenging task to reflect upon the Church from the vantage point of its *perichoretic* mode of life in the context of its relationship with the wider world, more specifically the Hindu nationalist milieu. The Church is rooted in the plenitude of the Triune God and, as such, the Church is a continuing manifestation of the mystery of God in Christ and the Holy Spirit. Its intended purpose, among other things, is to proclaim the fullness of life that God has engendered to the entire world –fullness of life that can be realised in the present context of fragmentation, isolationism and ostracism only in, and through our conscious and consistent efforts to build relationship across boundaries. The Christian perception of the plenitude of the Trinity, incarnation and the Pentecost experience obviously disclose God's initiative of integrating or reassembling the otherwise hostile humanity to God's communion of *perichoretic* intimacy and, in turn, to be in communion with each other. If the reality of the Church is thus understood, then it necessitates us to transcend the usual community discourse in order to see the pressing need of communion[141] because of the inherent difficulties in the contemporary particularist discourses, which, instead of providing a viable alternative to the previous universalist discourse, has, in fact, turned out to be more and more exclusive and inward looking, as we have seen in the community discourse. Therefore, as an integrative principle, we would neither subscribe to the grand universalism nor do we allow ourselves to be carried away by the narrow particularism; rather we intend to concentrate on a third middle way where we could discern the cry of the people of God for "credible signposts" to realize a truly human communion that would engender peace, harmony and good will among human beings as a whole.

Within our public space today we can glean the mobilization of three distinctive voices that attempt to influence and shape public opinion side by side. *First,* there is an ideology of freedom, which presupposes that human freedom can be accomplished only by affirming complete human autonomy, which excludes centrality and authority.[142] *Second,* there is an ideology that insists (often forcibly) that religion and religious tenets (especially certain particular interpretation of the same) must become the essential ingredients and that alone must influence and shape public space, opinion and culture. Contemporary Hindu nationalist situation in India, the Islamic jihads and other similar movements fall within this category. *Third,* there is also a voice that insists upon making a distinction between the temporal and the spiritual, and stresses the need for keeping them in tension, i.e., while disallowing one to usurp the authority and power of the other, yet bringing them in a dialogical relationship that would lend a critical voice to the shaping of the public space for the benefit of humanity. Luther's 'two-kingdom' theory, for instance, is posited on this principle and we can see most 'secular voices' advocating this principle (though not explicitly subscribing to Luther) over against Hindutva's overt insistence on Hindu dominance in the Indian public space today.

We have noted earlier that the Reformer's 'two-kingdom' theory emerged in the context of papacy's usurpation of political powers and the abuses of its power for selfish ends that had turned out to be pernicious to the voiceless. The basic principle on which he constructed this doctrine is: *dualism of the opposites* or *unity of the opposites* or *distinction and integration*, in which the clear distinction is between the proper limits of the spiritual and temporal realms and the integration is their effective functioning for the welfare of the common people. Hindu nationalism, on the contrary, is a dominant religiously laced political voice, which is relentless in its effort to assume power in order to reestablish and reshape the public space for the sake of the Hindu elites. It is precisely for this reason that we strongly and trenchantly argue for making a distinction between religion and temporal authority and yet without divorcing them, and shutting them up in their own autonomous realms because the need of the hour is to hold them in a dialogical relationship if we intend to forge a harmonious human existence. The Church is placed in this context and it has to become an interlocutor between these two realms in the current Indian public space. It is here that we try to argue for *perichoretic* communion as a relevant mode of discourse that would forge relationship of love as an integrative principle among variegated human communities whom we identify as the 'people of God' because, according to the Reformer, "since this is common to all, differences in outward life causes no offense"[143].

Christianity is also characterised by extended communion *vis-à-vis* those who adhere to Jesus and his teachings without formally subscribing themselves to the institutional Church. Rajaram Mohun Roy, K. C. Sen, M. K. Gandhi, Subba Rao, and a host of others formed this sort of communion in the past and there are such adherents of Jesus in the secular world even today. M. M. Thomas, for instance, brings to light this sort of communion through conversion (without changing one's religion) through the example of R. K. Karanjia (Editor, *Blitz* Bombay) who converted "to faith in Christ and his fellowship with believers in Christ without conversion from Zoroastrian to Christian community".[144] It is for the 'official' Church to grapple with the question of extending its ministry of building relationship with those who do not formally subscribe to membership in the visible Church. It must be an essential mission agenda of the Church in the twenty-first century. Similarly, Herbert Hoefer's seminal study on the non-baptised believers throws a challenge to the Indian Church to break free from its traditional ghettos and enter into the world of these 'believers' with appropriate forms of ministry, so that the idea of the *perichoretic* communion becomes real in their life. In order to accomplish this task ecclesia needs to make a shift from its misplaced emphasis on the rigid structures to the reality of the people of God.

People of God and the Church

Rightly understood, Church as the body of Christ is the exemplary *perichoretic* communion of God's people on earth. This is possible only when the Church's priorities are put into proper perspective.

Given, the current precarious situation, it could no longer hold on to its structural elements. Rather it is important that the Church transcends its captivities to the structures and institutions, and demonstrates its priority for the people of God over the structures. Doyle opines that communion ecclesiology understands Church as a "communion" among human beings and God; it places its primary emphasis on "relationship" as against the overly institutional approaches; and it fosters a creative, dynamic and healthy interplay between diversity and unity, i.e., between the local and the universal Church. It is a Church that practices love, acceptance, forgiveness, commitment, and intimacy. It is the expression of the Church's sharing in the communion, love and life of God who is Trinity in unity, i.e., the plenitude of the communion in Godhead.[145] The Reformer's thoughts on the Church demonstrate this mode of ecclesiological discourse. In his understanding of the work of the Spirit in the Church, he affirms that Christ remains with his Church through the Spirit who leads and guides the Church into all truth. An important point Luther brings out is that the history and the reality of the empirical ecclesiastical structure is not free from but under the judgment of God. In other words, Luther raises a polemical question as to whether the structure of papacy, canon law and the magisterium truly came from the Spirit. Of course, this polemic must be understood as conditioned by his struggle with Rome and the polemical situation it created. Nevertheless, his polemic implies that the true Church is neither conditioned by nor contingent on the structures, but found in the communion of the faithful – a definite preferential option for the people of God over the structures.

Luther's theology of the cross provided perspective to his ecclesiology, which teaches that the true *perichoretic* communion of the faithful, the body of Christ, is not fully identical with its historical form. It is rather hidden under it, complemented by the theology of resurrection, which informs that God has preserved the Church even under the institutionalised structure, i.e., papacy. Here, he came to realise that the true Church could not be preserved by replacing the existing structure with another one; rather by the Gospel and the Sacraments.[146] Obviously, it was a corrective of the erroneous perception of the Spirit's leadership in the Church in hierarchical or supernatural evolutionist terms. The obvious inference is that the Church is neither a supernatural nor a merely humanly evolved community; rather it is a communion – an event or happening by the continuing work of the Holy Spirit. It is a communion of the faithful, patterned after the Divine Communion, i.e., the perfect Trinitarian relationship between the Father, the Son and the Holy Spirit, which, thus, designates the supreme mode of *perichoretic* relationship and the Church is mandated to give visible and tangible expression to this relationship on earth. In this communion, differences and multiplicity are not obliterated or assimilated or excluded but embraced and celebrated. If this is the ideal Church, then, we need to acknowledge that the contemporary Churches across the globe display demoralisation than the true image of the Church. Martin E. Marty, for instance, painfully asserts:

> Serious leaders in evangelical Protestantism have also more recently begun to express dismay as their movement has been increasingly exposed to the acids of modernity... A new religious consumerism, they say, replaces a concern for the cost of discipleship. The market orientation of religion in the current revival leads it to cater to individuals but not to build community.[147]

In Luther's thoughts on the Church, the idea of communion bears certain specific connotations. *First,* he understands communion in terms of participation – participation of the believers in the benefits of grace, and together with other saints, the adverse and favourable situations of life. This communion involves in sharing of goods among the believers, giving and receiving of the fellow believers, becoming one with all others, and living and working for one another. Luther puts this aspect of Christian living succinctly as follows: "I am...a participant and a co-partner in all the blessings it possesses".[148] The communion we seek is not formed out of any ascriptions; it is not hierarchically structured and, therefore, it is a more open communion that shares its life with the society, i.e., with the people in need. This communion consciously and consistently works for unity (even of the opposites) and never for isolation, ostracism, or fragmentation. It is not an exclusive communion of the bona fide believers. Rather it opens itself up to be in communion with the wider society, fully participating in the benefits and misfortunes of the people. It raises a pertinent question: What is Church's attitude towards Hindutva's hate-filled, hostile and violent reactions against the Church? In response, I would categorically affirm that, following the basic Christian principles and values, the *perichoretic* communion presently conjured up is not reactive but proactive, i.e., it continues to work for the benefit of even its detractors, true to its central principle of the *unity of the opposite*.

Second, this communion *happens* and continues to exist because its foundation is Christ's sacrificial love, which embraces believers as one body or "one loaf" with Christ and therefore also with each other. Luther asks: "Therefore, since the spirit of Christ dwells in the Christians, by means of which brothers become co-heirs, one body, and citizens of Christ, how is it possible for us not to be participants in all the benefits of Christ?"[149] In this sense, then, everyone who finds him/herself in the communion is no longer self-centered, self-seeking and autonomous, but Christ-centered, communion-oriented and mutually responsible. The depth of the meaning of this delineation of the Church can be appreciated only when we realise that Christians across the globe derive their identity and meaning of their Christian existence in and through this communion, because this communion (not the structures, because the structures in all of history are engaged in controlling the graces for self interest and, hence, vitiated) imparts all the graces to the believers and to humanity in general freely as Christ has offered himself freely not for the Church but for the entire world. In a brilliant text the Reformer captures the salience of the Christian Church:

> The Church is…the divine, the heavenly, the noblest brotherhood;…the communion of saints in which we are all brothers and sisters, so closely united that a closer relationship cannot be conceived for here we have one Baptism, one Christ, one sacrament, one food one gospel, one faith, one spirit, one spiritual body [Eph. 4:4f], and each person is a member of the other [Rom 12:5]". [150]

Here, we need to remind ourselves that if we fail to capture such a holistic vision of ecclesia in its true spirit, we are going to remain *exclusive communities* having no openness towards the 'other'. It is precisely for this reason, we need to resent against the idea of the Church as "peoples' movement".[151] While recognising the rationale behind such a conception of ecclesia from concrete historical situations mostly characterised by human contradictions, my discomfort emanates from the very fact that such a perception of the Church is theologically not viable because it puts too much strictures around the Church and makes it an exclusive human institution, diminishing the Church's ability to embrace differences. Further, it vitiates the double character of the Church as a Sacramental and exemplary reality

Third, the Church, the body of Christ, the communion of the saints, is an open communion that embraces the 'other' and celebrates 'differences' as God's way of dealing with God's creation as a whole. If this is true, then, ecclesia is essentially and necessarily an integrative communion that always engages in building bridges across boundaries, even across apparently opposing categories, following Christ who did the ministry of integrating humanity and the creation with God and, thereby, paved the way for mutually responsible and responsive human collective, overcoming the forces that work for the polarisation of people on the basis of certain human made structures.

Fourth, to be true to the ideal of the body of Christ, i.e., the communion of saints, ecclesia is (and must be) built on the principle of equality, which has found its clearest expression in the Reformer's thoughts on the Church. In the face of papacy's corruption and abuses of power, the Reformer found the Biblical symbols of cross, justification, Baptism and priesthood of all believers as critical to counter the ecclesiastical power point, and they provided a firm basis for the reform movement of the Church. An important purpose of the movement itself was the reform of the structures of the Church for the service of the Gospel and the people of God. Luther's incisive discovery here is the *equality of the believers* within the communion by virtue of the synthesis of Baptism and Royal priesthood. In Baptism, i.e., by the act of putting on Christ to be the new creation, everyone becomes a priest along with Christ, the chief priest, and all the members of the body of Christ stand on equal footing. The priesthood of all believers was a brilliant tool that provided an alternative or new consciousness to the believers over against the hierarchical structure of the Church that had ushered in a consciousness of higher and lower humans even within the Church. Luther's new interpretation of the priesthood was founded on the principle of service or servanthood. It obviously suggests that the priority is for the people of God gathered by the Word through the Spirit and held together around the Sacraments, and the structures are rendered credibility only insofar as they exist for the service of the Gospel and the people. An important characteristic of Luther's explication of the ministry of the Church is that power is vested with the people and the priest, who is called and vested with the priestly responsibilities of the congregation, exercises the priestly functions only as the representative of the rest of the congregation.[152] The universal priesthood of all believers, thus, divests all tendencies of religious individualism, self-centeredness and hierarchy, and invests its entire force with the reality of the communion.

For various historical reasons, the Church has concentrated too much on the centralised structures and paid only scant attention to the people of God, especially the disenfranchised. Now, for theological reasons, the focus must be on the people of God, the locus of communion. It is appropriate to recall two vital concerns we identified in the course of this study, namely, the crisis of identity and meaning, and human misery, especially in the context of Hindu nationalism. These crises diminish the possibilities for human beings to meaningfully participate in communion building because the dividing lines of dichotomy are clearly drawn between the 'we' and the 'other' – a notorious framework in which the 'other' is always placed at the receiving end. Hindu nationalism, for instance, operates on the basis of a clearly drawn dividing line, which has identified the Church as the definite 'other' and demands that the Church either subjects itself to the corporatist Hindu identity or remains as a permanent alien.

At this point, I also recognise the efforts taken by intellectuals to identify and affirm Christianity as Indian. A recent edited book has the provocative title: *Christianity is Indian.*[153] Introducing the book, the editor affirms: "Indigenous Independent Church Movements represent a vigorous and rapidly expanding section of Christianity in India today. They are demonstrations of the translatability of the Gospel, an authentic Indian incarnation of Christian faith".[154] At the outset, we commend the efforts of the guild of theologians who contributed twenty-seven essays with a view to give a new expression to Indian Christianity. However, it is problematic on certain basic grounds: (i) When Christian faith itself is regarded as alien and Christians' loyalty to the nation is called into question, what impact is this approach going to make in changing the attitude of Hindutva forces towards Indian Christians? (ii) If Christianity is Indian, where is the need for an *Indian* incarnation of Christian faith? (iii) When the contributors to this volume themselves identified a number of *independent* Church groups, where is the possibility of the emergence of *an* indigenous community? These issues once again reiterate the need for understanding the Church from a communion framework.

Our perception of ecclesia as *perichoretic communion* enhances the scope of the vulnerable to meaningfully participate in building communion for the following reasons:

(i) In contrast to Hindutva's social ostracism, *perichoretic communion* operates from the vantage point of embrace. It works relentlessly to integrate different categories through a network of interwoven relationships.

(ii) When the phenomenon of caste discrimination is a vexing problem, not only in the wider Indian society but also within the Church, *perichoretic communion* offers a viable model for authentic human existence because *perichoresis* does not categorise human beings into higher and lower humans. It embraces cultural differences as an occasion to celebrate, for it emanates from its faith in God who is Trinity in unity. Here, communion of the faithful with God and with fellow human beings, irrespective of their differences, is gelled together by the principle of *perichoretic* integration. In an ethos of *perichoretic* experience, human problems are not approached as 'their' problems; but as 'our' problems to be collectively dealt with because the predominant concern of this communion is loving relationship.

(iii) In the world context of women's subordination, this model understands ecclesia in a new light. It readily recognises that half (or even more) of its priesthood *vis-à-vis* the women are co-partners with God in its mission for the world. Therefore, this is a relevant model that empowers the socially and culturally disenfranchised to be the subjects of history. Letty Russell offers a brilliant critique of women's subordinate situation through her volume, *The Church in the Round.* She posits 'Round Table' as an important posture of the Church in the contemporary situation.[155]

(iv) In a world that is fragmenting and hurting, communion ecclesiology promotes loving relationship,[156] following the light that shines from the Trinitarian relationship of God, the light that was brought to this world by Jesus Christ.

Today we require the truth and plenitude of the Trinity as a model for our reflection on the oneness or unity of the Church and its mission to the world. The sovereign monarchical episcopate was the governing model of the Church for ages. In this model the conception of God is mostly governed by an image of a sovereign monarch, a model developed by Ignatius of Antioch with the underlying notion: 'one bishop', 'one Church'. In this model, God was essentially viewed to be a monarch and, hence, the Church on earth also must have a corresponding monarch. Within Roman Catholicism, this monarchical episcopate achieved its heightened expression in the doctrine of papal infallibility.[157] It was a system that dominated not only the doctrine of God but also provided enough impetus to patriarchal system of human relationships. The doctrine of Trinity, on the contrary, helps us to make a break with radical monotheism that lends credence to the monarchical model of ecclesial life and mission, as the Trinitarian model places its emphasis on the Church as the communion of the believers. As Cyprian stated, the Church is "a people brought into unity from the unity of the Father, the Son and the Holy Spirit".[158]

As Robert W. Jenson understands, the unity of the Church foreshadows the unity of humanity as a whole – a unity that God intends to work out through the Church, for in the Trinity "we find a unity which presupposes and gives ultimate value to relationship, reciprocity, and mutuality between members in a loving communion of equals".[159] The apostolicity of the Church, then, is the continuation of God's sending God's Son and the Spirit because the Church is 'a people' who are God's elects to serve the Triune God for the benefit of all people. Without doubt, this is the missionary nature of the Church and it certainly raises a fundamental question as to whether the Church must engage in its missionary activity today in India, especially in the context of Hindutva's acute hostility and resistance to the Church's mission.

Describing the Church, Robert Jenson aptly states: "the first gatherings of believers were gatherings of missionaries".[160] We have observed in the third chapter of this study that the missionary nature is fundamental to the Church and without which it would have died out. Braaten is quite emphatic on the missionary nature of the Church in all ages as he argues:

> If we surrender this missionary identity of the Church, we will be left to serve some other Gods [other than the Trinitarian God], perhaps the pagan gods of blood and soil, the gods of our race, or land, or class, or gender. We are commissioned to speak in the name of the triune God. We are authorized to speak *to* this God in worship, to speak *for* this God in proclamations, and to speak *about* this God in theology. Apart from the God of the Gospel, our talk will revolve around someone else. The Bible calls this idolatry [Emphases as in the text].[161]

This is a real challenge to the Indian Church because the only way the Church can maintain its relationship with the wider society is in and through its missions and it is an open question before the Church as to what kind of mission it can evolve in the present context. Whatever the choices that the Church makes, it has to be faithful to its evangelical mission, i.e., its commitment to build intimate relationship across boundaries because in its origin it was characterised by the re-assembling of the dispersed and the disenfranchised, as we found in the Pentecost experience whose theological root is the principle of *love* – the love of God manifested on the cross of Christ.

Ecclesia and the Principle of Love – Bible and the Reformer

The Biblical understanding of love encapsulates potential theological substance to re-construe ecclesia in the context of the intolerant Hindu nationalism. From a Biblical point of view, the law in its entirety has been summarised in terms of love – love for God and love for the neighbor. The central Christian affirmation that "God so loved the world" (John 3:16) is nothing but the affirmation of God's love for humanity and the wider creation. It is this love that made our communion with God possible through the cross and it invites us to engage in the ministry of building communion on the principle of *perichoretic* love. In a situation of conflicting and hurting human relationships, especially Hindutva's continuous attempts to inflict injury to the 'other', it is the principle of love that provides the basis for the Church's existence as the communion of the faithful. It is a way of God's dealing with God's creation and it must enable us to derive meaning and identity and strive to dispel human misery.

The Biblical perception of love does not imply some sort of overt kindness and mere absence of physical abuse. Rather it allows individuals derive their dignity and identity within human collectives and urges them to make positive contributions towards building up of the true values of collective consciousness. We need to realize that depravity of human dignity and identity is an important factor that stands as a disruptive force in the way of communal harmony.[162] A major tenet of human existence based on the principle of love is the true urge and concern to seek the welfare of the 'other', which must be the foundation from which one can move out to conceive human collective living. As Amartya Sen aptly puts it, seeking the welfare of the 'other' is not simple altruism; rather it is a trajectory of "our attention from the notion of *being identical to oneself* to that of *sharing an identity with others*" [Emphases as in the text].[163] Love for the 'other' opens up the possibilities of the great many ways in which human beings relate to each other. It challenges our usual penchant to engage in well-defined and formalised programmes that intend to promote "amity among civilizations", "dialogue between different religions", "inter-community conversations" and so on, which mostly remain as academic enterprises. Thus, love for the 'other' is pivotal in human collectives where exchange of thoughts and interaction of humans is not smothered by hostilities, hatreds, fears, prejudices, and other similar setbacks; rather love is mutually beneficial.

Love for the 'other' has the potential to liberate humans from fanaticism, more specifically related to caste, creed and ethnicity. This mode of love is the opposite of selfishness and vested interest, which are contrary to truth. Selfishness or vested interest is filled with evil and it is the breeding ground of evil and suffering. Its fundamental character is to foster evil, and hence, it is the opposite of love and peace. Thus it can be argued that despite all the penchant for our social activism and rhetorics of structural changes; and in spite of all the euphoria over the newfound wisdom of social reasoning in the recent times that repudiates individualism in order to foster 'community-consciousness', the long awaited justice, peace, amity, and harmony in human collective existence still remain elusive from our grasp because we human beings miserably failed to hold on to the fundamental principle of love in the public sphere. Contemporary public sphere seems to be a virtual battleground of competitive selves, where identities are defined in oppositional terms with certain pernicious modes of discourse.[164] On the contrary, true love engages itself in de-centering and de-essentializing of one's own identity; it perceives reality not in dichotomous terms but in terms of communion; it engages in border-crossing; and it allows space for multiple voices. It entails that we need to re-discover the principle of love for the 'other' in our theological agenda in the twenty-first century, which has the potential to integrate variegated human communities and collectives towards the realization of the new heaven and new earth.

The central thrust of the Biblical message hinges on God's self-offering for the renewal and regeneration of human existence from degeneration, fragmentation, hostility, hatred, and hurt. The Biblical story of creation and fall, God's covenant relationship with God's people, the incarnation, the life, teachings and ministry of Jesus, the cross, the teachings of the Apostles, and the eschatological hope of new creation have all in them strong emphases of the principle of love. Without this love the Biblical story would remain a naïve account, completely disjuncted from human existential situation, having no relevance to our journey towards the fullness life. God's covenant relationship as detailed in the Bible indisputably relates God's passionate desire for humans to be in communion with God and with the fellow creation (Gen 3:15; 9:8 – 17). Israel's moral code *vis-à-vis* the Decalogue, as interpreted by Jesus with its vertical and horizontal dimensions of love, epitomizes the principle of love. Jesus' parable of the 'Good Samaritan' (Luke 10:25-37) is a treasure house of theological truths and the central thrust of the story is that it is love for the 'other' that drew the Samaritan to the wounded man to render a helping hand at the most crucial time of need. It further demonstrates the conflict between self-interest and seeking the welfare of the 'other': self-interest indulges in self-alienation from the victimised and seeking the welfare of the 'other' moves out to integrate with the weak, vulnerable and the suffering, even from among the dominant. If ecclesia is to be relevant to the contemporary context, then, it has to take hold of this vital component in its theological and mission agenda.

An important strand of the stimulus of Luther's theological thinking sprang from his intense reflections on love and he counsels:

> The love and benevolence which Christ has shown towards us should move us to esteem one another highly and dearly for the sake of Christ, who dwells in us. I must not look down on anyone because of his imperfections. On the contrary I should think: My Lord dwells in this weak vessel and honors him with His presence. If then, Christ considers him worthy of favour and sincere affection and has given him as great an interest in Himself as He has given me, I must accord him respect and honor as the living temple and seat of my Lord. What difference does it make to you how lowly the seat is on which the Lord sits? If it is not too lowly for Him to sit on and honor with His presence, Why should you, His servant, not honor it?[165]

Undeniably, this is a fertile text that has enormous implications today in our ecclesiological reflections, more particularly to the issues of justice, amity and equality. It raises startling questions: Can a true Christian alienate him/herself from the weak and vulnerable?

Can the dominant within the Church deny the vulnerable brothers and sisters equal respect, dignity and honor and still claim that they are Christians? What are we going to offer to promote true values of human collective existence? The Reformer's explication of the doctrine of justification points unmistakably to the principle of love, which was a counter-model to the medieval understanding of God as a righteous judge and its insistence on appeasing the wrathful God through appropriate penances.[166] Arguably, then, the Reformer's theological/ecclesiological expositions have strong traces of the Biblical principle of love (justification, cross, *communio*, sacraments, priesthood/servanthood, equality of the believers, caring for each other, bearing each other's burdens and so on). To Luther, it was an important way to dispel the misery of the weak and find one's identity and meaning as a member of the body of Christ.

When Hindutva continues to hurl its invectives against the vulnerable, more specifically to the religious and ethno-cultural minorities, perpetuating fragmentation and hostilities and inflicting more injuries; when it trains its armories against them to avenge for the past 'errors'; when it attempts to assimilate and/or exclude them by way of imposing its corporatist Hindu identity; and when it indulges in gruesome and barbarous violence against the vulnerable Christians, the Church's response can neither be uncritical activism (a kind of 'paying back in the same coin') nor can it be passive submission, but rather a middle-third path, i.e., a mode of existence that would clearly demonstrate a different *perichoretic* lifestyle of embrace as an alternative, a counter-consciousness and a resistance to the tendencies to erase difference or plurality and exclude or annihilate the 'other'. These delineations, then, configure on one particular question: What visible and tangible form does the *perichoretic* communion assume in the contemporary Indian public space? Of course, what it envisages is not a grand canopy that shelters different structures; it is not a conglomerate of communions; it is not a communion of communities; and it is not an already finished circle either. Rather, it is a *communion of God's people* organized around the principle of *perichoresis,* which is the truth and plenitude of the Trinitarian communion of the Divine. It fosters and preserves a new lifestyle of *accepting (even the most) unacceptable* without prejudice and discrimination as exemplified by the Divine acceptance of the humans (infidels and enemies) in Christ. If this is the nature of the Church, its function must correspond to this nature.

Mission of the Church in the Context of Hindu Nationalism

The mission of the Church in India is a seriously debated issue, not only from within the Church but also from outside. My purpose in this section is not to draw a blueprint for the mission of the Indian Church but to propose certain principles that would enable the Church to design its mission for the twenty-first century. Of course, I am not suggesting that the Indian Church should, without question, endorse every aspect of the development of ideas presented here. On the contrary, they must be critically evaluated and reconsidered in light of the emerging situations. What I present here are reflections that express a deep-rooted concern and passion pertaining to the living context of the Indian Christians and the fate of the secular fabric of the nation as a whole. It suggests that the Indian Church has a far more challenging task ahead. Since our theological reflection on the Church has emerged from the context of Hindu nationalism, it is appropriate to begin our discussion on the mission of the Church with a crucial question: What can be the possible attitude of the Indian Church towards the extremist Hindutva forces who express extreme anger, hatred and enmity, and seek to unleash violence against Christians under every possible pretext? A relevant answer to this question must emerge from the living context of the Church, and it must be able to provide adequate theological substance to the mission of the Church. However, in order to derive a viable answer to the above question, I would like to delve into some of the principles on which the Church had responded to similar situations.

Christian Faith and Church's Mission

Christian faith is not founded on simple cause and effect mechanism; it is not built on retributive justice either; and certainly it is not posited on retaliatory ethics. On the contrary, it is founded on grace and forgiveness, and Christianity ceases to exist without this foundation. It is God's way of dealing with hostility and restoring relationship – a way that points to the reconciliation and healing of the world.

The fundamental substance of this relationship, as Luther brought to light, is the divine acceptance of the unacceptable or infidels, i.e., God's acceptance of the fallen humanity into God's communion on account of Jesus Christ. It entails that the Church's mission, whatever mode it assumes, must emanate from this foundation. Two crucial points are in place here. *First*, under no circumstance can retaliatory ethics be the basis or foundation of the Church's life and mission. It implies that when the external situation is hostile, especially when Hindutva forces let loose violence against Christians, the Church's response cannot be violent retaliation. *Second*, the Church, in any situation, must not aspire for temporal power, because history tells us that whenever religion usurped temporal power, it became dangerous to human existence. Instances are numerous in history – Constantine's embrace of Christianity, Papal authority over temporal domain, the Reformer's delegation of ecclesiastical powers to the princes, Islamic theocracy, and contemporary Hindu nationalism – and they have all proved to be disastrous. Such instances remind us of a warning given by George Santayana a century ago: "Those who do not remember the past are condemned to repeat it".[167] This does not in any way mean to promote a culture of silence or submission. The Reformer's distinction between the spiritual and temporal realms is a strong reminder for our Christian existence in India today. It does not teach the Church to be locked up in its own domain (a model adopted by the majority Lutherans in Germany during Nazi regime); rather it tells us that the Church must be able to offer a critical voice in the midst of injustice, brokenness, oppression, and marginalization because, as Tillich asserted, the Church has the spiritual sword to judge and transcend the present situation. The Indian Church has offered this critical voice and it is this critical voice that has largely earned the wrath of the Hindutva forces. What, then, can be the mission of the Church?

Our ecclesiological task is to discover those elements, which sustained the Church in the midst of hostility and motivated the early community of believers to move ahead with unflinching determination to proclaim that "in Christ God was reconciling the world to himself" (2 Cor. 5:19) in a fragmented world. Further, according to the New Testament, God has entrusted this ministry of reconciliation to us, making us the "ambassadors for Christ" so that we might beckon the world in Christ's behalf to "be reconciled with God" (2 Cor. 5:20). Therefore, the onus is with the Church to be God's instrument of reconciliation in this world. To put it differently, in nature and function, doctrine and practice, and worship and teaching, the Indian Church must clearly demonstrate that it stands for the task of building communion and it will not compromise, dilute or water down this purpose whether the dominant Hindu world recognizes this genuine purpose of the Church or not.

The primitive Christian Church, when it was placed in the midst of acute hostility and persecution never attempted to use force for self-defense. Rather, being rooted in faith in the Lord, the early Church demonstrated a different attitude, namely, denial of the (ways of the) world, enduring suffering and caring for the needy, following the example of the cross. In other words, when the external factors were hostile to the faith community, the believers were engaged in an act of strengthening their fellowship through their intimacy with Christ and with each other – to be sure this intimacy provided them the energy to withstand the external hostility and engage in mission. Luther consistently argued for self-restraint on the face of suffering. Undoubtedly, this attitude of the early Church and also of Luther has a strong Biblical foundation (Mt 5:38-45; Rom 12:14-21, I Thess. 5:15 cf. Mt 26:51f), which repudiates violence as a means of redressal.[168] Therefore, the fundamental mission of the Church in the contemporary context is to proclaim the intimate relationship that is embodied in communion, so that in the place of hatred, hostility, animosity, brokenness, mutual distrust, and mutual destruction, this intimate relationship shall prevail. Thus, the true inner strength of the Church is this intimacy that holds the believers together in Christ transcending all geographical, ethnic, cultural, regional and linguistic boundaries, and not its numerical growth, worldwide expansion, and fantastic administrative and power structures.

The mission/ministry of the Church is necessarily and essentially the outcome of its nature and structure and our understanding of the nature of ecclesia is *perichoretic* communion inspired by and patterned after the tri-unity of God. The fundamental theological substance of the Church's mission is, thus, provided by the plenitude of the Trinitarian relationship that exists between the three persons of the Trinity. Within the Trinity, even though there are three persons, they share the same substance and equality of status. Obviously, the persons within the Trinity are not hierarchically ordered and that is the reason why we are told that they are co-equal, co-eternal and con-substantial, which implies that there is no inner contradiction or tension within the Trinity with regard to the divine will, purpose and activities. Christian faith further affirms that one among the three persons – the Son/the eternal *Logos* – became concretised in history (Heb. 2: 14-15), which is commonly referred to as *God's self-manifestation in Jesus Christ for all humanity*. Rightly understood, the reality of the Divine *Logos* taking human form is an extension of the Divine communion and an invitation to humans to be part of this communion.[169] The Biblical image of the 'body' used to refer to the Church unambiguously illustrates the truth of the believers' being integrated into the body of Christ, the incarnate person of the Trinity.

The believers' being in communion as the body of Christ is irrefutably attested by the symbols of 'adoption' (Rom. 8:15, 23; 9:4; Gal. 4:5; Eph. 1:5) and 'inheritance' (Gal. 3:18; Eph. 1:8; Col. 3:24; 1 Pet. 1:4).[170] These symbols unmistakably point to the fact that by virtue of their adoption on account of Christ, the believers are entitled to inherit all that is in store for Christ. Admittedly, then, if Christ is in intimate communion with the Father and the Spirit, a believer also inherits that communion on account of his/her being incorporated into the body of Christ. God's being in Trinity is not an exclusive community, rather an open communion that is always willing to embrace the 'other', which, in the event of Christ's incarnation, means God's embrace of the ungodly and the infidels (Rom. 5:10). This perception of open communion suggests that the Church can never be an exclusive entity or an island in the world. Rather, it is a veritable sign and an instrument of the transformation of the world. We have reason to believe this because ecclesia could embrace differences within its communion, for the Bible speaks of the Church as the new creation composed of Jews and Gentiles (Eph. 2:15; Col. 3:11). Therefore, true to its Christian character, the Church essentially is and ought to be an open *perichoretic* communion, the body of Christ. If this is the true nature of the Church, then, its mission ought to correspond to its nature.

A communion ecclesiology believes in the *equality of the people of God*, which is the salience of the true nature of ecclesia. We have discussed at length as to how the Reformer tried to retrieve the idea of equality of the believers in Christ through his doctrines of 'Justification', 'Royal Priesthood' and 'Office of the Ministry' of the Church. For him, every person – from an ordinary believer to the pope – standing under the grace of God stands on equal footing with all others. In 1842, C. F. W. Walther, a zealous missionary pastor of the LCMS, in one of his sermons attempted to recapture the perfect equality of the believers within the Church thus:

> The Church which Christ has established on earth ought to be marked by perfect equality. It should never be set up as an earthly government. In the Church no one should be on top, no one superior, no one first, no one the lord or master. This is one of the fundamental doctrines of all Christendom. Each has the same Baptism, the same faith, the same Christ, the same righteousness, the same hope of eternal, heavenly blessing of salvation in Christ... Great harm, therefore, has always come when individuals desire to be lords in the Church. There was total equality at the time of apostles, along with the most pleasant and splendid blessings. At that time, all Christians were regarded as spiritual priests, and no one was oppressed.[171]

In a caste-ridden society like that of ours, the idea of equality of all believers provides a clear pointer and a new consciousness for the people to affirm their equality. This is a radical, revolutionary and fertile doctrine of the Church, which engenders true substance to re-vision ecclesia as a *perichoretic* communion and its mission primarily as proclaiming God's gracious provision of opening up the new possibility of ending hostility, restoring relationship and living as equal heirs of the benefit of this grace. This is the true spirit of communion, which is made possible by Church's constant struggle to be faithful to God's grace and empowerment for true '*koinonia*', even though it often falls short of its own ideal of communion. Taken the equality of the believers seriously, the Church, as Stanley

Hauerwas described, is 'the truest possible human communion'[172] because (a) it is founded on the Trinitarian communion; and (b) it came into existence because of God's intention to bring into being a universal communion of love. This is a new life of sharing and caring that is predicated on the embrace of differences, more specifically of the 'other'.

What raises the morale of ecclesia above everything is the gift of the power of the integrating grace of God, which continues to empower the life of communion and its mission to the world. Perhaps the best demonstration of the earliest communion can be seen in *Acts*, which is something totally new, engendered by the work of God through the outpouring of the Holy Spirit.[173] The Reformer understood this as the noblest and truest brother/sisterhood, in which everything is held in common – both divine grace and material blessings. As Ronaldo Muñoz aptly described:

> There are today...in Latin America and...in European and American cultures, Christians who are trying to live out, through the power of God's grace, the intention of love...[T]hese groups are already living the communion between God and human beings, and between human beings themselves, that constitute the most essential content of the kingdom. They are living it imperfectly in the chiaroscuro of faith and with sinful defects, but they are living it in a real way. This is the deepest underlying secret of the Church's life.[174]

Is this not the very life of Jesus Christ, the risen Lord, transmitted to us by the Spirit?

Church as an Instrument of Healing and Reconciliation

God's initiative to renew the fallen humanity from death and destruction to a new life is important for ecclesiology. Luther understands Christ event as the sublimest expression of God's *feeling* towards the sinful humanity. The life of Jesus is a bridge-building event between God and humanity and it prefigured the destruction of the powers that enslaved humanity – the most decisive event of reconciliation, redemption and healing. Christ's work is not his own work carried out in isolation, but the divine work to reconcile humanity with God.[175] It is a decisive work of God in which God redemptively dealt with God's creation in Christ.[176] In the midst of death, destruction, brokenness, and incertitude (the work of demonic forces), "Christ is nothing else than *pure life*" with which he smothered death and pointed to the new life.[177] It implies that ecclesia, being the body of Christ, bears this mark of redemption or new life, in the first place, and acts as a mediator of this renewed life as an interlocutor between God and humanity, in the second place. This has serious implications for the Church today, which the Reformer explains in his passionate expression: "wonderful exchange"[178] – the highest expression of *perichoresis.* Christ has made himself one with humanity in love and takes everything that is ours (sin, agony of death and so on) upon himself and gives us everything that belongs to him (his innocence, righteousness, and blessedness) as our own. This is a model that could potentially guide the Church in a world of fragmentation and mutual hostility. Ecclesia, in this sense, is a 'sacramental' and an 'exemplary' reality. As Luther explains, Christ's work is a sacrament insofar as it essentially deals with sin and an example insofar as the Church follows after Christ by suffering. The Reformer clearly asserts that Christ's sufferings must be dealt with not only in terms of words and appearances but honestly in terms of life. Does Christ's passion and death automatically put an end to all the works of the demonic forces? The Reformer's answer to this question is in the negative. For him, Christ's work is not an already finished task, but an ongoing battle until the end of the world because the demonic forces continue to wage their war against the people of God in history.

The inner constitution of the communion of believers signifies the renewed life of the believers that God had engendered on account of Christ, and, as the second letter to the Corinthian Church declares (5:18-21), God uses ecclesia in and through its ministry of reconciliation as God's instrument for the renewal of the whole of humanity,[179] which can be categorised as the 'incarnational principle' in which Christ, Church, Sacraments, and Ministry are understood as the continuation of God's saving activity for the entire world. However, this aspect of ecclesial life might not be greeted with any sign of acceptance by the hardcore Hindutva forces that always wait for pretexts to intimidate the Church and the Christians.[180] There are deliberate attempts to call into question the credibility of the ongoing mission works of the Indian Church: medical mission, education, social awareness programmes that had contributed and still contribute a great deal in the area of nation building, the newly initiated works like inter-faith dialogue and peace initiatives, initiatives on justice issues and gender concerns and other important works. Hindutva reiterates its stereotypical opinion that these works are aimed at gaining more conversion. In this context, it becomes imperative for the Church to be healed of its own fragmentation and to come together as a communion to express its solidarity with the victimised, both within and without. Implicitly, then, there must be a definite visible expression of the healing of the brokenness of the Church that alone can lend credibility to the mission of the Church – mission that offers hope to the fragmented world.

It is a nagging question indeed as to what kind of hope of reconciliation and healing can the Church (itself a fragmented reality) offer to a broken world? In other words, what is the content of the reconciliation we propose, which could take tangible form in the midst of vengefulness, hatred, hostility, and human impulse to annihilate the 'other'? What I endeavour here is to make some tentative, but vital, proposals for the Church's mission in the twenty-first century, specifically attuned to our central thrust of the Church's mission as building *perichoretic* relationships across boundaries. There is a general tendency in many of the modern theological discourses on Church's mission to lay emphasis on the divine work of reconciliation and the Church's work as an extension of God's work in Christ.[181] It requires us to devote a great deal of our intellectual energy to the portrayal of the reconciling work of God as it is disclosed in the divine work of redemption, which describes the purposiveness of the Triune God for the world. My central proposition here is that the true Church is a 'healed and reconciled' communion of believers, in and through Jesus Christ, which, in turn, is an instrument of providing spiritual resources to the healing and reconciliation of the world. As Timothy Gorringe observes, the purpose of the Church of Christ is to offer a messianic "home" or basis to humanity[182] by remaining faithful to its call, commitment and vocation.

A closely related proposal to the above is that the contemporary Indian Church urgently requires a renewed 'theology of embrace'. This proposal is more in line with the central Christian faith affirmation that clings to 'God's acceptance of the infidels', which the Reformer unearthed in terms of 'justification' and contextualised it in his struggle against the stronghold of papacy over the people's lives. A more contemporary theological expression of this reconciliatory mission of the Church can be found in the works of Miraslov Volf. According to him, God's unconditional embrace of the hostile humanity (Rom. 6:10) into God's communion serves as a model for the way the Christians must relate with other human beings.[183] This is a facilitating mission of the Church to orient the world towards the consummation of the 'final reconciliation',[184] since we do not have a grand narrative of the *telos* of reconciliation. This is what a responsible theology is expected to accomplish.

One final proposal that I intend to make in this study is that, given the present milieu of acute hostility and human impulse to annihilate the 'other' with impunity, the Church of Christ must be able to create an ambience of *metanoia* – a *metanoia* as represented in the book of Revelation, which states: "But I have this against you, that you have abandoned the love that you had at first. Remember then from what you have fallen; repent, and do the works you did at first" (2:4-5). As Volf understands, repentance implies resisting the enticing power of sin and allowing the 'new order of God's rule' to be established, more specifically, in human hearts.[185] This perception of repentance in relation to reconciliation and healing might elicit two major criticisms: (a) it might be criticised as individualistic; and (b) it might also be criticised as an 'instrumentalist' view of the Church, in which the Church is viewed as a facilitator of breaking the psychological barriers to reconciliation and healing. Obviously, the liberationist strand of theology would find it difficult to throw its weight behind this view because this does not overtly deal with structures. But I would like to lend support to this view of *metanoia* towards healing and reconciliation of the world because vengefulness, hostility, hatred, and human impulse to annihilate the 'other' are not merely structural and/or law-and-order problems, rather they represent the problems of human mental attitude, which must be dealt with at that level. Here, I like to recall Dalai Lama's speech in which the Tibetan spiritual leader had dwelt upon the importance of dealing with human mental attitude for social transformation. Implicitly, then, a complete transformation of the world is possible not simply by transforming the structures, but by *metanoia*, at the personal and collective levels, which involves primarily human mental attitude towards the 'other'. To conclude, while affirming the need for breaking the mental/psychological barriers, I do not deny the need for structural changes. Conversely, what I propose here is that the breaking of the psychological barrier must be translated into ecclesial praxis. And only then, can we realize the true transformation of the world – a clear depiction of which is represented by Jesus' encounter with Zacchaeus (Luke 19:1-10).

Church's Role in the Life of the Nation

Our age has witnessed (and continues to witness) some of the most gruesome violent incidents, flared up by communal frenzy in India and terror attacks across the globe by extremist forces, in which the victims in most cases are the innocent people. It implies that while people look for religion to beget tranquility and peace, it gives birth to terror.[186] The most painful reality in most of the instances of communal violence and terror attacks is that it is religious sentiments that incite these crimes against humanity. Such situations normally arise from an alleged threat to one community's hegemony or even authority from the 'other'. That is the reason why those who indulge in violent rioting and brutal killing do so in the name of God. It happened during the medieval period in the form of crusades; during Luther's time it occurred in the fateful peasant revolt in the name of God; Islamic terror outfits vouch their inhuman acts as a service to God; and contemporary Hindu fundamentalists incite violence as a means to protect the Hindu dharma and Raj. It brings us closer to the issue of religion-state relationship and the way Luther endeavored to understand the complexity and sensitivity of this issue.

What we call the issue of religion (or Church-State relationship) is not a recent phenomenon.[187] But it became an issue of serious debate after the emergence of nationalism and democracy as modes of political discourse. Prior to this phenomenon, the issue was the relationship between Church and the empire or kingdom. Quite interestingly, in the modern democratic system of governance, power is abstract and mostly bureaucratic. In contrast, the rule of the ancient empires and kingdoms was personal and often authoritarian. The ancient emperors, kings and queens exercised tremendous powers and they were often equated to gods and goddesses.[188] As the report study on the Church-State relationship by the LCMS points out: "Above the empires and states of history stands *one* everlasting divine authority to whom *all* are accountable – even kings and queens, presidents, and dictators. And so, while kings and empires pass from the scene, the church continues to proclaim God's divine authority."[189]

But the way Jesus radicalised and reconstructed the notion of this divine authority is a crucial point to ponder over, because Jesus' interpretation of God's authority or the kingdom of God has a universal connotation with an eschatological meaning. We should not immediately hasten to conclude that the Church is the custodian of the kingdom of God on earth. Jesus resisted such temptation by refusing to reconstitute the Hebrew understanding of God's rule through an earthly king, and thereby he refused to particularise divine power to any single location (John 18:33-37). Jesus, however, never commanded his disciples to alienate themselves from the state; rather he commanded them to be active participants in the affairs of the state (Mt. 22:21). From this vantage point, as explained by Jesus, particular state has certain authority and it is our duty to submit to temporal authority within the given limits, which, in principle, is to enhance human life. But the real life-enhancing power lies in the power of the Gospel and faith and not in the particularised temporal powers of the world because the Gospel has the power to penetrate, transcend and judge both spiritual and temporal domains of human existence. Understood thus, according to Jesus, the kingdom of God is open to all (Mk 4:30 – 32). It was this understanding of the power of the Gospel that engendered courage to the early Christians to face persecutions and still remain faithful to the Gospel.

A proper Christian approach to temporal power, thus, must be a more balanced one. A Christian lives in the world and contributes his/her part to the building up of the state insofar as the state acts as an instrument of God for the good of the citizens, and at the same time, a Christian transcends the world and does not conform to the ways of the corrupt world and worldly structures (Rom 12:2) that trample upon human welfare, twist justice, and exploit the disenfranchised for self aggrandisement. Only such an approach can enable the Church to offer its critical voice in the midst of human contradictions. The intention of Luther's two-kingdom teaching was to make the people of God aware of this critical role of the Church. To put it in practical terms, when the dominant powers indulge in discriminating and exploiting the weak, the Church cannot remain silent; when millions of human beings created in God's own image live in dehumanized conditions, the Church has to be on the side of the victims; and when women are treated with so much discrimination, the Church must use its spiritual resources to raise its critical voice against such discriminations. It is a way of building relationship with the disenfranchised and a way of truth. Of course, standing on the truth would certainly invite the wrath of vested interests, and Hindutva's diatribes against the Church can perhaps be the result of its anger against truth. Hindutva's hostility, however, must not discourage Christians because they have two powerful symbols that reinforce their faith: *first*, the symbol of the plenitude of the Trinity that is the foundation of their being in *perichoretic* communion; and *second*, the symbol of Christ, the one who held on to truth and laid down his life for the healing and reconciliation of the world.

Summary

Hindu nationalism views the Christians, the Church, its mission and missionaries (overseas and indigenous missions) in India, and all modes of Christian theological discourses through the political lens with a strong sense of suspicion as if Christianity is up to debilitate the (Hindu) nation. This is obviously a baseless insinuation perpetrated by Hindutva as part of its hate campaign against the Church. This allusion, however, is not intended to project the Church as a perfect institution. Certainly there are a number of areas in its life and mission that need to undergo thorough transformation. To cite a few examples: the fragmented expressions of the worldwide Church with mutual condemnation[190] that vitiates the very basis of communion; the deep-rooted caste consciousness among sections of Indian Christians that contributes to the prolonged misery of the marginalized even within the Church; Church's tolerance of corruption within its own boundaries; and the aggressive evangelism aimed solely at 'soul winning'. Further, during the colonial period, the triumphalistic language of Christian theology, often with colonial expression, did promote a negative view of the religious and cultural practices of India, though this view did not go unchallenged. In the last three to four decades, in particular, there emerged newer and broader perceptions of the mission and ministry of the Church, which are mostly rejected by the Hindutva adherents.

It is heartening at the same time to note that the Church has undergone notable transformation in a number of areas of its life and mission. Christianity as a religion does not provide any scope to usurp temporal powers. Its Master's voice and/or mandate, "My kingdom is not of this world" (John 18:36 NKJV; the NRSV translates as "My kingdom is not from the world") still lingers (and it must linger) on in the consciousness of the Christians. To identify the Christians in India either as a vote-bank or as a formidable political force is an aberration. It is a minority communion, demographically scattered all over India, though not evenly. The oft-cited examples of Mizoram and Nagaland as 'Christian states' can be true only in the sense that Christians constitute the majority of the population of these geographically small states. But then, these states are not Christian theocracies, and certainly not ruled by the Church. Rather, they are administered in letter and spirit by the secular democratic norms as enshrined in the Indian constitution as a part of the Indian nation. Further, Hindutva forces often cite the example of Papacy usurping the temporal powers, but they fail to acknowledge that even in this case the Church itself took the lead in resisting such unholy alliance, which is demonstrated clearly by the Protestant Reformation. An important feature of Christian history is that Christian theology has shown the courage time and again to challenge the Church whenever it indulged in espousing secular power.

The primitive Christian Church, when it was placed in the midst of acute hostility and persecution never attempted to retaliate or indulge in using force for self-defense. Rather, being rooted in its faith in its Lord, the early Church demonstrated a different attitude, namely, denial of the (ways of the) world, enduring suffering and caring for the needy, following the example of the cross. In other words, when the external factors were hostile to the faith community, the believers were engaged in an act of strengthening their communion through their intimacy with Christ and with each other. Luther consistently argues for self-restraint in the face of suffering. Undoubtedly, this attitude has a strong Biblical foundation (Mt 5:38-45; Rom 12:14-21, I Thess. 5:15 cf. Mt 26:51f), which repudiates violence as a means of redressal.

Luther's fundamental understanding of the Church as *communio sanctorum* did provide an alternative consciousness to the people when the medieval Church usurped political power and became an instrument of oppression of the vulnerable. His reconstruction of the theology of the Church exhibits certain crucial traits that are helpful for our ongoing reflections on the Church in the contemporary Indian context: (a) it is rooted in the Scripture; (b) it is founded on the Church's faith in the truth and plenitude of the Trinity; (c) in his perception, the essential nature of the Church is the "communion of the faithful", which stands for loving, mutual and intimate relationship; (d) as such, ecclesia moves away from exclusion to embrace. In our attempt to reflect on the self-understanding of the Indian Church and its ongoing mission in the current Hindu nationalist milieu, our consciousness never became captive to a kind of a *reactive* ecclesiology. Rather our thoughts have been guarded by the Reformer's principle of the *unity of the opposites*, which is a fertile *proactive* theological principle that had potentially guided our thoughts towards construing the Church as a *perichoretic communion of the people of God.*

Notes

1 John D. Zizioulas, *Being as Communion: Studies in Personhood and the Church* (Crestwood, New York: St Vladimir's Seminary Press, 1997), p. 15.

2 A. C. Kannambirathinam, "Vidiyalai Ethirnōkki" ("In Anticipation of the Dawn"), in *Uzhaippin Uyarvum Manithanēya Mānpum,*

[*The Greatness of Hard Work and the Characteristics of Humaneness*], (Chennai: New Century Book House, 4th edition, 2006), p. 66.

3 Luther also added 'the office of the keys', the public ministry by call, public prayer and worship, and the public bearing of the cross. See Martin Luther, "On the Councils and the Church" (1539) *LW* 41, pp. 148-168; WA 50, pp. 509-524. For a different view on this issue, see Gerhard O. Forde, "The Word That Kills and Makes Alive" in Carl E. Braaten and Robert W. Jenson, eds., *Marks of the Body of Christ* (op. cit.).

4 In Luther's own words: "I know and am assured, by the grace of God, that I am more learned in the Scriptures than all the sophists and the papists". *LW* 40, p. 55; *WA* 15, p. 216. "[N]o one is bound to believe more than what is based in Scripture". *LW* 32, p. 96; *WA* 7, p. 453.

5 According to Luther, theology has essentially to do with the knowledge of God and the humans. Its twofold theme, therefore, is 'human guilt' and 'God's saving act in Christ'. "The proper subject of theology is man guilty of sin and condemned, and God the Justifier and Savior of man the sinner. Whatever is asked or discussed in theology outside this subject, is error and poison." *LW* 12, p. 310; *WA* 40, p. 327.

6 *Unity of the opposites* is a dialectical principle first proposed by the Milesian Philosophers of the 6th century BCE and their contemporary Heraclitus of Ephesus. See V. J. McGill and W. T. Parry, "The Unity of Opposites: A Dialectical Principle" *Science & Society*, Vol. 12, No. 4 (Fall 1948), p. 418 of 418-444.

7 For a cryptic view of this sort of construing the Church, see Leonardo Boff, *Ecclesiogenesis: The Base Communities Reinvent the Church*, Tr. by Robert Barr (Maryknoll, New York: Orbis Books, 1986); and Craig Van Gelder, *The Essence of the Church: A Community Created by the Spirit* (Grand Rapids, Michigan: Baker Books, 2002).

8 See Alasdair MacIntyre, *After Virtue: A Study in Moral Theory* (Notre Dame: University of Notre Dame Press, 1984), pp. 216ff.

9 Frank G. Kirkpatrick, *Community: A Trinity of Models* (Washington: Georgetown University Press, 1986). Much of the material in this section is drawn from this source.

10 See Thomas Hobbes, *Leviathan, Or the Matter, Form and Power of a Commonwealth Ecclesiastical and Civil*, ed. by Michael Oakeshott (New York: Collier Books, 1962).

11 See John Locke, *The Second Treatise of Government*, ed. with an introduction by Thomas P. Peardon (Indianapolis: Bobbs-Merrill, 1952).

12 Robert Nisbet, *The Social Philosophers: Community and Conflict in Western Thought* (New York: Washington Square Press, 1982), p. 26.
13 John Locke, *The Second Treatise of Government*, pp. 38-78.
14 Kirkpatrick, *Community*, pp. 24f. There are several other influential names that figure in this kind of theorizing: Jeremy Bentham (1748-1832) *A Fragment on Government*; James Mill (1773-1836) *An Essay on Government;* Adam Smith (1723-1790) *An Inquiry into the Nature and Causes of the Wealth of Nations*; and Jeans-Jacques Rousseau (1712-1778) *The Social Contract*. See Ibid., pp. 34-55.
15 Frank G. Kirkpatrick, "Toward a Metaphysic of Community" *Scottish Journal of Theology*, Vol. 38 (1985), pp. 565f.
16 Kirkpatrick, "Toward a Metaphysic of Community", p. 570.
17 Kirkpatrick, *Community*, pp. 67f.
18 Charles Taylor, *Hegel and Modern Society* (Cambridge: Cambridge University Press, 1979), pp. 85-87.
19 Charles Taylor, *Hegel and Modern Society*, p. 86.
20 M. Rader, *Marx's Interpretation of History*, Tr. M. Nocolaus (London: Penguin Books, 1973), pp. 57ff.
21 David McLellan, ed., *Karl Marx: Selected Writings* (Oxford: Oxford University Press, 1977), p. 115.
22 Kirkpatrick, *Community*, p. 94.
23 Kirkpatrick, *Community*, pp. 94-95.
24 Ever since Descartes, certain strands of philosophy came to appropriate reality in dichotomous terms – mind and matter, reason and emotion, and the natural and supernatural. Process metaphysics repudiated this dualism and attempted to view reality in an organic relationship. See Kirkpatrick, *Community*, p. 100. For a discussion on Whiteheadian and later Process thinking, see Christopher Duraisingh, "Science, Whitehead, and New Perspectives on Reality" *Bangalore Theological Forum*, Vol. IV, No. 1 (1972), pp. 31-54.
25 A. N. Whitehead, *Process and Reality: Essays in Cosmology* (New York: Free Press, 1978), p. 18.
26 A. N. Whitehead, *Process and Reality*, p. 209.
27 Christopher Duraisingh, "Science, Whitehead, and New Perspectives on Reality", p. 37.
28 A. N. Whitehead, *Process and Reality*, p. 110.
29 Victor Lowe, "Whitehead's Metaphysical System" in Delwin Brown, Ralph E. James, Jr., and Gene Reeves, eds., *Process Philosophy and Christian Thought* (Indianapolis: Bobbs-Merrill, 1971), p. 4.
30 Kirkpatrick, *Community*, p. 103.

31 A. N. Whitehead, *Process and Reality*, pp. 214f.
32 Kirkpatrick, *Community*, p. 111.
33 Stanley Hauerwas, *A Community of Character: Toward a Constructive Christian Social Ethics* (Notre Dame: University of Notre Dame Press, 1981), p. 80.
34 Martin Buber, *I and Thou*, Tr. by Ronald Gregor Smith (New York: Charles Scribner's Sons, 2nd edition, 1958). Normally it is taken for granted that the "I-Thou" model is a contribution from Martin Buber. But in fact it was first brought out by Ludwig Feuerbach. See his seminal work: *The Essence of Christianity* (New York: C. Blanchard, 1855), p. 208.
35 Kirkpatrick, *Community*, pp. 141-143.
36 See T.N. Madan, *Modern Myths, Locked Minds: Secularism and Fundamentalism in India* (Delhi: Oxford University Press, 1998).
37 A phrase borrowed from M. M. Thomas, "The Open Church" in Mathai Zachariah, ed., *The Church: A Peoples' Movement* (Nagpur: NCCI, 1975), p. 63.
38 M. M. Thomas, "The Open Church", pp. 63ff.
39 As caricatured by James P. Alter and Herbert Jai Singh, *The Church in Delhi* (Delhi: NCCI, 1961), p. 95.
40 See M. M. Thomas, "The Open Church", p. 63.
41 Volf argues that a "Post-confessional Christianity" is in the making wherein there is a phenomenal decline of rigid denominationalism. See Miroslav Volf, *After Our Likeness: The Church as the Image of the Trinity* (Grand Rapids: Wm B. Eerdmans, 1998), p. 19. Also see Robert Wuthnow, *The Restructuring of American Religion, Society and Faith* (Princeton: Princeton University Press, 1988), pp. 71-99.
42 This poses a real problem to identify Indian Christians as a "community". See Frederick S. Downs, "The Search for Integrative Principle" in Kanichikattil Francis, ed., *Church in Context: Essays in Honour of Mathias Mundadan CMI* (Bangalore: Dharmaram Publications, 1996), pp. 21-30. See also John C. B. Webster, "The Identity of the Indian Christians", pp. 56-71 in the above volume.
43 The term communalism in America, for instance, has a positive connotation, which invites people for "fellow feeling and to a rather cherishable attribute of good will and neighbourliness". See Dipanker Gupta, "Between Ethnicity and Communalism: The Significance of the Nation-State" in Ravinder Kaur, ed., *Religion, Violence and Political Mobilization in South Asia*, p. 79.
44 Dipanker Gupta, "Between Ethnicity and Communalism" , p. 79.

45 Hindutva invokes the ideology of 'Vedic Golden Age' in order to legitimize its claim of Hindu supremacy. Savarkar, *Six Glorious Epochs of Indian History*; and Dayananda Saraswati, *Rigvedadi Bhasya Bhumika (Introduction to the Commentary on the Vedas)* Tr. by G. Ram (Meerut: Bharath Prakasan, 1925).

46 John H. Leith, ed., *Creeds of the Churches* (Atlanta: John Knox Press, 1982), p. 33.

47 Avery Dulles, *Models of the Church* (New York: Image Books, 1978), p. 133.

48 Stanley J. Grenz, "Ecclesiology", p. 261. The Reformers, while accepting the essential marks of the Church, nevertheless, regarded that such an appeal could not solve the ecclesiological problem. For them, the description of the Church in terms of "one, holy, catholic and apostolic" did not delineate where in fact the true Church was to be found. Hence, they focused on two other rudiments: the Word and Sacraments, which they found to be true signs of the Church in its visible form. See Paul D. L. Avis, *The Church in the Theology of the Reformers* (Atlanta: John Knox Press, 1981), p. 8.

49 Stanley Hauerwas criticizes this tendency and argues that making Christianity into a set of beliefs is a strategy "to legitimate the false universalism of liberalism". See Stanley Hauerwas, *After Christendom: How the Church is to Behave if Freedom, Justice and a Christian Nation are Bad Ideas* (Nashville: Abingdon Press, 1991), pp. 15f.

50 Johannes A. Van der Van, *Ecclesiology in Context* (Grand Rapids, Michigan: Wm. B. Eerdmans, 1993).

51 James Thoppil, *Towards an Asian Ecclesiology*, p. 227.

52 George A. Lindbeck, *Nature of Doctrine: Religion and Theology in a Postliberal Age* (London: SPCK, 1984), pp. 15-39.

53 Stanley J. Grenz, 'Ecclesiology", pp. 260-264.

54 As Catherine Keller affirms, "Religion…activates connection. It 'ties together', binding up the wounds of breaking worlds. It is the bridging, bonding process at the heart of the things". See *From a Broken Web: Separation, Sexism and Self* (Boston: Beacon Press, 1986), p. 219. It is applicable to the Church also.

55 Christopher Duraisingh, "Contextual and Catholic: Conditions for Cross-Cultural Hermeneutics" *Anglican Theological Review*, Vol. 82, No. 4 (Fall 2000), p. 683 (679-701).

56 As quoted in Christopher Duraisingh, "Contextual and Catholic", p. 683 from Philip Potter, Report of the General Secretary, WCC Central Committee (Geneva, July/august 1977), Doc. 18, p. 9.

57 See Dennis M. Doyle, *Communion Ecclesiology: Visions and Versions* (Maryknoll, New York: Orbis Books, 2000); John D. Zizioulas, *Being as Communion*; Miroslav Volf, *After Our Likeness*; Ian T. Douglas, ed., *Waging Reconciliation*; Wilhelm M. Hermann, *The Communion of the Christian with God: Described on the Basis of Luther's Statements*, ed. by Robert T. Voelkel (Philadelphia: Fortress Press, 1971); Michael Welker, *What Happens in Holy Communion?* Tr. by John F. Hoffmeyer (Grand Rapids, Michigan: William B. Eerdmans, 2000); Letty M. Russell, *Church in the Round: Feminist Interpretation of the Church* (Louisville, Kentucky: John Knox Press, 1993) & Miroslav Volf and Michael Welker, eds., *God's Life in Trinity* (Minneapolis: Fortress Press, 2006).

58 Alexander Belopopsky, "Between Chaos and Kairos: Churches, Ecumenism and the World Council of Churches in Central and Eastern Europe 1989-2003" *The Ecumenical Review*, Vol. 56, No.1 (Jan 2004), pp. 77-83; Emilio Castro, *A Passion for Unity: Essays on Ecumenical Hopes and Challenges* (Geneva: World Council of Churches Publications, 1992); and Samuel Kobia, *Called to One Hope: A New Ecumenical Epoch* (Thiruvalla: CSS, 2006).

59 See John D. Zizioulas, *Being as Communion*. Here, the author brings to light the deep-rooted communion mode of discourse inherent in the early Church and Patristic writings. See also Dennis M. Doyle, *Communion Ecclesiology: Visions and Versions*, p. 1.

60 See his famous thesis: *simul iustus et peccator* (sinner and saint simultaneously) – an idea that is quite rampant in his thinking. See *WA* 56, p. 70, 272; *LCC* 15, p.127 / *WA* 57, p. 165; *LCC* 15, 127 / *LW* 27, pp. 230f; *WA* 2, pp. 496f / *LW* 32, p. 173; *WA* 8, p. 173. (See the expressions like: "Even though I am indeed a sinner yet I am not a sinner". "No Christian has sin, and all have sins".)

61 See Jurgen Moltmann, *The Trinity and the Kingdom of God: The Doctrine of God*, Tr. By Margaret Kohl from German (London: SCM Press, 1981), pp. 174-178.

62 Jean Vanier, *Community and Growth*, p.1.

63 Dennis M. Doyle, *Communion Ecclesiology*, p. 1.

64 David Clark, *Yes to Life* (London: Collins/Fount, 1987), p. 22.

65 Source: HT – TV, 06 March 2009.

66 See Christopher Duraisingh, "Encountering Difference in a Plural World", pp. 190-207.

67 John S. Dunne, *The Way of all the Earth: Experiments in Truth and Religion* (New York: Macmillan Publishing Company, 1972), pp. ix ff.

68 Dennis M. Doyle, *Communion Ecclesiology*, p. 5.

69 John Ford, "Koinonia and Roman Catholic Theology" *Ecumenical Trends*, Vol. 26, (1997), pp. 42ff.

70 John D. Zizioulas, *Being as Communion*, p. 224.

71 See Peter Gay, ed., *The Enlightenment: A Comprehensive Anthology*, p. 384.

72 See Gustavo Gutierrez, *A Theology of Liberation*, pp. 6-19.

73 See R. J. Bernstein, *The New Constellation: The Ethical-Political Horizons of Modernity/Postmodernity* (Cambridge: Cambridge University Press, 1991), pp. 14f.

74 See Paul Ricour, *Hermeneutics and Human Sciences: Essays on Language, Action and Interpretation* (Cambridge: Cambridge University Press, 1981), pp. 44f.

75 "Relationship or intimacy" is one of the major concerns that finds passionate expression in a number of recent studies. The fundamental human aspiration is to find a way of common human existence of mutual caring and not destruction. See Leroy S. Rouner, *To Be at Home: Christianity, Civil Religion and World Community* (op. cit.) and Lothar Bauerochse, *Learning to Live Together: Interchurch Partnerships as Ecumenical Communities of Learning* (Geneva: WCC Publications, 2001).

76 Leonardo Boff, *Trinity and Society*, Tr. Paul Burns (Maryknoll, New York: Orbis Books, 1988), p. 158.

77 As Craig Van Gelder understands, "the Church is both a social organization and a spiritual community". *The Essence of the Church*, p. 25. Here in this volume, Gelder uses the term "social" to refer to a "human community of persons in relationship with one another".

78 *Book of Concord,* p. 417; WA 30^{I}, p. 190; also see *LW* 35, pp. 52ff; *WA* 2, pp. 744ff. Cf. Hans Küng, *The Church*, pp. 3-39. Küng affirms a dual nature of the Church and his treatment serves as a brilliant introduction to this transition in ecclesiological discussions.

79 Paul C. McGlasson, *Invitation to Dogmatic Theology: A Canonical Approach* (Grand Rapids, Michigan: Brazos Press, 2006), p. 16.

80 For a discussion on the historical/theological root of the Trinity, see Robert Jenson, *The Triune Identity* (Philadelphia: Fortress Press, 1982).

81 John Macquarrie, *Principles of Christian Theology* (London: SCM Press, 6th print, 1986), pp. 190ff.

82 Robert W. Jenson, *Systematic Theology* Vol. I, pp. 44ff.

83 Luther appropriated the *Athanasian Creed* as "a protective symbol" of the *Apostles' Creed*, see "The Symbols or Creeds of the Christian Faith", *LW* 34, pp. 202-228; *WA* 50, pp. 262-285.

84 The creeds offer us the fundamental Trinitarian faith affirmation of the Christian Church. A brilliant exposition of the Trinity can be seen in the *Athanasian Creed*, a creedal statement composed during the early sixth century CE, probably by a disciple of St. Augustine (probably St. Caesarius of Arles). For the historical background of this creed, see J. N. D. Kelley, *The Athanasian Creed* (London: Adam & Charles Black, 1964), pp. 48f. See also Edgar C. S. Gibson, *The Three Creeds* (London, New York, Bombay, and Calcutta: Longmans, Green, And Co., 1909), pp. 181-279. See *Book of Concord*, "Smalcald Articles" (1536), articles 1 & 2, p. 262.

85 J. N. D. Kelley, *The Athanasian Creed*, pp. 17-20.

86 See the creed vv. 3-6.

87 Ibid., vv. 7-14. Obviously these two warnings are directed against two controversial teachings, namely, Sabellianism and Arianism. While the former confounded the three persons, i.e., confused them by affirming that the distinction between the three persons of the Trinity was merely one of character, and that they are personally to be identified, the latter split asunder the substance by its rejection of the *homoousios* of the Son. Hence v. 5 is directed against Sabellianism and v. 6 against Arianism. See Edgar C. S. Gibson, *The Three Creeds*, p. 212.

88 See the text vv. 21-24.

89 J. N.D. Kelley, *The Athanasian Creed*, pp. 75.

90 See the text vv. 25-27.

91 See St. Augustine, *De Trinitate*, 5: 6f.

92 See v. 23 of the Athanasian Creed.

93 St. Augustine, *De Trinitate*, 5:12.

94 Robert W. Jenson, *Systematic Theology* Vol. I, "The Pneumatological Problem", pp. 146-161.

95 Michael Buckley, *At the Origins of Modern Atheism* (New Havens: Yale University Press, 1987), pp. 71ff.

96 Lesslie Newbigin, "Trinity as Public Truth" in Kevin J. Vanhoozer, ed., *The Trinity in a Pluralistic Age: Theological Essays on Culture and Religion* (Grand Rapid, Michigan: Wm B. Eerdmans, 1997), pp. 1-8. Also see Jürgen Moltman, *The Trinity and the Kingdom of God* (London: SCM Press, 1981).

97 Lesslie Newbigin, "Trinity as Public Truth", pp. 5f.

98 Lesslie Newbigin, *Trinitarian Faith and Today's Mission* (Richmond: John Knox Press, 1963), pp. 9-31.
99 Carl E. Braaten, *No Other Gospel: Christianity among the World's Religions* (Minneapolis: Fortress Press, 1992), p. 109.
100 Quoted in Carl E. Braaten, *No Other Gospel*, p. 105 from Karl Rhaner, *The Trinity*, Tr. by Joseph Donceel (New York: Herder and Herder, 1970), pp. 10-11.
101 Quoted in Carl E. Braaten, *No Other Gospel*, p. 106.
102 Carl E. Braaten, *No Other Gospel*, pp. 108-109.
103 John Macquarrie, *Principles of Christian Theology*, p. 194.
104 Ambrose, *De spiritu sancto* I, pp. 159-160.
105 As Michael Ipgrave argues, Trinitarianism is conceivably a resource not only for Christians but also for the wider world. *Trinity and Inter Faith Dialogue: Plenitude and Plurality*, Religion and Discourse Series Vol. 14 (Bern: Peter Lang, 2003), p. 24.
106 "…for I have not spoken on my own, but the Father who sent me has himself given me a commandment about what to say and what to speak…What I speak, therefore, I speak just as the Father has told me" (John 12: 49-50). "Whoever has seen me has seen the Father…Do you not believe that I am in the Father and the Father is in me?...Believe me that I am in the Father and the Father is in me;…" (John 14:9-11). "And I will ask the Father, and he will give you another advocate, to be with you forever. This is the Spirit of truth…" (John 14:16-17)
107 See F. F. Bruce, *The Gospel of John: Introduction, Exposition and Notes* (London: Pickering Paperbacks, 1983), pp. 1-16; and Raymond E. Brown, *The Gospel according to John (I-XII)*, Vol. 1 (New York: Doubleday, 1966), pp. xli ff.
108 *Book of Concord*, p. 292.
109 See Paul Althaus, *The Theology of Martin Luther*, p. 199.
110 As Luther understands: "Scripture…cleverly proves that there are three persons and one God. For I would believe neither the writings of Augustine nor the teachers of the Church unless the New and the Old Testaments would clearly show this doctrine of the Trinity". As cited in Paul Althus, *The Theology of Martin Luther*, p. 199 from *WA* 39^{II}, p. 305.
111 Of course, women and feminist theologians take offense at the use of the term "Lord's Supper" because the term 'Lord' connotes the male, and hence, they find this as a tool to marginalize women. For a brief discussion, see Astrid Lobo Gajiwala, "The Passion of the Womb:

Women Re-living the Eucharist" in Francis Gonsalves, ed., *Body, Bread, Blood*, pp. 119-132. See also Monika Hellwig, *The Eucharist and the Hunger of the World* (London: Sheed & Ward, 1992).

112 Michael Welker, *What Happens in Holy Communion?* (op. cit.), pp. 2f.

113 Michael Welker, *What Happens in Holy Communion?*, p. 59.

114 See *Book of Concord*, p. 448.

115 For further discussion on the significance of the Eucharist, see Michael G. Lawler, *Symbol and Sacrament: A Contemporary Sacramental Theology* (New York: Paulist Press, 1987).

116 *LW* 35, p. 57f; *WA* 2, p. 747. Luther describes the Lord's Supper as the Sacrament of the community (*Gemeinde*) and affirms that, in the primitive Church, communion was the sign, which enabled the believers to recognize each other.

117 *LW* 35, 51; *WA* 2, p. 743.

118 *LW* 35, pp. 55-61; *WA* 2, pp. 745-750.

119 *LW* 22, p. 26; *WA* 47, p. 558.

120 *LW* 22, p. 26; *WA* 47, p. 559.

121 *LW* 37, p. 60; *WA* 23, p. 137.

122 *LW* 26, p. 95; *WA* 40^{I}, p. 175.

123 As quoted by Dennis M. Doyle, *Communion Ecclesiology*, p. 1.

124 Dennis M. Doyle, *Communion Ecclesiology*, p. 6.

125 Dennis M. Doyle, *Communion Ecclesiology*, p. 21.

126 Roman Catholicism emphasizes the sacramental reality of the Church, which of course is not absent in other modes of discourse on the Church. For a Roman Catholic understanding of ecclesia, See Edward Schillebeeckx, *Christ the Sacrament of Encounter with God*, Tr. Paul Barrett (New York: Sheed and Ward, 1963); and Karl Rhaner, *The Church and the Sacraments*, Tr. by W. J. O'Hara (Freiburg: Herder, 1963).

127 See *LW* 2, pp. 210ff; *WA* 42, pp. 474ff. A modern understanding of Babel and Pentecost in relation to communion ecclesiology can be found in the Roman Catholic theologian Jean-Marie Tillard, *Church of Churches: The Ecclesiology of Communion*, Tr. by R. C. De Peaux (Collegeville, MN: Liturgical Press, 1992). Of course, Tillard points to the fact that the historical critical approach does raise skepticisms about the authenticity of such an interpretation as, according to this school, it is most unlikely that the author of *Luke-Acts* had the story of Babel in his mind while composing the story of Pentecost (Ibid. pp. 6ff).

128 *LW* 2, p. 215; *WA* 42, pp. 413-414.
129 Jean-Marie Tillard, *Church of Churches*, pp. 93ff.
130 *LW* 37, p. 372; *WA* 26, p. 509.
131 Friedrich Schleiermacher, *The Christian Faith* (Edinburgh: T & T Clark, 1928.)
132 Dennis M. Doyle, *Communion Ecclesiology*, pp. 23-28.
133 Friedrich Schliermacher, *The Christian Faith*, pp. 358-369.
134 Friedrich Schleiermacher, *Christian Faith*, pp. 26-29, 62-70; 358-373. Also see Schleiermacher, *On Religion: Addresses in Response to Its Cultured Critics*, Tr. by Torrence N. Tice (Richmond: John Knox Press, 1969), pp. 127-129.
135 Friedrich Schliermacher, *The Christian Faith*, pp. 526f.
136 Friedrich Schliermacher, *The Christian Faith*, pp. 638-660.
137 See Miraslov Volf, *After Our Likeness: The Church as the Image of the Trinity* (op.cit.); Volf, "'The Trinity is Our Social Program': The Doctrine of the Trinity and the Shape of Our Social Engagement", *Modern Theology* Vol. 14 (July 1998), pp. 403-423; Volf, "Trinity, Unity, Primacy: On the Trinitarian Nature of Ecclesial Unity and Its Implications for the Question of Primacy" in James F. Puglisi, ed., *Petrine Ministry and the Unity of the Church* (Collegeville, MN: Liturgical Press, 1999), pp. 171-184.
138 Volf, "'The Trinity is Our Social Program', pp. 405ff.
139 As quoted by D. M. Doyle, *Communion Ecclesiology*, p. 165 from John Quinn, "The Exercise of the Primacy and the Costly Call to Unity" in Phyllis Zagano and Terrence W. Tilley, ed., *The Exercise of the Primacy: Continuing Dialogue* (New York: Crossroad, 1998), pp. 1-28 at p. 25.
140 Miraslov Volf, *After Our Likeness: The Church as the Image of the Trinity*, pp. 133-134.
141 One of the aspects of communion ecclesiology is to posit ecclesia as the "communion of Christian communities". See Evelyn Montario, SC, *Church and Culture: Communion in Pluralism* (Delhi: ISPCK, 2004), pp. 14-31.
142 Lesslie Newbigin, "The Trinity as Public Truth", in *The Trinity in a Pluralistic Age*, p. 1.
143 *LW* 2, p. 215; *WA* 42, pp. 413-414.
144 M. M. Thomas, "The Church – The Fellowship of the Baptized and the Unbaptised", in *The Church's Mission and Post-Modern Humanism* (op. cit.), pp. 155-161. See also the interview with Karanjia in *Light of Life*, Feb 1995: "Face to Face", pp. 31-34.
145 Dennis M. Doyle, *Communion Ecclesiology*, p. 13.

146 *LW* 13, p. 90; *WA* 40^{III}, p. 505.

147 Martin E. Marty, *The Public Church: Mainline-Evangelical-Catholic* (NY: Crossroad, 1981), p. ix.

148 *Book of Concord*, p. 417; WA 30^{I}, p. 190.

149 *LW* 31, p. 190; *WA* 1, p. 593.

150 *LW* 35, p. 70; *WA* 2, p. 756.

151 See P. Victor Premsagar, "The Church: A Peoples' Movement (I), pp. 102-111 & M. J. Joseph, "The Church: A Peoples' Movement (II), pp. 112-119 in Mathai Zachariah, ed., *The Church: A Peoples' Movement* (Nagpur: NCCI, 1975). Also see Leonardo Boff, *Ecclesiogenesis*; and Dale T. Irvin and Scott W. Sunquist, *History of the World Christian movement*, Vol. I *Earliest Christianity to 1453.*

152 *LW* 24, p. 87; *WA* 45, p. 540.

153 Roger E. Hedlund, ed., *Christianity is Indian: The Emergence of an Indigenous Community* (Delhi: MIIS & ISPCK, 2004).

154 Ibid., p. xv.

155 Letty M. Russell, *Church in the Round: Feminist Interpretation of the Church.*

156 With reference to Jn. 15:13-15 & Lk. 7:34, there are scholars who understand this *loving relationship* in terms of *friendship* and as a means to resistance. To have an understanding of the depth of friendship and its relevance, see Jürgen Moltmann, *The Church in the Power of the Spirit*, pp. 156-204; Eberhard Bethge, *Friendship and Resistance: Essays on Dietrich Bonheoffer* (Geneva: WCC/Wm B. Erdmans, 1995); and Deryck Sherrifs, *The Friendship of the Lord* (Carlisle, Cumburia, UK: Paternoster Press, 1996).

157 See Carl E. Braaten, *No Other Gospel*, p. 115.

158 As quoted by Carl E. Braaten, *No Other Gospel*, pp. 115-116.

159 Carl E. Braaten, *No Other Gospel*, p. 116.

160 Robert W. Jenson, *The Triune Identity* (Philadelphia: Fortress Press, 1982), p. 29.

161 Carl E. Braaten, *No Other Gospel*, pp. 116-117.

162 H. Lindgren, *An Introduction to Social Psychology* (New York: John Wiley and Sons, 1969), p. 163.

163 Amartya Sen, *Identity and Violence*, p. xii.

164 See Christopher Duraisingh, "Encountering Difference", pp. 187ff.

165 As quoted in *What Luther Says: An Anthology* Vol. II, Compiled by Ewald M. Plass (Saint Louis, Missouri: Concordia Publishing House, 2nd Print, 1972), p. 667.

166 See Paul Tillich, *A History of Christian Thought*, pp. 227ff. Luther countered this position with his understanding of 'justification', which imbued a counter consciousness that had a potential appeal among the common people as it engendered a new meaning to be truly human. Wilhelm Hermann argues that the Protestant Church, even though it loyally voices justification, has, in fact, long since betrayed the Reformer's insight. See Robert T. Voelkel, "Introduction" in Wilhelm Hermann, *The Communion of the Christian with God*, ed. by R.T. Voelkel (Philadelphia: Fortress Press, 1971), p. xxx.

167 George Santayana, *The Life of Reason* (New York: Charles Scribner's Sons, 1906), p. 284.

168 Wolfhart Pannenberg, *The Church*, Tr. Keith Crim (Philadelphia: Westminster Press, 1983), pp. 10ff.

169 Paul C. McGlasson, *Invitation to Dogmatic Theology*, p. 148.

170 For brief discussion on the Biblical doctrines of 'adoption' and 'inheritance', see Henry Clarence Thiessen, *Lectures in Systematic Theology* (Grand Rapids, Michigan: Wm B. Eerdmans, 2006, First published 1949), pp. 282-286.

171 C. F. Walther, "Bringing Souls to Christ: Every Christian's Desire and Duty" *Missio Apostolica*, Vol. VI, No. 1, Issue No. 11 (May 1998), pp. 6-12 at 6f.

172 Stanley Hauerwas, *A Community of Character: Towards a Constructive Christian Social Ethic* (Notre Dame: University of Notre Dame Press, 1981), p. 2.

173 L. S. Thornton, *The Common Life in the Body of Christ* (London: Dacre Press, 1946), p. 6.

174 As quoted by Frank G. Kirkpatrick, *Community*, p. 228 from Ronaldo Muñoz, "Ecclesiology in Latin America" in Sergio Torres and John Eagleson, eds., *The Challenge of Basic Christian Communities* – Papers from the International Ecumenical Congress of Theology (Feb. 20-March 02, 1980), Sao Paulo, Brazil (Maryknoll, New York: Orbis Books, 1981), p. 156.

175 See Luther's explanation to the second article of the *Apostle's Creed* in his *Small* and *Large Catechism* in *Book of Concord*, pp. 345 & 413ff.

176 *LW* 36, p. 177; *WA* 8, p. 519. In this and other similar texts, Luther uses 'reconciliatory or redemptive' language interchangeably: "God is reconciled" and "we are reconciled with God".

177 *LW* 26, p.282; *WA* 40^{I}, p. 440.

178 *LW* 31, pp. 189 ff, 351f; *WA* 1, p. 593.

179 The Church's mission, both local and global, clearly points to the fact that despite all the weaknesses of the Church, God has been using the Church as a vital instrument of change. The Reformation movement, for instance, had not only engendered the three strands of confessional movements: Protestant Reformation (Lutheran, Reformed and Anglican Traditions), the Radical Reformation (Anabaptists, Spiritualists and Rationalists), and the Catholic Reformation, but also played a crucial role in determining the political and religious shape of Western Europe and its colonies. David V. N. Bagchi, "Reformation" in Trevor A. Hart et al., eds., *A Dictionary of Historical Theology*, pp. 462-466 Cf. Robert Schreiter, *The New Catholicity: Theology Between the Global and the Local* (Maryknoll, New York: Orbis Books, 1997), pp. 122-127.

180 The violence in Kandhamal, Orissa, is an important indicator of this trend. Unfortunately, a section of the media took a partisan attitude, which insinuated the idea that the "widespread religious conversions" taking place in Orissa as the "root-cause" for the violence. See the editorial "Dark portents in Orissa" *The New Indian Express* (27 August 2008), p. 10. Such misinformation campaign obscures the ground realities in Orissa – the utter poverty and the caste structure that never allow any space for the poor to climb the economic ladder, the growing intolerance on the part of the extremist wing of Hindu religion, and the "soft" attitude of the State Government (in which the BJP was a partner) towards the violent agitators. In this whole drama, conversion has become a pretext and the killing of the swami has been interpreted as the provocation. The Church is almost left on its own to stage demonstrations across the country to register its voice of protest against such organized violence. There are also attempts to curtail this freedom of peaceful protest, which is made clear from the BJP Government's decision to send 'show cause notices' to more than 2000 Christian schools and colleges across Karnataka that remained closed on 29 August 2008 in protest against the attacks on Christians in Orissa. See *The New Indian Express* (30 August 2008), p. 3.

181 See, for instance, the following works: G. Jones, *Embodying Forgiveness: A Theological Analysis* (Grand Rapid, Michigan: Wm B. Eerdmans, 1995); Miraslov Volf, *Exclusion and Embrace: A Theological Exploration of Identity, Otherness, and Reconciliation* (Nashville: Abingdon Press, 1996); Rowan Williams, *The Truce of God* (London: Fount, 1983); and W. Wink, *When the Powers Fall: Reconciliation in the Healing of Nations* (Minneapolis:, Fortress Press, 1998).

182 Timothy Gorringe, *God's Just Vengeance: Crime, Violence and the Rhetoric of Salvation* (Cambridge, UK: Cambridge University Press, 1996), p. 263.

183 See Miraslov Volf, *Exclusion and Embrace.* In this volume, Volf urges the priority of reconciliation over liberation, which closely corresponds with what Carl E. Bratten advocates, which we noted earlier.

184 Miraslov Volf, *Exclusion and Embrace*, p. 109.

185 Miraslov Volf, *Exclusion and Embrace*, p. 116.

186 Mark Juergensmeyer, *Terror in the Mind of God: The Global Rise of Religious Violence* (Delhi: Oxford University Press, 2nd Impression, 2002), p. 5

187 To understand my own position on the issue of Religion-State interface, see R. Sahayadhas, "Religion-State Relationship: Significance of a Middle-Path in Contemporary India" *Bangalore Theological Forum*, Vol. XLIII, No. 1 (June 2011), pp. 55-82.

188 See Ethelbert Stauffer, *Christ and the* Caesars, Tr. K. R. Gregor Smith (London: SCM Press, 1955) & Edward Gibbon, *The Decline and Fall of Roman Empire* Vol. 1 (New York: The Modern Library, n.d.).

189 *Render Unto Caesar…and Unto God*, p. 7.

190 To understand the mutual condemnations within Christianity, see the following the texts: H. George Anderson et al. eds., *Lutherans and Catholics in Dialogue*, Vol. VII "Justification by Faith" (Minneapolis: Augsburg Publishing House, 1985); Karl Lehmann and Wolfhart Pannenberg, eds., *The Condemnations of the Reformation Era, Do They Still Divide?* (Minneapolis: Augsburg Publishing House, 1989); and George A. Lindbeck and Vilmos Vajta, *The Role of the Augsburg Confession: Catholic and Lutheran Views* (Philadelphia: Fortress Press, 1982).

Chapter Seven

CONCLUSION

Church Amidst Intransigent Hindu Nationalist Discourse

Hindutva is alive, active and waiting for the next opportunity to enunciate itself as the strongest political power in the country. In December 2012, I stayed at Kottayam, Kerala, for three days in connection with a pedagogical seminar. Kottayam is one of the strong holds of Christianity in south India, especially with its culture being influenced by a strong presence of Syrian Christians. While travelling in Kottayam, I noticed a poster which read: "*Hindutvam Bhārathathintre Ātmāvu*" (Hindutva is the soul of India). Hindutva decks itself up with newer meanings in tune with the emergent discourses in the public domain. A very recent example is the interpretation that in India "Hindutva is the 'true synonym' for secularism and is liberal as it embraces all other religions."[1] It is a re-echo of what L. K. Advani had hinted in *The Times of India* (20 April 2010) that Hindutva and secularism were the same. This new trend is indicative of a major new shift in the Hindutva discourse, i.e., a shift from its criticism of Indian secularism as "pseudo secularism" to an identification of Hindutva as secularism.

It appears that the 'secular' forces in contemporary Indian politics are being weakened by both actual and perceptional scandals of corruption and nepotism. It would pave the way for the reinforcement of Hindu nationalist politics as a dominant and decisive force in the public sphere. One can also discern new trajectories occurring within Hindutva that would easily thrust Hindutva into the *inclusive* bogey with the claim that Hindutva is inclusive of 'most' religions. Whether the Hindutva brand of inclusivism is a truly unconditional inclusivism is a critically important issue because the Church of Christ, I believe, would be relentless in its resistance to Hindutva's homogenising drive. Therefore the signs are that the Church might continue to be an 'other' and an 'outsider' to be ostracized in Hindutva's perception.[2] These are indications and also ominous signs that the days ahead are going to be challenging for Indian secular politics and also for the minority Christians. The future of the life and mission of the Indian Church in this changing milieu is contingent on the promise of the Gospel of Jesus Christ, which not only empowers the Church to face these challenges, but also offers credible signposts for the Christians to move into the unknown and uncertain future with confidence and courage.

Church as the *Perichoretic Communion:* Promise of the Gospel

I believe that the image of the Church as the *perichoretic communion of the people of God* based on the perichoretic intimacy of the Trinity, which we have reconstructed through our critical interaction with Luther's thoughts, has its own inner strength to witness to the Gospel of Jesus Christ in our context. Klaus Nürnberger identifies two "experiential components" in Luther's theology that are vitally important in any context: (i) "the actual experience of life in its exhilarating richness and its disconcerting ambiguity"; and (ii) the reassurance that "What ultimately carries our life forward is not pitted against us but in our favour".[3] What he affirms here is that, having been reassured of the divine favour in extreme conditions of adversity, "we are invited to accept the gifts of reality with a joyful heart and raise a stubborn protest against the incongruencies and predicaments we face in reality".[4] Obviously, this study has been done from within the crisis situation created by Hindutva and it lends a definite voice of protest against the incongruencies of Hindu nationalism.

Luther's thoughts on the Church, especially the way he worked them out from within his central theological principle of *unity of the opposites* or *distinction and integration*, are far more sensible to our living context because the principle of the unity of the opposites forms the core of the Christian Gospel and hence, also of Christian theology irrespective of the form or mode it assumes in any context. The twin effects of this fertile theological principle, derived directly from the Gospel, are notable here.

First, it was an authentic theological principle that provided Luther with necessary tools and even spur to critique the existent structures of the Church and society; and it has the same effect today in our own context when Hindutva is relentless in construing reality in oppositional terms and benchmarking people as *insiders* and *outsiders*. For, I believe that the future of the world is contingent on casting the variegated and even opposing forces (both at the local and global level) *across* each other and *not against* each other. The Church of Christ has a critically important role to play in this mission of putting peoples, communities, cultures, and even civilizations across each other. This is my passionate approach throughout this study and even when distinctions were made between different particularities, they were not intended to lock up and confine the individual entities within their own independent domains; rather to unite them with all that make them different. In other words, what we urgently require is a new hermeneutic of *nearness* over against the predominant human tendency of *distancing* from or *setting-at-a-distance* of the 'other'. Here, we need to take cognizance of the fact that the tendency to distance dangerously pitches humans, groups, communities, and civilizations irreconcilably against each other. *The second* effect of this theological principle is its ability to reassure the people of God who live in the midst of acutely adverse situations, like the Christian community in India, about the *perichoretic intimacy* of the Divine that embraces even the infidels and most ungodly. I think it was this principle that provided the nascent Church the assurance of God's initiative to end hostility and enhance life, life in all its fullness; and the same principle is capable of providing a new consciousness to the Indian Christians to affirm their identity as *Christians* and continue their ministry of healing and reconciliation amidst the intransigent Hindu nationalist discourse. It empowers the faith community to stand in protest against all forces that perpetuate hatred and resist all tendencies to pitch people and communities against each other. It is from this vantage point that I would like to view the issue of religion-state interface in contemporary India

Religion-State Interface Today

The Church and the state of Luther's time were so confounded that the Church with relative ease usurped temporal powers for its advantage, leading to a disastrous trend of moral and spiritual decadence and the exploitation of the vulnerable. Further, the inert and hierarchically ordered Church structure with higher and lower humans in accordance with the moral/spiritual standing of the members had serious consequences to human existence. There was a general tendency to elevate the priestly class to a higher status than the ordinary believers due to their moral/spiritual achievements. The Church was also a powerful institution that could wield its enormous powers, both on the religious and temporal affairs across its boundaries. In such a situation, Luther was able to glean a decisive theological principle – two kingdom principle – in order to critique and challenge his own Church.

I believe that we require this effect of the Christian Gospel in our public domain today, for we live in a similar situation in India now. The Hindutva forces are relentless in their attempt to capture political power through the instrumentation of the dominant religion. We have already noted that Hindu nationalism is not built on the platform of social justice but on the well being of the Hindu elites. It implies that if Hindutva captures political power it would aggravate the crisis of identity and meaning of the differently 'others' and the misery of the weak and the vulnerable, for it will continue to promote the interest of the elite-led-Hindu-nation putting the weak and the vulnerable (including the distinctively different minorities) under enormous pressure. Incidentally, when the Church became politically powerful and arbitrary, there was strong resentment and resistance from within the Church itself as exemplified by the Reformation movement. However, the emergence of such an organised protest from within Hinduism is most unlikely even if Hindutva turns out to be arbitrary and authoritarian. This was made clear when the innocent Christians were brutalised in Kandhamal and the Churches were attacked in Karnataka. It impels us to look for an alternative

Hindutva's aggressive politics of fusing the dominant religion with the secular state.

Possibility of a Middle Third Way

Thus, in the context of Hindutva's overt and even aggressive discourse on confounding religion and state, especially within the doctrines of nationalism and patriotism by placing the nation before the self, I am more and more inclined to re-signify the Reformer's conception of religion and state as two realms of God's activity (two-kingdom theory). Of course, I would immediately hasten to add that this attempt is not to divorce or separate them, as often misunderstood and wrongly applied by some of the later Lutherans, rather to clearly understand their proper limits and to make them work for the welfare of the people. It would provide a sure middle third way to negotiate the current tensed situation of the Indian public domain – a tension between homogeneity and heterogeneity – and proffer a veritable counter consciousness to the people to stand firm against any ideology that would become detrimental to the freedom of human faith and life. Undeniably, this is a reliable insight the Reformer re-discovered from his intense study of the Scripture and re-inscribed in his reconstruction of the theology of the Church. It was his concerted and self-conscious effort to drive home the vital point that it is the people of God who constitute the Church, and not the structures.

Luther's lived experience of the crisis situation, both within the Church and society, became a fertile ground of theological reasoning in which he came to view reality in *dialectical* terms over against the *oppositional* conception of reality, which was a predominant trend during his time. Luther's was a strong enough theological gesture to make clear distinctions between the variegated categories he encountered, not to divorce them into separate or autonomous domains for self-perpetuation, but to affirm genuine differences as typical of those entities and to embrace them to be in intimate relationship, for it is the way God deals with God's creation. Ecclesia, in any context, must represent this mode of construing reality as it is capable of providing the basic theological orientation and existential courage to the faith communities when they face adverse situations today. Of course, Hindutva is also involved in an exercise of *distinction* **or** *integration*. It is a kind of an *either-or* discourse, i.e., it ***either*** makes distinctions to confine or lock up particular entities within their own realms, so that it could easily identify and ostracize or annihilate those particularities intending to be different ***or*** it integrates different particularities into its construal of a Hindu nation by erasing the differences. It is in this milieu we need to appreciate the relevance of perceiving reality dialectically, especially from within the principle of the *unity of the opposites*, for it turns out to be a firm, conscious and active protest against the rigid, homogenizing, ascriptive and reactionary discourse of Hindutva. And I am sure the image of ecclesia as the *perichoretic* communion of the people of God becomes more sensible as we negotiate the intransigent Hindu nationalist discourse.

Significance of the *Perichoretic* Communion

Perichoretic intimacy is rooted in the communion of the persons of the Trinity with their fundamental characteristics of consubstantiality, co-equality and coeternity, and harmony of will and purpose. This truth and plenitude of the divine reality finds its concrete expression in the Christ event, which represents God's unconditional acceptance of the otherwise unacceptable humans, i.e., it declares that in Jesus Christ God reconciles the world to God's self without weighing its merits. It has opened up a new and reliable way for us humans to be in (*perichoretic*) communion with God, irrespective of our moral/spiritual/social accomplishments. In turn, it is an exhortation to all those who came to experience this *perichoretic* intimacy with the Divine in Christ to forge this *perichoretic* communion across boundaries by embracing 'others', even those who are unacceptable. It is a new lifestyle that represents and points to the new quality of life of freedom and dignity God endows to every person. The most significant aspect of this sort of ecclesial speech is its power and propensity to critique the asymmetric power relations that are typical of contemporary religious and social institutions.

It entails that we humans find our identity not in isolation as individuals but as human collectives with a commitment to live responsibly as a *perichoretic* communion of the people of God created by the Spirit, continuously nourished by Divine graces such as the Word and Sacraments. Further, it suggests that we become mature sons and daughters of God to be God's representatives on earth to continue the ministry of building communion across boundaries, especially in contexts of brokenness, meaninglessness, fragmentation, mutual hatred, and hostility. Needless to say that it is in the spirit of genuine *perichoretic* intimacy that we can live in peace and harmony, and in this process, the Church, as God's communion of the faithful, fully participates in God's creative authority, redemptive concern, and holistic vision for the world. All these are possible because of the fact that the Gospel of Christ engenders equality and human dignity to all irrespective of their social standing. It implies that no one is a slave to the structures; rather structures and those who are placed in authority are valued only insofar as they serve, empower, and enhance the lives of others. This is down to earth and practical theology and never an abstract, detached or speculative theology. Our Churches, our society and politics need to re-discover this propensity of the Gospel, for which Luther pointed the way.

A key feature of the Reformer's theological articulations is his most creative way of engaging with traditional Christian doctrinal constructions in his practical and down to earth approach to theology. In his reform process it turned out to be a successful venture. Instances are numerous: his contextualization of the doctrine of *justification*; his re-interpretation of the doctrine of the *priesthood of all believers*, locating it within the ambit of servanthood based on the model of Christ; the idea of equality he tried to incorporate into the otherwise inert office of the ministry of Roman Catholicism through his 'representative' language; his understanding of the word of God in terms of Law and Gospel; and his re-construction of the spiritual and temporal as two realms of God's activity. Luther's reconstruction of these and other dogmatic constructions of the Church unmistakably points to the fact that Christian theologians worth the salt must necessarily engage with the dogmatic constructions. Of course, I would add a caution that this endeavour is not to perpetuate a kind of *dogmatism* but to create an attitude to be critically rooted in the dogmatic/doctrinal constructions of the Church. In this sense, this study invites readers, especially those who denounce Church doctrines as irrelevant, to take a relook at those vital teachings of the Church. It is critically important when we negotiate the tough terrains of antagonism, so that we can be reassured with these vital resources to re-construe our Christian (human) existence within the ambit of the *perichoretic* intimacy of the Divine.

Hindutva avowedly proposes to enunciate traditional Hinduism as the only way of life for all those who intend to be part of this nation and those who refuse to subscribe to this arbitrary, authoritarian, and totalizing authority of Hindu religion cannot find a rightful place in this nation. It works with the principle of "nation first and self next"; it repudiates the principle of "unity in diversity" and expends its energy to find "unity in uniformity or homogeneity", undermining the pluralistic texture of India. The perichoretic communion ecclesiology in this precarious milieu undercuts Hindutva's ascriptive mode of discourse that is floated towards re-construing a totalitarian Hindu nation, demanding the citizens to place the nation before the self. It has been acknowledged that the Reformer's interpretation of the Gospel penetrated deep into the traditional discourses, which had placed their exorbitant emphases on the structures submerging the true human faces under those inert structures. In other words, structures stood as determinative factors of human existence, making humans captive to those monstrous structures. Today, it becomes an urgent need to retrieve 'people of God' from those structures because true relationship of intimacy and harmony are possible only in and through the *perichoretic* communion of the people, not in and through the structures. Truly, our construal of ecclesia as *perichoretic communion* engenders an authentically new voice in contradistinction to the dominant voice of Hindutva. It is an ecclesiology that always seeks for the 'other' to embrace and never attempts to exclude or annihilate the 'other'. It is built on a set of relationships, inspired by the *perichoretic* communion of the Trinity. Here I would like to reaffirm that amidst the unprecedented troubles and suffering perpetrated by the Hindutva brigades, the Church gets revitalized to affirm itself as a *perichoretic* communion of the people of God vested with the mission of building relationships across boundaries in a world that exhibits ominous signs of self-destruction due to mutual hatred and hostility. In this task, the Church of Christ stands as a "credible signpost" that points to the possibility of a truly humane communion amidst all that attempts to divide, fragment and destroy.[5]

As Hindutva is relentless in its strategies to sanitize India of those who resist its project of re-construing India as an exclusively *Hindu Rashtra* based solely on Brahminic Hinduism;[6] as Hindutva moves ahead with unflinching determination to obliterate the pluralistic texture of India in order to lump the different civilizations into one single ascriptive mould of Hindu civilization through a kind of re-civilizationlism, i.e., its meticulous endeavours to transform the multi-civilisational texture of India into a uni-civilisational ambience; and as we are given to encounter Hindutva's insidious discourse on reality in oppositional terms, I have attempted to show that a *perichoretic communion ecclesiology*, which is a fundamental feature of the Reformer's thought on the Church, is a viable and relevant mode of discourse on the Church because it is the basic ecclesiology, which understands Church as having been built on a set of mutual relationships, and Church's mission as building *perichoretic* relationships across boundaries.

While defining a Hindu, V. D. Savarkar cleverly drew a sharp dividing line between those who have the right to be *in* and those who forfeit their right and must be *out* of India.[7] Two important outcomes of such an innovative description merit our attention here: (i) a renewed vigour to unify or consolidate Hindus transcending the caste distinctions; and (ii) bitter hatred and enmity towards those who are adjudged to be out.[8] While the former is engaged in an exercise of assimilation of differences of caste, culture, ethnicity, and religion by lumping all these variegated categories into a single ascriptive mould, the latter provides the necessary legitimation for the Hindutva brigades to assume the role of self-styled 'cultural policing'[9] of those who prefer to be different. Therefore, it is not difficult to understand that when Hindutva seeks to let loose violence against Christians, it is the anger over Christians' determination to be different that invites the wrath of the Hindutva warriors. The important point here is that this is but an introverted, inward looking, and self-styled interpretation of Hindu religion for narrow political gains – a trend that esentialises the self and polarises communities and pitches people against each other with rigidly erected boundaries around its own construal of the nation. Conversely, our construal of ecclesia as the *perichoretic communion* of the people of God transcends this mode of narrowly particularised, essentialised and rigidified discourse on reality. It views reality from the vantage point of loving relationship – relationship with God, within the Church, with other people and with the world. It is a *perichoretic* relationship that springs forth from the Trinitarian foundation of the Church and inspired by the intimacy *par excellence*, which is characteristic of the Trinitarian communion of the Divine. Therefore, the *perichoretic* communion is an ecclesial reality, 'an image of the way in which God exists'.[10]

As the Indian Church negotiates the Hindu nationalist situation, perhaps its most aggressive form in the contemporary times, we need to bear in mind some of the emergent concerns for our further reflection on the Church. The ideological substance of Hindutva has virtually disseminated into almost all facets of Indian life. Even though there are opinions today, which maintain that, within the Indian polity, the Church and the secular forces are on the one side and the BJP on the other,[11] and even though there is some amount of truth in it, the tragic reality is that the religious minorities, especially Christians, and secular forces are disunited and their voice is divided. Kuruvachira is right in his observations that (a) there is a general "perception gap" among many Indians as they fail to realize that they are being encircled by a totalitarian ideology and if it is not resisted, then, there is no way they can escape their impending colonisation by this ideology; and (b) India requires another "independence movement in order to restore its secular credibility".[12] The emergence of UPA as a majority coalition (consisting of a number of secular minded political parties) after the 2009 General elections did provide us with some glimpses of hope that secularism still have the public acceptance in India. But, then, the critical question before us is: how long can such political maneuverings resist the strong political currents of Hindutva? The reason is that after three years in governance, the UPA appears to be weakened owing to various reasons. The Church must be alert to these new developments.

Church in the Public Domain

The life and mission of the Indian Church, I believe, is vitally important at this juncture of the troubled times. A more qualitative and relevant manifestation of the life and public witness of the Church would be more effective in the contemporary context of Hindu nationalism in India. It is so because the Church is the sign and instrument of the new life God had engendered to the entire humanity in Jesus Christ. It is a life of loving relationship and not hostility; it is a life of mutual acceptance and embrace and not exclusion or annihilation; and it is a life that proffers a "credible sign" that a truly human communion is still possible in the midst of all that divides us. Ecclesiology here implies the twin tasks: arriving at a self-understanding of the nature and function of the Church in the given context and empowering the Church to self-consciously and critically negotiate the religiously charged political currents of India; and engaging in its mission of proclaiming the sanctity and fullness of life for all.

I have pointed out various models of religion (Church)-state interface that had been attempted in the past. There were instances in which the religion was ruling the state and, in our times, we come across nations follow (Islamic) theocracy. Hindu nationalism is certainly the latest one that strives to enunciate itself as a theocratic state (though not overtly). It has to be noted that in most cases of theocratic rules or religiously ruled states, it is the religious extremists who dominate and worsen the miseries of humanity. Hindu nationalism is going to be no different if it is catapulted to power with absolute majority.[13] It would be helpful here to highlight the way the Reformer understood the Church-State relationship, which had close semblance to that of the early Church, especially when the Church was constantly targeted with utter hostility and scorn. In the midst of acute hostility and persecution, the early communion of believers adopted a policy of denial of the ways of the world and to proclaim the Gospel of God's redeeming acceptance of humanity in Christ. There were three principles with which the early Church faced the hostile situation: (a) denial of the (distorted) ways of the world and bearing the cross in order to follow Christ (Rom. 12:2;

Mark 8:34); (b) non-violent resistance to hostility and yet active engagement in mission (Acts 5:40-42); and (c) active involvement in the socio-political life without aspiring for temporal power (Mt. 22:21; John 18:36f).

This particularly Christian attitude was adopted self-consciously for theological and/or spiritual reasons. *First*, there was an urgency among the early believers to proclaim the Gospel 'to the end of the earth' before the imminent Parousia when all that was worldly would be transformed towards the reign of Christ. Therefore the predominant concern was not to get entangled in this world of death and decay. *Second*, Jesus himself reversed and reconstructed the retaliatory law into a law of love – love of God and love of neighbour as one's self. *Third*, their Master's voice that 'his kingdom was not from this world' might have served as a deterrent to any aspiration for political power. Therefore, it can be iterated that the Christian consciousness was constituted not by retaliatory ethics but by love ethics, which their master had so passionately taught them (John 14-17). To put it differently, it was an ethics that never annihilates, ostracizes or excludes the 'other'; rather always embraces the other in a spirit of loving relationship for which Jesus Christ has shown the way. These theological factors are crucial for our understanding of the early Christian attitude towards the temporal authority and for our own reflections on religion-state relationship today.

It raises an important question as to: How are we going to deal with Hindutva's unflinching efforts and struggles to wrap up an unchallengeable political power? The issue of religion-state relationship, thus, cannot be solved with a simple *either-or* answer due to its complexity. It is our responsibility to wrestle with the issue in our reflections on the Church. There is a fundamental principle that is inherent in Luther's two-kingdom theory, i.e., 'setting religion at a distance' from temporal authority. To put it in contemporary terms, the idea of 'keeping religion away from politics' is in the air for quite some time in India. Theoretically speaking, Church (or religion) is bestowed with the necessary means to redeem 'power' from its present captivity under the dominant. However, it is apt to ask here whether any religious institution in the world has transcended the lure of power. The answer is not very encouraging. I believe that it is this aspect that drove the teachers of the past to advocate what I call a 'self-restraint' involvement of the Church in politics. Certainly, the above positions do not suggest a political non-intervention or asceticism for the Church (and other religions as well). Rather, they advocate that while playing an active role in politics, religion must refrain from usurping secular or temporal power, basically because of the notion that power corrupts. Contemporary Hindu nationalism proves this apprehension beyond doubt, because it hinges on the essentialisation of Vedic Hindu tenets. The best course for religion in relation to state politics, especially in a multi-civilisational context with multiple faith persuasions in the public domain, is to render a critical voice towards just governance with the power of the spiritual resources.

India is a secular democratic nation and its true beauty is the co-existence of diverse categories as one nation. If secular democracy is a best-preferred mode of governance in world politics, India, despite all its failures, is the best product of democratic politics the world over, because it is the largest and culturally most diversified nation state to take democracy seriously in the modern world. Is secular democracy contingent on a dominant, elite, educated middle class? Or is it a global human possibility even among illiterate, poor, agrarian village folks? The Indian experiment and experience tell the world that it is a human possibility irrespective of human social standing. Therefore, if secular democracy succeeds in India against all odds, it would be a test case for the rest of the world to emulate. After analyzing various democracies of the world, L. S. Rouner opines, "If it [the Indian experiment] succeeds, there will be evidence that it is possible for people of radically diverse religious and cultural backgrounds to live together in the minimal harmony necessary for a world community. If it does not succeed, there will be major additional evidence for what we always suspected: that the instinct for hate is deeper in us than the instinct of harmony; and that the prospect for human cooperation in a world community is not good".[14] It points to the need for a *perichoretic intimacy* that can hold distinctively different individuals, groups, communities, cultures, civilizations, faith persuasions, and even ideologies together in harmony. If the Indian Church can aid this achievement, it will certainly add a new volume in the annals of world history as a story of God's communion-building work in contemporary world history.

Notes

1 It was a strong statement made by Ram Madhav, an RSS spokesperson, in an interview on 20 June 2012 in reaction to the opinion of Nitish Kumar, the Bihar chief minister, that the prime ministerial candidate in the 2014 general elections must be a secular person. Nitish Kumar has of course aired his opinion in resentment to the projection of Narendra Modi as the prime ministerial candidate.

2 John Zavos, *The Emergence of Hindu Nationalism in India* (op. cit.), p. 211.

3 Klaus Nürnberger, *Martin Luther's Message for Us Today*, pp. 309-310.

4 Klaus Nürnberger, *Martin Luther's Message for Us Today*, p. 310.

5 It is said that the Hindu middle class dream of a strong, powerful and sovereign nation on a par with some of the "Christian" Western countries. In this process, they tend to regard religion as having provided the necessary substance for the sovereign status of those countries. In order to achieve this goal, the most essential component is a definite geographical territory. We can better understand such ideological concepts as: nation, patriotism, fatherland, and holy land (*punyabhoo*), if we perceive them in the above light. Consequently, Hindutva becomes intolerant and even assumes a fascist mode when it comes to realize that there are communities and various segments of people who impinge upon their comfort. A typical example cited in this regard is the *Shiv Sena's* demand to drive out all the beggars from the city of Mumbai. See Sathish Deshpande, *Contemporary India*, p. 87.

6 Sanitization of India happens at two levels now: *first*, sanitizing the nation of the 'enemies', i.e., the non-conforming minorities; and *second*, disciplining those 'Indians' who indulge in overstepping the Hindu culture in order to adopt western culture. This is made clear by the recent activities of the hitherto unknown *Sri Ram Sene* in Mangalore. The *Sene's* latest threat is: to disrupt the Valentine's Day celebrations by forcefully dragging lovers found on the street and get them married. The *Sene* chief, Pramod Mutalik, had also never failed to spit venom

on the Church when he said: "It's okay if Valentine's Day celebrations are confined to Churches". See Ravi S. Joshi, "Mutalik or Brutalik" *The New Indian Express* (Bangalore: Sunday, 08 February 2009), p. 8. On the whole, the *Sangh Parivar* is turning the BJP ruled states into a Hindutva laboratory whose formidable effect will go a long way in shaping the nation's future if it is not tamed now.

7 K. P. Aleaz makes an important observation. According to him, "previously attempts had been made to define Hindus on the basis of religious beliefs, but Savarkar emphasized the cultural and historical aspects in the definition of a Hindu". K. P. Aleaz, "Religious Tensions and Dialogical Opportunities in India Today" in Samson Prabhakar, ed., *Overcoming Violence* (Bangalore: SATHRI/BTESSC, 2004), p. 15.

8 This hatred and enmity, particularly against Christians, came to the open through a series of violent attacks against Churches, chapels, Christian worship places and institutions that included brutal killings, gang-rape of nuns and so on from Christmas in 1998 in Gujarath. There were even bomb blasts inside Churches in Andhra and Goa. All these were carried out with the charges of the *Sangh Parivar* that the Christian missionaries have been indulging in "forced conversion". The most tragic part of this is that even the then Prime Minister, A. B. Vajbayee, did accord credibility to the allegations of the *Parivar* by calling for a national debate on conversion. See *NCC Review*, Vol. CXIX, No. 1 (Jan 1999).

9 This expression became popular in the wake of the recent (24 Jan 2009) outrage against women at Amnesia Pub in Mangalore by the *Sri Rama Sene* activists. Their outrage and angry utterances clearly tell us that the Hindutva forces are intolerant of people's choice to be different. We need to note the kind of justifications offered by Mutalik (the *Sene* chief), its activists and the belated condemnations that came from the ranks of the BJP. According to a *Sene* activist, the attack was carried out because the behaviour of the victims was *contrary to Hindu way of life*. The media categorized this atrocity as the "Talibanization of India" (Sources: CNN-IBN, NDTV and Times Now since 25 January 2009).

10 John D. Zizioulas, *Being as Communion*, p. 15.

11 See Swapan Dasgupta, "Orissa Can be Cured Only from within", *The New Indian Express* (Monday Nov. 24, 2008), p. 11.

12 J. Kuruvachira, *Roots of Hindutva*, pp. 293f.

13 See, for instance, the statement of the then BJP President, Rajnath Singh that the BJP will enact law to build Ram Mandir if it is voted to power with absolute majority, which is the "*nistha and astha*" (determination and faith) of the party. *The New Indian Express* (08 February 2009), p. 1. See also the editorial: "It's the Temple plank, again", *The New Indian Express* (09 February 2009), p. 10. Implicitly then, the BJP's topmost priority is not fair governance of the state, but to build the iconic Ram Temple, which would be a referral point to the self-esteem of the Hindu elite.

14 Leroy S. Rouner, *To be at Home*, p. 79.

SELECT BIBLIOGRAPHY

Primary Sources: Martin Luther

The various pieces of writings of Martin Luther cited here come from two sources: the English translation of his writings comes from the American Edition of *Luther's Works*, published by St. Louis: Concordia Publishing House; Philadelphia: Muhlenberg Press; and Philadelphia: Fortress Press. Those pieces from the English edition are cited as: *LW*, Vol. No., Publisher and Page Numbers. Their corresponding original writings of Luther in German and Latin are cited from *D. Martin Luthers Werke*. Kritische Gesamtausgabe: Weimer 1883ff. They are cited as: *WA*, Vol. No. and Page Numbers after every entry from English.

Luther, Martin. *Lectures on Genesis 1 – 5* (*LW* 1), Translated and edited by Jaroslav Pelican. St. Louis: Concordia Publishing House, 1958 (*WA* 42, pp. 3-263).

____________ *Lectures on Genesis 5 – 14* (*LW* 2), Translated and edited by Jaroslav Pelican. St. Louis: Concordia Publishing House, 1960 (*WA* 42, pp. 264-549).

____________ *Lectures on Genesis 26 – 30* (*LW* 5), tr. & ed. by Jaroslav Pelican. St. Louis: Concordia Publishing House, 1968 (*WA* 43, pp. 431-695).

____________ *First Lectures on the Psalms 1 – 75* (*LW* 10), Tr. & ed. by Hilton C. Oswald. St. Louis: Concordia Publishing House, 1974 (*WA* 3).

______________ *Lectures on Psalms 76 – 126* (*LW* 11), Tr. & ed. by Hilton C. Oswald. St. Louis: Concordia Publishing House, 1976 (*WA* 3 & 4).

______________ *Lectures on Isaiah 1 – 39* (*LW* 16), Tr. & ed. by Hilton C. Oswald. St. Louis: Concordia Publishing House, 1965 (*WA* 31^{II}, pp. 3-260).

______________ *Lectures on Isaiah 40 – 66* (*LW* 17), Tr. & ed. by Hilton C. Oswald. St. Louis: Concordia Publishing House, 1976 (*WA* 31^{II}, pp. 261-585).

______________ *Lectures on Minor Prophets* (*LW* 19), Tr. & ed. by Hilton C. Oswald. St. Louis: Concordia Publishing House, 1974 (*WA* 13, pp. 185-251; 424 – 448; 19, pp. 185-251; 345- 435).

______________ *Treatise on the Last Words of David – 2 Samuel 23:1 – 7* (*LW* 15), Tr. & ed. by Jaroslav Pelikan. St. Louis Concordia Publishing House, 1972, pp. 267-352 (*WA* 54, pp. 28-100).

______________ *Lectures on Romans* (*LW* 25), Tr. ed. by Hilton Oswald, St Louis: Concordia Publishing House, 1972 (*WA* 56, pp. 4-528).

______________ *Lectures on Galatians 1 – 4* (*LW* 26), Tr. ed. by Jaroslav Pelikan, St Louis: Concordia Publishing House, 1963 (*WA* 40^{I}, pp. 41-688).

______________ *Lectures on Galatians 5 – 6* (*LW* 27), Tr. ed. by Jaroslav Pelikan, St Louis: Concordia Publishing House, 1964 (*WA* 40^{II}, pp. 2-184).

______________ *Disputation against Scholastic Theology – 1517* (*LW* 31), Tr. & ed. by Harold J. Grimm. Philadelphia: Muhlenberg Press, 1957, pp. 5-16 (WA 1, pp. 221-228).

______________ *Ninety-five Thesis* – 1517 (*LW* 31), Tr. ed. by C. M. Jacobs, Philadelphia: Muhlenberg Press, 1957, pp. 17-34 (WA 1, pp. 233-238).

______________ *Heidelberg Disputation – 1518* (*LW* 31), Tr. & ed. by Harold J. Grimm. Philadelphia: Muhlenberg Press, 1957, pp. 35-70 (*WA* 1, pp. 353-374).

____________ *Explanations of the Ninety-five Theses – 1518* (*LW* 31), Tr. by Carl W. Folkemer. Philadelphia: Muhlenberg Press, 1957, pp. 79-252 (*WA* 1, pp. 525-628).

____________ *Two Kinds of Righteousness – 1519* (*LW* 31), Tr. by Lowell J. Satre. Philadelphia: Muhlenberg Press, 1957, pp. 297-306 (*WA* 2, pp. 145-252).

____________ *Freedom of a Christian* – 1520 (*LW* 31), Tr. by W. A. Lambert. Philadelphia: Muhlenberg Press, 1957, pp. 329-377 (*WA* 7, pp. 49-73).

____________ *Luther at Diet of Worms* (*LW* 32), tr. by George Forell. Philadelphia: Muhlenberg Press, 1958, pp. 101-132 (*WA* 7, pp. 814-857).

____________ *Bondage of the Will* – 1526 (*LW* 33), Tr. by Philiphs S. Watson. Philadelphia: Muhlenberg Press, 1972, pp. 5-295 (*WA* 18, pp. 600-787).

____________ *Theses Concerning Faith and Law* – 1535 (*LW* 34), Tr. by Lewis W. Spitz. Philadelphia: Muhlenberg Press, 1960, pp. 109-131 (*WA* 39^{I}, pp. 44-62).

____________ *The Disputation Concerning Man* – 1536 (*LW* 34), Tr. by Lewis W. Spitz. Philadelphia: Muhlenberg Press, 1960, pp. 135-144 (*WA* 39^{I}, pp. 174-180).

____________ *The Disputation Concerning Justification* – 1536 (*LW* 34), Tr. by Lewis W. Spitz. Philadelphia: Muhlenberg Press, 1960, pp. 147-196 (*WA* 39^{I}, pp. 82-126).

____________ *The Three Symbols or Creeds of the Christian Faith* (*LW* 34), Tr. by Robert R. Heifner. Philadelphia: Muhlenberg Press, 1960, pp. 202-228 (*WA* 50, pp. 262-285).

____________ *The Sacrament of Penance* – 1519 (*LW* 35), Tr. by Theodore E. Bachmann. Philadelphia: Muhlenberg Press, 1960, pp. 5-22 (*WA* 2, pp. 714-723).

____________ *The Holy and Blessed Sacrament of Baptism* – 1519 (*LW 35)*, Tr. by Charles M. Jacob. Philadelphia: Muhlenberg Press, 1960, pp. 23-43 (*WA* 2, pp. 727-737).

_____________ *The Blessed Sacrament of the Holy and True Body of Christ and the Brotherhoods* (1519), Tr. by Jeremiaj J. Schindel, *LW* 35, Philadelphia: Muhlenberg Press, 1965, pp. 45-78 (*WA* 2, pp. 742-758).

_____________ *A Treatise on the New Testament, That Is, The Holy Mass* (1520), tr. by Jeremiah J. Schindel, *LW* 35, Philadelphia: Muhlenberg Press, 1960, pp. 75-111(*WA* 6, pp. 353-378).

_____________ *The Babylonian Captivity of the Church* (1520), Tr. by A. T. W. Steinhauser, *LW* 36, Philadelphia: Muhlenberg Press, pp. 3-126 (*WA* 6, pp. 497-573).

_____________ *The Misuse of the Mass* (1521), Tr. by Frederick C. Ahrens, *LW* 36, Philadelphia: Muhlenberg Press, 1959, pp. 127-230 (*WA* 8, pp. 482-563).

_____________ *Receiving Both Kinds in the Sacrament* (1522), Tr. by Abdel Ross Wentz, *LW* 36, Philadelphia: Muhlenberg Press, 1959, pp. 231-267 (*WA* 11, pp. 431-456).

_____________ *Confessions Concerning Christ's Supper* (1528), Tr. by Robert H. Fischer, *LW* 37, Philadelphia: Muhlenberg Press, 1961, pp. 151-372 (*WA* 26, pp. 261-509).

_____________ *The Private Mass and the Consecration of Priests* (1533), Tr. by Martin E. Lehmann, *LW* 38, Philadelphia: Fortress Press, 1971, pp. 139-214 (*WA* 38, pp. 195-256).

_____________ *Against the Spiritual Estate of the Pope and the Falsely So Called* (1522), Tr. by. Eric W. Gritsch and Ruth C. Gritsch, *LW* 39, Philadelphia: Fortress Press, 1970, pp. 239-300 (*WA* 10^{II}, pp. 105-158).

_____________ *The Keys* (1530), Tr. by Earl Bayer and Conrad Bergendorf, *LW* 40, Philadelphia: Muhlenberg Press, 1967, pp. 321-378 (*WA* 30^{II}, pp. 465-507).

_____________ *On the Councils and the Church* (1539), Tr. by Charles M. Jacobs, *LW* 41, Philadelphia: Fortress Press, 1969, pp. 3-178 (*WA* 50, 509-653).

______________ *A Meditation on Christ's Passion* (15190, Tr. by Martin E. Bertram, *LW* 42, Philadelphia: Fortress Press, 1969, pp. 3-14 (*WA* 2, pp. 136-142).

______________ *A Sermon on Preparing to Die* (1519), Tr. by Martin E. Bertram, *LW* 42, Philadelphia: Fortress Press, 1969, 95-116 (*WA* 2, pp. 685-697).

______________ *Fourteen Consolations* (1520), Tr. by Martin H. Bertram, *LW* 42, Philadelphia: Fortress Press, 1969, pp. 117-166 (*WA* 6, pp. 104-134).

______________ *Treatise on Good Works* (1520), Tr. by W. A. Lambert, *LW* 44, Philadelphia: Fortress Press, 1966, pp. 15-114 (*WA* 6, pp. 202-276).

______________ *To the Christian Nobility of the German Nation Concerning the Reform of the Christian Estate* (1520), Tr. by Charles M. Jacobs, *LW* 44, Philadelphia: Fortress Press, 1966, pp. 115-229 (*WA* 6, pp. 404-469).

______________ *A Sincere Admonition by Martin Luther to all Christians to Guard against Insurrection and Rebellion* (1522), Tr. by W. A. Lambert, *LW* 45, Philadelphia: Muhlenberg Press, 1962, pp. 51-74 (*WA* 8, pp. 676-687).

______________ *Temporal Authority: To What Extent It Should be Obeyed* (1523), Tr. by J. J. Schindel, *LW* 45, Philadelphia: Muhlenberg Press, 1962, pp. 75–130 (*WA* 11, pp. 245-280).

______________ *Ordinance of a Common Chest: Fraternal Agreement on the Common Chest of the Entire Assembly at Leising* (1523), Tr. by T. W. Steinhauser, *LW* 45, Philadelphia: Muhlenberg Press, 1962, pp. 159-194 (*WA* 12, pp. 11-30).

______________ *Admonition to Peace: A Reply to the Twelve Articles of the Peasants in Swabia* (1525), Tr. by Charles M. Jacobs, *LW* 46, Philadelphia: Fortress Press, 1967, pp. 3-44 (*WA* 18, 291-334).

______________ *Against the Robbing and Murdering Hordes of Peasants* (1525), Tr. by C. M. Jacobs, *LW* 46, Philadelphia: Fortress Press, 1967, pp. 3-44 (*WA* 18, pp. 357-361).

_____________ *An Open Letter to the Harsh Book against the Peasants* (1525), Tr. by C. M. Jacobs, *LW* 46, Philadelphia: Fortress Press, 1967, pp. 57-85 (*WA*18, pp. 384-401).

_____________ *Concerning the Ministry*, Tr. by Conrad Bergendoff, *LW* 40, Philadelphia: Muhlenberg Press, 1958, pp. 7-44 (*WA* 12, pp.169-195).

_____________ *That a Christian Assembly or Congregation has the right to Judge All Teachings and to Call, Appoint, and Dismiss Teachers, Established and Proved from Scripture* (1523), Tr. by Eric W. and Ruth C. Gritsch, *LW* 39, Philadelphia: Fortress Press, 1970, pp. 75-85 (*WA* 11, pp. 408-416).

_____________ *On the Jews and Their Lies* (1543), Tr. by Martin H. Bertram *LW* 47, Philadelphia: Fortress Press, 1971), pp. 123-306 (*WA* 53, pp. 417-552).

_____________ *Trade and Usury* (15 24), Tr. by Charles M. Jacob, *LW* 45, Philadelphia: Muhlenberg Press, 1962, pp. 245-310 (*WA* 15, pp. 293-322).

Secondary Sources

Abraham, K. C. ed. *Ecumenism in Asia*. Bangalore: ATESEA & BTE-SSC, 1999.

Advani, L. K. *My Country, My Life*. Delhi: Rupa & Co., 2008.

Akkara, Anto. *Kandhamal: A Blot on Indian Secularism*. Delhi: Media House, 2009.

Alberoni, Francesco. *Movement and Institution*. New York: Columbia University Press, 1984.

Aloysius, G. *Nationalism without a Nation in India*. Delhi: Oxford University Press, 1997.

Alter, James P. and Herbert Jai Singh. *The Church in Delhi*. Delhi: NCCI, 1961.

Althaus, Paul. *The Ethics of Martin Luther*, Tr. by Robert Schultz. Philadelphia: Fortress Press, 1972.

Althaus, Paul. *The Theology of Martin Luther*, Tr. by Robert C. Schultz. Philadelphia: Fortress Press, 1966.

Anderson, Benedict. *Imagined Communities.* New York: Verso, 7th Impression 1996.

Anderson, Bernhard W. *Understanding the Old Testament.* London: Prentice-Hall, 1966.

Anderson, H. George et al. eds. *Lutherans and Catholics in Dialogue*, Vol. VII "Justification by Faith". Minneapolis: Augsburg Publishing House, 1985.

Arokiasamy S. and G. Gispert-Sauch. eds. *Liberation in Asia: Theological Perspectives.* Delhi: Vidhyajyoti Faculty of Theology, 1987.

Atkinson, James. "Introduction to Luther's *To the Christian Nobility of the German Nation Concerning the Reform of the Christian Estate, 1520*" in *Selected Writings of Martin Luther*, ed. by T. G. Tappert & Tr. by C. M. Jacob, Vol. 1. Philadelphia: Fortress Press, 1967.

Atkinson, James. *Rome and Reformation Today: How Luther speaks to the New Situation.* Oxford: Latimer House, 1982.

Augustine, John S. ed. *Religious Fundamentalism: An Asian Perspective* (Bangalore: SATHRI/CCA/ WARC, 1993).

Augustine, St. *The City of God*, ed. by R. V. Tasker. London: J. M. Dent & Sons, 1957.

Avis, Paul D. L. *The Church in the Theology of the Reformers.* Atlanta: John Knox Press, 1981.

Bainton, Roland H. *Here I Stand: A Life of Martin Luther.* Nashville: Abingdon Press, 1959.

Bainton, Roland H. *Christendom: A Short History of Christianity and Its Impact on Western Civilization*, Vol. I. New York: Harper & Row, 1966.

Banks, Robert. *Paul's Idea of Community.* Massachusetts: Hendrickson Publishers, 1994.

Barnett, Paul. *Finding the Historical Christ*, After Jesus, Vol. 3. Grand Rapids: Wm B. Eerdmans, 2009.

Basham, A. L. *The Wonder that was India*. Fontana: Collins, 1975.

Basu, Praphullachandra. *Indo-Aryan Polity during the Period of the Rig Veda*. Allahabad: The Pioneer Press, 1919.

Basu, Shamita. *Religious Revivalism as Nationalist Discourse: Swami Vivekananda and New Hinduism in Nineteenth-Century Bengal*. Delhi: Oxford University Press, 2002.

Bauer, Walter. *Orthodoxy and Heresy in Earliest Christianity*. Philadelphia: Fortress Press, 1971, 1st in 1934.

Bauerochse, Lothar. *Learning to Live Together: Interchurch Partnerships as Ecumenical Communities of Learning*. Geneva: WCC, 2001.

Bellah, Robert N. et al. *Habits of the Heart: Individualism and Commitment in American life*. New York: Harper and Row, 1986.

Bendix, Reinhard. *Max Weber: An Intellectual Portrait*. Berkeley, California: University of California Press, 1977.

Berger, Peter L. *Invitation to Sociology: A Humanistic Perspective*. New York: Doubleday, 1963.

Berger, Ronald. *Fathoming the Holocaust: A Social Problems Approach*. New York: Aldine De Gruyter, 2002.

Berkeley. Robert F. and Sarah A. Edwards. eds. *Christology in Dialogue*. Cleveland: Pilgrim Press, 1993.

Bernstein, R. J. *The New Constellation: The Ethical-Political Horizons of Modernity/ Postmodernity*. Cambridge: Cambridge University Press, 1991.

Bethge, Eberhard und Martin Greschat. eds. *Der Holocaust und die Protestanten*. Frankfurt: Athanaum, 1998.

Bethge, Eberhard. *Friendship and Resistance: Essays on Dietrich Bonheoffer*. Geneva: WCC/Wm B. Erdmans, 1995.

Bhasker, Roy. *Reflections on Meta-Reality: Transcendence, Emancipation and Everyday Life*. New Delhi: Sage Publications, 2002.

Bhattacharyya, Prabhakar. *Fanaticism*. Kolkata: Samik Prakashan, 2004.

Bigler, Robert M. *The Politics of German Protestantism: The Rise of the Protestant Church Elite in Prussia, 1815-1848*. Berkeley, CA: University of California Press, 1972.

Boff, Leonardo. *Ecclesiogenesis: The Base Communities Reinvent the Church*, Tr. by Robert Barr. Maryknoll, New York: Orbis Books, 1986.

Boff, Leonardo. *Trinity and Society*, Tr. Paul Burns. Maryknoll, NY: Orbis Books, 1988.

Bonhoeffer, Dietrich. *The cost of Discipleship*. Thiruvalla: Suvartha Bhavan, Indian Print, 2001.

Bornkamm, Gunther. *Early Christian Experience*. New York: Harper and Row, 1969.

Bose, Sugata and Ayesha Jalal, eds. *Nationalism, Democracy & Development*. Delhi: Oxford University Press, 1998).

Bose, Sugata. ed. *South Asia and World Capitalism*. Delhi: Oxford University Press, 1990.

Bowersock, G. *Martyrdom and Rome*. Cambridge: Cambridge University Press, 1995.

Braaten, Carl E. and Robert W. Jenson. eds. *Marks of the Body of Christ*. Grand Rapids, Michigan: Wm B. Eerdmans, 1999.

Braaten, Carl E. *No Other Gospel: Christianity among the World's Religions*. Minneapolis: Fortress Press, 1992.

Braaten, Carl E. *Principles of Lutheran Theology*. Philadelphia: Fortress Press, 1983.

Brandt, Walther I. *Introduction to Luther's Trade and Usury, 1524* in *Selected Writings of Martin Luther*, Vol. III. Philadelphia: Fortress Press, 1967.

Branick, Vincent. *The House Church in the Writings of Paul*. Wilmington, USA: Michael Glacier, 1989.

Broadie, Alexander. "Duns Scotus and William Ockham" in Evans, G. R. ed. *The Medieval Theologians*. Oxford: Blackwell, 2001.

Brown, Colin. *Philosophy and the Christian Faith*. Illinois: Inter Varsity Press, 1968.

Brown, Ralph E., James, Jr., and Gene Reeves, eds. *Process Philosophy and Christian Thought*. Indianapolis: Bobbs-Merrill, 1971.

Brown, Raymond E. *The Gospel according to John (I-XII)*. New York: Doubleday, 1966.

Brown, Robert McAfee. *The Significance of the Church*. Philadelphia: The Westminster Press, nd.

Bruce, F. F. *The Gospel of John: Introduction, Exposition and Notes*. London: Pickering Paperbacks, 1983.

Buber, Martin. *I and Thou*, Tr. by Ronald Gregor Smith. New York: Charles Scribner's Sons, 2nd edition, 1958.

Buckley, Michael. *At the Origins of Modern Atheism*. New Havens: Yale University Press, 1987.

Bultmann, Rudolf. *Theology of the New Testament*. London: SCM Press, 1965.

Calhoun, C. *Critical Social Theory: Culture, History and the Challenges of Difference*. Oxford: Blackwell, 1995.

Cameron, A. *Christianity and the Rhetoric of the Empire: the Development of Christian Discourse*. Berkeley, CA: University of California Press, 1991.

Carl E. Braaten, *The Apostolic Imperative: Nature and Aim of the Church's Mission and Ministry*. Minneapolis: Augsburg Publishing House, 1985.

Carmichael, Kay. *Sin and Forgiveness: New Responses in a Changing World*. Aldershot, England: Ashgate, 2003.

Castro, Emilio. *A Passion for Unity: Essays on Ecumenical Hopes and Challenges*. Geneva: World Council of Churches, 1992.

Chadwick, Owen. *The Reformation*. London: Penguin Books, 1972.

Chandran, Joshua Russell. *The Church in Mission: Some Reflections*. Madras: CLS, 1991.

Chatterjee, Partha. *A Possible India: Essays in Political Criticism*. Delhi: Oxford University Press, 1998.

Chatterjee, Partha. *The Nation and Its Fragments: Colonial and Postcolonial Histories*. Delhi: Oxford University Press, 1995.

Chatterjee, Partha. *The Nation and Its Fragments: Colonial and Postcolonial Histories*. Delhi: Oxford University Press, 1995.

Chazan, Robert. *European Jewry and the First Crusade*. Berkeley, CA: University of California Press, 1986.

Cheetham, Nicholas. *Keepers of the Keys: A History of Popes from St. Peter to John Paul II*. New York: Charles Scribner's Sons, 1983.

Chen, Kuan-Hsing. ed. *Trajectories: Inter-Asia Cultural Studies*. London and New York: Routledge, 1998.

Chowgule, Ashok V. *Christianity in India: The Hindutva Perspective*. Mumbai: Hindu Vivek Kendra, 1999.

Clark G. and T. Rajak. eds. *Philosophy and Power in the Graeco-Roman World*. Oxford: Oxford University Press, 1995.

Clark, David. *Yes to Life*. London: Collins/Fount, 1987.

Clark, Gillian. *Christianity and the Roman Society*. Cambridge, UK: Cambridge University Press, 2004.

Collison, J. G. F. "Issues in the History of Biblical Hermeneutics: A Protestant Perspective" in Downs, Frederick S. and Eric J. Lott. eds. *What is God Factor? Sermons and Writings of Frank Collison*. Delhi: ISPCK, 1999.

Connor, Walter. *Ethnonationalism: The Quest for Understanding*. Princeton: Princeton University Press, 1994.

Conzelmann, Hans. *Outline of the Theology of the New Testament*. London: SCM Press, 1969.

Cox, Harvey. *Fire from Heaven*. Massachusetts: Addison Wesley Publishing, 1995.

Cox, Harvey. *Religion in the Secular City*. New York: Simon & Schuster, 1984.

Cox, Harvey. *The Secular City*. London: SCM Press, 1965.

Cranz, F. Edward. *An Essay on the Development of Luther's Thought on justice, Law, and Society* Issued as an extra number of the *Harvard Theological Review*. Cambridge: Harvard University Press, 1959.

D'Arcy, Martin C. *Humanism and Christianity*. New York: An Nal Book, 1969.

der Veer, Peter Van. *Gods on Earth: Religious Experience and Identity in Ayodhya*. Delhi: Oxford University Press, 1997.

der Veer, Peter van. R*eligious Nationalisms: Hindus and Muslims in India*. Delhi: Oxford university Press, 1996.

Deshpande B. V. and S. R. Ramaswamy, *Dr. Hedgewar, the Epoch Maker*. Bangalore: Sahitya Sindhu, 1981.

Deshpande, Satish. *Contemporary India: A Sociological View*. Delhi: Viking, 2003.

Dillenberger, John and Claude Welch, *Protestant Christianity*. New York: Charles Scribner's Sons, 1954.

Dodd, Charles Harold. *Parables of the Kingdom*. London: Nisbet & Co., 1936.

Douglas, Ian T. ed. *Waging Reconciliation: God's Mission in a Time of Globalization and Crisis*. New York: Church Publishing Incorporated, 2002.

Douglas, Ian T. ed. *Waging Reconciliation: God's Mission in a Time of Globalization and Crisis*. New York: Church Publishing Incorporated, 2002.

Doyle, Dennis M. *Communion Ecclesiology: Visions and Versions*. Maryknoll. New York: Orbis Books, 2000.

Dresden, Sem. *Humanism in the Renaissance*, Tr. from Dutch by Margaret King. London: World University Library, 1968.

D'Sa, Thomas. ed. *The Church in India in the Emerging Third Millennium*. Bangalore: NBCLC, 2005.

Duffy, Eamon. *Saints and Sinners: A History of Popes*. New Haven: Yale University Press, 1997.

Dulles, Avery. *Models of the Church*. New York: Random House, 2002, 1st 1978.

Dunne, John S. *The Way of all the Earth: Experiments in Truth and Religion*. New York: Macmillan Publishing Company, 1972.

Durant, Will. *The Reformation*. New York: Simon and Schuster, 1957.

Dyke, Arthur J. *Rethinking Rights and Responsibilities: The Moral Bonds of Community*. Cleveland. OH: Pilgrim Press, 1992.

Ebeling, Gerhard. *Luther: An Introduction to His Thought*. London: Collins, 1970.

Edwards Jr., Mark U. *Luther's Last Battles: Politics and Polemics, 1531-46*. Ithaca. New York: Cornell University Press, 1983.

Elert, Werner. *The Structure of Lutheranism*. St. Louis, Missouri: Concordia Publishing House, 1962.

Ellis, M. H. and Otto Maduro. eds. *The Future of Liberation Theology* Maryknoll. New York: Orbis Books, 1989.

Elton, G. R. ed. *Renaissance and Reformation: 1300-1648*. New York: Macmillan, 6th Printing, 1966.

Elton, G. R. *Reform and Reformation, England 1517-1559*. Oxford: Blackwell, 1999.

Engels, Friedrich. *The Peasants' War in Germany*, Tr. by Moissaye J. Olgin. London: George Allen & Unwin, 1926.

Ericksen, Robert P. *Theologians under Hitler: Gerhard Kittel, Paul Althaus and Emmanuel Hirsch*. New Haven: Yale University Press, 1985.

Erikson, Eric H. *Young Man Luther: A Study in Psychoanalysis and History*. New York: Norton, 1958.

Eusebius, *The History of the Church from Christ to Constantine*, Tr. by G. A. Williamson. Minneapolis: Augsburg Publishing House, 1975.

Fagerberg, Holsten. *A New Look at the Lutheran Confessions (1529-1537)*, Tr. by Gene J. Lund. St. Louis, Missouri: CPH, 1972.

Farquhar, J. N. *Modern Religious Movements in India*. Delhi: Munshram Manoharlal, 1967, 1st in 1915.

Fergusson, David. *Community, Liberalism and Christian Ethics*. Cambridge. UK: Cambridge University Press, 1998.

Feuerbach. Ludwig. *The Essence of Christianity*. New York: C. Blanchard, 1855.

Fletcher, Richard. *The Barbarian Conversion: From Paganism to Christianity*. New York: Henry Holt, 1997.

Flew, Newton. *Jesus and His Church: A study of the Idea of the Ecclesia in the New Testament*. London: Epworth Press, 1938.

Foerster, Werner. ed. *Gnosis: A Selection of Gnostic Texts*, 2 Vols. Oxford: Clarendon Press, 1972-74.

Forde, Gerhard O. *On Being a Theologian of the Cross: Reflections on Luther's Heidelberg Disputation, 1518*. Grand Rapids: Wm B. Eerdmans, 1997.

Forde, Gerhard O. *Where God Meets Man: Luther's Down-to-Earth Approach to the Gospel*. Minneapolis: Augsburg Publishing House, 1972.

Francis, Kanichikattil. ed. *Church in Context: Essays in Honour of Mathias Mundadan CMI*. Bangalore: Dharmaram Publications, 1996.

Frank, Katherine. *Indira: The Life of Indira Nehru Gandhi*. Houghton: Mifflin Company, 2002.

Gadamer, Hans-Georg. *Truth and Method*. New York: Crossroad, 1975.

Gandhi, M. K. *To the Hindus and Muslims*, ed. by Anand T. Hingorani. Allahabad: Law Journal Press, 1942.

Gelder, Craig Van. *The Essence of the Church: A Community Created by the Spirit*. Grand Rapids, Michigan: Baker Books, 2002.

Gellner, Ernest. *Nations and Nationalism*. Oxford, UK, Cambridge, USA: Blackwell, 1996.

George, K. M. *Christianity in India through the Centuries*. Secundrabad, India: Authentic Media, 2007.

Gibbon, Edward. *A History of the Christian Church*. ed. by Williston Walter et al. New York: Charles Scribner's Sons, 1985.

Gibbon, Edward. *The Decline and Fall of Roman Empire* Vol. 1. New York: The Modern Library, n. d.

Gibson, Edgar C. S. *The Three Creeds*. London, New York, Bombay, and Calcutta: Longmans, Green, And Co., 1909.

Gilson, Etienne. *History of Christian Philosophy in the Middle Ages*. London: Sheed and Ward, 1955.

Golwalkar, Madhav Sadashiv. *We, or Our Nationhood Defined.* Nagpur: Bharat Prakashan, 1939.

Golwalkar, Madhav Sadashiv. *Bunch of Thoughts*. Bangalore: Sahitya Sindhu, Reprint, 1996.

Gorringe, Timothy. *God's Just Vengeance: Crime, Violence and the Rhetoric of Salvation*. Cambridge, UK: Cambridge University Press, 1996.

Gould, G. *The Desert Fathers and Monastic community*. Oxford, UK: Oxford University Press, 1993.

Grant, Robert M. ed. *Gnosticism: A Source Book of Heretical Writings from the Early Christian Period.* New York: Harper & Brothers, 1961.

Gratsch, Edward. J. *Aquinas' Summa: An Introduction and Interpretation*. Bangalore: TPI, 1990.

Greenslade, S. L. *Schism in the Early Church*. London: SCM Press, 1953.

Grey, Mary C. *Prophecy and Mysticism: The Heart of Postmodern Church*. Edinburgh: T & T Clark, 1997.

Gritsch, E. W. "Introduction" in *Luther's Works* Vol.39. Philadelphia: Fortress Press, 1970.

Guthrie, Donald. *New Testament Theology*. England: Inter-Varsity Press, 1981.

Gutierrez, Gustavo. *A Theology of Liberation: History, Politics and Salvation*. London: SCM Press, 1974.

Habermas, Jürgen. *Structural Transformation of the Public Sphere: An Inquiry into a Category of Bourgeois Society*. Cambridge, Massachusetts: MIT, 1989.

Hägglund, Bengt. *History of Theology*, Tr by Gene J. Lund. Saint Louis: Concordia Publishing House, 3rd Edition, 1968.

Hansen, Thomas Blom and Christphe Jaffrelot, eds. *The BJP and the Compulsions of Politics in India.* Delhi: Oxford University Press, 2004.

Hansen, Thomas Blom. *The Saffron Wave: Democracy and Hindu Nationalism in Modern India.* Delhi: Oxford University Press, 2004.

Hares, W. P. *History of the Christian Church of the first Six Centuries.* Madras: CLS, 2nd ed. 1975.

Harnack, Adolf von. *Militia Christi: The Christian Religion and the Military in the First Three Centuries*, Tr. by David McInnes Gracie. Philadelphia: Fortress Press, 1981.

Hart, Trevor A. ed. *The Dictionary of Historical Theology.* Grand Rapid, Michigan: Wm B Eerdmans, 2000.

Harvey, David. *The Condition of Postmodernity.* Oxford: Basil Blackwell, 1990.

Hastings, Adrian. *The Construction of Nationhood: Ethnicity, Religion & Nationalism.* Cambridge: Cambridge University Press, 1997.

Hauerwas, Stanley. *A Community of Character: Toward a Constructive Christian Social Ethics.* Notre Dame: University of Notre Dame Press, 1981.

Hauerwas, Stanley. *After Christendom: How the Church is to Behave if Freedom, Justice and a Christian Nation are Bad Ideas.* Nashville: Abingdon Press, 1991.

Hay, Stephen. ed. *Sources of Indian Tradition* Vol. II. New York: Columbia University Press, 1988.

Haynes, D. *Rhetoric and Ritual in Colonial India: The Shaping of a Public Culture in Surat City, 1852-1928.* Berkeley, CA: University of California Press, 1991.

Hedlund, Roger E. ed. *Christianity is Indian: The Emergence of an Indigenous Community.* Delhi: MIIS & ISPCK, 2004.

Heimsath, Charles H. *Indian Nationalism and Hindu Social Reforms*. Princeton: Princeton University Press, 1964.

Hellwig, Monika. *The Eucharist and the Hunger of the World*. London: Sheed & Ward, 1992.

Herman, Stewart. *The Rebirth of the German Church*. New York: Harper and Row, 1946.

Hermann, Wilhelm M. *The Communion of the Christian with God: Described on the Basis of Luther's Statements*, ed. by Robert T. Voelkel. Philadelphia: Fortress Press, 1971.

Hermanns M. and K. L. Fernandes. *Hinduism and Tribal Culture: An Anthropological Verdict on the Niyogi Report*. Bombay: CAB, 1957.

Hindu Nationalism and Indian Politics. Delhi: Oxford University Press, A 'three books in one volume' edition, 2004.

Hobbes, Thomas. *Leviathan, Or the Matter, Form and Power of a Commonwealth Ecclesiastical and Civil*, ed. by Michael Oakeshott. New York: Collier Books, 1962.

Hobsbawm, Eric. *Nations and Nationalism Since 1780*. Cambridge, UK: Cambridge University Press, 1990.

Hoefer, Herbert E. *Churchless Christianity*. Madras: Gurukul, 1991 / Revised edition – Pasadena. CA: William Carey Library, 2001.

Hoefer, Herbert. ed. *The Augsburg Confession and Ecumenism in India*. Madras: Gurukul, 1980.

Hogg, A. G. *The Christian Message to the Hindu*, in Eric Sharpe, ed., *The Theology of A. G. Hogg*. Madras: CLS, 1971.

Holloway, Richard. *On Forgiveness: How Can We Forgive the Unforgivable?* Edinburgh: Canongate Books, 2003.

Holze, Heinrich. ed. *The Church as Communion: Lutheran Contributions to Ecclesiology*. Geneva: LWF, 1997.

Hultgren, Arland J. and Steven A. Haggmark. eds. *The Earliest Christian Heretics: Readings from Their Opponents*. Minneapolis: Fortress Press, 1996.

Huntington, Samuel P. *The Clash of Civilizations and the Remaking of the World Order*. New York: Simon & Schuster, 1996.

Hussain, Abid. *The National Culture of India*. Bombay: Asia Publishing House, 2nd ed. 1961.

Ilaiah, Kancha. *Why I am Not a Hindu: A Sudra Critique of Hindutva Philosophy, Culture and Political Economy*. Delhi: Batkal & Sen 2001.

Inden, Ronald. *Imagining India*. Oxford: Basil Blackwell, 1990.

Ipgrave, Michael. *Trinity and Inter Faith Dialogue: Plenitude and Plurality*, Religion and Discourse Series Vol. 14. Bern: Peter Lang, 2003.

Irenaeus. *Against Heresies*, Tr. by Dominic J. Unger. New York: Paulist Press, 1992.

Irvin, Dale T. and Scott W. Sunquist. *History of the World Christian Movement* Vol. I *Earliest Christianity to 1453*. Bangalore: TPI 2004.

Jaeger, Werner. *Early Christianity and Greek Paideia*. London: Harvard University Press, 1961.

Jaffrelot, Christophe. ed. *The Sangh Parivar: A Reader*. Delhi: Oxford University Press, 2005.

Jenkins, Daniel. *The Strangeness of the Church*. New York: Doubleday, 1955.

Jenson, Robert W. *The Triune Identity*. Philadelphia: Fortress Press, 1982.

John Panicker, P. L. *Gandhi on Pluralism and Communalism*. Delhi: ISPCK, 2006.

Johnston, George. *The Doctrine of the Church*. London: Oxford University Press, 1943.

Jones, E. Stanley. *Christ at the Round Table*. Lucknow: Lucknow Publishing House, Reprint 2007 of 1928.

Jones, G. *Embodying Forgiveness: A Theological Analysis*. Grand Rapid, Michigan: Wm B. Eerdmans, 1995.

Jorez, Jerald C. and Paul T. McCain. eds. *Church and Ministry*. St. Louis, Missouri: LCMS, 1998.

Juergensmayer, Mark. *Religious Nationalism Confronts the Secular State*. Delhi: Oxford University Press, 1994.

Juergensmeyer, Mark. *Terror in the Mind of God: The Global Rise of Religious Violence*. Delhi: Oxford University Press, 2nd Impression, 2002.

Kakar, Sudhir. *The Colours of Violence*. Delhi: Penguin Books, 1995.

Kannambirathinam, A. C. "Vidiyalai Ethirnōkki" ("In Anticipation of the Dawn"), in *Uzhaippin Uyarvum Manithanēya Mānpum*, [*Greatness of Hard Work and Characteristics of Humaneness*]. Chennai: New Century Book House, 4th edition, 2006.

Kant, Immanuel. "*Was ist Aufklärung?*" (What is Enlightenment?) in Gay, Peter. ed. *The Enlightenment: A Comprehensive Anthology*. New York: Simon and Schuster, 1973.

Kaur, Ravinder. ed. *Religion, Violence and Political Mobilization in South Asia*. New Delhi, Thousand Oaks, CA & London: Sage Publications, 2005.

Keller. Catherine. *From a Broken Web: Separation, Sexism and Self.* Boston: Beacon Press, 1986.

Kelley, J. N. D. *The Athanasian Creed*. London: Adam & Charles Black, 1964.

Khadduri, Majid and H. J. Liebesny. eds. *Law in the Middle East* Vol. I. Washington: Richmond William Byrd Press, 1955.

Kim, Sung Ho. *Max Weber's Politics of Civil Society*. Cambridge, UK: Cambridge University Press, 2004.

Kirkpatrick, Frank G. *Community: A Trinity of Models*. Washington: Georgetown University Press, 1986.

Kishwar, Madhu. *Religion at the Service of Nationalism and Other Essays*. Delhi: Oxford University Press, 1998.

Kitamori, Kazoh. *The Theology of the Pain of God*. London: SCM Press, 1966.

Kittleson, James M. *Luther the Reformer*. Minneapolis: Augsburg Publishing House, 1986.

Kobia, Samuel. *Called to One Hope: A New Ecumenical Epoch*. Thiruvalla: CSS, 2007.

Kolb, Robert. *Luther's Way of Thinking: Introductory Essays*. Trivandrum: Luther Academy India, 2006.

Kopf, David. *British Orientalism and the Bengal Renaissance: The Dynamics of Indian Modernization 1793-1835*. Berkeley: University of California Press, 1969.

Kothari, Rajni. *Communalism in Indian Politics*. Delhi: Rainbow Publishers, 1998.

Krieger, David J. *The New Universalism: Foundation for a Global Theology*. Maryknoll, New York: Orbis Books, 1991.

Kümmel, Werner Georg. *Promise and Fulfillment: The Eschatological Message of Jesus*. London: SCM Press, 1961.

Küng, Hans and David Tracy. eds. *Paradigm Change in Theology*. Edinburgh: T & T Clark, 1989.

Küng, Hans. *Christianity: Essence, History, Future*. New York: Continuum, 1995.

Küng, Hans. *The Church*. London: Burns & Oates, 1968.

Kuruvachira, J. *Roots of Hindutva: A Critical Study of Hindu Fundamentalism and Nationalism*. Delhi: Media House, 2005.

Ladd, George Eldon. *The Presence of the Future: Eschatology of Biblical Realism*. Grand Rapids, Michigan: Wm B. Eerdmans, 1974.

Laing, Mark T. B. ed. *Nationalism and Hindutva: A Christian Response* – Papers from 10th CMS Conference. Delhi: CMS/UBS/ISPCK, 2005.

Lakeland, Paul. *Postmodernity: Christian Identity in a Fragmented Age*. Minneapolis: Fortress Press, 1997.

Larson, Gerald James. *India's Agony over Religion*. Delhi: Oxford University Press, 1997.

Lash, Nicholas. *Theology on the Way to Emmaus*. London: SCM Press, 1986.

Lasswell, Harold and Harlan Cleveland. eds. *The Ethic of Power: The Interplay of Religion, Philosophy, and Politics.* New York: Harper and Brothers, 1962.

Latourette, Kenneth Scott. *History of Christianity*. London: Eyre and Spottishwoods, 1953.

Lau, Franz. *Luther*, Tr. by Robert H. Fischer. Philadelphia: Westminster Press, 1963.

Lawler, Michael G. *Symbol and Sacrament: A Contemporary Sacramental Theology*. New York: Paulist Press, 1987.

Lazareth, William H. *Luther on the Christian Home: An Application of the Social Ethics of the Reformation*. Philadelphia: Muhlenberg Press, 1960.

Leff, Gordon. *Medieval Thought: From Augustine to Ockham*. Middlesex: Penguin, 1958.

Lehmann, Karl and Wolfhart Pannenberg. eds. *The Condemnations of the Reformation Era, Do They Still Divide?* Minneapolis: Augsburg Publishing House, 1989.

Leith, John H. ed. *Creeds of the Churches*. Atlanta: John Knox Press, 1982.

Lhose, Bernard. *Martin Luther's Theology: Its Systematic and Historic Development*. Minneapolis: University of Minnesota Press, 1999.

Lienemann-Perrin, Christine. et al. eds. *Reformed and Ecumenical: On Being Reformed in Ecumenical Encounters*. Amsterdam – Atlanta: Rodopi, 2000.

Lindbeck, George A. and Vilmos Vajta, *The Role of the Augsburg Confession: Catholic and Lutheran Views*. Philadelphia: Fortress Press, 1982.

Lindbeck, George A. *Nature of Doctrine: Religion and Theology in a Postliberal Age*. London: SPCK, 1984.

Lindgren, H. *An Introduction to Social Psychology*. New York: John Wiley and Sons, 1969.

Locke, John. *The Second Treatise of Government*, ed. with an introduction by Thomas P. Peardon. Indianapolis: Bobbs-Merrill, 1952.

Loisy, Alfred. *The Gospel and the Church*. Philadelphia: Fortress Press, 1976.

Lott, Eric. *Religious Faith, Human Identity: Dangerous Dynamics in Global &Indian life*. Bangalore: ATC/UTC, 2005.

MacIntyre, Alasdair. *After Virtue: A Study in Moral Theory*. Notre Dame: University of Notre Dame Press, 1984.

MacMullen, Ramsay. *Christianizing the Roman Empire*. New Haven: Yale University Press, 1984.

Macquarrie, John. *Principles of Christian Theology*. London: SCM Press, 6th print, 1986.

Madan, T.N. *Modern Myths, Locked Minds: Secularism and Fundamentalism in India* Delhi: Oxford University Press, 1998.

Maier, Christoph. *Preaching the Crusades: Mendicant Friars and the Cross in the Thirteenth Century*. Cambridge: Cambridge University Press, 1994.

Malik, Yogendra K. and V. B. Singh. *Hindu Nationalists in India: The Rise of Bharatiya Janata Party*. Delhi: Vistaar Publications, 1994.

Manadev, Pradeep. *Communalism in India: A Paradigm Shift to Indian Politics*. Delhi: Authors Press.

Marcus, George E. and Michael M. J. Fischer. *Anthropology as Cultural Critique: An Experimental Moment in the Human Sciences*. Chicago: University of Chicago Press, 2nd edition, 1999.

Markus, Robert. *The End of Ancient Christianity*. New York: Cambridge University Press, 5th Print, 1997.

Marty, Martin E. *The Public Church: Mainline-Evangelical-Catholic*. New York: Crossroad, 1981.

Martyr, St. Justin. *The Fathers of the Church*, Vol. 6, Tr. by Thomas B. Falls. New York: Christian Heritage, 1949.

Marx, Karl. "Preface to a Contribution to the Critique of Political Economy" in *Karl Marx and Frederick Engels: Selected Works*. New York: International Publishers, 1969.

Masselos, Jim. *Nationalism on Indian Subcontinent: An Introductory History*. Melbourne, Australia: Thomas Nelson, 1972.

Mathew, C. V. *The Saffron Mission*. Delhi: ISPCK, 1999.

McGlasson, Paul C. *Invitation to Dogmatic Theology: A Canonical Approach*. Grand Rapids, Michigan: Brazos Press, 2006.

McGrath, Alister E. *An Introduction to Christianity*. Cambridge, USA & Oxford. UK: Blackwell, 1997.

McGrath, Alister E. *Justification by Faith*. Grand Rapids. Michigan: Zondervan, 1998.

Mckelvey, R. J. *The New Temple: The Church in the New Testament*. London: Oxford University Press, 1969.

McLellan, David. ed. *Karl Marx: Selected Writings*. Oxford: Oxford University Press, 1977.

Mead, G. Herbert. *Mind, Self and Society*. Chicago: University of Chicago Press, 1962.

Meyer, Carl S. ed. *Luther for an Ecumenical Age*. Saint Louis: Concordia Publishing House 1967.

Michael, Robert. *Holy Hatred: Christianity, Antisemitism, and the Holocaust*. New York: Palgrave Macmillan, 2006.

Minear, Paul S. *Images of the Church in the New Testament*. Louisville, KY: Westminster John Knox Press, 1960.

Mishra, B. B. *The Indian Middle Classes: Their Growth in Modern Times*. London: Oxford University Press, 1961.

Moltmann, Jürgen. *The Church in the Power of the Spirit*. New York: Harper & Row, 1977.

Moltmann, Jürgen. *The Trinity and the Kingdom of God: The Doctrine of God*, Tr. By Margaret Kohl from German. London: SCM Press, 1981.

Monterio, Evelyn. *Church and Culture: Communion in Pluralism*. Delhi: ISPCK, 2004.

Montserata, D. ed. *Changing Bodies, Changing Meaning: Studies on the Human Body in Late Antiquity*. London: SCM Press, 1998

Morris-Jones, W. H. *The Government and Politics of India*. Bombay: B.I. Publications, 1964.

Mudge, Lewis S. *Rethinking the Beloved Community: Ecclesiology, Hermeneutics, Social Theory*. Geneva: WCC, 2000.

Nandy, Ashis. *The Intimate Enemy: Loss and Recovery of Self under Colonialism*. Delhi: Oxford University Press, 1983.

Nandy, Ashis. *Bonfire of Creeds*. Delhi: Oxford University Press, 2004.

Nehru, Jawaharlal. *The Discovery of India*. Delhi: Penguin Books, 2004, first in 1946.

Newbigin, Lesslie. *Trinitarian Faith and Today's Mission*. Richmond: John Knox Press, 1963.

Ngien, Dennis. *The Suffering of God According to Martin Luther's 'Theologia Crucis'*. New York: Peter Lang, 1995.

Nickle, K. F. *The Collection: A Study in Paul's Strategy*. London: SCM Press, 1966.

Niebhur, H. Richard. *The Social Sources of Denominationalism*. New York: Meridian Books, 4th Printing, 1960.

Niebhur, H. Richard. *Christ and Culture*. London: Faber and Faber, 1951.

Nisbet, Robert. *The Social Philosophers: Community and Conflict in Western Thought*. New York: Washington Square Press, 1982.

Novak, Michael. *The Rise of the Untenable Ethnics*. New York: Macmillan, 1972.

Nürnberger, Klaus. *Martin Luther's Message for Us Today: A Perspective from the South*. Pieter-Martizburg: Cluster Publications, 2005.

Oberman, Heiko A. *Luther: Man Between God and the Devil*. New York: Image Books, 1992.

Painadath, S. ed. *Jesus and Society: Selected Writings of Sebastian Kappen*, Vol. 1. Delhi: ISPCK, 2002.

Palkivala, N. A. *We, the People*. Bombay: Strand Book Stall, 4th print, 1984.

Pandey, Gyanendra. *The Construction of Communalism in Colonial North India*. Delhi: Oxford University Press, 1992.

Panikkar, K. N. *Before the Night Falls: Forebodings of Fascism in India*. Bangalore: Books for Change, 2003.

Pannenberg, Wolfhart. *The Church*, Tr. Keith Crim. Philadelphia: Westminster Press, 1983.

Park, Andrew Sung. *The Wounded Heart of God: The Asian Concept of Han and the Christian Concept of Sin*. Nashville: Abingdon Press, 1993.

Pelikan, Jaroslav. *Luther the Expositor: Introduction to the Reformer's Exegetical Writings*. St. Louis: Concordia Publishing House, 1959.

Perkins, J. *The Suffering Self: Pain and Narrative Representation in the Early Christian Era*. London: SCM Press, 1995.

Perrin, Norman. *The New Testament: An Introduction*. New York: Harcourt Brace, 1974.

Pesch, Otto Hermann. *The God Question in Thomas Aquinas and Martin Luther*. Philadelphia: Fortress Press, 1972.

Philips, Derek L. *Looking Backward: A Critical Appraisal of Communitarian Thought*. Princeton, CA: Princeton University Press, 1993.

Prabhakar, Samson. ed. *Inter-Play of Religion, Politics and Communalism in India*. Bangalore: BTESSC/SATHRI, 2004.

Prabhakar, Samson. ed. *Overcoming Violence*. Bangalore: SATHRI/BTESSC, 2004.

Prasad, Bimal. *Pathway to India's Partition: The Foundations of Muslim Nationalism* Part I. Delhi: Manohar Publications, 1999.

Preus, Robert. *Justification and Rome*. Saint Louis: Concordia Academic Press, 1997.

Puglisi, James F. ed. *Petrine Ministry and the Unity of the Church.* Collegeville, MN: Liturgical Press, 1999.

Punyani, Ram. *Fascism of Sangh Parivar.* Delhi: Media House, 2000.

Rader, M. *Marx's Interpretation of History*, Tr. M. Nocolaus. London: Penguin Books, 1973.

Radhakrishnan, Sarvapalli. *Our Heritage.* Delhi: Hind Pocket Books, 1973.

Radhakrishnan, Sarvapalli. *The Heart of Hindusthan.* Madras: G. A. Natesan & Co., 1932.

Radice, W. ed. *Swami Vivekananda and the Modernization of Hinduism.* Delhi: Oxford University Press, 1998.

Raju, T. Swami. *Christian Responses to Plurality of Religion.* Bangalore: BTESSC/SATHRI, 2006.

Religious Conversions: Frequently Asked Questions. Bombay: Hindu Vivek Kendra, 1999.

Rhaner, Karl. *The Church and the Sacraments*, Tr. by W. J. O'Hara. Freiburg: Herder, 1963.

Rhaner, Karl. *The Trinity*, Tr. by Joseph Donceel. New York: Herder and Herder, 1970.

Richards, Lawrence O. *A Practical Theology of Spirituality.* Grand Rapids, Michigan: Academic Books, 1987.

Richardson, Cyril C. ed. *Early Christian Fathers*, Library of Christian Classics Vol. 1. Philadelphia: Westminster Press, 1953.

Ricour, Paul. *Hermeneutics and Human Sciences: Essays on Language, Action and Interpretation.* Cambridge: Cambridge University Press, 1981.

Ridderbos, Herman. N. *The Coming of the Kingdom.* Grand Rapids, Michigan: Wm B. Eerdmans, 1997.

Roberts, Alexander and James Donaldson. eds. *The Ante-Nicene Fathers*, 10 Vols. 1st in 1885-97 and reprinted by Peabody, Massachusetts: Hendrickson Publishers, 1994.

Robinson, James M. ed. *The Nag Hammadi Library in English*. San Francisco: Harper Collins, 3rd edition, 1988.

Rossel, Jacques. *The Roots of Western Europe: An Essay on Interpretation of Cultures During the First Nine Centuries A.D.* Bangalore: ATC, 2001.

Rouner, Leroy S. *To be at Home: Christianity, Civil Religion, and World Community*. Boston: Beacon Press, 1991.

Rupp, Gordon. *Martin Luther and the Jews*. London: Council of Christians and Jews, 1972.

Russell, Letty M. *Church in the Round: Feminist Interpretation of the Church*. Louisville, Kentucky: John Knox Press, 1993.

Said, Edward. *Culture and Imperialism*. New York: Alfred Knopf, 1993.

Said, Edward. *Orientalism*. New York: Vintage Books, 1979.

Samuel, V. C. *The Council of Chalcedon Re-examined: A Historical Theological Survey*. Delhi: ISPCK, 2001.

Sandel, Michael. *Liberalism and the Limits of Justice*. Cambridge, UK: Cambridge University Press, 1998.

Santayana, George. *The Life of Reason*. New York: Charles Scribner's Sons, 1906.

Saraswati, Dayananda. *Rigvedadi Bhasya Bhumika (Introduction to the Commentary on the Vedas)*, Tr. by G. Ram. Meerut: Bharath Prakasan, 1925.

Sasse, Hermann. *This Is My Body: Luther's Contention for the Real Presence in the Sacrament of the Altar*. Minneapolis: Augsburg Publishing House, 1959.

Savarkar, Vinayak Damodhar. *Hindu Sangathan: Its Ideology and Immediate Programme*. Bombay: Hindu Vivek Kendra, 1940.

Savarkar, Vinayak Damodhar. *Hindutva: Who Is a Hindu?* Bombay: Veer Savarkar Prakasan, 6th ed. 1989.

Savarkar, Vinayak Damodhar. *Six Glorious Epochs of Indian History*. Bombay: Bal Savarkar Publishers, 1971.

Schillebeeckx, Edward. *Christ the Sacrament of Encounter with God*, Tr. Paul Barrett. New York: Sheed and Ward, 1963.

Schleiermacher, Friedrich, *On Religion: Addresses in Response to Its Cultured Critics*, Tr. by Torrence N. Tice. Richmond: John Knox Press, 1969.

Schleiermacher, Friedrich. *The Christian Faith*. Edinburgh: T & T Clark, 1928.

Schnackenburgh, R. *The Church in the New Testament*. London: Burnes and Oates, 1965.

Scholder, Klaus. *A Requiem for Hitler and Other New Perspectives on the German Church Struggle*, Tr. by John Bowden. London: SCM Press, 1989.

Scholder, Klaus. *The Churches and the Third Reich,* Vol. 1, *Preliminary History and the Times of Illusion 1918-1934*, Tr. by John Bowden Philadelphia: Fortress Press, 1988.

Schreiter, Robert *Reconciliation: Mission and Ministry in a Changing World Order*. Maryknoll, New York: Orbis Books, 1992.

Schreiter, Robert. *The New Catholicity: Theology between the Global and Local.* Maryknoll, New York: Orbis Books, 1997.

Schweizer, Eduard. *Church Order in the New Testament.* Napervile: Alec R. Allenson, 1961.

Segundo, Juan Luis. *Grace and Human Condition*. Maryknoll, NY: Orbis Books, 1973.

Sen, Amartya. *The Argumentative Indian: Writings on Indian Culture, History and Identity*. London: Penguin Books, 2005.

Sen, Amatya. *Identity and Violence: The Illusion of Destiny*. London: Penguin Books, 2006.

Setalvad, M. C. *Secularism*, Patel Memorial Lecture. Delhi: Ministry of Information and Broadcasting, Govt. of India, 1965.

Shaw, T. *The burden of the Flesh: Fasting and Sexuality in early Christianity*. Minneapolis: University of Minnesota Press, 1998.

Sherrifs, Deryck. *The Friendship of the Lord.* Carlisle, Cumburia: Paternoster Press, 1996.

Shourie, Arun. *Harvesting Our Souls: Missionaries, Their Design, Their Claims*. Delhi: ASA, 2001.

Shourie, Arun. *Missionaries in India: Continuities, Changes, Dilemmas* Delhi: ASA Publications, 1994.

Shütz, John H. "Introduction" in Theissen, Gerd. *The Social Settings of Pauline Christianity*. Edinburgh: T & T Clark, 1982.

Sinha, V. K. ed. *Secularism in India*. Bombay: Lalvani Publishing House, 1968.

Skarsaune, Oscar. *Incarnation: Myth or Fact?* St. Louis, Missouri: Concordia Publishing House, 1991.

Smith, Donald Eugene. *India as a Secular State*. Princeton: Princeton University Press, 1963.

Soares, A. ed. *Truth Shall Prevail: Reply to Niyogi Committee*. Bombay: CAB, 1957.

Sobrino, Jon. *Christology at the Crossroads – A Latin American approach*, Tr. by John Drury. Maryknoll, New York: Orbis Books, 1978.

Sobrino, Jon. *Jesus the Liberator: A Historical-Theological Reading of Jesus of Nazareth*, Tr. by Paul Burns and Francis McDonagh. Kent: Burns & Oates, 1994.

Srinivas, M. N. *Caste: Its Twentieth Century Avatar*. Delhi: Viking, 1996.

Stark, Rodney. *For the Glory of God: How Monotheism let to Reformations, Science, Witch-Hunts, and the End of Slavery*. Princeton and Oxford: Princeton University Press, 2003.

Stark, Rodney. *One True God: Historical Consequences of Monotheism*. Princeton: Princeton University Press, 2001.

Stauffer, Ethelbert. *Christ and the* Caesars, Tr. K. R. Gregor Smith. London: SCM Press, 1955.

Steinmetz, David C. *Luther in Context*. Grand Rapids, Michigan: Baker Press, 1995.

Stern, R. W. *Changing India*. Cambridge, UK: Cambridge University Press, 2nd ed., 2003.

Sugirtharajah, R. S. *Asian Biblical Hermeneutics and Postcolonialism*. Sheffield: Sheffield Academic Press, 1999.

Sugirtharajah, R. S. *Postcolonial Criticism and Biblical Interpretation*. Oxford, Oxford University Press, 2002.

Tagore, Rabindranath. *A Vision for India's History*. Calcutta: Vishvabharathi, 1951.

Tappert, Theodore G. *Book of Concord*. Philadelphia: Fortress Press, 1959.

Taylor, Charles. *Hegel and Modern Society*. Cambridge, UK: Cambridge University Press, 1979.

Tertullian Adversus Marcionem, 2 Vols., Tr. by Ernest Evans. Oxford: Clarendon Press, 1972.

Thapar, Romila. ed. *India: Another Millennium?* Delhi: Penguin Books, 2001.

The Complete Works of swami Vivekananda. Calcutta: Advaita Ashrama, 10th ed. 1963.

The Formula of Agreement in Confessional Lutheran Perspective. St. Louis, Missouri: CTCR, LCMS, 1999.

The Joint Declaration on the Doctrine of Justification in the Confessional Lutheran Perspective. St. Louis, Missouri: CTCR- LCMS, 1999.

Theertha, Swami Dharma. *The Menace of Hindu Imperialism*. Lahore: Happy Home Publications, 1946.

Thiessen, Henry Clarence. *Lectures in Systematic Theology*. Grand Rapids, Michigan: Wm B. Eerdmans, 2006, First published 1949.

Thomas, M. M. *Church's Mission and Postmodern Humanism – Collection of Essays & Talks*. Tiruvalla: CSS & ISPCK, 1996.

Thornton, L. S. *The Common Life in the Body of Christ*. London: Dacre Press, 1946.

Tillard, Jean-Marie. *Church of Churches: The Ecclesiology of Communion*, Tr. by R. C. De Peaux. Collegeville, MN: Liturgical Press, 1992.

Tilley, M. *Donatist Martyr Stories: The Church in Conflict in Roman North Africa*. Liverpool: Liverpool University Press, 1996.

Tillich, Paul. *A History of Christian Thought*. New York: Simon and Schuster, 1968.

Tillich, Paul. *Perspectives on 19th and 20th Century Protestant Theology*. New York: Harper and Row Publishers, 1967.

Tillich, Paul. *The Courage to Be*. New Haven: Yale University Press, 5th printing, 1954.

Tillich, Paul. *The Protestant Era*, Tr. by James Luther Adam. Chicago: Phoenix Books, 1963.

Torres, Sergio and John Eagleson. eds. *The Challenge of Basic Christian Communities* – Papers from the International Ecumenical Congress of Theology. Feb. 20-March 02, 1980. Sao Paulo, Brazil. Maryknoll, New York: Orbis Books, 1981.

Trueman Carl R. and R. Scott Clark. eds. *Protestant Scholasticism: Essays in Reassessment*. Great Britain: Paternoster, 2005.

Tutu, Desmond *No Future without Forgiveness*. London: Rider, 1999.

Upadhyay, V. S. and V. P. Sharma. *Contemporary Indian Society*. Delhi: Amol Publications, 1995.

Uuras, Sarnivaara. *Luther Discovers the Gospel: New Light upon Luther's Way from Medieval Catholicism to Evangelical Faith*. St. Louis, Missouri: Concordia Publishing House, 1951.

Van der Van, Johannes A. *Ecclesiology in Context*. Grand Rapids, Michigan: Wm. B. Eerdmans, 1993.

Vanhoozer, Kevin J. ed. *The Trinity in a Pluralistic Age: Theological Essays on Culture and Religion*. Grand Rapid, Michigan: Wm B. Eerdmans, 1997.

Vivekananda, Swami. *The East and the West*. Calcutta: Advaita Ashrama, 1963.

Volf, Miraslov. *Exclusion and Embrace: A Theological Exploration of Identity, Otherness, and Reconciliation*. Nashville: Abingdon Press, 1996.

Volf, Miroslav. *After Our Likeness: The Church as the Image of the Trinity*. Grand Rapids: Wm B. Eerdmans, 1998.

Volf. Miroslav and Michael Welker. eds. *God's Life in Trinity*. Minneapolis: Fortress Press, 2006.

Volkmar, Lloyd B. *Luther's Response to Violence: Why the Reformer Hurled His Harsh 'No!' Against the Peasants*. New York: Vantage Press, 1974.

von Loewenich, Walther. *Luther's Theology of the Cross*. Belfast: Christian Journals Limited, 1976.

Waddell, Helen. *Desert Fathers*. London: Constable & Co., 1936.

Watson, Philip S. *Let God be God! An Interpretation of the Theology of Martin Luther*. Philadelphia: Muhlenberg Press, 1947.

Weaver, Rebecca Harden. *Divine Grace and Human Agency: A study of the Semi-Pelagian Controversy*. Macon: Mercer University Press, 1996.

Weber, Max. *The Protestant Ethic and the Spirit of Capitalism*, Tr. by Talcott Parsons. London York: Routledge, 1992.

Weber, Max. *The Sociology of Religion*, Tr. by Ephraim Fischof with an Introduction by Talcott Parsons. London: Methuen & Co., 1963.

Welker, Michael. *What Happens in Holy Communion?* Tr. by John F. Hoffmeyer. Grand Rapids, Michigan: William B. Eerdmans, 2000.

What Luther Says: An Anthology Vol. II, Compiled by Ewald M. Plass. Saint Louis, Missouri: Concordia Publishing House, 2nd Print, 1972.

Whitehead, Alfred North. *Process and Reality: Essays in Cosmology*. New York: Free Press, 1978.

Whitehead, Alfred North. *Religion in the Making*. Cambridge: Cambridge University Press, 1927.

Williams, Rowan. *The Truce of God*. London: Fount, 1983.

Wilson, Richard A. *The Politics of Truth and Reconciliation in South Africa: Legitimizing the Post-Apartheid State*. Cambridge, UK: Cambridge University Press, 2001.

Wingate, Andrew. *The Church and Conversion: A Study of Recent Conversions to and from Christianity in the Tamil Area of South India*. Delhi: ISPCK, 1997.

Wink, Walter. *When the Powers Fall: Reconciliation in the Healing of Nations*. Minneapolis: Fortress Press, 1998.

Wolpert, Stanley. *A New History of India*. Delhi: Oxford University Press, 1993.

Woodhead, Linda. *An Introduction to Christianity*. Cambridge, UK: Cambridge University Press, 2004.

Wuthnow, Robert. *Communities of Discourse: Ideology and Social Structure in the Reformation, the Enlightenment, and European Socialism*. Cambridge: Harvard University Press, 1989.

Wuthnow, Robert. *The Restructuring of American Religion, Society and Faith*. Princeton: Princeton University Press, 1988.

Zachariah, Mathai. *Beyond Ecumenism: A journey into Light*. Thiruvalla: CSS, 2002.

Zachariah, Mathai. ed. *The Church: A Peoples' Movement*. Nagpur: NCCI, 1975.

Zagano, Phyllis and Terrence W. Tilley, eds. *The Exercise of the Primacy: Continuing Dialogue*. New York: Crossroad, 1998.

Zavos, John. *The Emergence of Hindu nationalism in India*. Delhi: Oxford University Press, 2004.

Zizioulas, John D. *Being as Communion: Studies in Personhood and the Church*. Crestwood, New York: St Vladimir's Seminary Press, 1997.

Select Articles from Journals and Books

Belopopsky, Alexander. "Between Chaos and Kairos: Churches, Ecumenism and the World Council of Churches in Central and Eastern Europe 1989-2003" *The Ecumenical Review*, Vol. 56, No.1 (Jan 2004), pp. 77-83.

Casolari, Marzia. "Hindutva's Foreign Tie-up in the 1930s: Archival Evidence" *Economic and Political Weekly* (22 Jan 2000), pp. 218-228.

Clarke, Sathianathan. "Viewing the Bible through the Eyes and Ears of Subalterns in India" *Biblical Interpretation* Vol. 10, No.3 (2002), pp. 245-266.

Clarke, Sathianathan. "Hindutva, Religious and Ethnocultural Minorities, and Indian-Christian Theology" *Harvard Theological Review* 95:2 (April 2002).

Duraisingh, Christopher. "Science, Whitehead, and New Perspectives on Reality" *Bangalore Theological Forum*, Vol. IV, No. 1 (1972), pp. 31-54.

Duraisingh, Christopher. "Contextual and Catholic: Conditions for Cross-Cultural Hermeneutics" *Anglican Theological Review*, Vol. 82, No. 4 (Fall 2000), pp. 679-701.

Ford, John "Koinonia and Roman Catholic Theology" *Ecumenical Trends*, Vol. 26, (1997), pp. 42ff.

Inden, Ronald. "Orientalist Constructions of India" *Modern Asian Studies* Vol. 20, No. 3, (1986), pp. 401-446.

Jathanna, O. V. "Ecclesiology in Context: Reflections from an Indian Perspective in the Light of Current Ecumenical Deliberations" *Bangalore Theological Forum* Vol. 28, Nos. 3-4 (Sep-Dec 1996), pp. 3-11

Jayaraj, B. "The People of God in the Priestly Source" *The Indian Journal of Theology* Vol. 28, Nos. 3 &4 (July - Dec 1979), pp. 129-130.

Johnson, Gordon. "Partition, Agitation and Congress: Bengal 1904 To 1908", *Modern Asian Studies*, Vol. 7, No. 3 (May 1973), pp. 533-588.

Johnson, Luke Timothy. "Making Connections: The Material Expression of Friendship in the New Testament" in *Interpretation* (April 2004), pp. 158-171.

Joseph, M. J. "The Church in Paul" *Indian Journal of Theology* Vol. 28, 3 -4 (July-Dec, 1979).

Kanungo, Pralay. "Hindutva's Fury against Christians in Orissa" *Economic and Political Weekly* (September 13, 2008), pp. 16-19.

Kirkpatrick, Frank G. "Toward a Metaphysic of Community" *Scottish Journal of Theology*, Vol. 38 (1985), pp. 565f.

Kolb, Robert. "Christian Civic Responsibility in an Age of Judgment", *Concordia Journal* Vol. 19, No. 1 (Jan 1993).

Macchia, Frank D. "Justification by New Creation: The Holy Spirit and the Doctrine by which the Church Stands or Falls," *Theology Today* Vol.58, No.2 (July 2001), p. 202.

Mariaselvam, M. "The Church according to the Prophetic Tradition" *The Indian Journal of Theology* Vol. 28, Nos. 3 &4 (July - Dec 1979), pp. 135-142.

Mbiti, John. "Christianity Tilts to the South: A New Challenge for Christian Ministry and Theological Education" *Indian Journal of Theology* Vol. 33, 1-3 (Jan-Sept, 1984), pp. 2ff

McLane, John R. "The Decision to Partition Bengal in 1905" *Indian Economic and Social History Review*, Vol. 2, No. 3 (July 1965), pp. 221-237.

Mehta, Pratap Bhanu. "The Rise of Judicial Sovereignty", *Journal of* Democracy, Vol. 18, No.2 (2007), pp. 70-83.

Nereparampil, Lucius. "The Church in the Johannine Literature" *Indian Journal of Theology* Vol. 28, Nos. 3 & 4 (July - Dec, 1979).

Pralay, Kanungo. "Hindutva's Fury against Christians in Orissa" *Economic and Political Weekly* (September 13, 2008), pp. 16-19.

Rajashekar, Paul. "Luther's Doctrine of Justification and Christian Social Responsibility in India" *Bangalore Theological Forum* Vol. XV, No. 3 (September - December, 1983), pp. 197-217.

Sahayadhas, R. "Religion-State Relationship: Significance of a Middle-Path in Contemporary India" *Bangalore Theological Forum*, Vol. XLIII, No. 1 (June 2011), pp. 55-82.

Sarkar, Sumit. "The Fascism of the Sangh Parivar" *Economic and Political Weekly* (30 Jan. 1993), pp. 163-167.

Smith, David S. "Luther's Contribution to Positive Individualism", *Concordia Journal* Vol. 22, No.3, (July 1996), pp. 263-278.

Spivak, Gayatri Chakravarty. "Can the Subaltern Speak?" in Carey Nelson and Larry Grossberg, eds., *Marxism and the Interpretation of Culture*. Uraba: University of Illinois Press, 1988, pp. 271-313.

Spivak, Gayatri Chakravarty. "Subaltern Studies: Deconstructing Historiography" in Ranajit Guha, ed., *Subaltern Studies IV*. Delhi: Oxford University Press, 1985, pp. 330-363.

Stephenson, John R. "The two Governments and the Two Kingdoms in Luther's Thought" *Scottish Journal of Theology* Vol. 34, No. 4 (August 1981) pp. 321ff.

Vellanickal, Mathew. "The Church in the Bible" *The Indian Journal of Theology* Vol. 28, Nos. 3 &4 (July - Dec 1979), pp. 109-115.

Volf, Miraslov. "'The Trinity is Our Social Program': The Doctrine of the Trinity and the Shape of Our Social Engagement", *Modern Theology* Vol. 14 (July 1998), pp. 403-423.

von Brück, Michael. "In Search of an Authentic Christian Life-Style: Luther and Monasticism" *Bangalore Theological Forum*, XV, 3 (Sept-Dec, 1983), pp. 218-236.

Walther, C. F. "Bringing Souls to Christ: Every Christian's Desire and Duty" *Missio Apostolica*, Vol. VI, No. 1, Issue No. 11 (May 1998), pp. 6-12.

Wesselschmidt, Quentin F."The Beginnings of the Papacy in the Early Church" *Concordia Journal* Vol. 29, No. 4 (October 2003), pp. 374-391.

Wollenburg, David. "Is There a God-Pleasing purpose to War?: An Introduction to *Just* War Concept" *Concordia Journal*, Vol.29, No. 1(January 2003), pp. 65-69.

Wriedt, Markus. "Luther on Call and Ordination: A Look at Luther and Ministry" *Concordia Journal*, Vol. 28,. No. 3 (July 2002), pp. 254-269.

Zwanepol, Klass "A Human God: Some Remarks on Luther's Christology" *Concordia Journal* Vol. 30, Nos. 1 & 2 (January – April 2004) pp. 40-53.

Encyclopaedia/Dictionary Articles and Reports

"Righteous Before God: An Agreement on the Doctrine of Justification", the full text of the document prepared by the Lutheran World Federation (LWF) in consultation with the Pontifical Council for Promoting Christian Unity (PCPCU), released in print form and in a Video film by the LWF, Nov. 1999.

Angell, Robert Cooley. "Social Integration" in David L. Sills, ed., *International Encyclopedia of the Social Sciences* Vol. 7. New York: The Macmillan Company & The Fortress Free Press, 1972, pp. 380-386.

Dyck, Cornelius J. "Anabaptism" in Mircea Eliade, ed., *Encyclopedia of Religion*, Vol. 1. New York: Macmillan Publishing Company, 1987, pp. 247-249.

Gill, Kenneth D. "Charismatic mission" in A. Scott Moreau, ed., *Evangelical Dictionary of World Missions*. Grand Rapids: Bakkar Book House, 2000, pp. 173-175.

Lovine, Donald L. "Cultural Integration" in David L. Sills, ed., *International Encyclopedia of the Social Sciences* Vol. 7. New York: The Macmillan Company & The Fortress Free Press, 1972, pp. 374-376.

Potter, Philip. "Report of the General Secretary - WCC Central Committee" Doc. 18, Geneva: July/august 1977.

Wainwright, "Augustine" in M. D. Law, ed., *Chambers Encyclopedia*, Vol. I (London: Geovrge Newnes, 1959), pp. 774-775.

Whitley, W. T. "Enthusiasts (Religious)" in James Hastings, ed., *Encyclopedia of Religion and Ethics* Vol. 5. New York: Charles Scribner's Sons, nd., pp. 317-321.

LIST OF SCRIPTURAL REFERENCES

Genesis	2:7; 3:15; 9:8-17; 11: 1-9; 12:1-8; 13: 2-18; 15:5, 6; 17:5, 27; Ch 21 & 22
Leviticus	4:3-5
2 Samuel	7:8-16; 8:15
2 Chronicles	20:7
Psalms	32: 1; 36:9; 18:50, 89:20; 110:4
Isaiah	Ch. 9 &11; 45:1; 65:17-25
Jeremiah	31:1, 31-34
Matthew	1:16; 5:38-45; 7: 17-21; 10: 7, 28; 13: 47f; 16:16, 18; Ch.19; 21:12; 22:15-22; 25:40; 26:51-52; 28:18-20
Mark	1:15; 4:30-32; 8: 34; 9:47; Ch.10; 11:15-17; 16:15-16
Luke	7: 34; 9: 23; 10:25-37; 16:16; Ch.18; 19:1-10 & 45-46; 22: 36
John	1:3, 12-14; 3:5, 6f; 3:16; 4:2; 10:16; 11:27; 15: 13-15, 26; 18: 10-11, 33-37; 19:10-11; 20:37
Acts	1:6; 2:1-11, 42-47; 4:18-20, 32; 5:27-29; 5: 40-42; 6: 1- 6; 7: 2-50; 10: 1-48; 11:27-30; 12:12-13; 15: 1 - 11, 28; 17: 5-9; 16: 15, 33; 18:18
Romans	4: 1-25; 5:10; 6:1-4, 8-13; 8:15, 23; 9:4; 10: 10, 12:1-2, 4, 14-21; 13: 1-7, 14

INDEX OF SUBJECTS

INDEX OF AUTHORS